+HC427.92 .T34313 1991

HC
427.92
T34313
1991

Tálas, Barna.
Economic reforms
and political
attempts in China,
1979-1989

Europe-Asia-Pacific Studies in Economy and Technology

Editorial Board
Thilo Graf Brockdorff
Per Fischer
Manfred Kulessa
Theodor Leuenberger
Dieter Schneidewind

Titles in the Series

Manfred Kulessa (Ed.)
The Newly Industrializing Economies of Asia

Theodor Leuenberger (Ed.)
Technology Transfer to Technology Management in China

Barna Tálas

Economic Reforms and Political Attempts in China 1979 - 1989

Springer-Verlag Berlin Heidelberg New York
London Paris Tokyo Hong Kong
Barcelona Budapest

Professor Dr. Sc. Econ. Barna Tálas
Institute of Economic Policy and Planning
Ministry of Finance
Sas utca 23
H-1051 Budapest, Hungary

English translation by
György Hajdu M. Sc. Econ.

English translation of the Summary by
Erzsébet Németh

Copy Editing by
Mary Schäfer

This publication was supported by a grant from the Hungarian Academy of Sciences and Soros Foundation as well as by a grant from the Deutsche Bank AG.

ISBN 3-540-54548-4 Springer-Verlag Berlin Heidelberg New York Tokyo
ISBN 0-387-54548-4 Springer-Verlag New York Heidelberg Berlin Tokyo

This work is subject to copyright. All rights are reserved, whether the whole or part of the material is concerned, specifically the rights of translation, reprinting, reuse of illustrations, recitation, broadcasting, reproduction on microfilms or in other ways, and storage in data banks. Duplication of this publication or parts thereof is only permitted under the provisions of the German Copyright Law of September 9, 1965, in its version of June 24, 1985, and a copyright fee must always be paid. Violations fall under the prosecution act of the German Copyright Law.

© Springer-Verlag Berlin · Heidelberg 1991
Printing in Germany

The use of registered names, trademarks, etc. in this publication does not imply, even in the absence of a specific statement, that such names are exempt from the relevant protective laws and regulations and therefore free for general use.

2142/7130-543210 - Printed on acid-free paper

PREFACE

In our quickly changing world, authors who are analyzing the social, economic, and political processes going on in different countries often find themselves in a situation where the development of processes they have already described take a turn in another direction before their work is in final form or appears in print. As a consequence, some of their statements are no longer valid. More rarely it occurs that after the writing of a book presenting a reform process covering 10 years (the writing itself taking one and a half years), exceptional events take place in the given country (within 1 or 2 months of the delivery of the manuscript) that indicate a sharp break in this process, one that makes it doubtful whether the process can continue along the same channel. This is what has happened to this text and to its author at the beginning of June, 1989, when in Beijing - after the brutal suppression of student demonstrations and of protests lasting several weeks - the General Secretary of the Communist Party of China, Zhao Ziyang, was relieved of his office and arrested, along with several other prominent representatives of reform policy and reform endeavors of the past decade. The manuscript of this book was handed over to the publisher on May 4, 1989, for editing. Immediately thereafter I left for nearly 2 months in the United States; consequently, I did not receive the manuscript again until in early July. (I followed the events in China in May and June via the reports of the various American television correspondents.)

At the end of July 1989 a group of experts discussed this manuscript at my former place of work, the Institute of Economic Planning of the Hungarian National Planning Office, where the writing of this monograph had been one of my tasks. The arguments advanced during the discussion in effect strenghtened my earlier opinion and conviction that, in spite of events and political developments that had taken place in the meantime, there was no need to modify or considerably rework the written text; it was only necessary to complete the chronological part of the book to include the events and developments of the summer of 1989. The essence of opinions and critical observations expressed at the discussion can be concisely summarized as follows:

The author gives an authentic and documented review of the Chinese economic and political reform processes and reform endeavors of the past decade - together with their antecedents, following up the actual events and actions. The different concepts and theoretical considerations aimed at solving the problems that have emerged in the meantime are reviewed in an analytical way and highlighted from several aspects. Nevertheless, facts remain facts, even though they may be interpreted differently from time to time, depending on changes in power relations. However, any interpretation inevitably reflects a subjective value judgement, the motives of which have a basically ideological origin in the present case. Consequently, the author, while also reporting the events that have taken place in the meantime, should essentially aim at putting down the facts, without commenting on them particularly. The facts speak for themselves.

Following the discussion this is what I did, completing the chronological part and adding only a few sentences to what I had written in certain chapters of the theoretical part, referring to the expected impacts of the events that occurred in the summer of 1989.

At the discussion the author's approach to the problem was criticized as being far too "China-centric"; it was noted that the method of international comparison is rarely employed. Moreover, far too great importance is attached to the various Chinese party documents and government decrees, as well as to the different manifestos of certain Chinese leaders from which extensive passages are quoted. As a result, less attention is paid and less space devoted to the analysis of real processes, that is, to the presentation of what, from among the resolutions and program declarations, has been realized and how. Some people found the manuscript's explanation of views and opinions expressed by Chinese economists and theoretical experts too detailed and unresolved. Others, in contrast, called the author to account for not indicating in each case by whom, when, and in what kind of publications or fora, these views were represented. In connection with this I should mention that the majority of experts were of the opinion that one of the major virtues of the manuscript consists in its multifaceted approach and in the varied presentations of the problems discussed. They stressed the thorough and accurate documentation of authentic opinions, which makes it possible to use the book in several ways - either as a handbook or as a textbook. Finally, there were also those who questioned why the author, having presented the different Chinese opinions and views, had not immediately added his own opinion and standpoint, as well as those of other foreign sinologists; especially in view of the fact that today there is already a wealth of literature on foreign evaluations of the 10--year Chinese reform process that would almost fill a library.

It will be task of the reader to decide whether these critical observations are well founded and reliable, taking into account the size of the book (which is already larger than optimal). Some of these opinions I myself regard as correct and worth keeping in mind. If I began to write this book just now, I would no doubt take these remarks into consideration. However, I could not afford to make any fundamental structural and contextual changes to the present manuscript - without considerably enlarging it - in a way that every requirement should be met at the same time. May it be said in my defense that the majority of the experts judged my work, even in its present form, to be thorough, authentic, and one long needed in the international literature, and its earliest possible publication was proposed - in English as well, if possible. The easy-flowing style and the very careful language of the Hungarian manuscript were also stressed, and this cannot be considered unimportant in the case of a scientific work intended for a larger public. Consequently, in connection with these preliminary remarks I wish to make the following comments.

First, in my opinion, the fundamental task and function of this work is to give a factual and authentic account of the economic and political reform process developed in China and its antecedents. This task can be resolved only if - in addition to describing the facts and events - above all the official and nonofficial Chinese standpoints and opininions, as well as ideas and endeavors of Chinese reform economists and reform politicians are made known. The task is not necessarily to describe the foreign reception and evaluation of the Chinese reform process, all the more as this depends essentially on one's standpoint and on the particular professional and political approach.

Second, it is difficult for a professional researcher on the subject of China to avoid the charge of being "China-centric." There is no question that a person who has been dealing with a country for almost four decades and knows its problems from the inside will approach every subject concerning the country in a way different from those who know the country only on the basis of superficial impressions, or perhaps only through their reading. Between 1951 and 1957, I spent - at first as a postgraduate student and later as a diplomat - seven full and almost uninterrupted years in the People's Republic of China, and I have made several visits there since then. I speak their language, I read the written characters of their idiom. I know their customs, and I have many old acquaintances and good friends who work as researchers of economics or social sciences, and university lecturers. In spite of these facts, I have never shut myself within the circle of Chinese problems, but have always considered the Chinese socioeconomic development as a part of the universal development of all mankind, the socioeconomic development of the past four decades there as an organic part of a special historical experiment, i.e. an attempt to avoid the capitalistic phase of socioeconomic development in underdeveloped countries. This was my approach during my research work as well, and will be obvious to anyone who looks over the list of my publications, reflecting the results of my activity as a researcher to date. I think that the reader can assure himself of this on the basis of this book alone.

Third, as regards the exaggeration and overstatement of the importance of the Chinese party documents and government decrees, as well as of the declarations of certain leaders, I am of the opinion that in a country such as China, where the direction and control of economic and political processes continue to be centralized in the hands of an extremely small circle of the party and state leadership, it is not entirely useless to become acquainted in detail with the essential documents and declarations which have been issued with the approval of this small group. Many times it is the way they are drafted or the very slight differences in emphasis found in them that make it possible for us to draw conclusions about the current situation, the established power relations or conflicts.

Fourth, I could not undertake to identify exactly the origin of the various Chinese views by name, title, and source, since these views do not generally reflect the opinion of one scholar or expert and not even that of certain research groups or institutes. They usually are opinions logically systematized and extracted from several hundred articles, reports, and speeches. They were published in the diverse dailies, weeklies, periodicals, collections of articles and annuals enumerated in the bibliography, not infrequently in the form of second-hand publications or abstracts of articles. However, the titles of the most significant and characteristic articles - together with the indication of the source and the author(s) - are also given either in the text or in footnotes.

As regards the "concealment" of my own opinion, this criticism does not entirely correspond with the facts, as the reader will soon see. In several cardinal theoretical and ideological questions - e.g., the evaluation of the historical role of the whole reform process, or the question of "the initial phase of Chinese socialism" or "the socialism with Chinese characteristics " - I have never made a secret of my own opinion, which diverges radically from the official standpoint of the Chinese leadership. Given the current situation, the publication of this book under my own name also represents a kind of stand and the espousal of the Chinese reform movement and of its most consistent representatives.

This last statement may require some explanation for readers who are not well acquainted with the miserable state of research on modern China in the past several decades. As political relations with the People's Republic of China grew worse in the 1960s and 1970s, it became rather widespread practice among the China researchers of the socialist countries to publish their works on China under assumed names, in order to avoid becoming personae non gratae, a standing which would have made it difficult for them to carry on their research work. In this regard I was no exception; between 1963 and 1982 I issued nearly 50 publications at home and abroad under my pen name: HIDASI, GÁBOR. Under this name I also published my two independent volumes of selected studies, first in Poland, in 1976, and later in Hungary, in 1979, entitled Economy and Doctrines of the Maoist' China and Economy and Policy in the People's Republic of China. As Gábor Hidasi, I also appeared as an expert for a decade in the foreign political broadcast programs of the Hungarian Radio. I gave up this practice eight years ago, acting out of conviction and in the expectation that, on the basis of the reforms and the developing of open-mindedness policy in China, once and for all an end would be put to the period when friends and enemies of the Chinese people are judged according to who wrote and said what about the leaders of the Communist Party of China and of the People's Republic of China, as well as about their policy. I hope that the reception and evaluation of this book in China will not shake, but rather confirm my conviction.

* * *

Finnaly, I would like to thank numerous friends and colleagues, whose kind assistance has made this publication possible in this series of Springer-Verlag. I am particularly grateful to my distinguished German friends and colleagues, first of all to Prof. Dr. Per Fischer and Prof. Dr. Willy Kraus, who called Springer-Verlag's attention to this work. Thanks are due to the institution and personalities who financed and actually performed the translation of this voluminous manuscript from Hungarian into English. This translation - in consequence of the special construction of the Hungarian language - proved to be almost as difficult as if it had been done from the Chinese. Last but not least, thanks are due to all those Chinese friends and colleagues with whom I had intensive discussions and exchanges of views about the problems treated in this book, in China and in Hungary, on several occasions, between 1979-1988.

Budapest, January 1991

Barna Tálas

Contents

PREFACE	V
INTRODUCTION	1
PART ONE	19

Chapter One
BRIEF HISTORICAL REVIEW 21

The Chinese People's Revolution and Socioeconomic Situation of China in 1949	21
Economic Restoration and Accomplishment of the New Democratic Revolution (1949-1952)	25
Launching the Socialist Transformation: The First 5-Year Plan (1953-1957)	28
The Great Leap Forward and the Period of Readjustment (1958-1960 and 1961-1965)	33
Ten Years of Turmoil (1966-1976)	43
"Seeking Ways and Means" (1977-1978)	51
Footnotes to Chapter One	56

Chapter Two
FORMATION AND ANNOUNCEMENT OF THE REFORM AND OPENING POLICY (1978-1979) 61

Situation of the Economy in 1978	61
The Domestic and External Political Situation in 1978	64
Third Plenary Session of the 11th Central Committee of the CPC: Turning Point in Chinese Internal Politics	67
Emergence of the Outlines of the New Economic Policy	71
The "Four-Word Directive": Announcement of the Reform and Opening Policy	75
Footnotes to Chapter Two	78

Chapter Three
DEVELOPMENT OF THE REFORM AND OPENING POLICY IN THE PERIOD
OF READJUSTMENT (1979-1982) — 82

Establishment of an Ideological-Political Platform for the
  Reform and Opening Policy — 84
Theoretical Foundation of the Reform and Opening Policy — 88
Rapid Reform of the Rural Economy — 93
Reform and Opening in Other Areas of the Economy — 95
First Results of Political Reform — 99
Result of the "Readjustment Policy" — 102
Footnotes to Chapter Three — 108

Chapter Four
STABILIZATION OF THE REFORM AND OPENING POLICY DURING PRE-
PARATION OF THE COMPREHENSIVE ECONOMIC REFORM (1982-1984) — 110

12th National Congress of the CPC: Approval of Reform and
  Opening Policy, Turn in Chinese Foreign Policy — 110
Further Development of Reform and Opening Policy — 115
  Organizational and legal foundations of the reform
    process — 115
  Rural economic reform — 118
  Reform of the turnover sphere — 122
  Attempts to develop economic regions centered around
    cities — 125
  Further broadening of entrepreneurial independence — 126
Elaboration of the Complex Draft on Comprehensive Economic
  Reform — 129
Third Plenary Session of the 12th CC of the CPC: Resolution
  on Reform of the Economic System — 134
Strengthening Extensive Growth Tendencies — 144
Footnotes to Chapter Four — 147

Chapter Five
PROBLEMS OF EQUILIBRIUM IN THE INTRODUCTORY STAGE OF COM-
PREHENSIVE ECONOMIC REFORM (1985-1986)   151

Preliminary Measures to Ease Introduction   151
Circumstances of Introduction in 1985   156
Slowdown in Growth Rate of Agricultural Production   162
National Conference of the CPC in 1985: First Manifestations
   of Differences in Views on Basic Reform Issues Among
   Highest Party Leaders   167
1986: Attempts to Establish Macroeconomic Equilibrium and
   to Increase Independence of Enterprises   176
Footnotes to Chapter Five   186

Chapter Six
SLOWDOWN OF THE REFORM PROCESS (1987-1988)   188

Hidden Attack on the Reform and Opening Policy Under the
   Pretext of Struggle Against "Bourgeois Liberalization"   188
Strengthening of Reform and Opening Policy at the 13th
   National Congress of the CPC   194
1988: The Critical Year of the Reform   201
Slowing Down of the Reform Process Beginning in the Autumn
   of 1988   209
Footnotes to Chapter Six   215

Chapter Seven
THE REFORM PROCESS COMES TO A SUDDEN HALT (1989)   219

Situation in China, Spring, 1989   219
Sudden Halt in the Summer of 1989   227
   The character of the student demonstrations in April
     and May   230
   Factors giving rise to the student demonstrations   232
   Students' demands   235
   Organizers and supporters of the student demonstrations   239
   Could the bloodshed have been avoided?   241

    What happened at Tienanmen Square?   243
Prospect for the Reform Process on the Eve of the 40th
    Anniversary of the Establishment of the PRC   245
Footnotes to Chapter Seven   250

PART TWO   251

Chapter Eight
THEORETICAL BASES OF CHINESE ECONOMIC REFORM   253

Choice of the Target Model   253
Theoretical Basis   257
Issues Under Discussion   262
  Present stage of Chinese social devolopment   263
  Target model of the economic reform   264
  Phases of the economic reform   265
  Keystone of the economic reform   267
  Reform of the ownership system   270
  Debates about the system of shares   272
  The contractual responsibility system   273
  Labor as a commodity   274
  On the nature of wage work   275
  Focal points of macroeconomic regulation   276
Formation of the Target System for Economic Reform   277
Footnotes to Chapter Eight   284

Chapter Nine
INSTRUMENTS OF ECONOMIC REFORM IN CHINA   286

Means of Political and Economic Leaders for Realizing
  Reform Goals   286
Instruments of Administrative Regulation   288
Economic Regulators   295
  The price system   296
  The wage system   301
Financial Regulators   305

Regulation of the issue of money	306
The state budget	306
Credit policy and interest rates	307
Policy on foreign exchange and exchange rates	310
Reform of Foreign Capital Investments and Trade	313
Administrative regulation of foreign economic activity	313
Indirect regulation through economic and financial regulators	316
Instruments for regulating the inflow of foreign capital	318
Other methods of opening to foreign economic activities	321
Footnote to Chapter Nine	322

Chapter Ten
TWO KEY ISSUES OF CHINESE ECONOMIC REFORM: MARKET BUILDING AND FORMS OF OWNERSHIP — 323

Position of Certain Market Elements in China Today	324
The commodity markets	324
The money and capital markets	327
The land and estate market	327
The labor market	329
Reform of the Ownership System	330
Transformation of the ownership structure	331
Development of diversified forms of ownership	334
Establishment of an adequate government policy on ownership	338
Footnotes to Chapter Ten	342

Chapter Eleven
CONCEPTS FOR REFORMING THE POLITICAL SYSTEM — 343

Main Deficiencies of Existing Political System	344
Standpoint and Resolution of the 13th Congress of the CPC in Connection with Political Reform	347
Separation of party and state	350
Delegation of power to lower levels	351
Reform of governmental organs	352

Reform of personnel and cadre work	352
Developing a system of social consultation and dialogue	355
Expanding democracy	355
Strengthening socialist law and order	356
Interdependence and Mutual Conditionality of Political and Economic Reforms	357
Footnotes to Chapter Eleven	361
SUMMARY	363
APPENDIX	381
Basic Indicators of Economic Growth in the People's Republic of China, 1952-1988	382
Main Structural Proportions of the Chinese National Economy, 1952-1988 (percent)	388
BIBLIOGRAPHY	391

List of Tables

Table 1. Distribution of the gross value of industrial output by size and ownership (in percent)	104
Table 2. Annual growth rate of the gross output value in productive branches (in percent)	106
Table 3. Distribution of retail trade by forms of ownership (in percent)	124
Table 4. Distribution of the gross output value of agricultural production by sub-branches (in percent and at current prices)	164
Table 5. Average per capita annual consumption by rural and urban populations of the most important foodstuffs (kg/head/year)	166
Table 6. Distribution of foreign capital investment according to use between 1979-1988	320
Table 7. Changes in the ownership structure of the Chinese economy	332

ABBREVIATIONS

BR	Beijing Review
CASS	Chinese Academy of Social Sciences
CC	Central Committee
CMEA	Council of Mutual Economic Assistance
CPC	Communist Party of China
CPLA	Chinese People's Liberation Army
CPPCC	Chinese People's Political Consultative Conference
CPSU	Communist Party of the Soviet Union
ESRIC	Economic System Reform Institute of China
GDR	German Democratic Republic
GNP	Gross National Product
Gosplan	State Planning Commission of the USSR
HAS	Hungarian Academy of Sciences
HSWP	Hungarian Socialist Workers' Party
ICBC	Industrial and Commercial Bank of China
JTGS	Jingji Tizhi Gaige Shouce (Handbook of the Reform of the Economic System)
MPS	Material Product System (Statistical accounting system of socialist countries)
NPC	National People's Congress
PB	Political Bureau
PBOC	People's Bank of China
PRC	People's Republic of China
RMB	Ren-Min Bi = People's Currency (The official name of the unit of the PRC's currency)
SC	State Council (The government of the PRC)
SEC	State Economic Commission of the SC
SNA	System of National Accounts
SPC	State Planning Commission of the SC
SRC	State Reform Commission of the SC
UN	United Nations
US(A)	United States (of America)
ZJN	Zhongguo Jingji Nianjian (Almanach of China's Economy)
ZTN	Zhongguo Tongji Nianjian (Statistical Yearbook of China)

INTRODUCTION

The people living in the country with the greatest population in the world - who have, for more than two thousand years, called themselves "Han" in their own language (that is, descendants of the Han empire, - have lived for more than two thousand years in the belief that their country is the center of the civilized world, and that their civilization is superior to that of the "barbarian" peoples living in other parts of the world. The name of China in Chinese is Zhongguo, that is, "middle country" which, in the final analysis, also reflects this "China-centered" image of the world. Since for thousands of years the Hans generally had contact only with the agrarian or nomadic peoples living in their immediate surroundings and with those in the archipelago of the South China sea, this belief in their superiority gradually became a conviction, supported by the fact that the peoples capable of forming a state beyond their frontiers - the Koreans and Japanese to the northeast, the Vietnamese to the south - had long acknowledged the superiority of the Chinese civilization, had adopted their writing system and customs as well as the basic system of ideas of their social order, i.e., Confucianism.

This situation changed somewhat beginning with the fourth century A.D. in consequence of the spread of Buddhism in China; following the teachings of Buddha, the Hans became acquainted with the Indian civilization and culture, and with the Sankskrit alphabet, which was essentially simpler than the Chinese characters, or ideograms. Nevertheless, Buddhism had to fight serious ideological obstacles in China, to wit: the traditional Confucian views, as well as Taoism, then organizing itself into a religion. This, among other things, explains why, in the final analysis, Buddhism was not able to win a large following in China; it had never become a state religion (as in Burma, Thailand, or in the Khmer and Laotian kingdoms). Not even versions mixed with elements of the local ancient religions developed, e.g., Lamaism in Tibet and Mongolia, or Zen-Buddhism in Japan.

The Chinese empire under the rule of a series of imperial dynasties, on the whole succesfuly resisted the renewed attacks and attempts at conquest by the "northern barbarians" (various nomadic tribes and their allies). In the middle of the thirteenth century, however, when the southern Song Empire was invaded by descendants of Genghis Khan, the Mongols conquered China within a few decades. In 1280, Khublai Khan already considered himself emperor of the whole Chinese empire and founded the Yuan (that is, Mongolian) dynasty, whose rule lasted 88 years. It was at that time, from the reports of Marco Polo, that the European countries first got direct and authentic information about the social order, developed economy, and trade of China under Mongolian rule, as well as about everyday life in this huge far-eastern empire. Chinese civilization at that time surpassed even those of the most developed European countries. After the Mongolian dynasty, again a Chinese house of rulers - the Ming dynasty - came to power and ruled for 276 years, from 1368 to 1644. Although in the first decades of Ming rule a new - and the last - upswing occurred in Chinese civilization, and the Chinese emperors sent maritime expeditions to explore the "Western world," this upswing came to a halt in approximately 1430, and the Chinese ships reached only the shores of East Africa.

Beginning with the early sixteenth century, European ships and merchants appeared more frequently in the South China and Yellow seas. The Portuguese succeeded in getting a foothold in Macao in 1557, and the island remains under Portuguese rule even today. The rule of the Ming dynasty was again overthrown by the "northern barbarians," this time by the natives of what is now northeastern China, the Manchus, who in 1644 founded the Qing, or Manchu dynasty and spread their rule in 40 years over all of China. Under the rule of Manchu emperors, lasting 268 years, the development of Chinese civilization lagged epochs behind the civilization and technical progress of the European and American nations, which were taking the road to capitalist social development, but the people living in China did not become aware of this fact till the middle of the nineteenth century. The Manchus, who conquered the Chinese, soon adopted the culture of their subjects, which was essentially more advanced than their own, including their writing, language, and customs, to the extent that by the end of their rule they had completely lost their national identity and had become dissolved in the huge sea of the Han population. This experience further strengthened the faith of the Han population in their own cultural superiority, even during the centuries when the Chinese civilization was fatefully lagging behind.

In the first and second Opium Wars of 1838-1842 and 1856-1860, the Manchu government suffered a crushing defeat at the hands of the British and French fleets and expeditionary forces. It was forced to open its ports and to conclude humiliating, inequitable treaties, as well as to pay huge amounts in "indemnities". This brought home to the Chinese that their techniques and art of warfare were obsolete and that, as a consequence, they were at the mercy of smaller European countries that were far away and had incomparably smaller populations. From then on, patriotically minded Chinese government officials made several attempts to convince the ruling dynasty of the necessity of "self-strengthening" and reforms, of the expediency of appropriating, as soon as possible, the latest achievements of "overseas" science and technology, above all in the interest of developing a modern ordnance industry. But these attempts failed, one after the other, because of the resistance of the imperial court, which feared for its own power and influence if economic and political reforms were enacted, if foreign technologies and ways of life were introduced and adopted. Nor did the revolutionary movements organized among the peasants and directed against the Manchus bring lasting success. The Taiping uprising that erupted in 1851 was finally suppressed, after 14 years of heroic fighting, by the government army with foreign help, and the young emperor of Taiping Tianguo (the Heavenly Empire of Peace and Tranquility) was executed, together with the peasant leaders of the uprising.

China, which had become the "sick man of Eastern Asia" did not become an exclusive colony of any foreign power in the second half of the nineteenth century, merely because it proved to be too big a slice for any of them, even in its disrupted and powerless state. Beyond that, the colonizing powers were jealous of each other and tried to prevent any one of them from getting one-sided advantages in this far-away empire. This is why they rather divided the country into spheres of interest: Britain increased its economic, political, and military influence in the Yangtze region, France in southern China, Germany in the Shandong province, and Tsarist Russia in Manchuria and the Liaodong peninsula, and they made attempts to acquire privileges mainly in these areas. After its sweeping victory in the Sino--Japanese War of 1894, also Japan - strengthened in the wake of the Meiji reform of 1867 - appeared among the foreign powers demanding Chinese territories and areas of influence. In the peace treaty of Simonosek, concluded in 1895, China renounced its privileges in Korea and ceded Taiwan and the Penghu islands to Japan. (In this treaty China also agreed to ceding the Liaodong peninsula, but Russia succeeded in preventing its realization at that time. It was only 10 years later, as a result of the Russo-Japanese War of 1904-1905, that the peninsula became Japanese.) As a result of these conquests and the increasing penetration of foreign capital, which could no longer be hindered, the feudal Chinese society with its particular features had become, by the second half of the nineteenth century, a society of half-feudal and half-colonial character.

The humiliations suffered promted the best of the patriotic Chinese intelligentsia, both at home and abroad, to evolve a new reform movement and to organize various anti-Manchu and anti-foreigner secret societies in the final years of the past century. Those backing the constitutional monarchy - headed by Kang Youwei and Liang Qichao - tried to win the young emperor, Guangxu, for their reform ideas. But the "hundred-day reform" of 1898 failed because of the resistance of the dowager empress Ci Xi and her clique. The so-called boxer rebellion, organized against the foreign intruders by the Society of the Fist Creating Justice and Peace (in Chinese: Yi He Tuan), was bloodily suppressed by the united expeditionary forces of eight foreign powers in the summer of 1900, and the retaliatory actions continued till April 1901. The Allied League, organized in 1905 by Dr. Sun Yat-sen among the Chinese students in the United States, Japan, and the European countries set as its goal the overthrow of Manchu rule through armed revolution and the realization of the three so-called people's principles: national indepencence, democracy, and public welfare. The first goal was finally achieved, after several unsuccessful uprisings, by the national revolutionary forces in 1911. On October 11, the Republic of China was founded in Wuchang (in middle-China) and at the end of December Dr. Sun Yat-sen was elected as its temporary president. But the other triple goal, i.e., the "three people's principles," was far from being realized. Power in the Republic of China was soon seized by feudal war lords and one of them, general Yuan Shikai, even attempted to proclaim himself emperor in 1915. Sun Yat-sen soon had to understand that in the achievement of his revolutionary national and democratic goals he could hardly reckon with the help of either the Chinese landlords and generals in power, or with that of the foreign powers supporting them and using them for their own purposes. This is why, from the end of 1917, the interest and attention of Sun Yat-sen turned increasingly to the revolutionary manifestations of the Chinese masses and to revolutionary Russia. "We have to go along the way of the Russians" was how he drew the final conclusion a few years later.

Following World War I, China suffered new wrongs and humiliation. At the Paris Peace Conference - in which representatives of the Republic of China also took part - the big powers decided to give the areas previously under German occupation in Shandong province to Japan. This decision evoked justified indignation among the patriotic Chinese masses. On May 4, 1919, the students of Beijing organized a demonstration at Tiananmen square in the center of the capital, and marched from there to the dwellings of the members of government who wanted to accept the Paris decision, and even beat up one of the ministers who tried to flee. The government commanded military and police troops to disperse the demonstrators, and 20 students were detained. News of this spread, and within a few days antigovernment protest marches were held in most large cities of China; in June these turned into protest strikes. In the demonstrations and strikes, besides students, teachers and other members of the intelligentsia participated, as well as merchants and broad masses of workers. Under the impact of the mass movements the government finally retreated and refused to sign the Treaty of Versailles. Since that time, in China the "May 4th movement" has been considered the push that started the new democratic, national revolution which later turned into the people's revolution and in which - for the first time in the history of China - also masses of workers participated.

The Communist Party of China (CPC) formed in July, 1921, joined the anti-imperialist national revolution, headed - until his death in March, 1925 - by Sun Yat-sen and the Kuomintang (meaning National Party), organized by him. In 1922 the communists - so advised by the Komintern - individually joined the Kuomintang and even held several leading posts there. The Komintern devoted great attention to the cause of the Chinese revolution from the very beginning and showed readiness to support it with all means at its disposal. Sun Yat-sen similarly showed great sympathy for the Russian revolution and its leaders from the beginning. In August 1923, the executive committee of the Kuomintang sent a delegation, headed by Chiang Kai-shek, to the Soviet Union, asking for help from the young Soviet state and the Komintern in organizing their revolutionary party and the army. After that many Soviet and other communist political and military advisers traveled to China and offered effective help in the reorganization of the Kuomintang and the organization of the revolutionary army, including the training of the officers of the new army. Beyond that, in various schools of the Soviet Union and the Komintern the cadres of the Kuomintang studied in great numbers - in addition to members of the CPC. (Among them was Chiang Ching-kuo, son and political heir of Chiang Kai-shek - later president of the Republic of China on Taiwan.)

In the first half of the 1920s China was extremely divided and fragmented, both politically and militarily. The center of the national revolutionary forces was in Canton (Guangzhou), in the south, where in those years Sun Yat-sen formed several revolutionary governments. The seaports (e.g., Shanghai, Qingdao, Tianjin and Dalian) were controlled by large foreign powers (namely, Great Britain, France, and Japan). The Chinese government acknowledged by the foreign powers was seated in Beijing, but in some parts of the country power was actually exercised by generals and war lords, who fought with each other and were paid by various foreign powers. Under such conditions, national unity - a precondition for achieving national independence - was attainable only through revolutionary civil wars.

The first of these civil wars was waged between 1925 and 1927. As a result of the so-called northern campaign started in the summer of 1926, the armed forces of the Kuomintang, led by Chiang Kai-shek, succeeded in bringing a significant part of the country under their control, after which the new Kuomintang government formed in Nanking (Nanjing) was soon recognized by every foreign power. But the price of this "gesture" was the break and bloody showdown with the communists, beginning in the spring of 1927 with the Shanghai massacre. The revolutionary powers led by the communists then - having learned a lesson from a few city uprisings that had failed - marched to the mountains of southern China and first created "revolutionary bases of operation" and later "soviet regions." At the same time, with insurgents forced to flee from the towns and local peasant insurgents they organized the Chinese Red Army. This was the beginning of the second revolutionary civil war, which ended only with the assault by Japan in 1937, perceived as a menace to the national existence of China as a whole.

In the period of the second revolutionary civil war the Communist Party of China suffered huge casualties among its members. Ousted from the large cities, it had lost its earlier base of the working masses and revolutionary intellectuals, and in a few years it thus became the party of the poor illiterate peasants of the mountain regions. This circumstance left an indelible print on the ideological and political development of the CPC, manifested - among other things - in its mistrust of the intelligentsia and its oppressive policy. In the first half of the 1930s the concerns of the CPC were aggravated by the fact that its relations with the Komintern had become increasingly tense. In the meantime, the Kuomintang government consolidated its power over the greater part of the country and controlled its whole economic life through the banks and the state-monopolistic enterprises of the "four big families" belonging to its ruling élite. Beginning in 1930, Chiang Kai-shek deployed ever bigger and better equipped military forces to eliminate the soviet regions. After having beaten off four "punitive expeditions" in 1934-1935, the CPC was forced to abandon its bases of operation in southern China. With its "Long March" of 12 500 km it succeeded in transferring a part of its military forces to the revolutionary base of operation in northern Shaanxi. During this march - at the party conference held in Cunyi - Mao Zedong was elected chairman of the CPC; he held this post for more than 40 years, until his death. From this point on, the CPC became increasingly independent of the Komintern's influence and of the Communist Party of the Soviet Union (CPSU). In the meantime, exploiting China's internal struggles, Japan occupied northeastern China in 1931 and, by enthroning there the last Manchu emperor, set up a puppet empire called Manchukuo. With this, northeastern China had become - similar to Korea and Taiwan - a colonial area of Japan. Japan was not satisfied with the annexation of China's northeastern provinces, and attacked China again in July 1937, with the intention of subjugating China as a whole. Thus, the War of Resistance against the Japanese intruders began. It only ended 8 years later, in the autumn of 1945, with the catastrophic defeat and unconditional surrender of Japan in the Second World War.

During the War of Resistance, the Kuomintang and the CPC suspended their enmity for some time and achieved a united front againts the Japanese. The armed forces of the two parties were put under common command, while the organizational independence of the armies was preserved. The Red Army units of China, then numbering a mere 45 000, obtained the name of Eighth Army of the national armed forces. The operational area of this army was the occupied zones east and south of the "liberated region" in the border area of northern Shaanxi, where the Japanese maintained significant military forces because of the rich coalfields and railway junctions. Among the more than 10 000 partisans fighting in the middle and southern provinces of the country another army under CPC command was organized and called the "New 4th Army". Owing to the fast advance of the Japanese, the Kuomintang government seated in Nanking was transferred first to Wuhan in December 1937 (in middle China) and then in October 1938 to Chungking (Chongqing) in Sichuan province. The CPC set up in Chungking a liaison office headed by Zhou Enlai, later prime minister and minister of foreign affairs of the People's Republic of China (PRC). Still, cooperation between the Kuomintang and the CPC was not smooth. Clashes between their armed forces became increasingly frequent after 1941. After the United States had entered the war in the Far East, both parties took a wait-and-see attitude; they gathered and reserved their forces for fighting the decisive war for power over the whole of China after the victory to be won by the allies over Japan.

In the years of the War of Resistance the army led by the CPC increased to one million, and in 1945 they already controlled 19 liberated regions with a population of more than 100 million. The puritan atmosphere of the liberated regions and the strict discipline of the communist troops were in such glaring contrast with the atmosphere and state of public affairs in the Kuomintang areas and armies that between 1942 and 1944 even the American military leadership and some American government circles contemplated whether it would not be more expedient and useful to spend the billions of dollars and military equipment that was being used to support the corrupted Kuomintang system on the modernization of the military forces led by the CPC and on increasing their fighting value. But this possibility was excluded in early 1945 and, following that, they did everything in their power to keep alive the demoralized system of Chiang Kai-shek.

After the capitulation of Japan the conflicts within the anti-Japanese national front immediately revived. The liberation of Manchuria by the Soviet Red Army brought the revolutionary forces under the influence of the CPC into a more advantageous position all over northeastern China, and they also participated in the disarming of the Japanese army. The powers victorious in the Second World War at that time still made combined efforts to prevent eruption of a new civil war in China, declared to be the fifth great power in the United Nations, so that a democratic coalition government acceptable to all parties might be established. Both parties strove to ward off these efforts; the Kuomintang trusted the weight and superior technical equipment of its forces, while the CPC hoped to become victorious through the discipline and revolutionary spirit of its army. (In the summer of 1946 the armed forces of the Kuomintang numbered 4.3 million, those of the CPC only 1.2 million, and there were huge differences in equipment in favor of the former.) Therefore, in July 1946 the Kuomintang launched a general offensive against the liberated regions to prevent further increase of the forces and influence of the CPC. With this the third revolutionary civil war began, which ended in 1949 with the complete collapse of the Kuomintang régime.

In the first year of the third revolutionary civil war the overpowering numerical and technical superiority of the government forces was still felt. The armed forces of the CPC - which then took the name of Chinese People's Liberation Army (CPLA) - were compelled to give up the overwhelming part of the liberated areas and bases of operation in the middle and the north of China and to regroup their troops into the provinces bordering on Mongolia and the Soviet Union in order to gain an adequately protected hinterland. In March 1947 the Kuomintang troops occupied Yenan, the seat of the border region of Shaanxi-Gansu-Ningxia, which had been a legendary center of revolutionary forces for a decade. But the war, extending into ever greater areas, soon exhausted the agressors who suffered increasing losses of life against the people's forces who enjoyed the support of the population. By the summer of 1947 the Kuomintang army already had lost more than one million men; these could be only partly replaced, even with the most violent conscription. The fighting spirit and morale of the peasants forced into the Kuomintang army rapidly declined - not least because of the ever more inhuman treatment they received. Massive desertion and changing sides to the people's forces became everyday occurrences. Nor was the situation any better in the hinterland of the Kuomintang. Despite massive American support, the economic and political situation deteriorated year by year and month by month. Inflation became galloping and assumed astronomical dimensions by the end of the war. In the summer of 1947 the units of the CPLA took the counter-offensive and not only reconquered the earlier liberated areas within a year, but deeply penetrated into the Kuomintang regions as well. By the summer of 1948 the CPLA was organized into a regular army and its troops started major liberating operations. In the so-called Liaoxi-Shenyang battle between September and November of 1948 the most important industrial centers of north-eastern China were liberated. Following that, between November 1948 and January 1949 - in the course of the Huaihai battle - the region between the Huai river and the Yellow Sea was cleared of Kuomintang troops. Simultaneously a third operation was taking place, in the framework of which the units of the CPLA liberated Tianjin and Beijing. By the spring of 1949 these three battles essentially decided the final outcome of the third revolutionary civil war (also called People's Liberation War). In April 1949 the people's armed forces crossed the Yangtse, and in 2 days they occupied the seat of the Kuomintang government: Nanjing. The government then fled to Canton (Guangzhou) but was ousted from there in October. The Kuomintang officials and their supporters, together with their families, were brought with American help to the island of Taiwan, as were the remnants of the defeated army. The sovereignty of the "Republic of China" extended thenceforth only to this island of 36 000 sq.km and to a few tiny islands off the coast of the mainland. On October 1, 1949, Mao Zedong declared the formation of "the People's Republic of China" from the balustrade of the former imperial palace's Gate of Heavenly Peace (in Chinese: Tiananmen). With this, one of the most painful periods in the recent history of China came to an end, through which the people languishing in a half-feudal, half-colonial state had suffered immeasurable pain and humiliation. But the trials of the Chinese people had not yet ended. The development of Chinese society under the leadership of the victorious revolutionary power, the CPC, took a direction which - from the perspective of 40 years - may be considered rather a violent attempt at overcoming socioeconomic backwardness "in a revolutionary way" which led to a historical blind alley than a deep-reaching modernization securing both national and social advancement.

* * *

Even this sketchy outline of China's history shows that in the identity-consciousness of the most populous nation of the world the greatness and stability of their culture and civilization as well as the moral superiority of the Chinese people were dominant for almost 2000 years. This awareness protected them against external influence and gave them the ability to resist and assimilate for so long. Until the appearance of the "foreign devils," the Chinese were not really interested in the outside world, all the more as the overwhelming majority of the people lived in close-knit local communities and had little contact even with neighboring towns. Only wars and natural disasters and famines following them at times forced a part of the population to leave their place of birth, resettle, or emigrate. From this way of life only merchants, soldiers, imperial officials, and students preparing for official examinations were excepted, those whose occupation or vocation entailed frequent changes of place. Even in the twentieth century, direct contacts with foreigners were established only by inhabitants of the large seaports, big cities, employees of foreign firms, and designated government officials.

Because of this seclusion from the outside world, even the most enlightened thinkers of China became aware late - one might say, too late - of the anachronistic nature of their social order, of the epochal backwardness of their economy, science, and technology and of the resulting need for deep social change and modernization. On the governmental level this recognition came only several decades later. In addition, by the time the patriotic Chinese intellectuals first reached this awareness around the turn of the century, beyond the internal obstacles to modernization, a number of external circumstances hindered China from powerfully addressing itself to the modernization of the country and to gradually overcoming the backwardness in civilization that had accumulated over the centuries.

It is well known that in the final decades of the nineteenth century some societies that had not yet reached bourgeois democracy through revolutionary transformation started on the road to capitalism, under the conditions of absolute feudal monarchies, with industrialization and reforms implemented from above and supported with the instruments of power of the state. Among them were Tsarist Russia and Japan and, to a certain extent, even the Austro-Hungarian empire and Germany. Along this road they made considerable progress in a few decades. Each of the countries mentioned had become significant factors in world politics and not insignificant factors in world economy by the turn of the century as large feudal-capitalist and/or imperialist powers. This historical opportunity was not given to China, because - beyond the fact that the Manchu court was shortsighted and conservative - an independent capitalist social development of national character conflicted above all with the colonizing efforts of the world powers, themselves capitalist, and met with their resistance. In spite of the faster rate of capitalization beginning at the time of the First World War, under the half-feudal, half-colonial conditions of the country the national and petty bourgeoisie were never in a position where they could succesfully achieve bourgeois democratic revolutionary change by relying on their own economic and political power and thus start Chinese society along the road to independent, national capitalist development. This is why the national revolution of Sun Yat-sen failed in spite of repeated starts and trials, and why this great Chinese revolutionary democrat and national hero searched at the end of his life - disappointed with the capitalist powers that were leading in the development of civilization - for possibilities and modes of cooperation and alliance with the masses of Chinese workers and peasants, and with the center of the international communist movement, the Komintern.

Nor did Chiang Kai-shek's compromise with the leading capitalist powers and his turning against the communists bring about the possibility for independent, national capitalist development and for closing the gap between China and the pioneering countries of the world. After 1927 a socioeconomic system became established in China which preserved throughout its half-feudal and half-colonial character; the feudal and imperialist exploitation and rule was complemented by the exploitation and rule of the so-called bureaucratic capital. (Bureaucratic capital meant in China the capital of the Chinese comprador bourgeoisie intertwined with foreign capital, and the "state-monopolist" capital hoarded by the leaders of the Kuomintang through the acquisition and filling of key government posts. Together, these amounted at the end of the 1940s to already nearly 80% of the total Chinese social capital.) This is why, after World War II, broad masses of the population became convinced that the development and rise of the Chinese nation could be achieved only by overthrowing the joint rule of feudalism, imperialism, and bureaucratic capital, that is, in the wake of the victory of a radical people's revolution. This recognition and conviction were decisive for the victory of the new democratic revolution led by the CPC, as the basic goal of this revolution was precisely the removal of these three obstacles.

The "new democratic revolution" (in Chinese: xin-minzhuzhuyi geming) was introduced into the terminology of Chinese Marxist literature as a category of political theory by Mao Zedong in the early 1940s, and at the end of the 1940s it was adopted by the international literature as well. Mao Zedong divided the Chinese revolution into two qualitatively different stages. The first stage was that of the new democratic revolution, in which the people's revolutionary forces, led by the CPC, basically solved the tasks of the bourgeois democratic revolution, in such a way that the second, socialist stage of the revolution must necessarily follow within a few decades. Between the two stages a new democratic society, of transitory nature, should come about in wich both socialist and nonsocialist elements as well as transitory and half-socialist ones may be found. (By socialist elements are meant the state-owned enterprises and economic units, and the collectively owned cooperative units; by nonsocialist elements are meant the units and enterprises remaining in private individual or capitalist ownership; and by half-socialist elements are meant the private and state joint enterprises operating in various state-capitalist forms as well as the cooperatives of lower type which distributed the income not only according to work, but also paid rent for the land and other means of production contributed.) The economic basis of this society is a form of the multisectoral market economy wherein the elements of a planned economy already appear and gather strength, the most important element of its system of superstructure being the state power of the people's democratic dictatorship. This relies mainly on the alliance of workers and peasants as well as on the alliance of classes coming about with the urban and rural petite bourgeoisie and the patriotic national bourgeoisie. This alliance of the four "revolutionary classes" is led by the CPC, also leaving certain room for the political activities of democratic parties and organizations of the allied classes, insofar as these acknowledge the leading role of the communist party. This is the most important difference from the bourgeois democratic revolutions led by the bourgeoisie, and from the parliamentary democracies that secure equal rights and chances for every party.

Elaboration of the strategic concept of the stages of the new democratic and socialist revolution reflected the sound recognition of the leaders of the CPC at that time that the communist party, which took upon itself the leadership of this revolution, could not set the carrying out of a socialist revolution and of socioeconomic changes of socialist nature as immediate goals for the radical people's revolution. Chinese industry was underdeveloped and the working class was extremely weak in terms of numbers; in addition, in China and in similar colonial, half-colonial, and half-feudal societies the national bourgeoisie proved to be unsuited to simultaneously lead the national liberation and bourgeois revolutions. Thus, instead, in the first stage of such revolutions all patriotic and democratic forces had to be rallied and their first efforts had to be aimed at achieving national independence and at solving, as soon as possible, the tasks of the bourgeois democratic revolution. This required above all liquidation of the rule of foreign capital and the closely related domestic comprador capital, consistent implementation of a radical land reform, and the establishment of a system of political power based on representation of the people.

In the Chinese concept of the new democratic revolution and a new democratic society it is not difficult to recognize the intention of demarcation from the Soviet road and the Stalinist model of socialist revolution and socialist construction; in a sense, it may also be conceived as a refutation of the latter as a model of general validity, mandatory for everyone. For a long time, the leaders of the CPSU actually interpreted the Chinese standpoint in this sense and did everything they could to get the leaders of the CPC revise and discard this Maoist concept as soon as possible, worked out with the claim to theoretical generalization and supporting the right to the existence of "particular development paths." The most curious thing in the whole matter is that the concept of necessarily constructing a new democratic society was revised and discarded by Mao Zedong himself, and this at a historical moment - in the spring of 1953, not long after Stalin's death, when he was no longer forced to do so by external circumstances. After that, the Soviet model of "socialist construction" and of "socialist industrialization" was fully accepted and followed in China, together with the utterly anti-Marxist and arbitrary Stalinist system of criteria for "laying the bases of socialism." It was in the wake of these that the "socialist" economic and political system also evolved in China which in a few decades became an almost insurmountable obstacle to the development of the forces of production, the free development of people's talents, the realization of the democratic and revolutionary goals and ideals. This is why a thorough change and reform of the economic and political systems has become a historical necessity in China, i.e., evolvement of the policy of reform and opening.

Attempts at economic and political reform started in China at the end of 1978. More than 10 years have passed since then. This book is about these 10-11 years, rich in events, showing equally achievements and failures and not lacking in dramatic turns, either. The closure of the manuscript coincided with the 40th anniversary of the existence of the People's Republic of China, and the events and developments of the past decade would be difficult to understand without a knowledge of their antecedents. Thus, beyond this sketchy historical outline, the first chapter of the book will highlight the most important events and stages in the socioeconomic and politico-ideological development during the first three decades of the existence of the PRC. The closing of the manuscript was facilitaded - strange as this may seem - by the dramatic events in China in the summer of 1989. These set a definitive limit to a stage in the course of economic reforms and political reform attempts that covered more than a decade. The thrust of the reforms had already suffered a break years earlier, and in the autumn of 1988 a rearrangement was begun within the framework of a recentralizing policy and administrative measures aimed at "improving the economic environment and rectifying the economic order" (in Chinese: zhili jingji huanjing yu zhengdun jingji zhixu). Suppression of the "counterrevolutionary disturbances" and then the restoration of "order and stability" essentially only crowned the process begun earlier of "readjustment" and "ordering". All this shows that, while clinging to the fiction of "existing socialism" and of the "socialist road," China has not managed to keep the vigorous economic and political reform process in motion; it has been stopped or restrained for a time. Nevertheless, in the foreseeable future even for China there is no other solution and way out of her abiguous and unstable situation but to continue and speed up again economic and political reform processes launched 11 years ago, namely in the direction determined on the 13th national congress of the CPC and in the reform programmes elaborated subsequently.

PART ONE

Chapter One
BRIEF HISTORICAL REVIEW

The Chinese People's Revolution and Socioeconomic Situation of China in 1949

As a result of armed fighting and repeated civil wars over several decades, the people's revolution gained a sweeping victory in China in 1949, and on October 1, the People's Republic of China was formed. The fight was led throughout by the communist party.

The Chinese people's revolution was an organic part of the radical people's revolutions of the twentieth century which today may already be called typical. They began with the Russian revolutions and set the goal of accelerating the modernization of countries and societies pushed to the periphery of capitalist world development, together with elimination of their backwardness in economy and civilization. These revolutions are composed of a particular mix and intertwining of the elements of three revolutionary processes of differing nature and historical function. Elements of the antifeudal bourgeois revolution, of the anti-imperialist national liberating revolution, and of the anti-capitalist proletarian revolution are equally represented. Where and when which revolutionary elements come to the fore and become preponderant depends on the direct and indirect impact and mutual effects of several objective and subjective, internal and external factors. In determining the character of these revolutions, however, it is by all means advisable to make a distinction between the declared and the real objectives as well as between the apparent and real processes.

The Chinese people's revolution was called a "new democratic" revolution by the Communist Party of China, which took upon itself its organization and direction. With this name they intended to emphasize the qualitative difference between the Chinese revolution and the bourgeois democratic revolutions of the old type. The aim of this revolution was something other than to pave the way for capitalistic social development, although as regards its basic tasks and historical function it resembled the bourgeois revolutions in many respects. It wanted to open the way for such a new democratic or people's democratic development which would necessarily lead to transition from the new democratic stage of revolution to the socialist one and thus, in the final analysis, open the road to establishing a socialist society in China.[1]

As a result of the victory of the people's revolution the development of Chinese society thus stepped from one transitory era - begun hardly more than 100 years earlier - into a new transitory era without having succesfully completed the historical task of the first one: transition from the Asian type of feudalism to capitalism. With this victory of 1949 such a transitory era began, following the ideology then achieving supremacy; its historical task and function should no longer have been to make the capitalist mode of production dominant, but rather to avoid capitalist development and to gradually surpass capitalism altogether. For this, however, both the objective and subjective conditions were missing at the moment the revolution was victorious. Thus the PRC faced a relatively long new democratic stage of social development, in the course of which - - relying on the state power of the people's democratic dictatorship and consistently implementing the tasks of the new democratic revolution - the objective and subjective, economic and social conditions for transition to its socialist stage were to be brought about gradually, chief among them the modernization of the Chinese civilization.

This long-term strategy of social development was truly reflected by the Common Program of the Chinese People's Political Consultative Conference (CPPCC), adopted in September, 1949, which functioned as a basic law of the country until the elaboration and approval, in 1954, of the Constitution of the PRC.[2] Accordingly: "The People's Republic of China is a New Democratic or a People's Democratic state. It carries out the people's democratic dictatorship led by the working class, based on the alliance of workers and peasants, und uniting all democratic classes and all nationalities in China. It opposes imperialism, feudalism, and bureaucratic capitalism and strives for the independence, democracy, peace, unity, prosperity and strength of China."[3]

In economic policy the Common Program advocated the boosting of production, reconciliation of social and individual interests, development and cooperation of every sector of the five-sector economy (state, cooperative, private capitalist, state capitalist and individual). It identified conclusion of the land reform and consolidation of the country's financial position as basic conditions for developing the forces of production and for industrializing the country.

The new people's state considered the national bourgeoisie - together with the urban and rural petty bourgeoisie - to be allies of the workers and peasants and provided for measures restricting them only in exceptional cases and situations. The rights of the nationalities were laid down in a separate chapter, establishing first of all that "all nationalities in the People's Republic of China shall have equal rights and duties,"[4] and where they were preponderant, it envisaged the creation and realization of territorial autonomy.

This shows that the Chinese people's revolution preserved its new democratic or people's democratic character, even following the formation of the PRC and - as against declarations made a few years later - in October 1949 it had not yet entered the stage of socialist revolution.

At the moment of its formation the PRC was the most populous country of the world but - as regards its level of economic development - one of the poorest and the most backward. China's land area amounted to hardly 7% of the world total, but even then more than half a billion people, more than 22% of the world total, lived there. Of the population of 542 million, 95% lived in the smaller, eastern part of the country, nearer to the sea; the total area of the country was 9.6 million sq.km. Almost 90% of the huge population lived in rural settlements. According to computations made by UN statisticians in 1949, the per capita national income was merely US $27 in China, while - according to the same methodology - in the same year it was US $57 in India, 100 in Japan, 269 in Hungary, 308 in the Soviet Union, 773 in the United Kingdom, and 1453 in the United States.[5]

When the PRC was founded, the country showed the chaotic picture of a society tired of and disarranged by wars, in a half-colonial and half-feudal state. Inflation reached astronomical figures, production attained barely half of the pre war level in industry and about two thirds of it in agriculture. In the generation of national income modern industry had a share of 6.3%, traditional small-scale industry 7.4%, agriculture 71.0%, and all other branches 15.3%.[6] Thus, the main place in the country's economy was occupied by small-scale agriculture, the peasants working with extremely obsolete production techniques and backward methods. The modern manufacturing industry, using mechanical techniques and technologically backward, showed several distorted, semi-colonial features, both in its structure and in its territorial location. It employed 2.5 million workers; i.e., the industrial proletariat did not attain 0.5% of the population. (Even including the wage earners employed in traditional trade and transportation, the Chinese working class hardly exceeded 15 million in 1949, i.e., 5% of the adult population.) The underdevelopment of the transportation network and the lack of modern means of transport - coupled with the devastating inflation - made the lack of a united national market even more palpable and also the huge differences in level of development between different parts of the country. Economic backwardness was most substantially and most immediately manifest in the extremely low living standards and miserable living conditions of the people, in widespread hunger and misery. The daily per capita consumption of calories hardly amounted to 1600 for the poor urban and rural inhabitants; in some places it was even lower in the period following the liberation, and under normal conditions this would have been equal to the daily calorie requirement of a 5 to 6-year-old child.

In the period period to the victory of the revolution and the following radical land reform almost 70% of the Chinese peasants were landless or owned only a minimum of land; they rented small plots from the landlords under cruel tenancy conditions. Millions of paupers, unable to live in the villages, tried to find work in the cities, but mostly they only increased the numbers of paupers in the urban slums living from occasional work, or of ragamuffins rallying in criminal gangs. The group of urban and rural exploiters - including their family members - hardly exceeded 10%-12% of the population; the landlord and rich peasant families each amounted to 4%-5% and the urban haute and medium bourgeoisie to 2%-3%. The petite bourgeois and white--collar groups (including the middle peasants, individual artisans, small merchants, physicians, teachers, students, and other intellectuals) made up 20%-22% of the population in villages and 30%-35% in towns. The number of those knowing how to read and write in pre-liberation China had not reached 20% in villages and 30% in cities; thus the national rate of illiteracy was approximately 80%.

Economic Restoration and Accomplishment of the New Democratic Revolution (1949-1952)

Following formation of the PRC, the economy was restored, the remaining tasks of the new democratic revolution were accomplished within relatively short time, by the end of 1952, in spite of the fact that this period included the eruption of the Korean war, with the direct participation of Chinese popular volunteers.

The newly established people's power, guided by the Central People's Government, brought about in a few months a relatively strong state economic sector which firmly controlled the key economic positions. The instruments used for this were expropriation of so-called bureaucratic capital (meaning that of the Kuomintang state-capitalist haute bourgoisie and of the comprador bourgeoisie intertwined with foreign capital), confiscation of property owned by foreign capitalists, and nationalization of the majority of banks and foreign trading companies. With the aid of these and a number of further measures it was possible to brake the inflation that had lasted for 12 years by the spring of 1950 and by the end of that year public finances were also balanced. Following this annual plans were worked out for the reconstruction of the economy, for the rational organization of production and distribution, of commodity trade, and of money circulation, as well as for the utilization and control of private capitalist industrial and commercial firms owned by the national bourgeoisie. In the villages, however, a radical land reform of historically unprecedented dimensions was implemented, an agrarian revolution from the basis upwards. In its course, 47 million hectares of land were distributed free of charge among more than 300 million landless peasants or those with only a minimum of land. This freed the earlier tenants from a land rent of 35 million tons of grain in physical terms. Moreover, in the course of the land reform the debts of poor peasants that had accumulated with landlords and rich usurer peasants - frequently over several generations - were cancelled. With this measure the material bases of feudal exploitation that had existed for thousands of years were once and for all abolished in China. The Chinese agriculture became one of typically small peasants, where the size of a plot hardly exceeded 1-1.5 hectares even in medium peasant families.

In consequence of the beginning of continuous production and the effective measures taken by the central organs of economic management, the economic and financial position of the country improved year by year and economic reconstruction was accomplished in almost every area by the end of 1952. Industrial output increased almost 2.5-fold in 3 years, and the value of agricultural production increased relative to 1949 by nearly 50%. The economic and technical aid provided by the Soviet Union played an important role in the reconstruction of industry and transportation during this period. In February 1950, on the signing of the treaty on friendship, alliance, and mutual aid between the two countries the Soviet government granted a commodity credit of US $300 million. The bulk of this sum was used for the rebuilding and technical reconstruction of 50 large Chinese factories. In place of the earlier Japanese and Soviet capital interests, joint Chinese-Soviet enterprises were founded and put into operation.

In the years of the reconstruction period the foreign economic relations of China changed radically and were rearranged. The share of the socialist countries in the foreign trade turnover of the country rose from 29% in 1950 to above 70% by 1952. The home trade turnover also expanded significantly: the purchases of the population increased in terms of value by 62% between 1950 and 1952. As a result of the stopping of inflation, growing chances for work, and the implementation of land reform, personal consumption increased in the cities by about 60% and in the villages by more than 30%. This meant that the daily per capita consumption of calories in 1952 was 2100 in the villages and around 2300 in the cities.

By the end of the reconstruction period a system of economic management and political institutions of the PRC became established which, as regards its basic features and organizational setup - with smaller or greater modifications and temporary functional disturbances or breaks - functioned for more than 30 years, albeit with ever diminishing efficiency. At the end of 1952 - with the cooperation of the experts and advisers of the State Planning Commission of the USSR (the Gosplan) - the State Planning Commission of the PRC was established; its main task was to elaborate annual and 5-year plans and to organize and monitor their implementation. The Chinese system of planning and economic management was based completely on Soviet experience and Soviet methodology, and its system of institutions was basically built on the pattern of the Soviet system of economic management institutions. The same may also be said of the system of political institutions, with the difference that in its setup and operation Chinese features and traditions also played a role. In this period the military or semimilitary nature of the newly organized public administration was still strongly felt in China; this derived from the fact that most of the leading cadre members had earlier held commanding posts in the Chinese People's Liberation Army.

Launching the Socialist Transformation: The First 5-Year Plan (1953-1957)

After the rapid and successfull implementation of economic reconstruction, the question of large-scale, planned socialist construction was put on the agenda also in China, in the context of industrialization of the country and the gradual "socialist transformation" of the nonsocialist sectors of the national economy. According to the general guidelines of the CPC issued for the period of transition, this was originally intended to be carried out during three 5-year plan periods, that is, up to 1967.[7] In fulfilling these tasks they believed - according to the then prevailing concept and terminology - they would be able to lay the "foundations of socialism" in China, just as it had been accomplished in the Soviet Union between 1928 and 1937.

Elaboration of the general guidelines for the "transition period" leading to socialism and its proclamation were closely related to the drafting of the first 5-year plan of the PRC and to the acquisition of the external - basically Soviet - help needed to realize the industrialization provided for in it. In the formation and modification of the Chinese strategy for transition to socialism as well as the dimensions and rate of socialist construction, the death of Stalin in the spring of 1953 played a detectable role. This event raised in the then leaders of the CPC, and particularly in Mao Zedong, the hope that if they developed socialism faster and more successfully than anyone else they might become the leader of the socialist world system and of the whole communist world movement.[8] This strategic concept was, for more than a decade, a determining factor in Chinese domestic and foreign policies.

Negotiations between the Chinese and the Soviet government regarding Soviet economic, technical, and financial help to be granted for the industrialization program of the first 5-year plan began in the autumn of 1952. Concrete results were achieved only in May 1953, when an agreement was signed to the effect that - in addition to the reconstruction and equipment of the 50 large factories already included in the 1950 treaty - the Soviet

Union would provide help in building and equipping a further 91 large new industrial establishments, as well as in starting up production (including the training of production managers and skilled workers). This agreement was published - for unknown reasons - not until September 1953, in the form of a letter of thanks addressed by Mao Zedong to G. M. Malenkov, then prime minister of the USSR. Negotiations continued for another year about further extending this aid, as a result of which in October 1954 - on the occasion of N. S. Khrushchev's first visit to China - a new complementary agreement was signed by the representatives of the two countries about the Soviet technical and financial aid to be granted for the construction and equipment of a further 15 large modern establishments and about increasing the dimensions of several other projects already under construction. As a result of all these agreements, also covering the value of military aid granted for the participation of China in the Korean war, between 1950 and 1954 the Soviet Union granted credit totalling 1.4 billion rubles; this amount was completely repaid by 1964.[9]

Because of the protracted negotiations with the Soviet Union, the first 5-year economic development plan of the PRC was not elaborated until the spring of 1955, and it was approved only at the second session of the National People's Congress (NPC) in July of that year. (The Congress had first convened in 1954.) Until then, the development of the economy was directed on the basis of annual national economic plans and budget estimates.

In the first 5-year plan period the overwhelming portion of resources and efforts was concentrated on creating a basis of modern big industry; 42.5% of total national investment was spent on the development of industry, in which heavy industry had a 85% share, and light industry 15%. The backbone of industrial investment projects were the 156 large production establishments constructed with Soviet help (they represented more than half of total investment input), and they belonged, almost without exception, to various branches of heavy industry. Some of them actually represented the appearance in China of a new industry, their technical level corresponding to the development level of the Soviet Union at that time. (It was in this period that the automobile, tractor, and airplane industries, the heavy machine tools industry, the power-plant and metallurgical equipment industries, and several branches of the chemical industry became established in China.)

From the investments of the first 5-year plan, agriculture and the related branches (forestry, water management, meteorology) received only a small share (7.1%), although this branch was the almost exclusive source of livelihood for more than 80% of the able-bodied population. The effects of this neglect of agricultural production manifested themselves in negative phenomena in the middle of the plan period: supply of the urban population with foodstuffs and of the light industry with raw and basic materials of agricultural origin became increasingly difficult. Efforts were made to overcome the difficulties partly by administrative measures, partly by accelerating the rate of collectivization in agriculture. (The administrative measures included mandatory and centralized state procurement and sale of the major agricultural products and rationing of the most important foodstuffs and industrial consumer goods.)

The first 5-year plan provided for a somewhat faster progress in the socialist transformation of the nonsocialist sectors of the economy in comparison to the general guidelines of the CPC for the period of transition. It set as its target that by the end of 1957 about half of the peasant farms in the earlier liberated areas, and about one third of those in the later liberated regions, should be amalgamated into producers' cooperatives of a semi-socialist nature; parallel to this, the organization of rural and urban artisans, and of individual carriers and retail merchants into various forms of cooperatives was to be started. In the case of private capitalist industry and trade, the plan made efforts to establish closer cooperation with the state sector, based on contractual relations (e.g., ordering of commodities, jobwork, outwork, procurement and sale on commission).[10] The establishment of joint, state-private ventures, on a higher level than these medium forms of Chinese state capitalism, presupposing a partnership in ownership relations, was only exceptionally provided for.

Following approval of the plan, however, the socialist transformation developed at a rate utterly different from the one planned. On the day following approval of the plan Mao Zedong convened a national party conference (of secretaries) at which he declared that in China's villages conditions had matured for accelerating socialist transformation. On his initiative, a nationwide movement aimed at socialist transformation began in the autumn of 1955. By the end of 1956 - i.e., in merely 1.5 years - more than 96% of the country's 118 million peasant farms were pushed into producers' cooperatives, and almost 88% of these became members of higher-type cooperatives with a completely socialist character. During the same period almost 92% of private artisans, nearly all individual carriers, about 96% of private retailers and caterers (cook-shops, snack-bars) entered cooperatives. In 1956, private capitalist industrial and commercial firms were uniformly transformed into state-private joint companies in every branch of the economy. The former owners were entitled - beyond the salary depending on their position - to a "fixed rent" for 5 years, corresponding to 5% of the value of their property taken into the joint venture; in principle a 25% "redemption" or "compensation" was envisaged for them in return for renouncing their property. (This right was prolonged in 1961 for a further 5 years.) Thus, for the last year of the plan period the remaining task in the field of socialist transformation was to consolidate the producers' cooperatives, cooperative shops, and catering enterprises, as well as the joint ventures of varying size and equipment that had all been established in a hurry. With this rapid and radical transformation of ownership relations one of the most important tasks of the transitory period leading to socialism was considered accomplished, in substance, and 10 years earlier than the deadline that had been set, it was declared that the foundations of socialism had been laid in China.

Despite this socialist transformation at a stormy rate, China's economic development was surprisingly fast and successful during the first 5-year plan period. On annual average, the national income increased by 8.9%, the total value of industrial output by 18%, that of agriculture by 4.5%. Within the generation of national income the share of industry increased from 19.5% in 1952 to 28.3% by 1957, while in the same period the share of agriculture fell from 57.7% to 46.8%. In the utilization of national income the ratio of accumulation to consumption hovered about 24:76, and under the then prevailing conditions this could be considered rational, almost optimal. During that plan period the value of retail trade within home trade increased by more than 70%, and foreign trade turnover by nearly 70%, 75% of foreign trade was transacted with the socialist countries, 55% of it with the Soviet Union. While in these years China received significant economic, technical, and financial aid from the more advanced socialist countries, above all from the Soviet Union, China itself provided considerable aid to the socialist countries devastated by war or suffering in any other way (1953: Korea, 1955: Vietnam, 1957: Hungary).

During the first 5-year plan the income and consumption level of the population increased at a slower rate than in the preceding period. The value of annual per capita consumption increased nationwide from 76 yuan in 1952 to 102 in 1957; this meant an increase from 62 to 79 yuan in the villages and from 148 to 205 yuan in the cities. Thus, the difference in per capita consumption between rural and urban dwellers became greater, from a ratio of 1:2.4 in 1952 to 1:2.6 by 1957. At the same time, the proportion of urban population within the total rose from 12.5% in 1952 to 15.4 in 1957 and the per capita calorie consumption increased to approximately 2200 in the villages and 2500 in the cities in 1957.

During the first 5-year plan period further significant changes occured in the Chinese economic and management system heading toward the traditional model of a planned economy. The scope of national economic planning was expanded and "the unified planning and management on various levels" was extended beyond the state sector to cover also cooperatives and the state-capitalist sector. Since by 1956 the individual and private-capitalist sectors had practically been liquidated, the government control of economic processes became general. The earlier indirect forms of management were gradually replaced by direct ones: mandatory plan targets, budget levies and subsidies, mandatory state procurement and sale, centralized allocation, and centrally determined prices. As a result, by the end of the plan period the already underdeveloped commodity and monetary relations as well as the regulatory role of the market were significantly restricted and suppressed. Eighty percent of the budget revenues flowed into the central budget and financed 75% of the budget expenses. Of the basic construction projects, 90% were financed by the state, and almost 80% of the investment projects financed from the budget were started and implemented on the basis of central decisions. It was in this period that the rigid centralized system of manpower management became established, under which firms were prohibited from recruiting workers directly; also, the regrouping of labor among firms without permission as well as the migration of rural workers into towns with the aim of individually finding jobs was prohibited, and this secured a privileged position for the workers of the state sector for many decades.[11] But all these changes took place in the framework of an economic growth which was relatively dynamic and entailed deep structural changes as well; the unified and centralized system of economic control and management still exhibited a rather large degree of flexibility, changeability and capacity for adjustment. Thus, from the point of view of controlling and guiding the economic processes, centralization was advantageous. At the same time, it was already becoming apparent that the development of vertical economic control would meet with serious difficulties in China, mainly because of the poor qualifications of lower-echelon cadres.

The Great Leap Forward and the Period of Readjustment (1958-1960 and 1961-1965)

Originally, 1958 should have been the first year of the second 5-year plan of national economic development, covering the years up to 1962. In reality, it is remembered as the first year of the elaboration and practical implementation of the arbitrary economic development concept of the "great leap," which had very grave consequences. The policy of the "great leap" was forced through for 3 years until, under the impact of the catastrophic economic situation and massive famine that had developed by the winter of 1960-1961, even the most stubborn of the Chinese leaders had to see that an urgent "readjustment" of this policy was needed. The elimination of the grave consequences of the "great leap" took 5 years, i.e., the length of a full 5-year plan. (For this period, however, no new 5-year plan was elaborated; the readjustment was carried on under annual plans.) This is why it is more expedient to discuss the two periods together in the same section in this brief historical review.

The guidelines for the second 5-year plan and its targets were reviewed by prime minister Zhou Enlai already at the 8th congress of the CPC, in September 1956. Thus by 1962 national income was to exceed the level attained in 1957 by 50%, the combined value of agricultural and industrial gross output by 75% (industry increasing by 100% and agriculture by 35%). The targets in physical terms were a steel output of 10.5 million (metric) tons, a coal output of 190-220 million tons, electrical energy 40-43 billion kWh, cotton fabrics 7.3-8 billion metres, grain 250 million tons, cotton 2.4 million tons envisaged for 1962. Retail trade turnover was to grow by 50%, the wage level of workers and other employees as well as the average income of peasants equally by 25%-30% between 1958 and 1962.

At the end of 1957 these targets - by no means low - no longer satisfied the Chinese leaders, who had become intoxicated with the fast and resounding success of socialist transformation. These leaders, headed by Mao Zedong, were convinced that the possibilities deriving from the fact that socialism had become a world system would allow a "big leap" of the Chinese economy, that is, its sudden rapid development over several years, if they were coupled with the particularly advantageous objective conditions of China, if the efforts were properly organized and managed, and if the proletarian internationalism were correctly interpreted. (By the possibilities offered by socialism as a world system, aid to China from the more advanced socialist countries was meant, and by China's advantageous conditions, richness in raw materials and primary energy, an almost inexhaustible supply of labor, and enthusiastic revolutionary masses ready to sacrifice were meant.) Beyond that, the leaders were of the opinion that complete collectivization and the communist principle of distribution according to need could be implemented in China even with a relatively low abundance of products (at the level of basic supply) because Chinese society had not gone through several centuries of capitalist development, and the Chinese people were therefore not infected by materialism, by the harmful spirit of egoism and bourgeois individualism. Thus, they believed that as a result of the "great leap" Chinese society could "catch up with Britain" in 10-15 years and carry out the transition from socialism into communism. These willful concepts derived partly from and fed on the false assumption that socialism had already been achieved, and partly from the mistaken interpretation of the theory of permanent revolution, as well as from an exorbitant exaggeration of the national features of the Chinese revolution and the particular nature of the Chinese masses.

The concept of the "Great Leap Forward" was first expounded in detail at the so-called second session of the 8th congress of the CPC, which convened in May 1958, by the then vice-chairman of the party, Liu Shaoqi; it took concrete form shortly afterwards in the raised targets and indicators of the second 5-year plan. The intent was to increase the national income of the country approximately fourfold in 5 years, the total value of industrial output 6.4-fold, and the production of agriculture 2.5-fold, relative to 1957. The level of steel output to be attained by 1962 was set at 80-100 million tons, the grain harvest first at 350 and then at 500 million tons. In the spring of 1958, Mao Zedong declared at the Chengdu conference of the central committee (CC) of the CPC: "Our 8-10 years will be equal to 40 years of the Soviet Union."

In the interest of achieving communism as soon as possible, first in the villages and then also in the cities, the CPC shifted to organizing production and every social activity in a military manner, and to building up a system of "war-communistic" supply, similar to that of the army. A new organizational unit, the "people's commune," was brought about, which was more socialist in nature and which initially provided a number of free services to it members (meals three times a day, two suits of clothes, free housing, collective care for children, the old, and the sick, etc.).

In the summer and autumn of 1958 the 740 000 recently founded agricultural producers' cooperatives were amalgamated into 26 000 rural people's communes within a few months. In the winter of 1958/1959 the organization of so-called street-communes was begun in the cities as well, mainly to provide work for those of the able-bodied population who did not have permanent jobs or had earlier performed only household work. From that time on the people's communes took on complex socioeconomic organizational forms and became basic units of local administration in the villages and the urban districts. Beyond the organization and management of local production they also managed local commodity trade, communal services, education and culture, as well as health care; furthermore, they attended to tasks delegated to the people's militia. The rural people's communes were engaged not only in agricultural production, but also in industrial activities (e.g., iron and steel melting in the so-called people's furnaces and extracting or mining); they also produced and repaired means of production and even performed construction work. Their organization and ownership relations were characterized by a treble division: commune, large producting team or brigade, and producing team.(Of the latter two, the first corresponded to the earlier producers' cooperatives, the second to their large teams or brigades.) The productive activities of the street communes operating in cities consisted mainly of outwork for industrial establishments and commercial enterprises, as well as complementary activities (e.g., waste processing, packaging).

In the winter of 1957/1958 construction on large-scale water management projects started (e.g., water reservoirs and irrigation channels) and afforestation and soil amelioration projects were begun. These factors undoubtedly contributed to the formation of people's communes. It soon turned out that works of such size and importance cannot be executed in a coordinated manner within the framework and with the forces of a single cooperative. It was also important that the Chinese party and government leadership wanted to increase the reliance on one's own forces and the self-sufficiency of the rural areas at any price, so that an ever greater portion of the state means could be used for the development of large industry under central management. This was beyond the proclamation of the policy of "walking with two legs" - a part of the policy of the "great leap" - the target of which was the simultaneous and parallel development of industry and agriculture, including heavy and light industry, central and local industry, and both modern large-scale industry based on modern technology and traditional small-scale industries working mainly with artisan methods.

In practice this policy had already become distorted by 1958; it became one-sided, mainly as a result of the nationwide iron and steel melting campaign, the so-called people's furnace movement. This was detrimental mainly for agricultural and light industrial production and led to food problems and to chronic shortages of several consumer goods as early as 1959. This period was also known as the peroid of the "three red flags" policy. The three were the "new general guideline," the "great leap," and the "people's commune," condensed into the slogan: "More, faster, better and more efficiently." Of the four aims only the first two were realized in practice, in the majority of cases at the expense of the latter two.

The "great leap" and the "three red flags" soon proved to lack any sound consideration and real calculation, and it was evident that their continuation and enforcement would only lead to ever graver consequences. The sounder part of the party leadership began to voice their doubts about the foundations of this policy already in the autumn of 1958 and made repeated attempts to ward off the menacing catastrophe. But their efforts were mostly unsuccesful, and in the autumn of 1959 a number of them were qualified as an "anti-party group" and were deprived of all leading positions and functions in the party and government apparatus. Although in the spring of 1959 Mao Zedong abdicated as president of the state, as party chairman he continued to be a determining factor in politics. Thus the policies of the "great leap" and of the "three red flags" were continued right up to the end of 1960, complemented by a similarly arbitrary and adventurous pseudorevolutionary foreign policy.

A "great leap" or continuous sudden development for several years occurred - at the price of great effort and much sacrifice - only in industry, mainly in heavy industry. In the other areas of the national economy the initial upswing, the spectacular results based on the massive cooperation of the labor force, were followed rather soon by ever graver failures and setbacks, owing to the forced rate, unplanned work, disorganization, and incompetence. In the last resort, even the sound targets originally set for 1962 were not implemented. Thus, from the viewpoint of modernization, the arbitrary experiment of the "great leap forward" proved to be a completely false track.

Difficulties emerged first in agriculture and in the villages. Although - thanks to the large-scale construction for water management and soil improvement carried out in the winter of 1957/1958 - there were indeed record harvests in 1958, the result was greatly exaggerated. In addition, a large part of the crop was wasted due to badly organized harvesting, and a large portion was consumed in a few months, as a result of the free meals that were introduced in the autumn and winter of 1958. Thus, in the spring of 1959 - owing partly to the lack of seed grain and partly to the hope that there would be greater yields on smaller areas - a large amount of acreage remained unsown, in consequence of which the harvest of 1959 fell to the level of 1955. Even more serious was the decline in agricultural production in 1960, to which, in addition to the decline in the labor zeal of peasants and poor organization, various natural disasters also contributed. As a consequence, the annual output of the most important agricultural products fell to the level of

8-9 years before. In the meantime, however, the population of China had increased by more than 100 million; therefore, the per capita quantity of grain was far below the consumption rations established in 1954. Thus, for the first time since the liberation, in the winter of 1960/1961 in some provinces and towns there was again famine. This was clearly reflected in later demographic statistics showing an almost 14 million drop in population from 1960 to 1961, mainly because of undernourishment and plagues. In these years the per capita daily calorie consumption fell to 1800 in the cities and to about 1600 in the villages. Beginning in 1961 - in consequence of the stimulating measures under the "adjustment policy" - harvests began to improve again, but they did not attain the "record" level of the first year of the "great leap" until 1966.

In industry the rapid development continued right up to 1960 though the rate diminished with every year. But the drive for quantitative results led to exhaustion here as well, to deteriorating quality, irrational management of labor and of the goods produced, to waste. Although in some industries (e.g., coal mining, electrical energy generation, ferrous metallurgy, machine building) outstanding results were attained in the first 2 or 3 years, from 1960 on decline was evident here, too. As a result, the output level of 1962 fell in most of them to that of 1957--1958, i.e., to the level before the "great leap." In the wake of the catastrophic decline in agricultural production the living standard of the population fell to a much greater extent, mainly due to the lack of consumer goods and the irrational rise in the rate of accumulation. (In 1959 the rate of accummulation within the national income available was 43.8%!)

In the first year of the "great leap" there was a significant upswing in the foreign trade of the PRC. The total turnover reached a "peak" approximating US $4.4 billion in 1959. Thereafter, it fell every year until 1962 and only began to rise beginning in 1963. Even so, it did not attain the 1959 level even in 1965. At the same time, the geographical division of Chinese foreign trade, or rather its division by groups of countries, changed radically. While in 1959 the share of socialist countries in the trade of the PRC was almost 70%, (the European countries of the Council of Mutual Economic Assistance, CMEA, accounting for about 65% of this) this share fell by 1965 to 30% (respectively 25%).

Thus, the arbitrary policy of the "great leap" - guided by big power and hegemonic striving - set China's economic development back by 8-10 years. It also upset the whole system of planned economy then prevailing, together with the basic production and distribution relations of the national economy. From then on - and for more than two decades - the PRC went along its own road of social and economic development, which was essentially different from that in the other socialist countries. Its most essential elements developed partly in the years of the "great leap", and partly in the following period of the "readjustment policy."

The aggravation of the economic situation in early 1961 made it clear that the economic policy pursued in the years of the "great leap" should be "readjusted" and the earlier arbitrary targets of economic development revised and radically reduced. The 9th plenary session of the 8th CC of the CPC, held in January 1961, laid down the guidelines to be followed in economic work in terms of "coordination, consolidation, complementation, and improvement". In his report to the 3rd session of the 2nd National People's Congress which convened in the spring of 1962, Prime Minister Zhou Enlai summed up the tasks of "readjustment" made necessary by the shifts in proportions in consequence of the "great leap" in ten points. (It followed from the "readjustment" nature of these tasks that the period was given the name of "readjustment policy." However, opinions are still divided on whether this period includes a full 5 years (1961-1965) or only the 3 years following the second 5-year plan period, i.e., 1963-1965.

Early in 1961, Mao Zedong himself recognized the graveness of the situation and issued the statement, which can be considered correct and topical even today, that in China "agriculture is the basis of the national economy and industry its leading factor." Accordingly, in the framework of the "readjustment policy" efforts were concentrated first of all on the reconstruction of agricultural production, and even the development of industrial production was mostly subordinated to this goal. In the program of "readjustment" agriculture thus took first place in the order of development priorities, light industry second, and heavy industry third. Investments were curbed in every field, except where new projects served partly the modern armament industry (including above all nuclear war techniques) and partly the development of agriculture (e.g., production of machines for agriculture, production of fertilizers).

In harmony with the new goals, the system of people's communes was reorganized. In the case of the rural communes the administrative scope of authority and the production and management tasks unrelated to agriculture were essentially reduced. Free meals were abolished, together with all other free services; income distribution according to units of work accomplished was restored; personal property that had been taken into the common farm was handed back (e.g., sewing machines, bicycles, carts, hand tools). Communes were forbidden to use the material and financial assets and labor of the producing teams or brigades (large teams) to support commune-level ventures or state investments without the consent of these brigades and teams. Household plots were given back to the peasants, the keeping of small animals was allowed, and cottage industry and various complementary rural activities were stimulated. Peasants were also allowed to dispose freely of any surplus product remaining after fulfillment of the delivery obligations which were determined for several years ahead. In some places successful experiments were already being made with the method of <u>métayage</u> carried on with in the framework of the family. (This method of "métayage" means that a part of the crops harvested goes to the owner of the land.) In the late 1970s and early 1980s this became widespread under the name of "production responsibility system under family contract". All this significantly expanded the rural commodity production and revived the free market which had died out almost completely in the preceding years. In the cities the so-called street communes were dissolved, and apartments were returned to their owners. The common catering units were liquidated, the network of shops was expanded, and several measures were taken to develop trade, handicrafts, and various services and to improve commodity supply. To alleviate the depressing housing situation that developed during the "great leap," between 1960 and 1962 about 30 million people - among them quite a few educated young adults - were sent to the villages to perform agricultural work. A considerable number of them were rural workers who had flowed into the cities in 1958-1959 to carry out the large-scale construction projects then started, but beyond that several million skilled urban workers and young intellectuals were also settled in the countryside, not infrequently for political reasons and for the purpose of "reeducation through work."

In a few years these measures brought the expected result. Beginning in 1963, the national economy started to emerge from the difficulties caused by the "great leap"; the basic national economic proportions began to improve and the per capita consumption and living standards of the population showed a gradually rising tendency. By 1965 the internal and external equilibrium of the national economy was essentially successfully restored. The volumes of production originally set as goals for 1962 were again attained in most branches of industry - this time under more balanced relations and essentially better technical and economic indicators. In agriculture, by 1965 the Chinese succeeded in surpassing the 1958 level in terms of the total value of output, but, in spite of concentrated efforts, the annual output of grain corresponded only to the 1957 level. As a consequence, the daily per capita calorie intake in 1965 reached only 2000 nationwide and hardly exceeded 2200 even in the cities. At the same time, industrial activities in the rural areas again took an upswing; under the slogan "reliance on one's own forces," small power plants and tool-producing and tool-repair workshops were established in large numbers, as were small plants producing fertilizers and materials for construction. In places well endowed with natural resources, the coal and ore mines as well as the ferrous metallurgical establishments that were the modernized form of the "people's furnaces" also remained. In addition, great efforts were made for a faster development of modern chemistry and particularly of man-made fibers. Suprising results were attained in creating the basis for the modern armament industry, particularly nuclear weapons. (It was in 1964 that the first nuclear device produced in China was exploded!) Thus, from the viewpoint of economic and technical modernization the years of the "policy of readjustment" brought significant results for China.

The achievements of the "readjustment policy" were, to a decisive extent, attributable to the sound and pragmatic economic policy which was implemented, mainly by the government organs of the PRC under the guidance of State President Liu Shaoqi, Prime Minister Zhou Enlai, Chief Secretary Deng Xiaoping, and Deputy Prime Minister Chen Yun. On the whole, from the viewpoint of development of the Chinese economy, this period was one of consolidation. Although the volume of national income stagnated, most areas of the economy showed significant structural rearrangement and qualitative development.

Ten Years of Turmoil (1966-1976)

Originally, 1966 was to have been the first year of the third 5--year development plan of the national economy. Instead, it became the first year of the "great proletarian cultural revolution." Already prior to that, at the first session of the 3rd NPC at the end of 1964, in his report to the congress on the work of the government, Prime Minister Zhou Enlai had outlined an economic development strategy for the three and a half decades till the end of the century, consisting of two stages. In the first stage (1966-1980), the period of the third, fourth, and fifth 5-year plans, the target was to gradually build up an independent and relatively complex industrial and national economic system. In the following two decades (i.e., still before the turn of the millenium) the goal was to complete the comprehensive modernization of agriculture, industry, and defense, as well as of science and technology, so that by the year

2000 the Chinese economy would lead the world in terms of absolute performance. This was the first time that the requirement of the so-called four modernizations was formulated; it was put on the agenda again only in the second half of the 1970s.

The situation of the Chinese economy at the beginning of 1966 seemed propitious for the implementation of such a grand strategy of economic development, although this concept was not free from arbitrary elements in many respects, either. In the last 3 years of the "readjustment period" (1963-1965) industrial and agricultural production increased dynamically, at a rate accelerating every year, while the basic proportions of the national economy and the most important technical and economic indicators were steadily improving, and the internal and external balance of the economy was also restored. The foreign economic relations of the PRC began to expand again, and a growing number of developed capitalist countries showed interest in establishing and developing economic, commercial, and technical-scientific cooperation. In the autumn of 1964 there also was some hope - although for a short time only - of achieving a compromise solution in Sino-Soviet relations, which had in the meantime deteriorated. All this strengthened the authority and influence within the CPC leadership of the realists and pragmatists who were successfully implementing the "readjustment policy," of the "moderates" who believed that modernization and opening towards the outside world were prime tasks.

But the nationalist, traditionalist, and radical "extremists" who rallied around Mao Zedong refused to accept this situation. They were not willing to renounce the continuation of socialist construction along the "particular path" begun in 1955 and enriched in 1958 by new elements, up to the point when it would gain general validity for every country developing within the framework of socialism and communism. These Chinese leaders considered the period of "readjustment policy" to be only a temporary, forced detour from the "revolutionary road," to which China must return as soon as possible. Otherwise, they feared, "modern revisionism" would gain the upper hand and social development would "take the road to the restoration of capitalism." Since, however, the advocates of this extreme view could not achieve this "reversion to the revolutionary road" in keeping with the official communist line because of the change in power relations, Mao Zedong and his small circle of trusted followers decided to spark an artificial "revolution", within the framework of which they intended to square with their political and ideological opponents who possessed firm positions in the party and state leadership.

The "great proletarian cultural revolution" which began in May 1966 pushed the country in a few months into anarchy and turmoil again; hardest hit were the administrative, industrial, and cultural centres. The "Red Guards" and "revolutionary rebels" or "insurgents" - recruited mostly from among fanatic secondary school or university students and uneducated workers and young peasants - first criticized and abused the leaders and cadres of various party and state organs and institutions of "walking along the road of capitalism" only on so-called dazibao's (wall newspapers with big ideograms), but 1 year later physical force and compulsion, shaming and humiliation were being used against them with growing frequency. As a consequence, tens of thousands of cadres perished from maltreatment or committed suicide in fear of it. The number of those sent to various reeducating schools or labor camps reached hundreds of thousands, and the number of intellectuals simply sent to the countryside to perform hard physical labor "under control of the masses" can only be measured in millions.

Beginning in 1968, in place of the destroyed party committees and leading government organs, so-called revolutionary committees were set up under the guidance of the army and with the participation of its cadres, in which soldiers, Red Guards, and "tested" revolutionary cadres were represented in equal proportions. All these anarchic phenomena were accompanied by extremely nationalistic anti-foreign and anti-Soviet manifestations, while the personality cult of the "great helmsman" assumed fearfully irrational dimensions.

The chaotic and anarchistic events and developments of the "cultural revolution" - despite the immeasurable harm done in the political and ideological sphere - did not have such grave and lasting consequences in the economic sphere as the policies of the "great leap" and, in general, of the "three red flags" had. Also the unbridled terror had comparatively fewer victims among the population than the famine of 1960/1961: On the one hand the "cultural revolution" did not extend simultaneously to all areas of the national economy, and not with the same intensity and, on the other hand, where it did evolve, it soon came under the control of the army, lest the fights between various groups should take on the dimensions of a civil war. In spite of this, production in several industries fell significantly in 1967 (by 15%-30%), mainly as a consequence of disorganized management, worsening transportation problems, and - in many places - protest strikes by workers. However, the agricultural harvest was rather good in that year, and this considerably counterbalanced the decline in industrial output. The decline in production continued in most areas into 1968, but on the whole - in spite of the 2-year decline - the volume of national income in 1968 still exceeded that of 1965.

Beginning in 1969, the economic development of the PRC took a more normal course, although the storms of the "cultural revolution" had not yet subsided. The 9th congress of the CPC was organized in April 1969, and its representatives were, of course, selected from among the "three revolutionary groups" that had gained power (soldiers, "rebels", and "tested" cadres). At the congress the personnel changes carried through in the first wave of the "cultural revolution" and the whole policy of the extremist Maoist leadership were approved. Marshal Lin Biao, minister of defense of the PRC, was "elected" deputy chairman of the party and official heir to Mao Zedong. With this, the first wave of the "cultural revolution" had essentially come to an end and, as a result, the "consolidation" of political power began. (Opinions are still divided about the nature of this power, both among the Chinese and foreign experts. There are some who called and still call it simply a "fascist dictatorship", others a "half-fascist, half-feudal dictatorship," and others, again, "Bonapartist" or "Maoist military-bureaucratic dictatorship."

But everyone agrees that this power did not correspond to the "people's democratic dictatorship" - considering either its class character or its nature - laid down in the constitution of the PRC.)

In 1970-1971 the group of pragmatic leaders who had weathered the storms of the "cultural revolution" and who rallied around Prime Minister Zhou Enlai made efforts to put the tasks of economic development into the fore and to convince Mao Zedong that, for China to achieve the status of a big power, the economic and military strengthening and modernization of China, as well as compromise with the leading power of "world imperialism," the United States, were indispensable. Thus, a situation had developed in which almost every interest and viewpoint - domestic and foreign policy, strategy and tactics - supported the idea that China should abandon its policy of isolation and attempt to carry on an active and open foreign policy. Circumstances for convincing Mao Zedong were propitious, because at that time some of the personalities nearest to him and enjoying his trust began to organize themselves with the aim of putting Mao Zedong out of the way (among them Lin Biao, the designated heir, and Chen Boda, Mao's personal secretary). As soon as this came to Mao Zedong's notice, his trust in Zhou Enlai again increased. It was with his help that the "conspiracy" of Lin Biao and his associates was unmasked, and this led finally to the death, in September 1971, of Lin Biao and his nearest family members. (According to official publications, Lin Biao - for fear of being unmasked - had tried to flee with his family and his aide-de-camp to the Soviet Union in an army plane, but that the plane had for some reason crashed into a mountain in Mongolia, exploded, and burnt out, together with the nine persons on board.)

The prehistory of this strange and unusual event i.e. the death of Lin Biao includes the fact that at the end of 1970 Mao Zedong sent a personal invitation to Richard Nixon, president of the USA, through Edgar Snow, an American reporter and an old man trusted by the Chinese leaders. And, for the first time in 10 years, Zhou Enlai published some comprehensive statistical data characterizing the performance of the national economy, which unambiguously indicated the intention of opening China toward the outer world. Then, in the spring of 1971, the so-called period of table-tennis diplomacy began, and in the summer Henry Kissinger, the chief national security adviser of President Nixon, unexpectedly appeared in Beijing in order to prepare for the official visit of the president. Since the leaders of the "left extremists" who rallied around Lin Biao were not successful in preventing the opening towards the leading imperialist power, the United States, they - allegedly - decided to resort to other measures: to the physical annihilation of Mao Zedong. According to these rumors, it was only after the third unsuccessful attempt that they tried to flee, and this ended in the air catastrophe.

The first attempt at "opening" in the early 1970s brought relatively quick and spectacular results. In the autumn of 1971 the PRC was at last able to occupy the place allotted to it in the UN, its specialized organizations, and in the Security Council. In February 1972 - on the occasion of President Nixon's visit to China - the guidelines for the normalization of Sino--American relations were laid down in the so-called Shanghai joint communiqué. The active policy of the PRC in establishing relations, the considerable amount of credit and aid granted to a definite circle of developing countries, and the first signs of approximation between China and the United States started a particular chain reaction among the capitalist countries. In 1971-1972 the number of countries that acknowledged the PRC and broke official diplomatic relations with the Republic of China in Taiwan suddenly increased among both the developed and developing capitalist countries, and a genuine race began to conquer the Chinese market. As a result, the total foreign trade of the PRC rose rather steeply between 1971 and 1974; as against US $4.6 billion in 1970 it reached US $14.6 billion by 1974. Obviously the oil price exploison of 1973 and the continuous devaluation of the dollar also played a role in this fast rise, but the basic factor was by all means the rising volume of trade. In 1975, however, the increase was already minimal even in nominal terms, while in real terms it diminished. The declining tendency continued until 1977, but the greatest drop in Chinese foreign trade - about 10% at current prices - occurred in the last year of the decade of "turmoil", 1976, which must also be remembered for several other events.

The domestic economy of the PRC in the first half of the 1970s showed a smoother growth, though at rates that fluctuated, almost year by year. The period between 1971 and 1975 is shown in Chinese statistical yearbooks and some publications as that of the "fourth 5-year plan", but this does not mean an actual plan period, any more than the terms "third" or "fifth 5-year plan period" do, as these "5-year plans" were never elaborated and accepted, not even in such preliminary form or outline as the guidelines of the second 5-year plan in 1956. Thus, the economic development between 1971 and 1975 can rather be compared to the results of the preceding 5 years (1966-1970). In the first half of the 1970s the rate of economic growth in almost every branch of material production was lower by a few percentage points, while at the same time - beyond the fast growth of foreign trade, already mentioned - the volume of productive investments increased significantly. This is why the rate of accumulation fluctuated in these years around 33% within the national income used. Fluctuating growth was characteristic of these years. The odd years were the peaks of the waves (1971, 1973, 1975) and the even ones the troughs (1972, 1974).

The internal political development of the PRC in the first half of the 1970s presented a picture somewhat different from that of domestic and foreign trade. After the explosion of the so-called Lin Biao affair, the "moderate" or "pragmatic" wing that rallied around Zhou Enlai attempted to exploit the conflicts between the "extremists" in order to consolidate its position and to rehabilitate and reinstall in their earlier positions the old cadres who had been reviled and removed in the first wave of the "cultural revolution". (Thus, for example, in April 1973 Deng Xiaoping was rehabilitated and appointed as deputy prime minister.) In spite of this, the "cultural revolutionist group" of the far left, particularly the "Shanghai group" (the "gang of four")[12] that constituted its hard core, continued to hold strong positions within the leading party bodies reorganized on a far-left ideological platform. At the 10th congress of the CPC in August 1973, the "four" succeeded - with the help of Kang Sheng, then deputy chairman of the party and head of the security service - in delimiting themselves from "Lin Biao's group of conspirators," who were qualified as "far right" and given eight further epithets. They started subversive activities and an ever more undisguised attack against the line and policy represented by Zhou Enlai. Thus began the second wave of the "cultural revolution," which lasted until October 1976, when the "gang of four" were arrested.

The second wave of the "cultural revolution," which began in 1974 with the campaign of "let us criticize Lin Biao and K'ung Fu-tzu (Confucius)," attained its peak after the death of Prime Minister Zhou Enlai in January 1976. Following the "Tienanmen square events" of April 5-6, 1976, it led to the renewed dismissal of a number of rehabilitated leaders - among them Deng Xiaoping - and their denunciation. In its wake the dynamism of the economy, on the upswing between 1971 and 1975, suffered a break, and in 1976 its performance diminished even in absolute terms. In the summer of 1976 there was a devastating earthquake in the vicinity of the town of Tanshan in Hebei province; hundreds of thousands were killed and millions were made homeless. Not long afterward, on September 9, 1976, came the event which - according to popular Chinese belief - had been "forecast" by the earthquake: "death of the emperor," "the end of the dynasty." This meant, of course, the death of the "great helmsman," Mao Zedong, one of the founders of the CPC, who had headed it for 41 of the 55 years of its existence. The historical figure and role of Mao Zedong may perhaps be best compered to Stalin's, with the difference that Mao was the Lenin, Stalin, and Trotsky of the Chinese party in one person (a partial ideological and political "relationship" with each of them can be shown). He was an extremely contradictory personality whose merit rested in his bringing the Chinese people's revolution to victory and consolidating the people's power. During the last two decades of his life, however, with his adventurous extreme-left policy, he pushed his revolutionary oeuvre, the People's Republic of China, almost to the brink of collapse on two occasions. After his death the way out of the extremely grave internal political and economic crisis was again found by those who had already success after the failure of the "great leap." (In the meantime, however, Zhou Enlai had died, Liu Shaoqi had fallen victim to the "cultural revolution," and this was the fate of quite a few others as well.) Of those who had survived the "cultural revolution," it was Deng Xiaoping who - with his particular acumen, boldness, and straightforwardness in this search for ways out of the mess, as well as with several other features not recognized earlier - excelled as a qualified leader. He soon became the most respected and most influential leader of the CPC. Thus, the 1976 earthquake this time signalled only the death of the "ruler," but not the end of the "dynasty"; forces were still present within the leadership of the CPC which were capable of leading the country and the society out of the critical situation.

"Seeking Ways and Means" (1977-1978)

The dramatic events that took place in the Beijing government quarters on the night of October 6, 1976, put an end to the growing influence and ever more thinly disguised efforts at autarchy of the "extreme left." Hardly 4 weeks after the death of the "great helmsman," by command of the acting chairman of the Political Commission of the CC, CPC (Prime Minister Hua Guofeng), and one of its deputy chairmen (Defense Minister Ye Jianying), four further members of the Standing Committee of the Political Bureau (PB) (the so-called gang of four) were arrested on the charge of "antistate conspiracy," among them Mao's widow, Jiang Qing. The arrest of the "four" was an extremely great blow for the "extreme left" orthodox Maoist forces that had gotten key positions within the CPC leadership as a result of the "cultural revolution." Their most extreme and best-organized group was eliminated, and so began a radical change in the political power relations established immediately after the death of Mao Zedong.

In the new power setting that developed following the arrest of the "four," for a time it was the "moderate" leaders of the army (headed by marshal Ye Jianying) and a few old leaders who had more easily weathered the "cultural revolution" (e.g., Chen Yun, later deputy party chairman, and between 1978 and 1987 first secretary of the central disciplinary and control commission of the CPC, as well as Li Xiannian, later president of the republic) who constituted the center, who balanced the scales. To their left were the "left" cadres who had risen in the "cultural revolution" and were capable of delimiting themselves from the "gang of four" (headed by Hua Guofeng, acting party chairman and prime minister), and to their right were the surviving leaders who had been shelved and defamed during the "cultural revolution" as "revisionists" or as "walking along the capitalist road." In the autumn of 1976 most of the latter were still in "home custody" or under "protective arrest,"[13] waiting for their rehabilitation. One of these was Deng Xiaoping, the most influential leader of China during the 1980s, who was again rehabilitated and reinstalled in all of his earlier offices and functions in July 1977, at the central committee meeting preceding the 11th congress of the CPC.

The 11th congress of the CPC was organized in August 1977. After the 10 years of "turmoil" it set as medium- and long-term goals the soonest possible restoration of "great order" and achievement of the "four modernizations" by the end of the century. Opinions were strongly divided regarding the ways and means by which these goals should be attained, but at that time their reality was not challenged. In both wings of the party leadership there were quite a few people who believed that the "four modernizations" and "closing the gap between China and the leading countries of the world" by the end of the century could be accomplished with a new "great leap." But, while those on the left wanted to achieve this with new mass movements in production ("Let us learn from Dazhai and Daqing")[14] and with new "cultural revolutions,"[15] those on the right thought that the guarantee was to be found in ever closer economic, commercial, technical, scientific, financial, and - last but not least - political and strategic cooperation, in establishing quasi-allied relationships with the United States, Japan, and the other developed capitalist countries. It was on the basis of such antecedents that - relying on the favorable experience of the upswing in 1977 - a 10-year national economic development program for 1976-1985 was worked out in the second half of 1977. (Work on the outlines of a development program of this nature had already started in the spring of 1975, but it was interrupted in 1976 due to "sabotage by the gang of four.") The program was submitted for discussion and approval to the first session of the 5th NPC (convened in February 1978) by Hua Guofeng, party chairman and prime minister, in his report on the work of the government. (At that time the discussion did not take place, but 1 year later the targets of the document were indeed thoroughly scrutinized, and finally, in 1980 at the third session of the 5th NPC, the targets of this development program were formally abandoned; in their place were the approved guidelines for the elaboration of the sixth 5-year plan, covering the years 1981--1985.

The "10-year national economic development program" - in harmony with the original ideas worked out in 1975 - put the emphasis on the "accelerated development of industry,"[16] and aimed at the further development of agriculture, mainly by "relying on one's own forces." For the 8-year period 1978-1985 the program provided for a more than 10% annual increase in the total value of industrial output and for an average of 4%-5% annual growth in the total value of agricultural production. Moreover, it set the targets to be attained by 1985 at 60 million tons in steel output and at about 400 million tons in grain production per annum. At the same time, government revenues and government expenditure on national economic investments were to grow - according to the estimates - at such a rate that their combined value would attain or approximate the order of magnitude of cumulated government revenues and expenditure on investments throughout the preceding 28 years.[17] According to some rumors, this order of magnitude would have been around 1000 billion yuan, and this would have been equal to the combined national income of the 3 years from 1978 to 1980.[18] Investments of such order of magnitude - distributed over 8 years and assuming a 7%-8% annual growth of the national income - would have required keeping the rate of accumulation at around 35%. Considering the level of consumption of the Chinese population at that time, this would have been difficult to bear. According to the targets of the program, the bulk of fixed capital investments would have been distributed among 120 big industrial and infrastructural establishments. Among these were ten ferrous metallurgical and nine nonferrous metallurgical plants, eight coal-mining bases, ten new crude oil and natural gas extracting establishments, 30 large power plants, six new railway lines, and five modern seaports. After the completion of these projects China was to posses 14 relatively strong industrial bases which would be rationally located. The program also provided for a number of concrete measures in the development of agriculture. The aims were to improve the conditions of management and the organization of work, to raise the standards of agrotechnical supply, and, as a result, to increase the yield per unit of land area.

In the years after its approval this "10-year program of national economic development" was much critized and discarded as a document "comprising irrealistic and arbitrary targets" and thus "still exhibiting the signs of leftish policy." Still, the basic goals included in it were, on the whole, fulfilled, with the exception of the quantity of steel output and the volume of state investments into fixed capital. This should be attributed mainly to the fact that, in spite of several attempts and assiduous efforts on the part of the Chinese economic and political leadership, economic growth of the extensive type could not be stopped. Thus, the way could not be opened for qualitative development and more efficient management. The causes were diverse and ramified. Both objective and subjective factors as well as the methods of economic management established in the preceding two decades played their roles.

As regards the objective causes, it is clear that in China, with the largest population of the world and the size of a continent, the reserves for economic growth of the extensive type are almost inexhaustible, given a certain level of economic and technical development. In consequence of the relatively fast growth of the population, employment problems became increasingly pressing by the end of the 1970s and this pushed the investment policy of the Chinese leadership toward one of expanding labor-intensive activities and creating vacancies and workplaces on a massive scale. At the same time, China had and still has huge unexplored and unexploited natural resources and deposits. Their utilization demands above all capital-intensive and slowly returning investments in research, extraction, and processing, as well as the development of an infrastructure. In order that China be able to bring about export capacities satisfying world market requirements in either the extracting or the manufacturing industries, a rapid modernization of production equipment would be needed, and China was unable to do this on its own. This is why the "opening outward" became unavoidable, i.e., the expansion of economic, technical, and financial cooperation with the developed countries of the world.

In the late 1970s, all these objective requirements were in sharp contrast to the practice of the Chinese economic policy and economic management system, which had for decades proclaimed the "reliance on their own forces" and which considered economic management to be above all a political task. In the period of the "cultural revolution" the organs of economic management and the economic units had become incapable - in consequence of the all-embracing party control - of weighing the viewpoints of economic efficiency and observing the requirements of quality. Most of the professionally qualified cadres were branded "rightist" and sent to perform manual work in order to be "reeducated". This is why in 1977-1978 even traditional planned economy could hardly be deemed to exist in China. The State Economic Commission, the State Planning Commission, the State Statistics Bureau, and the various specialized ministries could be restaffed with rehabilitated cadres only beginning with the autumn of 1977. Thus, before reform of the economic management system could be started in China, the traditional system of institutions of planned economy had to be restored, together with the earlier methods of planning, also taking into account the practice, which has been established in the meantime, of decentralized economic management.

Footnotes to Chapter One

1. For a more detailed and authentic picture see Mao Zedong: "The Chinese Revolution and the Chinese Communist Party" (December 1939) and "On the New Democracy" (January 1940). In: Mao Zedong Xuanji, Di er juan. Beijing, 1952, pp 591- -625 and 633-382.
2. In: Liu Suinian, Wu Qungan (eds) China's Socialist Economy. An Outline of History (1949-1984). Beijing Review, Beijing, 1986, pp 487-500
3. Ibid., p 488
4. Ibid., p 489
5. National Income in Several Countries. Working Papers of the UN Statistical Commission. New York 1955, pp 175-176
6. Weida de shinian. Renmin Chubansi, Beijing, 1959, p 198
7. See: "Mobilizing all forces, let us fight to build our country into a big power." In: Theses for studying the general guidelines of the CPC for the period of transition. (Prepared by the agitation section of the CC of CPC in December 1953, and approved by the CC, CPC; circulated as internal material within party and state organs)
8. See a study written by the author in 1977: "A Kínai Kommunista Párt átmeneti időszakra szóló általános irányvonala kidolgozásának néhány tisztázatlan mozzanatáról - Egy történelmi fordulópont koncepcionális hátteréhez." (About some unclear features in the elaboration of the general guidelines of the CPC for the period of transition - To the conceptual background of a historical turning point.) In: Gábor Hidasi: Gazdaság és politika a Kínai Népköztásaságban (Economy and Politics in the PRC), Kossuth Kiadó, Budapest, 1979, pp 331-351
9. See Liu Suinian, Wu Qungan (eds.) 1986: op.cit., o 125

10. <u>Jobwork</u> means that a party gives materials to another one for being processed and then only pays for the processing. In the case of <u>outwork</u> the processing is usually done in small workshops or households
11. Employees in the Chinese state sector - in contrast to those working in other sectors - receive full-scope social security benefits (sick pay, old-age pension), 2 weeks of paid leave annually, recreation and meals at reduced prices, housing allocations, medical care, sports and cultural facilities. Their children can be placed in enterprise nurseries and kindergartens. On retirement - in the case of manual workers - the enterprise is obliged to employ their children in their place (if demanded). Their wages are usually higher than those in identical jobs in the collective ownership sector, and they can be dismissed only in exceptional cases (criminal act or deliberate damage). This is why the privileged position of state employees in China is called figuratively the "iron rice bowl ("tie fanwan" in Chinese): it never breaks and is always filled with rice, no matter how its owner works.
12. The so-called "gang of four" consisted of the following persons: Wang Hongwen, deputy chairman of the CC, CPC, member of the standing committee of the PB; Zhang Chunqiao, deputy prime minister, member of the standing committee of the PB; Jiang Qing, member of the PB of the CC, CPC, widow of Mao Zedong; Yao Wenyuan, member of the PB of the CC, CPC, head of the agitation and propaganda section of the CC, CPC. All of them stemmed originally from Shanghai, or had filled different leading posts there earlier.
13. Some of the leaders - among them Deng Xiaoping - succeeded in leaving Beijing in the autumn of 1976 and found refuge and protection with the moderate commanders of the southern army group.
14. The slogan: "Let us learn from Dazhai and Daqing" had been issued by Mao Zedong in the early 1970s in the spirit of "reliance on one's own forces." The commune-brigade of Dazhai in Shaanxi province became famous (and later infa-

mous) because its members irrigated their fields without outside help and thus multiplied their harvest yields. In 1973 the head of the brigade, Chen Younggui, was elected member of the PB of the CC, CPC, and not much later he was appointed deputy prime minister. (He was relieved of both functions in the autumn of 1980.) With the purpose of spreading their methods, two national conferences were organized - in the autumn of 1975 and at the end of 1976 - with the slogan: "Let us learn form Dazhai in agriculture." At the latter conference the main report about modernization in agriculture was delivered by Hua Guofeng, chairman of the party.

Daqing is the oil field with the greatest yield in China, having an annual production of 50 million tons. One of the oil-drilling brigades there became an example to be followed because its members saved a drilling tower from collapse and explosion by risking their lives in a windstorm. Under the slogan: "Let us learn in industry from Daqing!," national industrial conferences were held in Daqing and in Beijing in April and May 1977, where the questions and tasks of the "four modernizations" were discussed. At these conferences, in addition to Hua Guofeng, Marshal Ye Jianying delivered a "basic report"; this dealt with the modernization of the armament industry and the army. It later turned out that the spectacular results of both brigades had been manipulated and exaggerated, similar to those of the "Stakhanov" brigades in several other countries.

15. At the 11th national congress of the CPC, held in August 1977, Hua Guofeng himself declared in his report that "political revolutions similar to the cultural revolution may take place even in the future several times." He justified the necessity of such revolutions with the theory of Mao Zedong about the "unavoidability of class struggle under conditions of the dictatorship of the proletariat." It is not difficult to detect the ideological relationship and connection between this "theory" of Mao Zedong and Stalin's "theory" that the class struggle would become more intense as socialism developed.

16. In the first half of 1975 - based on a proposition by Zhou Enlai and Deng Xiaoping - the experts of the State Planning Commission compiled a document addressing "some questions of accelerating the development of industry." This document was discussed at one of the sessions of the State Council, presided over by Deng Xiaoping. Deng himself made some remarks on the document. In this the need for setting out from the demands of agriculture, major development of foreign trade (i.e., industrial development aimed partly at exports), scientific research and technological development in enterprises, improvement of quality and of management, establishment of a system of normative regulation and a system of responsibilities, as well as the consistent assertion of the principle of distribution according to work done were emphasized. The document and, even more, the proposals of Deng Xiaoping soon became the targets of a new ideological attack by the "gang of four." In November 1975, the "four" started a nationwide political campaign to "beat off the rightist deviation attempting to reverse correct decisions," which in a few months grew into the open movement of "Let us critizice Deng!" After the "Tienanmen square events" of April 5, 1976, Deng Xiaoping was again deprived of all functions and was held in house arrest until the death of Mao Zedong. After the return of Deng Xiaoping into the leadership, the said document was again put forward and work with it continued. By July 1978, the CC, CPC, commissioned the elaboration of a draft resolution, consisting of 30 chapters, about some questions of accelerating industrial development, but in the end it was not submitted to the plenary session of the CC. (See: Decision of the Central Comittee of the Communist Party of China on some questions concerning the acceleration of industrial development (draft), (July 1978). In: Almanac of China's Economy, 1981. Eurasic Press, New York and Hong Kong, 1982, pp 175-193

17. Renmin Ribao, March 7, 1978
18. Deputy Party Chairman and Deputy Prime Minister Li Xiannian declared to Japanese businessmen that the total value of na-

tional economic investments envisaged in the plans would reach 1000 billion yuan by 1985; at the then official rate of exchange, this corresponded to US $645 billion (US $100 = 155 RMB). China Trade Report, December 1978, p 2

General Notes to all chapters:
It is noted at this place that such economic-statistical concepts and indicators as e.g. national income generated or available, total social product, total or combined value of agricultural and industrial output are - in comformity with the statistical and planning methods of China - value indicators according to the Material Product System (MPS). Beginning with the 1980s, Chinese statistics also produce computations of the gross national product (GNP) that is, also use the methodology of the System of National Account (SNA). The main interrelations between the two systems may be seen from the following table:

I. Total Social Product (MPS)
   + Net Product (Value Added) and Depreciation Allowance in Non-material Production
   - Intermediate output of Material and Non-material Production (Material Consumption)
   = Gross Domestic Product (SNA)
II. National Income (MPS)
   + Net Product of the Non-material Production Sphere
   - Intermediate Output of the Non-material Sphere (for the Material Production)
   = Net Domestic Product at Market Prices (SNA)

Chapter Two
FORMATION AND ANNOUNCEMENT OT THE REFORM AND OPENING POLICY
(1978-1979)

Situation of the Economy in 1978

In October 1978 the People's Republic of China entered its 30th year of existence. As is clear from the preceding brief historical review, these 30 years abounded in both successes and failures. Although in these three decades Chinese society made significant progress in modernization, civilization, and economic and cultural development, the political leadership was by no means able to rest on its laurels, whether their achievements were compared with the socioeconomic development of other East-Asian and Southeast-Asian countries in the vicinity or with China's own potential development possibilities. It was no mere coincidence that some of the Chinese leaders had even earlier spoken about a "lost decade" and estimated that China's lag in technology behind the pioneering countries was about 50 years, adding that the abyss separating China from them had not narrowed in the decade from 1967 to 1976, but rather deepened and widened.[1]

The national income produced in the PRC in 1978 exceeded 300 billion yuan; that is, it had increased 7.7-fold relative to 1949 and 4.5-fold relative to 1952 (at comparable prices). Even so, the per capita national income was only 313 yuan in 1978, which, at the then prevailing exchange rate (1.72 RMB = 1 US $), corresponded to US $182. Even if computed at the purchasing power parity, this was a per capita national income of hardly more than US $200, or a per capita GNP of US $230. This was much below the average for the developing countries at that time (US $400), and with this the PRC occupied the 140th place in the corresponding list of the more than 160 members of the UN. In the generation of national income industry, employing about 50 million people, had a share of 49.4%, while agriculture (with 294 million employees) contributed only 32.8%; the other branches, employing about 25 million people (construction, transport and communications, trade) contributed 17.8%. These shares are a good illustration of the huge differences in labor productivity between industry and agriculture, and the resulting low income-producing capacity of agriculture. The net output value per agricultural employee in 1978 (362 yuan) was 7.8 times smaller than the corresponding figure in industry (2816 yuan). But the real difference was much greater since, according to the then prevailing statistical accounting system, the value of agricultural output also included that of rural industries and of all complementary activities. It is well known that the productivity of those working in the rural industries was even at that time 2-3 times higher than productivity in plant production. On the user side of the national income, accumulation had a 36.5% share in 1978, the third highest value after 43.8% in 1959 and 39.6% in 1960 in these three decades. This irrationally high rate of accumulation was a consequence not only of the slow development and traditional backwardness of agricultural production, but mainly of the "socialist industrialization," with development of heavy industry its first priority.

The combined gross output value of industry and agriculture increased by 1978 to 13.8 times that in 1949 and to 5.8 times that in 1952 (at comparable prices). These combined figures derive from a 39.8-fold (16-fold) growth of industrial production and from a 3.4-fold (2.3-fold) growth of agriculture in the preceding 29 (26) years. It follows that the growth rate of industrial output exceeded that of agriculture 11.6-fold between 1950 and 1978 and sevenfold between 1953 and 1978, and this made the backwardness of agriculture even more conspicuous and depressing. But in the same three decades a similar disproportion was evident within industrial production between heavy and light industries, or between the branches producing means of production and those turning out consumer goods. While the total output value of heavy industrial production increased 91.8-fold relative to that in 1949 and 27.8-fold relative to 1952, the corresponding figures for light industry during the same period were "only" 20.8-fold and 9.7-fold respectively. That is, the growth rate of heavy industry between 1950 and 1978 was 4.4

times, between 1953 and 1978 almost 2.9 times higher than that of light industry . Looking at the combined gross output value of industry and agriculture, agriculture had a 27.8% share, light industry 31.1% and heavy industry 41.1% in 1978; these ratios were 43.3:31.2:25.5 in 1957 and 37.3:32.3:30.4 in 1965. Looking at the total output value of industry, the percentual shares of light and heavy industry in 1978 were 43.1:56.9, as against 55:45 in 1957 and 51.6:48.4 in 1965. According to opinions of Chinese economists - considering the present level of development, structure, and other conditions of the Chinese economy - with the former a ratio of equal thirds and with the latter one of 50:50 seems optimal. The chronic and substantial lag of the growth rates of agriculture and light industry behind those of heavy industry resulted in growing volumes of products unsuited for personal consumption (basic materials, intermediary goods, machinery, and equipment). As a consequence, the share in the end use of products spent on investment and stockpiling, i.e., in the last resort on accumulation, necessarily increased. Thus, the irrationally high rate of accumulation (mostly above 30%) may also be considered as a necessary concomitant of the classical "socialist industrialization."

In 1978, with employment of nearly 400 million, there were almost 20 million people "waiting for work" in the big cities of China, mostly those who had completed the lower forms (classes) of the secondary school but were unable to continue learning or to learn a trade on their own. In the rural areas the number of the "underemployed", that is, "latent unemployed," was estimated at about five times the previous figure, that is, about 100 million. The majority were absorbed in the 1980s by the fast expansion of rural industrial activities. The average net income per peasant inhabitant in 1978 was merely 134 yuan, compared with a per capita income of 316 yuan for urban dwellers. At the same time, the floor area per capita was 8.1 m^2 in villages and 4.2 m^2 in cities. The daily per capita calorie consumption in 1978 was 2700 in cities but only 2200 in villages, with an average daily protein consumption of 80g and 70g respectively. However,

90% of the protein was of plant origin; per capita meat consumption in that year was merely 6 kg in villages and around 12 kg in cities.

Nevertheless, as regards the quantitative indicators, 1978 was a year of record performances. It was the first year that the national income exceeded 300 billion yuan and the annual grain harvest 300 million tons. The situation was similar with industrial production: for the statistically recorded important industrial products the highest results were attained in 1978 - with the exception of metal-working machine tools. This was attributable mainly to the accelerated rate of economic growth in both industry and agriculture. As a result, the value of the global social product (a gross indicator) increased at comparable prices by 13.1%, and that of the (net) national income by 12.3%. The improving economic situation and the rise in living standard by more than 6% in both cities and villages created an atmosphere favorable for active home and foreign policies and for the preparation and initiation of the necessary "adjustments" and "reform steps". The rehabilitated leaders, headed by Deputy Chairman Deng Xiaoping, who wanted to abolish the burden of the "cultural revolution" as soon as possible and aimed at a radical change in the politics of the CPC, tried to exploit this favorable situation to the maximum.

The Domestic and External Political Situation in 1978

Looking back on the most important events and developments of 1978 after 10 years, it may be stated that they served - almost without exception - the preparation and partial trial of the new economic policy guideline (the so-called four-word directive)[2] that was announced in the following year and of the policy of "opening outwards - enlivening the economy at home." This also shows that those who prepared for political change acted most deliberately and in a planned manner, and that, in the final analysis, they were the initiators and directors of the events and processes. To quote a few examples:

In the provinces Anhui and Sichuan - led by First Party Secretaries Wan Li and Zhao Ziyang - essential changes in agricultural policy were made as early as in the winter of 1977/1978. The autonomy of the lowest organizational units of the rural people's communes, the producing teams, was increased. They were allowed to divide production tasks between smaller groups or even large families and to trust that they be performed by these groups or families in the form of production under contract (small-group or family contract production responsibility system). At the same time, the area of household plots was increased, and the keeping of animals on these plots and other complementary rural activities (including the organization and operation of industrial workshops) were materially and financially stimulated. Rural and urban free markets were opened for the sale of peasant products that exceeded their contractual obligations or goods produced on the household plots, naturally at free-market prices developing according to supply and demand.

In Beijing several national staff conferences were held in the spring, summer, and autumn of 1978 for those working in science, education, literature, and the arts, as well as for the political officers of the army and the institutions of the State Council, dealing with questions of foreign economic policy. At these conferences Deng Xiaoping, Li Xinnian, and others severely criticized the situation that had developed in the wake of the "cultural revolution" and urged immediate radical measures and reforms.

In May 1978, great interest was aroused by a theoretical article written by a professor at Nanking University, entitled: "The sole criterion for checking truth is the practice." It was first published in the communiqués of the Central Party School of the CC, CPC, but shortly thereafter it was taken over by the daily, Guangming Ribao. Following that, the view of "two whatevers,"[3] earlier voiced by Hua Guofeng, was publicly criticized. One year earlier it had already been called a "non-Marxist thesis" by Deng Xiaoping among a narrow circle of party leaders.

The pragmatic wing of the CPC leadership, headed by Deng Xiaoping, considered the development of the forces of production to be a task that took precedence over all others. To this end they made efforts to significantly liberalize domestic and economic policies and intended to carry out a large-scale "opening" in foreign policy. In the course of 1978 they made a great endeavor to remove the obstacles to the expansion of relations with the political and economic centres of the developed capitalist world (United States, Japan, Western Europe), and to lay down the principles and norms for these relations in international contracts and bilateral agreements. It was within this framework that a general trade contract was signed with the European Community in April 1978; in August a treaty of peace and friendship was signed with Japan, and in December mutual and unconditional diplomatic recognition with the United States was announced. In the wake of the latter, relations between the two countries became normalized in every respect as of January 1, 1979. During the same period, Chinese relations with the Socialist Republic of Vietnam and the People's Republic of Albania (formerly the closest ally of the PRC) deteriorated and even degenerated into enmity, while further steps were taken by China to develop and strengthen relations and cooperation with the Korean Peoples's Democratic Republic, the Socialist Republic of Rumania, and the Socialist Federal Republic of Yugoslavia. Some steps were also taken toward normalization of relations with other Eastern European countries (e.g., in the autumn of 1978 it was indicated that, if there were agreement, it was intended to send a delegation of well-known Chinese economists to Hungary in order to study the experiences with the preparation and introduction of economic reform). However, these negotiations were soon broken off under the impact of the warlike events on the Sino-Vietnamese frontier.

The spectacular results in improving the domestic economic situation and in developing international relations, as well as the consolidation of the international position of the PRC in the wake of normalizing its interstate relations with the leading powers and power groups of the developed capitalist world, greatly increased the influence and respect within the Chinese leadership of the pragmatic wing led by Deng Xiaoping. Hua

Guofeng was increasingly forced to adapt to the guidelines of this group, in both domestic politics and ideology. In the interest of faster economic and scientific-technological progress and of securing smooth cooperation with the developed capitalist countries, this group demanded "liberation of thought", expansion of democracy, official recognition that the "cultural revolution" had been a mistaken concept right from the beginning, and public condemnation of its methods, as well as dismissal of the cadres that had risen to power during the "cultural revolution" and thus occupied various leading posts. Simultaneously, the cadres who had been dismissed and reviled or even executed during the same period were to be completely rehabilited. In this situation, Party Chairman Hua Guofeng and other "left"-motivated leaders of the CPC were forced into tactical maneuvers to counterbalance the influence of this group. Nevertheless, they were not able to prevent the radical turn in domestic policies; their power, influence, and "rearguard fight" sufficed only to brake the transformation process and to put off certain personnel changes and rehabilitation.

Third Plenary Session of the 11th Central Committee of the CPC: Turning Point in Chinese Internal Politics

The first serious showdown between the orthodox Maoist, "extreme left" and "cultural revolutionary" cadres rallying around Party Chairman Hua Guofeng and the rehabilitated cadres loyal to Deng Xiaoping occurred at the 3rd plenary session of the 11th CC, CPC, held in December 1978. This plenary session was qualified a few years later as a "historical turning point" and a "milestone" - and not without reason. As a matter of fact, this plenary session started all the processes which put an end to the excesses of the "extreme left" policies over two decades and which finally led to the emergence and consolidation of the policies of reform and opening. But at the time all this was not yet so clear and unambiguous. In fact, considering the events at the plenary session and the documents that were there accepted, the external observer had the feeling and impression that at this session a particular compromise and transitory balance was achieved between the orthodox Maoist and the pragmatic wings of the Chinese party leadership. In its course the centrist powers[4] between them obtained the most advantageous position, since they "balanced the scales" and were able to exert moderation in both directions in the interest of protecting and preserving unity.

What actually happened at this famous plenary session? Certainly, Deng Xiaoping and the pragmatic group of rehabilitated leaders wanted above all to attain an unconditional condemnation of the "cultural revolution" and its qualification as an "extreme-left" deviation, along with the immediate and final rehabilitation of its every victim and persecuted person. Hua Guofeng and the orthodox Maoist group of cadres who had risen and taken over leading posts in the "cultural revolution" were aware that their political career would soon come to an end if the former group succeeded in attaining its goals at the plenary session. This is why they resorted to such tactical maneuvering, which changed the political and ideological power relations within the leading party bodies in a direction favorable for them, and which undoubtedly helped them to remain in power positions for 2 or 3 years. While in several less cardinal questions they yielded to the demands of the pragmatic wing, as regards the condemnation and liquidation of the "extreme leftish" trend, they took the standpoint that this should not begin with the "cultural revolution" but rather with the "great leap," as the roots of this policy reached back to the second half of the 1950s. It was related to this tactic that at the 3rd plenary session of the 11th CC of the CPC - to the surprise of many - it was not Liu Shaoqi, former state president and party deputy chairman, counting as the number one victim of the "cultural revolution," who was rehabilitated, but mainly those personalities who had confronted Mao Zedong's "extreme leftish" and arbitrary political guideline much before the "cultural revolution" (e.g., Peng Dehuai, Zhang Wentian, Huang Kecheng, Bo Yibo, Tao Zhou). This circumstance could not fail to have an impact on the further shaping of the political and ideological image of the CPC and on the whole development of the PRC.

Although the plenary session passed a resolution to the effect that "... the stress of the party's work should shift to socialist modernization,"[5] the greatest attention was paid to the diversified development of agriculture. The session represented the view that "... the whole party should concentrate its main energy and efforts on advancing agriculture as fast as possible, because agriculture, the foundation of the national economy, has been seriously damaged in recent years and remains weak on the whole."[6] It was recognized that if agriculture did not develop at a faster pace, the upset proportions and equilibrium of the national economy could not be "adjusted" and rehabilitated, and raising the living standard would be out of question. But this was far from being in agreement with the earlier development concept of the pragmatic wing, which was based on the assumption that the developed capitalist countries were interested mainly in strengthening the military potential of China, with China taking an anti-Soviet platform, and in the joint exploitation of its natural resources. Thus they placed the emphasis on development and modernization of industries related to armaments and to the extraction of raw materials, as well as on creating the scientific-technological and infrastructural background needed for faster development.

The 3rd plenary session of the 11th CC, CPC, devoted great attention to expanding the democratic rights of the masses, the freedom of criticism, and, in general, to widening democracy and restoring the legal system. The problems of whether "practice is the sole criterion for testing truth" and whether "truth should indeed be sought by setting out from the facts" were dicussed at length. Most of the participants took the view that this was "of far-reaching significance in encouraging comrades of the whole party and all people of the country to emancipate their thinking and follow the correct ideological line. For a party, a country, or a nation, if everything had to be done according to books and thinking became ossified, progress would become impossible, life itself would stop, and the party and country would perish."[7]

Nevertheless, the session declared emphatically that "... the great feats of Comrade Mao Zedong in the protracted revolutionary struggle are indelible. Without his outstanding leadership and without Mao Zedong's Thought, it is most likely that the Chinese revolution would not have been victorious up to the presert." ... "Comrade Mao Zedong, was a great Marxist", but at the same time "... it would not be Marxist to demand that a revolutionary leader be free of all shortcomings and errors. It also would not conform to Comrade Mao Zedong's consistent evaluation of himself."[8] In the opinion of the plenary session: "... the cultural revolution should also be viewed historically, scientifically, and in a down-to-earth way." As for the shortcomings and mistakes that had been made in the actual course of the revolution, they were to be summed up at the appropriate time as experience and lessons so as to unify the views of the whole party and the people of the whole country. However, there should be no haste about it,"[9] read a publication about the 3rd plenary session of the 11th CC.

These events show that in December 1978 a particular compromise was reached among the representatives of different trends within the highest leadership of the CPC. This compromise and the new power relations that formed in their wake already created greater possibilities for considering issues from all sides and for the activation of healthier forces earnestly wishing to learn from the mistakes that had been made. Among those who were eager to learn from the past - also reagarding their Marxist education - were several highly qualified policymakers, ideologues, economic and cultural, theoretical and practical experts, scientists, artists, and pedagogues, whose chances of being published in the Chinese press increased dramatically beginning in the spring of 1979. Thereafter, in conformity with the principle: "let us search for truth by setting out from facts," several articles and studies were published in Chinese dailies and various social science periodicals which attempted to summarize the positive and negative experiences of socio-economic development throughout the preceding three decades, and to draw the theoretical and practical conclusions therefrom in order to more exactly determine the further tasks of development and to select or elaborate the appropriate tools and methods.

Emergence of the Outlinees of the New Economic Policy

Following the session, the main goal was to achieve rapid results in agricultural production and an upswing in rural economy. Relying on the favorable experiences gained in the provinces Anhui and Sichuan, the CC of the CPC worked out and published in January 1979 a document entitled: "On some questions of accelerating agricultural development (draft resolution)." This prescribed that the rights of ownership and self-management of the people's communes, production brigades, and production teams should be respected and protected. Their assets, means of production, and inventory, as well as the labor available to them, must not be used, expropriated, or "regrouped" without compensation. The household plots, complementary family occupations, and free-market trade of the members of communes were to be regarded as necessary complements of the socialist economy and not as the "tail of capitalism" which had to be "cut off" as soon as possible. At the same time, the brand "cap" of "landlord" or "rich peasant" was removed from 4.4 million people in Chinese villages.[10] In March, the state procurement prices for 18 basic agricultural products were raised - on average by 24.8% - among them cereals, cotton, vegetable oils, and live pigs, and this raised the net income of peasants in itself by about 7 billion yuan in 1979. In addition, for producers who offered their surplus products - after meeting their commitments undertaken in the production contracts - to the state procurement agencies, a further 50% "premium" was promised above the raised procurement price. At the end of September, the document approved at the 4th plenary session of the CC, CPC, held September 25-28 was also published. It was entitled: "Resolution of the CC, CPC, on some questions of accelerating agricultural development," and it summed up the most important related tasks in 25 points. With its concrete measures this resolution greatly increased the productive activity of peasants and started the changes which in a few years radically transformed the picture of Chinese agriculture and Chinese villages, which had stagnated for decades. Thus, in China as well, the reform process began with agriculture and the rural economy, and rapid and striking success was achieved relatively soon.

The debate that developed within the CPC leadership in the spring of 1979 - soon after the end of the "restricted war operations" that had been started with the aim of "reprimanding" Vietnam - was of outstanding importance. It dealt with whether the economic policy that had been accepted a year earlier and had been pursued since then was correct. Some of the expcricnced economic leaders and rehabilitated economists who had been drawn into the leadership at the 3rd plenary session of December 1978 proved with convincing arguments - supported by concrete analyses and computations - that the 10-year economic development program approved at the first session of the 5th NPC in February 1978 (for the implementation of which less than 8 years were available), or those who had elaborated it, had not reckoned realistically with the actual state of the Chinese economy, with the disproportions that had developed in the preceding 10-12 years, or with the bureaucratic rigidity and cumbersomeness of the Chinese system of planning and economic management. They warned the political leadership that the repeated setting of new unfounded and unattainable targets and the drive to achieve them would - similar to the "great leap" - soon lead to new grave disproportions and a decline in the living standard. This would again provoke the dissatisfaction of the working masses, who had had enough of continuous promises and useless efforts. The Chinese people wanted to live better, not merely in the next century or the next millennium, but in the next few years and decades, since "ten thousand years of happiness" had already been promised them in the late 1950s "after 3 years of strenuous work." In the course of the debate sharp criticism was voiced, directed at those working out the development program, who - not reckoning with realities and the objective laws of economic development - had visions of a kind of new "great leap." They had believed - so it was said - that the complicated and difficult task of modernizing Chinese industry could be solved by building a few hundred or even a few thousand large modern establishments, but they had paid hardly any attention to the modernization of the more than 350 thousand existing industrial plants.

These criticisms were raised not merely, and not even primarily, against party chairman Hua Guofeng (who, in his capacity as prime minister, had submitted the criticized program to the first session of the 5th NPC), but also against Deng Xiaoping, who was known to have commissioned the elaboration of the program of "accelerated development and modernization" of Chinese industry in the autumn of 1975.[11] (An organic part of the program was the establishment of close economic, commercial, scientific-technological, and financial cooperation with the most advanced capitalist countries and groups of countries, that is, the policy of "opening outward," from which the pragmatic Chinese leaders hoped a sudden acceleration of the "four modernizations." Deng Xiaoping tried to ward off this thinly veiled criticism and to shift it onto others, partly by emphasizing even more strongly the scientific and technological backwardness of China and the dangers deriving from seclusion, and partly by formulating, as the first among the Chinese leaders, the "four cardinal principles"[12] on which they had to absolutely insist in the course of implementing the "four modernizations," and which have ever since served as terms of reference, appearing in almost every important party document.

In the course of the debate the most respected and most authoritative economists and theoretical experts pointed out that without deep social, economic, political, and ideological reforms and without a radical transformation of the existing system of economic management, all active factors could not be mobilized in China and a successful solution of the tasks of economic and social development that were put on the agenda was out of the question. They proposed that, instead of the risky experiment with a repeated "great leap", a new "adjustment" period of at least 3 years be inserted into the development process of the Chinese economy. In the course of this period the disproportions and irrational features that had developed in the preceding years could be eliminated and adjusted. They also emphasized that the "four modernizations" had to set out from the particular conditions of the country and that China's "socialist character" had to be preserved unconditionally.

As a result of this debate, in the spring of 1979 - hardly 1 year after the approval of the "10-year development program" - the targets of the plan document were revised and some of the investment and industrial development estimates figuring in it were radically reduced. In the course of this revision the Chinese foreign trade organs were forced to suspend "indefinitely" the signing of 32 contracts that had already been discussed with Japanese firms in every detail, the combined value of which approximated US $2.8 billion. Following that, several other negotiations - in some cases of even greater value - about purchases of complete production plants with American, Japanese, and Western-European partners were suspended. In the next few years also the foreign trade of the PRC with the Eastern European countries, on the upswing in 1978, temporarily declined. Finally, at the second session of the 5th NPC, held in June 1979, Prime Minister Hua Guofeng, chairman of the CPC, announced that "readjustment, reformation,[*] consolidation, and improvement" of the national economy would take at least 3 years (including 1979); thus the "adjustment period" would extend into the fifth 5-year plan period covering the years 1981-1985.

After a break of almost 20 years, following the session of the NPC an official publication was issued about the fulfillment of the national economic development plan of the PRC in the preceding year. Also, on the basis of the reports read at the

---

[*] In official English translations made by Chinese the verb _gaige_, the first meaning of which is "reform", is rendered here and in other contexts as "restructuring." The author disagrees with this, and throughout the text the terms "reform" or "reformation" will be used as terms corresponding to _gaige_.

session, concrete information was given about the targets of national economic development for 1979, the balance of the state budget of 1978, and the budget estimates for 1979. Thus, the second session of the 5th NPC was a turning point in several respects and greatly contributed to providing information for foreign observers and Sinologists about the actual situation of the Chinese economy from authentic sources.

The "Four-Word Directive": Announcement of the Reform and Opening Policy

The new economic policy guideline characterized by the terms "readjustment, reformation, consolidation, improvement" as points of emphasis (henceforth: "four-word directive")[13] was announced at a working conference convened in April 1979 by the CC, CPC. More closely, this guideline meant the following: (a) "adjustment" of the basic national economic proportions that had been upset in the wake of the "extreme leftist" economic policy pursued under the "cultural revolution;" (b) "reformation" of the overcentralized, rigid, bureaucratic system of economic management that had developed in the preceding decades; (c) "consolidation" of the enterprise management system disarranged by the various political and ideological movements (campaigns); and (d) "improvement" of production standards, technology, economy, and management of the existing enterprises. (In this latter respect, raising of the standards meant for several years only the "restoration" of earlier standards, because in 1979 the technicoeconomic parameters and efficiency indicators of production and trade in most industries still lagged significantly behind the levels that had already been attained in 1965, the year preceding the "cultural revolution.")

At this meeting Li Xinnian, party deputy chairman and member of the standing committee of the PB, pointed out on behalf of the CC that the system of economic management then functioning had many deficiencies and that its gradual reformation was unavoidable. As the most important of the deficiencies he pointed out the overcentralization of guidance and management, the rigidity and meticulousness of planning, and the resultant passive behavior of central and local organs, enterprises, and workers; i.e., he showed that the economic system in force was hamstringing the activity, creativity, and initiative of economic organizations and workers. It was also formulated at this conference that the situation could best be changed and improved if the established relations of production and the whole superstructure were adjusted to the requirements raised by the development of the forces of production, and, if the objective laws of economy were allowed to assert themselves and even were deliberately used in economic management.

At the conference of the CC, CPC, held in April 1979 the questions related to the reform of the Chinese economic system were discussed in depth, and in a first approximation, the following principles were laid down:

1. Planned economy is of prime importance in the whole national economy but, at the same time, serious attention has to be paid to the complementary role of market regulation. The production and allocation of products important for the national economy and for public welfare have to be centrally planned and the prices of these products have to be centrally set. As regards all other products, the enterprises determine the volume of output themselves, depending on the development of market supply and demand, and they organize production and selling themselves. In some cases prices are shaped by the state, in others also by the enterprises themselves - moving within certain limits and adjusting to the market demand and supply relations - thus enabling competition between firms.

2. Enterprise autonomy should be expanded, and the material interest of workers should be made dependent on the management results of the given enterprise. Every enterprise is obliged to keep strict cost accounting, in the course of which the principle of distribution according to work done has to be consistently asserted.

3. In conformity with the principle of central leadership and management by levels, the management authority of the central and the local organs has to be clearly delimited. The elabora-

tion and issuing of plans, measures, and legal rules affecting the whole of the national economy have to be concentrated with the central organs. These central organs should also manage the large-scale construction investment, the material supply of large plants that are of key importance for the country, as well as their production and selling activities. The central organs have to support the local ones in attending to the tasks entrusted them.

4. The organization and structure of public administration have to be simplified; the use of economic tools and methods in economic management has to be learned. Various specialized large enterprises and associations of enterprises have to be organized to promote specialization and cooperation, and the system of economic contracts has to be broadened.

The conference also pointed out that, parallel with the implementation of the partial reforms, conscientious fact-finding, research, analysis, experimentation, and preparatory work were needed, and it suggested that a relatively comprehensive draft of a reform also had to be elaborated.

It was in the spirit of this conference and according to the principles there formulated that the preliminary ideas and concepts relating to the reform of the Chinese economic system began to take shape and discussion was started. The necessary domestic and international data and experience were collected and processed, and, in their wake, the target model of Chinese economic reform and its system of goals were gradually elaborated. To organize and direct this work the Financial and Economic Committee of the State Council of the PRC formed a research group to engage in the reform of the economic system. It mobilized a relatively wide circle of theoretical and practical experts, started research projects of significant volume to find facts and disclose interrelations, and organized conferences, debates, and study tours on various themes. This is how, in the autumn of 1979, a small group of Chinese theoretical economists and social scientists came to pay their first visit to Hungary.[14] Their goal was to become directly acquainted with and to discuss the theoretical problems, practical questions, and experiences related to the preparation and introduction of the new system of management and the functioning of the new economic mechanism in this country.

The policy of "opening outward" was not yet formally announced in 1979; merely the first steps were taken on the road leading to the formulation of this policy. Thus, e.g., in July 1979 the CC of the CPC allowed the party committees of the provinces Guangdong and Fujian "to carry on special policy in the field of foreign economic activity and to take flexible measures."[15] On August 13, 1979, the State Council issued a decree "On some questions of the large-scale development of foreign trade increasing the foreign exchange revenues." This extended the foreign trade authority of local authorities and enterprises, introduced a system whereby a fixed portion of foreign exchange revenues deriving from exports could be retained by the local foreign trade organs and productive enterprises, and prescribed preferential customs clearing procedures for import goods promoting exports.[16]

As a result of all these developments, the main outlines of the new economic policy began to emerge in mid-1979, the backbone of which initially was "adjustment" of the basic national economic proportions upset in the preceding period. As it evolved, however, the tasks related to the reform of the existing economic system and to "opening outward" came increasingly to the fore, so much so that now the whole period since 1979 is called in China "the period of reform and opening."

Footnotes to Chapter Two

1. In the course of an interview in the autumn of 1977, Deng Xiaoping estimated that China lagged behind the scientific and technological level of the developed industrial countries by about 50 years, and declared that the abyss separating China from the pioneering countries had not narrowed in the past decade but had even widened. See: Han Suyin: Interview with Deng Xiaoping, deputy chairman of the CPC. Der Spie-

gel, 1977, no.48, and Harrison Salisbury: Chinese leaders consider the past decade as lost. New York Times, November 5, 1977.
2. The "four-word directive" announced in the spring of 1979 took its name from the four words in which the main tasks of the new economic policy guideline were summed up. These were: readjustment, reformation, consolidation, improvement.
3. The thesis of "two whatevers" was published on February 7, 1977, as a common editorial in Renmin Ribao, Hongqi, and Jiefangjun Bao, under the title: "Let us carefully study the documents and grasp the decisive links." This meant: "Whatever is decided by Chairman Mao, we consistently support it, and whatever directive has been given by Chairman Mao, we unswervingly hold to it." In criticizing this thesis, Deng Xiaoping made efforts to dispel the faith in the infallibilitiy of Mao and the dogmatic atmosphere of the constant references to him.
4. At that time the centrist forces of the Chinese party leadership included Deputy Party Chairmen Ye Jianying, Li Xiannian, Chen Yun, and those rehabilitated in December 1978: Peng Zhen, Huang Kecheng, and Bo Yibo.
5. Liu Suinian, Wu Qungan (eds.) 1986: op. cit., p 564
6. Ibid, p 570
7. Ibid, p 575
8. Ibid, p 575
9. Ibid, p 575
10. As a matter of fact, "cap" here means the branding itself. The term derives from the old Chinese custom that once criminals or rebels had been caught, they were led or carried to the place where they lived wearing a high paper cap on which their names and crimes were written. This traditional form of public humiliation was especially common after the liberation as well, particularly at times of mass political campaigns. "Taking off the cap" meant that the old classification and detrimental distinction had ceased.
11. The document mentioned in footnote 15 to Chap. One is meant. It was entitled: "On some questions concerning the accelera-

tion of industrial development" and summed up the tasks involved in 70 points.

12. The "four principles" were the following: adherence to the socialist road, adherence to the dictatorship of the proletariat (a few years later, the term "dictatorship of the proletariat" was replaced by "people's democratic dictatorship"), adherence to the leadership of the communist party, and adherence to Marxism-Leninism and Mao Zedong Thought. Deng Xiaoping expounded these four principles on March 30, 1979, at the theoretical conference of the party, in his speech entitled: "Let us adhere to the four principles." His aim was to define the points of orientation and the limits to which the idcological dcbatc could go in the search for expedient ways and means of modernization.

13. This guideline is called in China the "eight-character guideline" because the four words are written in Chinese with four times two, i.e., with altogether eight characters (tiao-zheng, gai-ge, zheng-dun, ti-gao).

14. Four leading scientists from the Chinese Academy of Social Sciences: deputy chairman Yu Guangyuan, director of the Marxism-Leninism-Mao Zedong Thought Institute; Su Shaozhi, deputy director of the same institute; Liu Guoguang, deputy director of the Economic Research Institute; and Huang Hai, head of section of the same institute, paid a visit to Hungary as guests of the ambassador of the PRC in Budapest. Their program of consultations was organized - with the consent and support of the competent authorities - by the Magyar Külügyi Intézet (Hungarian Institute of Foreign Affairs), involving the research institutes engaged in the theoretical and practical problems of the reform of economic management and the economic management organs. During the almost 4 weeks of their visit several consultations were held which also showed the pitfalls of Hungarian economic reform. In addition, the guests visited several industrial enterprises, agricultural producers' cooperatives, and wholesale and retail firms. They reported on their experiences in several articles and lectures, in addition to mak-

ing an official report on the study tour. Their notes on the consultations were also published in the summer of 1981 in a 350 page book (246 000 characters) under the title: "Report on the investigation of the Hungarian economic system." The book was in circulation exclusively in China.
15. Dangdai Zhongguo de jingji tizhi gaige (Reform of the economic system of present-day China) Beijing, 1984, p 782.
16. Ibid.

Chapter Three
DEVELOPMENT OF THE REFORM AND OPENING POLICY IN THE PERIOD OF READJUSTMENT (1979-1982)

At the outset it was envisaged that the implementation of the economic policy objectives formulated in terms of the "four-word directive" would require 3 years or somewhat longer. Thus it was clear at the start that the implementation of the tasks of "readjustment, reformation, consolidation, and improvement" would reach well into the sixth 5-year plan period covering the years 1981-1985. Since the points of emphasis of the new economic policy guideline were - particularly in the initial phase - mainly "adjustment" and partly "consolidation," the tasks of "reformation" could generally be addressed in this phase in only partial and experimental frameworks. The only exceptions were agriculture and the rural economy in general; in certain provinces such reform processes - partly spontaneous and partly directed - were started as early as 1978. Later, under the impact of measures taken in the meantime and of party resolutions, the latter reform processes evolved at a fast rate and spread all over the country.

The change in economic policy also had an impact on the elaboration of the plan for medium-term economic development and of the long-term strategy for economic development. Elaboration of the sixth 5-year plan was delayed, for example, because of unclear priorities and concepts, the growing uncertainty regarding numerous factors and the personnel changes in leading positions of management. Its final form was not worked out until the autumn of 1982; i.e. in the first 2 years of the plan period only annual plans were in force. In spite of this, the 5-year plan actually approved at the 5th session of the 5th NPC, held in December 1982, soon proved to be too cautious and underplanned, so much so that its most important targets were already attained the following year (1983), and by 1984 all its objectives were by far overfulfilled. Thus, we have sufficient justification for calling the 4-year period between 1979 and 1982 the period of "readjustment policy," as it may be considered a well-

-delimitable, particular phase in Chinese economic development and economic policy on grounds of objective criteria.

In order to let the policy of reform and opening take shape as soon as possible, and to smoothly implement it, in this phase the still numerous obstacles - mainly in the political and ideological spheres - had to be gradually removed. At the same time, firm theoretical and ideological bases had to be established for the policy of reform and opening which would make it clear to both the cadres and the wide masses that one could no longer live and manage in the old accustomed ways, that outside the policy of reform and opening there was no other way to raise the standards of the Chinese nation and society, to ensure the prosperity of every group and individual. At the same time, the tens of millions of Chinese cadres who had been educated on the intellectual food of dogmatic Marxism-Leninism and "Mao Zedong Thought" had to be convinced that this policy was not a turning against these ideas; that, on the contrary, it meant the further development and creative application of these ideas to the requirements of the age and to Chinese realities. At the same time, the practical implementation of the policy of reform and opening had to be boldly started in every area where the political conditions were already mature, or where the various reform measures were forced by life itself, by the requirements of economic development. Thus, in 1979 the reform of the rural economy was already taking place on a national scale, and beginning with 1980 various partial or experimental reform measures were taken in various other fields of the national economy. Parallel to that - in the 4 years from 1979 to 1982 - the complex task of readjusting the basic national economic proportions was also successfully completed. As a consequence, in the first half of the 1980s the Chinese economy started on a development that was more dynamic and more balanced than ever before.

At the 3rd plenary session of the 11th CC, CPC, held in December 1978, and following it at consultations and conferences organized by the CC for party and government leaders of various levels, significant progress was made and there was a more realistic judgement of the social, economic, political, and ideological situation of China and of the development and the distortions in all these fields in former decades. Still, an honest and relentless facing of the past, an unbiased analysis of the deficiencies and crimes, and the identification of those responsible for all these were still missing. Nor was it any clearer what stage the PRC had reached in its development towards socialism in the three decades full of grave distortions and, setting out from it, what kind of goals had to be worked out and attained with the social, economic, and political reforms.

Establishment of an Ideological-Political Platform for the Reform and Opening Policy

The first serious attempt at solving the first task and "settling the debt" was made by the Chinese leadership at the end of September 1979, at the 4th plenary session of the 11th CC of the CPC. It discussed and approved - among other things - the text of the speech that was to be delivered by Ye Jianying, deputy chairman of the CPC and member of the standing committee of the PB, on the occasion of the 30th anniversary of the founding of the PRC, at a mass meeting. This anniversary forced the Chinese leadership - still greatly divided and of heterogeneous composition - to make a summary evaluation, acceptable to every faction, about the development of the PRC over three decades and provide in this framework some explanation for the grave mistakes, arbitrary measures, and unlawful acts of the different periods. This was by no means a simple task, as at that time the leadership of the CPC still included a large number of leading cadres - headed by Party Chairman Hua Guofeng - who had risen during the "cultural revolution" by faithfully serving the then ruling policy and who were thus themselves responsible for those mistakes. At the same time, as a result of the rehabilitations in the meantime, there was a growing number of leading cadres who had been vilified during the "cultural revolution" and thus quite naturally demanded that the policies of that period and the "extreme left" ideology supporting that policy should be definitely and finally condemned, and in this framework the personal responsibility of Mao Zedong should be established and declared. Thus, as regards the evaluation of the past, only a compromise could be reached even at this 4th plenary session of the CC, CPC. The participants themselves considered the evaluation "preliminary," indicating at the same time that "at an appropriate date an official assessment of the history of the past 30 years has to be made, above all of the 10 years of the cultural revolution, in the framework of a conference to be convened for this purpose."[1] This was accomplished with some degree of success little more than one and a half years later, at the 6th plenary session of the 11th CC in June 1981, and the debate on the evaluation of the past ended - at least for some time. Still, the evaluation given at the 4th plenary session represented substantial progress on the road towards disclosing the actual causes of the grave distortions in the socioeconomic development of China and the policy of the CPC. This session considerably accelerated the process of eliminating the ideological and political impacts of the "cultural revolution."

The later events were as follows: In February 1980, at the 5th plenary session of the 11th CC, the number-one target and victim of the "cultural revolution": State President and Party Deputy Chairman Liu Shaoqi was rehabilitated - he had been the main adversary of Mao Zedong. At the same time, Zhao Ziyang and Hu Yaobang - designated heirs of Hua Guofeng to his posts of prime minister and party chairman - were elected members of the highest leading bodies of the party, while five prominent left--extremist cadres of the cultural revolution were removed. In March 1980 the CC, CPC created a drafting commission to clarify some questions of party history after the liberation and to elaborate the related text of the draft resolution. The commission performed this work in 15 months and discussed in the meantime several versions of the text. Deng Xiaoping contributed on several occasions and made various proposals. (The document itself was approved at the 6th plenary session of the CC, held in June 1981 and was published on July 1981, the 60th anniversary of the founding of the CPC.)

At the 3rd session of the 5th NPC, held between August 30 and September 10, 1980, Party Chairman Hua Guofeng was relieved of his post as prime minister and Zhao Ziyang was appointed in his place. In the documents of the session - including the report of Hua Guofeng - the term "cultural revolution" appeared for the first time in China in this form, that is, in quotation marks, indicating the essential change in the evaluation of this period. The further changes in personnel and regrouping of cadres approved at the session considerably strengthened the position of the group of reformist, pragmatic leaders who rallied around Deng Xiaoping also within the government apparatus. Following that, in November 1980, the persons belonging to the "Lin Biao conspiracy group" and the "gang of four" were put on trial before a "special court"; among them was Mao Zedong's widow, Jiang Qing. After a public trial lasting more than 2 months - also broadcast on television - all main defendants were condemned: Jiang Qing and Zhang Chunqiao received "suspended" death sentences, the other eight persons imprisonment for 16-18 years.

The task of facing the past and official evaluation of the "cultural revolution" was performed by the 6th plenary session of the CC, CPC, held in June 1981. It approved a lengthy resolution on certain questions of party history after the liberation.[2] After a brief survey of the 28 years preceding the liberation and the most important events of the 32 years following it, the policy of the party was evaluated in a breakdown of four phases (1949-1956, 1957-1966, 1966-1976, 1976-1981), and the mistakes that had been made were pointed out. Following this, the "historical place of comrade Mao Zedong and Mao Zedong Thought" were discussed in five points, which made up almost one quarter of the length of the resolution of 38 points. It emerges from the debates of the draft resolution that this proved to be the task most difficult to solve. Finally, a Janus-faced solution was chosen. On the one hand, it acknowledged Mao Zedong's outstanding role and service in the victory of the Chinese revolution and in establishing the foundations of socialism; on the other hand, it pointed out the grave mistakes he committed in the last two decades of his life. On the whole, however, the resolution took the view his merits outdid his mistakes, and thus, "Comrade Mao Zedong was a great Marxist and a great proletarian revolutionary, strategist and theorist."[3] This evaluation did not prove to be durable, although the offical evaluation has never been changed. Until the summer of 1989 quotations from and references to Mao Zedong were rarely found in Chinese theoretical and ideological literature. More frequently, he was mentioned as an "outstanding" person of a vanishing period who had distorted the theory and practice of socialism. An effort was made to cleanse the notion of "Mao Zedong Thought" - which remained, along with the ideology of Marxism-Leninism, the ideological and political basis and guideline for the activities of the CPC - from the undesirable distortions that had occurred in various periods with a declaration that: "Mao Zedong Thought is Marxism-Leninism applied and developed in China; it constitutes a correct theory, a body of correct principles and a summary of the experiences that have been confirmed in the practice of the Chinese revolution, and is a crystallization of the collective wisdom of the Chinese Communist Party."[4] With this a formula "Mao Zedong Thought" was delimited partly from Mao Zedong himself, partly from all the elements which had proven to be erroneous and which had to be gotten rid of in the interest of further progress and development. The 12th congress of the CPC, held in September 1982, fully adopted this pragmatic approach to "Mao Zedong Thought" and expressed it by repeating, word for word, the above definition of "Mao Zedong Thought" in the modified organization rules of the party (the party constitution).

Besides approving the resolution on some questions of party history after the liberation, the 6th plenary session of the 11th CC also made new changes in the leadership of the party bodies. The most important of these was the removal of Hua Guofeng from his position as chairman of the CC and of the Military Committee of the CC. Hu Yaobang was elected party chairman and Deng Xiaoping chairman of the Military Committee. Thus the composition of the Standing Committee of the Political

Bureau and of the Presidium of the CC changed in consequence of the redistribution of functions as follows: chairman was Hu Yaobang; deputy chairmen were Ye Jianying, Zhao Ziyang, Li Xiannian, Chen Yun, and Hua Guofeng. The latter was finnaly removed from the highest leadership at the 12th congress of the CPC.

As a result of all these events and personnel changes, in 2 years a relatively unified ideological and political platform was created in China for the evolution of the policy of reform and opening. During this time, the theoretical and practical experts committed to the policy of reform and opening were not idle, either; in the ever more favorable atmosphere they performed outstanding work both in the theoretical foundation of this policy and in the practical implementation of the necessary and possible, partial and experimental reforms and of the "opening outward."

Theoretical Foundation of the Reform and Opening Policy

For a theoretical foundation of the reform and opening policy the first question that had to be clarified was what stage had been attained in social development as a result of three decades of "building socialism" - full of grave distortions - and, relying on this basis, what target model could and should be set as a strategic goal of the necessary social, economic, and political reforms.

The offical view in the late 1970s was that through the "socialist transformations," carried out in the mid-1950s and concluded by the end of 1956, the socioeconomic development of China had completed the basic tasks of the transitory period leading to socialism: it had made dominant, almost exclusive, the two basic forms of social ownership: the state (or the whole people) and the collective (group) property. As a result, socialist relations of production predominated; that is, Chinese society became socialist in its character. Since, however, the attained level of the forces of production, and the material and cultural living standards of the population were still rather low in China, in spite of the socialist transformations, Chinese society was in the developmental stage of "underdeveloped socialism." From this it could enter the stage of "developed socialism" only after completion of the "four modernizations," i.e., after modernization of agriculture, industry, defense, science and technology. The belief was that this goal could, on the whole, be attained by the end of the century, the turn of the millenium.

In early 1979 the CC, CPC, and the Chinese Academy of Social Sciences (CASS) organized a theoretical conference at which a group of Marxist social science researchers voiced the opinion that in determining the social character of a society one could not set out merely from the transformation of ownership relations, nor could some kind of automatism be assumed to exist between the legal act of changing the form of ownership and the coming about of socialist relations of production. Formal socialization is, namely, not identical with the actual socialization of the production and work processes, the latter being basically the result of the development of the forces of production. Therefore, in their opinion, Chinese society was - in spite of the actual changes in ownership relations - still in the transitory stage leading to socialism, and thus the phase called "underdeveloped socialism" in China was actually a part of the long historical transition leading to socialism.

This concept was most clearly expounded by two leading fellows of the Marxism-Leninism - Mao Zedong Thought Institute of the CASS: Su Shaozhi and Feng Lanrui, and was published in the theoretical periodical Jingji Yanjiu (no. 5, 1979) in their common work entitled: "Question of the stages in social development after the proletariat has come to power." They justified their standpoint by stating that, although the two main forms of public property, state and collective ownership, had indeed become predominant in China as a result of socialist transformations, yet, because of the underdevelopment of the forces of production these forms of ownership could not properly function. Small-scale production and work processes were still widespread, and on this account the real socialization of the production and work processes had not and could not have taken place in the overwhelming part of the economy. Because of the low productivity of social labor, even today products are not available in a quantity and quality that would allow the assertion of the socialist principle of distribution according to work done and thus, when satisfying the basic needs of the population, it is the levelling distribution: "eating from the big common kettle," that is, egalitarianism, which is characteristic of Chinese society. In consequence of the relative underdevelopment of the forces of production, the technological lag of a whole era, small-scale production will be needed in China for quite some time to come. This requires the development of individual and small-group forms of ownership best conforming to it and even the involvement of foreign and domestic private capital in the interest of accelerating technical progress and acquiring modern management know-how, in the form of partly joint state and private ventures, partly capitalist private enterprises. Thus, in China the development of a multisector economy should be aimed at; this is not characteristic of socialism, but of the economy of the period of transition.

However convincing these arguments may have been for some of the social scientists and theoretical economists, the majority kept to the official party opinion, according to which, in spite of every distortion and backwardness, Chinese society was not in a transitory stage but had been a socialist society ever since 1957. It is not difficult to recognize that in this cardinal theoretical question - similar to that of the other ruling communist parties - the standpoint of the CPC did not move a jot from the anti-Marxist and unscientific system of criteria for "laying the bases of socialism" which had been "theoretically" developed by Joseph Stalin in the second half of the 1930s. This led to the "confusion of social formation"[5] with grave theoretical and practical consequences which even the parties advocating and implementing the most radical social, economic, and political reforms dared not admit to the masses. At the latest, the 13th congress of the CPC, the only development was that the term "underdeveloped socialism" was replaced by the term "initial stage of socialism," and an attempt was made to give a fuller explanation for the concrete contents of this notion and to attribute theoretical importance to the notion itself. Otherwise, the fact that the substance does not lie in the name is well exemplified by an article of another participant in the 1979 debate, Jiang Chunzi. He published it in the periodical Jingji Yanjiu (no. 10, 1979) under the title: "Scientific behavior towards scientific socialism." He stated that for the name of the transitory stage extending from the basic socialist transformation of ownership of the means of production to the first phase of communism, in addition to the terms "underdeveloped socialism," used in China, and "noncomplete socialism," applied in the People's Democratic Republic of Korea, the terms "immature socialism," "incomplete socialism," "intermediate phases of socialism," or "early socialism" may also be considered. To this list may be added the terms "formal socialism," earlier used in Vietnam, and "presocialism," which I tried to introduce myself in the early 1980s, all of which were intended to call attention to the qualitative difference between the notion of socialism as defined by scientific socialism and the Marxian theory of social formations as well as so-called existing socialism.

Besides consideration of the theory of formations, a lively discussion evolved at that time, particularly among theoretical economists. The subjects involved were the role that the law of value should play in a socialist economy, the substance of the basic law of socialism, the goal of socialist production, the law of the planned and proportional development of the national economy, the interpretation of dynamic and complex equilibrium, and the expedient methods for and possibilities of asserting the principle of material interest and distribution according to work done in practice. In the course of the discussion many experts emphasized the necessity of studying other countries that were working to establish socialism, with special regard to national features and the experiences with attaining the central targets of economic development with various methods and instruments of economic management. Some voiced the opinion that the experiences in industrial development and modernization of some Far-Eastern and Southeast-Asian countries were most relevant for China. They said that the historical traditions of these countries, their earlier social structure, the mentality of their inhabitants were - in spite of the different character of their political pattern - much nearer to those of China than conditions in this respect of either the Soviet Union or the Eastern-European countries. As a result of the debate, the standpoint was adopted and officially approved that China had to realize a modernization setting out from the particular conditions of the country, but relying on socialist principles as regards both its contents and character, and its systems of society and economic management had to be adjusted to the requirements of this socialist modernization. As a result, the Chinese theoretical and practical experts engaged in developing the policy of reform and opening in the early 1980s became even more interested in the experiences of the Eastern-European socialist countries with their own economic and political reforms. This later found expression in the more frequent and regular study tours and professional consultations.[6]

The target model of economic reform was selected essentially as a result of the theoretical debates of 1979. This will be reviewed in greater detail in a later chapter of this book. Here it need only be mentioned that the choice fell to a model organically linking plan and market, more precisely, on an organic linking of regulation through plan and through the market, which was at that time called by some Chinese economists the "Hungarian model." This is the explanation for the fact that in the period of preparing for the comprehensive reform the greatest and most intensive interest was exhibited toward the reform of economic management in Hungary, and that, among the materials translated into Chinese from the economic literature of the Eastern-European socialist countries, the works of Hungarian authors are the most numerous.

Rapid Reform of the Rural Economy

In the wake of the initiatives taken in the provinces of Anhui and Sichuan and the measures taken after the 3rd plenary session of the 11th CC, CPC (reviewed above) and, particularly, after publication of the party resolution "On some questions concerning the acceleration of agricultural development," approved at the 4th plenary session of the 11th CC, held in September 1979, a nationwide movement developed to reform the earlier system of control and management of the rural economy.

In the winter of 1978/1979, as has been mentioned, in the provinces of Sichuan, with 100 million inhabitants, and Anhui, with 50 million - with the support of the local party leaders Zhao Ziyang and Wan Li new methods and forms of an experimental nature were introduced in the organization and production of agriculture. The substance of these changes was that earlier - in the framework of producing teams directed by the producing brigades of the rural people's communes and constituting their self-accounting units - the collectively performed productive work and other complementary tasks were broken down first to smaller groups and later to family communities and were entrusted completely to these small communities with conditions stipulated in contracts signed for this purpose. Since the small groups or families undertook responsibility for adequate quantity and quality of production and other work in contractual form, this system was called "system of contractual responsibility for production" (in Chinese: chengbao shengchan zerenzhi).

Since the party resolution on questions of accelerating agricultural development - the draft of which was published in January 1979 - embraced and supported this initiative, the system spread like wildfire to other regions and provinces of the country. In the framework of this system the responsibility of the lowest organizational units of the rural people's communes, of the producing teams, significantly increased, since it was they who concluded the contracts with the small groups or families. These contracts stipulated exactly what commitments under what conditions the contracting parties took upon themselves, and in what proportion they shared in the output or income. With regard to crops and animal husbandry this meant clarification of the following points:

1. In what quantity and under what conditions the collective farms made available to the peasants the necessary means of production (arable land or plantation, seed stock, small machines, breeding stock, fodder, vehicles, etc.) and services (machine work, irrigation, plant protection, veterinary supply, storage, transport, etc.)

2. In what quantity and quality, at what date, and at what prices the producers were obliged to hand over the produce or live animals to the producing team. (These latter commitments were jointly established by the contracting parties on the basis of earlier average yields of several years on the land area or plantation made available to them, or of the animal breeding station, while as regards prices the current state procurement prices were authoritative.)

3. What amounts the enterprising peasants were obliged to contribute to the development and welfare funds of the collective farm taking into consideration the number of family members, their composition, and other social factors.

Beyond these commitments, the enterprising peasants were free to dispose of their labor and time as they wished; they scheduled the time spent on production and determined the order in which work was performed themselves. At the same time - and this was the greatest incentive offered by the change - they were free to dispose of the total volume of output above the quantity to be sold under the contract. They could consume it, feed it to their animals, or sell it on the free market. They could also sell it to the state procurement agencies, in which case they received a premium much exceeding the official procurement price (by 20%-50%). All that gave a big impetus to the spread of these new forms of peasant ventures.

While the decentralized system of production management and work organization was gradually spreading, several special forms and variants of the contractual production reponsibility system came about in China's different agricultural regions. They differed from each other mostly as regards with whom the contracts for enterprise were concluded (group, family, or individual) and for what purpose (production or the performing of special skilled work), and also in how autonomously the entrepreneurs fulfilled these contracts - how independent of the producing team. As a consequence, in Chinese publications of those times the description of six or eight concrete forms can be found, and the names they were given are quite diversified, depending on local usage. Beginning in 1981, however, it was rather the family enterprises that began to spread and became generalized, as regards both production and work performance. By 1982 this process had been completed in the whole country, and this necessarily meant that the system of rural people's communes established in earlier decades had to be radically changed. This was accomplished in the next 2 years (1983/1984) partly through the reform of public administration and partly through the reorganization of the rural economy.

Reform and Opening in Other Areas of the Economy

The ideological, political, and theoretical developments of 1979 and the rapid reform of the system of rural economy and its success, as measured by the growing agricultural production and rising peasant incomes, stimulated development of the reform and opening policy also in other areas of the economy and in social activity.

The first steps of reform in industrial production were aimed at improving the management conditions of state enterprises, at expanding enterprise autonomy, and at the normative regulation of the management of fixed and circulating assets of enterprises. In July 1979, the State Council issued five decrees with the aim of making the management of state enterprises more organized and regulated, and thus more efficient.[7] These decrees were aimed at linking economic interests, economic efficiency, and economic responsibility on the one hand, and the interests of the state, of the enterprise, and of the individual on the other. A further aim was to increase enterprise autonomy, i.e., to create a situation where enterprises were not hamstrung. In January 1980 a new decree of the State Council regulated the mode of determining the portion of profit to be left with the state enterprises in industry, distinguishing between the portions retainable from the basic profit (as established in the preceding year) and from the increment of profit attained in the current year. In July 1980, the number of industrial state enterprises experimentally working with greater autonomy already exceeded 6600, which meant about 16% of all state enterprises. At the same time, these enterprises contributed 60% of the total value of output of the state industry and 70% of its total profit payments to the budget. On the basis of this greater autonomy, in order to ease the delimitation of enterprises by branches and by areas, and to develop cooperation between enterprises operating under different control organs, in July 1980 the State Council issued a temporary decree promoting the formation of economic unions. On the same basis, various forms of self-accounting (independent accounting), undertaking a definite profit payment, and other contractual forms of management appeared from 1981 on with experimental character; they began to spread only in the second half of the 1980s.

In order to bring about more rational proportions between economic sectors belonging to different forms of ownership and to reduce urban unemployment, significant efforts were made to stimulate and expand collective and individual ventures, particularly in medium-sized and large cities, but also in small and rural towns. In addition, the number of industrial plants, construction enterprises, and other servicing units established by people's communes or their producing brigades with their own resources began to grow in the villages. They were aimed above all at the local employment of labor forces that became redundant in agricultural production.

To regulate the incomes of individual entrepreneurs the 3rd session of the NPC, held in September 1980, approved the "Individual income tax law of the PRC," according to which a tax was levied only on incomes of 400 yuan/month and more, at progressive rates of 15%-45%. (The 45% rate related to incomes above 12 000 yuan/month.) In view of the fact that at the time the law was passed the average monthly wage of workers and white-collar employees was approximately 80 yuan, the upper limit of tax-free personal income was rather generously determined, and this obviously had a stimulating impact on individual ventures. But the average income of individual entrepreneurs - particularly in the early in the early 1980s - was only one and a half or two times that of workers and white--collar employees.

The initial steps made in investment under the reform policy tried to change the system of nonrepayable investment allocations from the state budget to state enterprises and to promote a shift toward financing from enterprise development funds complemented by middle- and long-term bank loans at low rates of interest. This goal was also served by the decrees issued by the State Council in July 1979 on the partial retaining of profit by industrial enterprises, on accelerated depreciation allowance, and on a more flexible use of the renewal and replacement fund. In the spring of 1981, however, the State Council was already forced to issue a few decrees on strengthening the planned management of basic investments and on restricting the size of investments, since some ministries and enterprises had embarked on too many projects at the same time, and in some cases had made oversized investments.

Since in the period of the "readjustment policy" a comprehensive reform of the earlier established system of wage payment could not be envisaged, an attempt was made to realize a wage payment better adjusted to performance, partly by introducing and spreading forms of piece work - where this was at all possible - and partly by expanding and further developing the system of premiums. A complementary decree of the State Council, issued in May 1981, prescribed that the sum of premiums payable in a year must not exceed the treble of the monthly wage and should range between one and two months' wages on average.

During the period of the "readjustment policy" significant progress was made in implementing the policy of "opening outward" and in reforming the management system of foreign economic relations. In August 1980, at the 15th session of the Standing Committee of the NPC, a decision was approved to create three "special economic zones" in Guangdong province and one in Fujian province. Two of the former three - Shenzhen and Zhuhai - border directly on Hong Kong and Macao, respectively; the third was created somewhat farther north, in an area constituting a part of the port Shantou. In the southern part of Fujian province it was a district of the town Xiamen, in the immediate vicinity of the island of Jinmen, belonging to Taiwan, that was designated for this purpose. Of these, the special economic zone of Shenzhen is the largest (327.5 km^2), within which a separate area was designated for the creation of industrial establishments. With decrees issued for this purpose, in these special economic zones advantageous conditions were created for foreign capital investment, to stimulate which, at the 3rd session of the 5th NPC (September 1980), "The income tax law of the PRC concerning joint ventures with Chinese and foreign investment" was approved; this set the income tax on joint ventures at 30% of the income earned, to which a local tax, amounting to 10% of the income tax paid, was added. (Thus, the actual tax rate was 33%.) From this tax liability various exemptions, differing with regard to amount and length of time could be obtained (e.g., import of advanced technology, production for export, development of backward areas - for 5-10 years.) By the end of 1982, foreign firms from 12 countries had invested altogether US $140 million in China and, as a result, 83 joint ventures were founded. The overwhelming majority (55 joint ventures) were from Hong Kong, and 44.3% of foreign investments were made by Chinese from Hong Kong. They were followed by American firms, with 11 joint ventures and 37% of total foreign investment. It was conspicuous that the most important trading partner of the PRC, Japan, figured on the list of foreign investors with a mere five joint ventures and only 5.4% of total investment.[8]

First Results of Political Reform

The question of reforming the political system was first raised by Deng Xiaoping on October 30, 1979, in his speech greeting the 4th national congress of Chinese writers and artists. He pointed out in this speech that, parallel to the large-scale development of the productive forces of socialism, also the economic and political systems of socialism had to be reformed and improved, a high degree of socialist democracy and a perfect socialist legal system had to be developed. He expounded his ideas in greater detail 10 months later, at an extended session of the Political Bureau of the CC, CPC, held in August 1980. Later it was published under the title: "The reform of the system of party and state leadership."[9]

This speech is still frequently referred to, and justly so. Deng Xiaoping pointed out in this speech, with a sharpness and detailedness unusual up to then with party leaders of socialist countries, the deficiencies and distortions of the management system developed in the preceding decades and passionately urged their quickest possible correction within the framework of a radical reform of the political system. He found the main faults and deficiencies of the existing political system in the following: (a) bureaucracy, (b) exaggerated concentration of power in the hands of a few people, (c) paternalistic behavior of the leaders, (d) lifelong tenure of those in leading positions, and (e) the various privileges of the leaders. At the same time, he outlined the most important tasks in connection with the political system. Since all these phenomena were in some form related to the feudal ways of reasoning and customs, one of the important tasks was to eliminate these feudal customs and the "mandarin style". A strong line should be taken, in his opinion, against the survival of the remnants of petty-bourgeois and bourgeois ideology, and also against anarchistic and extremist individual views and forms of behavior.

The most important tasks were identified by Deng Xiaoping in this speech in the following five points:

1. By modifying the constitution of the PRC, a constitutional guarantee should be created to prevent the exaggerated concentration of power.

2. At the next party congress a central advisory body should be created comprising the veteran cadres with outstanding merits and experience.

3. An effective order of work should be established for the State Council and for the local government organs on different levels; their autonomy (also toward the party) should be increased.

4. Introduction of the assembly of workers and white-collar employees or their representatives with every enterprise and institution in order to control the work of leaders.

5. Assertion on every level of party committees of the principle linking collective leadership and division of labor with personal responsibility.

Later, this speech of Deng Xiaoping was qualified as a document introducing a program which set the direction, principles, and main contents of the reform of the Chinese political system for a long time ahead, together with the related tasks of the next period.

In the spirit of this document, the CC of the CPC sent out a circular to the party committees in January 1981, in which it proposed to consider, in filling the leading posts of government organs of different levels, consistent assertion of certain viewpoints: introduction of young cadres, the increase of professional competence and qualification and consideration of persons outside the party in addition to deserving party members. By including in this work the educational institutions, efforts were made to elaborate the professional criteria for filling posts in various units of government administration and economic management, in order that later the filling of such posts could be made dependent on the winning of tenders and the passing of various professional examinations.

The reform of the institutions of government administration and the cadre system gathered momentum in 1982. At the 22nd session of the Standing Committee of the 5th NPC in March 1982, prime minister Zhao Ziyang delivered a report about the structural reform of the State Council.[10] Thereafter, the "streamlining" of the central government organs was carried out in 3 months. In its framework the number of ministries, government committees, and bureaus was reduced - by means of amalgamation, reorganization and dismissals - from 98 to 52. The number of people employed in these institutions dropped from 49 000 to 32 000, i. e., by more than one third. Significant reorganizations and staff reductions were implemented also in the structure and apparatus of government organs of provinces, towns of province rank, autonomous regions and units subordinated to them. As a result, the number of officials and cadres working in the institutions of public administration dropped from about 600 000 to about 400 000. The reorganizations involved a significant movement of cadres, and a rather large number of middle-aged (40-50 years) cadres with higher qualifications received leading jobs. As a result, the average age of members of leading bodies significantly diminished, and their level of qualification increased. Parallel with this, work was begun to elaborate the system and conditions for the retirement of aged leaders.

The 12th congress of the CPC, which convened in September 1982, was a serious step forward in the realization of the reform proposals made by Deng Xiaoping in August 1980. On the one hand, in preparation for the congress and in conformity with the resolution of the PB of the CC passed on April 23, 1980, it was decided that aged comrades who had lost their capacity for work should not be proposed as delegates to the 12th congress or as members of the CC. On the other hand, at the congress itself - through a modification of the party constitution - institutional forms and possibilities were created for the decent retirement of respected old leaders. According to Article 22 of the new party constitution, a Central Advisory Commission was created. "The Party's Central Advisory Commission acts as a political assistant and consultant to the Central Committee. Members of the Central Advisory Commission must have a party standing of 40 years or more, have rendered considerable service to the Party, have fairly rich experience in leadership and enjoy fairly high prestige inside and outside the Party";[11] so reads the new party constitution approved in September 1982. At the congress a Central Advisory Commission of 160 members was set up, and Deng Xiaoping was elected its chairman. (At that time he was still a member of the Standing Committee of the PB and also chairman of the Military Committee of the CC.) With similar purpose and character, advisory commissions were formed also with the party committees and government bodies on different levels, and this significantly accelerated the rejuvenation of the leading staff in these bodies and institutions. In the mid-1980s the institution of advisory commissions also developed in some large enterprises and educational and scientific institutions.

Result of the "Readjustment Policy"

Under the impact and as a result of the "readjustment policy," initiated in 1979, the basic structural proportions of the Chinese national economy improved significantly. As heavy industry and agriculture changed places in the order of priorities of the main productive branches (formerly: heavy industry - light industry - agriculture), agriculture became the main branch of the economy to be developed. It was followed by light industry, which had been similarly neglected in the preceding one and a half decades. Heavy industry - having enjoyed absolute priority in the traditional concept of socialist industrialization - was thus pressed into third place. As a result, within the combined gross output value of industrial and agricultural production the shares of agriculture, light industry, and heavy industry became almost balanced (33.6%-33.4%-33.0%). Most Chinese economists were of the opinion that, given the level of development of the Chinese economy, these were most rational proportions. (In 1978 the corresponding proportions had been 27.8%-31.1%-41.1%).

Structural proportions within industry were also favorably modified in the period of the "readjustment policy." As regards the weight of the two main groups - light and heavy industries -

within total industrial production, this also became balanced by 1982 (50.2% and 49.8%), approximating thus the proportion of 50:50 considered to be ideal. In 1978 the corresponding proportions still were 43.1:56.9. Within the structure by branches, the shares of the food industry and the textile industry increased relative to 1978 by 2.5 and 3.0 percentage points (from 11.1% to 13.6% and from 12.5% to 15.5%, while the share of the engineering industry fell by almost as much, i.e., by 5.3 percentage points (from 27.3% to 22.0%, computed by the gross value of output. In the 4 years mentioned, the shares of the other branches did not change considerably. However, a significant change occurred in these years in the number and size of industrial enterprises, and there was also some change in the distribution of industrial production by forms of ownership. While in 1978 there were 348 000 industrial enterprises operating in China, in 1982 their number approximated 390 000. Within that, the number of large and medium-sized enterprises increased from 4400 to 5400, while that of small firms from 343 600 to 383 200. The number of state-owned enterprises increased only by 2100 (from 84 000 to 86 100); that of industrial enterprises in collective ownership rose from 264 000 to 302 000. Within this figure, it was the number of the commune-level industrial enterprises of rural people's communes that increased the fastest: from 164 000 to 186 000. Growth was even faster with regard to the number of industrial establishments created at the level of the producing brigades of the communes (from about 600 000 to nearly 820 000). However, until 1984, the output value of the latter was included statistically in the total value of agricultural production; that is, it was recorded as complementary production in agriculture. Table 1 shows shares of enterprises of varying size and various forms of ownership in the total value of industrial output in 1982.

Table 1. Distribution of the gross value of industrial output by size and ownership (in percent)*

	1980	1982
Total value of industrial output	100.0	100.0
By size: Large enterprises	25.1	26.1
Medium-sized enterprises	18.1	18.4
Small enterprises	56.8	55.5
By ownership:		
State enterprises	78.7	77.8
Collective enterprises	20.7	21.4
- of which: commune level	5.6	6.4
Other forms of ownership	0.6	0.8

* For 1978 statistical data are not available in such a breakdown

Source: Zhongguo Tongji Nianjian 1981, 1983. Beijing, pp 208, 222. (Statistical Yearbook of China)

In consequence of the fast growth rate of rural complementary activities, within it particularly of those on the brigade level, the structural proportions within agriculture also underwent significant changes. Within the total value of agricultural production the share of plant cultivation diminished from 67.8% in 1978 to 62.8% in 1982, i.e., by 5 full percentage points. On the other hand, the share of animal husbandry increased from 13.2% to 15.5% and that of complementary activities from 14.6% to 15.9%. As a part of the latter, the share of brigade-level industrial production showed practically no change (11.7% and 11.6%). This unchanged weight indicates that the value of brigade-level industrial production increased on the whole at the same rate as that of agricultural production, while the number of workshops increased considerably. During the same period the shares of forestry and fishing - similarly included in agriculture - changed from 3.0% to 4.1% and from 1.4% to 1.7% respectively.

The share of the other productive branches of the economy in the total value of social product[12] hardly changed during the "readjustment policy." The proportion of construction rose from

8.3% in 1978 to 9.1% in 1982, while the shares of transport and communications and of trade fell from 3.0% to 2.8% and from 6.4% to 5.8%, respectively. Both of these pairs of figures indicate an unsatisfactory development of productive infrastructure and services.

The other fundamental objective of the "readjustment policy" was to bring about rational and optimal relations between accumulation and consumption within the national income. In the first 5-year period (1953-1957) their ratio was around 25:75. At that time - when the large-scale and planned socialist industrialization was started - this also permitted a considerable rise in the living standard of the population, perceptible for all social groups. This is why a considerable number of Chinese economists consider this ratio to be optimal at the present stage of economic development, up to the year 2000. In the 3 years of the "great leap," starting in 1958, and then in almost every year of the 1970s, the rate of accumulation remained throughout above 30%, even reaching 36.5% in 1978. In the third year of the "readjustment policy," 1981, this fell to 28.3%, and in 1982 it was 28.8%. (The rising tendency continued in the following years and in 1985 the rate of accumulation again attained 35.2%.

As a result of the "readjustment," the domestic equilibrium of the PRC's economy also developed in a favorable manner. The deficit of the state budget fell from 15.5% in 1979 to 2.3% in 1981, and it remained at that level in 1982. A not negligible factor in reducing the deficit - along with increased revenues - was the reduction of defense expenditures, and their maintenance at this reduced level thereafter. Thus the share of these expenses within the total declined from 17.5% in 1979 to 15.1% in 1981 and it was 15.3% in 1982. (In the following years the decline in military expenditures was even more spectacular.)

In consequence of the curbing of imports and other, sometimes very drastic, restrictive measures carried out in the early 1980s, by 1982 the foreign economic balance of the PRC became consolidated. Against a deficit of US $2.1 billion in 1979, the balance of trade was zero in 1981, and in 1982 it showed a surplus of US $3 billion. During the same period, exports increased (at current prices) from US $13.6 billion in 1979 to US $22.3 billion by 1982, imports from US $15.7 billion to US $19.3 billion. The foreign exchange reserve of the PRC increased from US $2.1 billion at the end of 1979 to US $11.1 billion by the end of 1982.

The Chinese economic leadership expected that the economic growth rate would significantly diminish during the "readjustment policy" and would not much exceed the annual growth rate of 6%-7%. (In agriculture they reckoned with an annual 4%-5% growth of the value of output and in industry with one of 6%-8%.) In reality, in the 4-year period 1979-1982, the total social product increased annually by an average of 7.8%, the national income by 6.7%, the total value of industrial production by 6.7%, and that of agricultural production by 5.9%. The growth of the value of gross output during the "readjustment policy" is shown in Table 2.

Table 2. Annual growth rate of the gross output value in productive branches (in percent)

	1979	1980	1981	1982
Industry	8.1	10.9	1.7	6.0
- Light	9.6	18.4	14.1	5.7
- Heavy	7.7	1.4	-4.7	9.8
Agriculture	6.4	-1.8	7.1	11.7
Crops	7.2	-0.5	5.9	10.3
Animal husbandry	14.6	7.0	5.9	13.2
Complementary activities	12.4	18.7	11.2	12.8
Construction	1.8	29.7	1.6	4.8
Transport, communications	2.5	4.1	3.2	15.4
Trade	6.9	0.6	19.0	4.8
Total Social Product	7.0	6.4	4.9	8.3

<u>Source:</u> Zhongguo Tongji Nianjian 1987, Beijing, pp 38, 45, 157. (Statistical Yearbook of China)

The table shows that, although growth rates approximating those planned were attained in the two main branches of production if the 4 years are averaged, in some years the growth rates showed rather large fluctuations, partly as an impact of the economic measures taken (in industry) and partly due to weather conditions (in agriculture). Approximation of the desired growth rate in industry was achieved only by curbing production in heavy industry drastically for almost 2 years, and this caused certain disturbances in the supply of materials and energy to manufacturers. The extremely adverse weather conditions of 1980 reduced agricultural production even in absolute terms. Conspicuous in Table 2 are also the "great leap" in the value of output in construction in 1980 (by almost 30%) and the almost 20% permanent increase in the gross value of commercial activities in 1981. The former was related to the sudden increase in investment and housing construction, the latter mainly to the rapid increase in production of consumer goods in light industry.

During the "readjustment policy" the income and consumption level of the population also increased significantly, particularly those of the rural population, which constituted 80% of the total. The average net income per peasant increased from 134 yuan in 1978 to 266 yuan in 1982, i.e., accounting for price increases, by nearly 32% in real terms. At the same time, the average wages of workers and white-collar employees rose from 614 yuan to 798 yuan, meaning a nominal increase of 30%, in real terms 13.6%. Between 1979 and 1982 the level of real consumption by rural inhabitants rose by 38.2%, that of the nonagricultural population by 14.5%. Thus, the consumption levels and living standards of rural and urban dwellers tended to approximate each other in this period. The living area per inhabitant in cities expanded from 4.4 m^2 in 1979 to 5.6 m^2 in 1982, while in villages it increased from 8.1 m^2 in 1978 to 10.7 m^2 in 1982. The average daily per capita calorie consumption approximated 3100 in cities in 1982, in villages 2700, compared with 2700 and 2200 calories respectively in 1978.

Footnotes to Chapter Three

1. Zhongguo Jingji Nianjin (henceforth: ZJN) 1981, Part II, p. 6
2. See: Resolution on certain questions in the history of our Party since the founding of the People's Republic of China. Adopted by the Sixth Plenary Session of the 11th Central Committee of the Communist Party of China. In: Almanac of China's Economy 1981. Eurasic Press, New York and Hong Kong, 1982, pp 75-104
3. Ibid., p. 94
4. Ibid., p. 95
5. The expression of "social formation" means in Marxian theory the forms of societies which - according this theory - regularly follow each other in the course of social development, thus slavery, feudalism, capitalism, socialism and, finnaly, communism.
6. In 1982 a delegation of economists, consisting of four members and headed by Liu Guoguang - which formerly also visited Hungary - studied the system of economic management and various reform measures for three weeks in the Soviet Union. Prior to that delegations of economists visited also Yugoslavia and Rumania with a similar purpose and afterwards also the GDR and Poland.
7. The five decrees were the following:
   - Decree on some questions related to expanding the autonomy in management of industrial state enterprises
   - Decree on the portion of profit retainable by industrial state enterprises
   - Temporary decree on the size of the depreciation allowance of fixed assets in industrial state enterprises and on the mode of utilization of the renewal and replacement fund
   - Temporary decree on the crediting of circulating assets in industrial state enterprises
   - Temporary decree on the tax to be levied on fixed assets of industrial state enterprises

   Source: Dangdai Zhongguo de jingji tizhi gaige. Beijing 1984, p 781

8. ZJN 1982, Part IV/ p 131
9. Selected Works of Deng Xiaoping (1975-1982). Foreign Language Press, Beijing, 1984, pp 302-325
10. ZJN 1982, Part II/pp 27-31
11. The Twelfth National Congress of the CPC (September 1982) Foreign Language Press, Beijing, 1982, p 112
12. The Total Value of Social Product or Total Social Product is an important index in the statistics of the Material Product System (MPS). It means the total results of material production in a certain period of time. It represents the aggregate total of the output value of the five material production sectors: agriculture, industry, construction, transport and commerce (including catering trades and goods supply and sale business). Among the social productive activities, agriculture, industry and construction directly produce material goods, while transport and commerce function as continuation of the process of production and create and add a portion of value to the total.

Chapter Four
STABILIZATION OF THE REFORM AND OPENING POLICY DURING PREPARATION OF THE COMPREHENSIVE ECONOMIC REFORM (1982-1984)

12th National Congress of the CPC: Approval of Reform and Opening Policy, Turn in Chinese Foreign Policy

The 12th national congress of the CPC was held in Beijing, September 1-11, 1982. One of the basic tasks of the congress was to approve the important political, ideological, organizational, and personnel changes which had taken place in the CPC since the preceding, 11th congress, held in August 1977 and, particularly, after the 3rd plenary session of the CC, CPC, in December 1978. Another task of the congress was to devise and formulate the party's long-term strategy for internal and external policies, the guidelines for socialist modernization of the economy and society, and for party work and party construction. In view of the nature of these tasks, this congress was qualified as being of historical importance at the moment it was opened. It was compared, in the history of the development of the CPC over more than six decades, to the 7th congress, held in 1945, which had laid the foundations for the victory of the new democratic revolution.[1]

Hu Yaobang, chairman of the CC (who at this congress, in line with the new party constitution, changed this post for that of general secretary), formulated the main tasks of the 12th congress as follows: "The mission of the present Party Congress is, through the summing up of the historic achievements of the past 6 years, to chart the correct course and define correct strategic steps, principles, and policies so that we can more throughly eliminate the negative consequences of the decade of domestic turmoil, make further progress, and create a new situation in all fields of socialist modernization."[2]

"Of the various tasks for bringing about an all-round new situation," the report to the congress put in first place pushing "forward the socialist modernization of China's economy. For this purpose, the Party has formulated the strategic objective, priorities and steps for our economic construction as well as a series of correct principles in a spirit of realism." So reads the first paragraph of Chap. II of the report to the congress, which discusses economic questions. The text then continues: "The general objective of China's economic construction for the two decades between 1981 and the end of this century is, while steadily working for more and better economic results, to quadruple the gross annual value of industrial and agricultural production - from 710 billion yuan in 1980 to 2800 billion yuan or so in 2000. This will place China in the front ranks of the countries of the world in terms of gross national income and the output of major industrial and agricultural products; it will represent an important advance in the modernization of her entire national economy; it will increase the income of her urban and rural population several times over; and the Chinese people will be comparatively well-off both materially and culturally. Although China's national income per capita will even then be relatively low, her economic strength and national defense capabilities will have grown considerably, compared with what they are today. Provided that we work hard and in a down--to-earth manner, and bring the superiority of the socialist system fuller into play, we can definitely attain our grand strategic objective.

From an overall point of view, what is most important in our effort to realize this objective in economic growth is to properly solve the problems of agriculture, energy, and transport and of education and science."[3]

The two introductory paragraphs of Chap. II of the report to the congress have been quoted at almost full length in order to convince the reader that the 12th congress of the CPC put first priority on the development of the forces of production and on implementing the tasks of the "four modernizations." The long--term strategic goal of economic construction was also a basically quantitative task: "to quadruple the gross annual value of industrial and agricultural production."

Thus, at that time the tasks related to the reform and opening policy were not yet so much at the center of attention as in the years to come; they were only briefly mentioned among the other tasks. For example, regarding the economic tasks of the years to follow, a further part of the chapter reads:

"In the period of the Sixth Five-Year Plan (1981-1985), we must continue unswervingly to carry out the principle of readjustment, reformation, consolidation, and improvement, practice strict economy, combat waste, and focus all economic work on the attainment of better economic results. We must devote our main efforts to readjusting the economic structure in various fields, streamlining, reorganizing and merging the existing enterprises and carrying out technical transformation in selected enterprises. At the same time we must consolidate and perfect the initial reform in the system of economic administration and work out at an early date the overall plan for reform and the measures for its implementation. During the Seventh Five-Year Plan (1986-1990), we shall carry out the technical transformation of enterprises on an extensive scale and gradually reform the system of economic administration, in addition to completing the rationalization of the organizational structure of enterprises and the economic structure in various fields."[4]

It may thus be seen that reform of the economic system appeared even in the report to the congress as an element of the tasks formulated in the "four-word directive." The policy of "opening outward" appears in an even more particular context in the framework of the principle: "persevering in self-reliance while expanding economic and technological exchanges with foreign countries." While the report stipulates that "it is our firm strategic principle to carry out the policy of opening to the outside world and expand technological exchanges with foreign countries in accordance with the principles of equality and mutual benefit," not long afterwards it states: "In no circumstances must we forget that capitalist countries and enterprises will never change their capitalist nature simply because they have economic and technological exchanges with us. While pursuing the policy of opening to the outside, we must guard against, and firmly resist, the corrosion of capitalist ideas and we must combat any worship of things foreign or fawning on foreigners."[5]

Among the principal questions of the economic policy to be followed, the congress also dealt with the problem of creating a multi-sector economy. It pointed out that "upholding the leading position of the state economy and developing diverse economic forms"[6] were necessary. As regards the principal problems of economic administration (management), it was emphasized that "correctly implementing the principle of the leading role of the planned economy and the supplementary role of market regulation" were needed. It pointed out in this context: "This is because diverse economic forms still exist in China and it is difficult to make precise estimates of the manifold and complex demands of society and of the productive capacity of a vast number of enterprises. But whether in mandatory planning or in guidance planning, we must strive to make it conform to the objective reality, constantly study changes in market supply and demand, consciously make use of the law of value and such economic levers as pricing, taxation, and credits to guide the enterprises in fulfilling state plans and give them varying degrees of power to make decisions as they see fit. Only in this way can state plans be supplemented and improved as required and in good time in the course of their implementation."[8]

"Correct application of the principle of ensuring the leading role of planned economy supplemented by market regulation is of fundamental importance to the reform of China's economic systems. We must correctly define the respective scope and limits of mandatory plans, guidance plans, and market regulation and, on the premise that basic stability of commodity prices is maintained, gradually reform the pricing system, price control measures, and the labor and wage systems, and establish an economic administrative system suited to China's conditions so as to ensure the healthy growth of the national economy."[9] This we can read further along in the chapter of the report which deals with economic questions.

All this clearly shows that the report of the CC, constituting the basis of the resolution adopted by the 12th congress of the CPC, reaffirmed and approved all the major questions of the reform of the economic system which had been raised at various expert consultations in the course of formulating the concept. At the same time, it may also be seen that in the working out of these principles also great restraint was exercised and the traditional concept of the operation of a socialist economy was asserted. (The latter is manifest particularly in the emphasis on the leading role of the state sector and on the determining role of planned economy.) At that time the guiding principle of Chinese economic reform had not yet been formulated, i.e., that in the current stage of development of Chinese society, socialist economy could not be anything else but a planned commodity economy, since the full development of commodity economy was an unavoidable phase of socioeconomic development and a necessary condition for modernizing the country.

The report of the congress continues with a discussion on such extraeconomic factors and conditions for attaining the long-term strategic objectives of Chinese social development as creation of a high-level socialist spiritual civilization, attaining a high level of socialist democracy, and carrying on autonomous, independent foreign policy, as well as the tasks of party construction and organization. Among these, the novel interpretation of the goals and principles of Chinese foreign policy was of outstanding importance. For the first time in many years, the leadership of the CPC did not emphasize the revolutionizing effect of the "great turmoil" in the world, or the "unavoidability of war"; rather, it voiced the conviction that: "Being internationalists, we are deeply aware that China's national interests cannot be fully realized in separation from the rest of mankind. Our adherence to an independent foreign policy accords with the discharging of our lofty international duty to safeguard world peace and promote human progress."[10] It was laid down that China does not depend on any big power or group of nations, does not yield to the pressure of any big power, and will preserve its independence in the future as well. At the same time, in conformity with the five principles of peaceful coexistence, it is willing to develop its relations and cooperation with every country of the world, including the socialist countries. Sino-Soviet relations were also intensively discussed, and three main obstacles to the normalization of relations were mentioned: (a) the stationing of significant military forces along the Sino-Soviet frontier and in the People's Republic of Mongolia; (b) the "military occupation" of Afghanistan; (c) the many-sided help given to Vietnam for the military occupation of Kampuchea. Their standpoint was formulated in the following terms: "If the Soviet authorities really have a sincere desire to improve relations with China and take practical steps to lift their threat to the security of our country, it will be possible for Sino-Soviet relations to move towards normalization. The friendship between the Chinese and the Soviet peoples is of long standing, and we will strive to safeguard and develop this friendship, no matter what Sino--Soviet state relations are like."[11]

It is known that, following the 12th congress of the CPC, interstate cooperation began to develop fast between the PRC and those Eastern-European countries with whom such relations had greatly deteriorated earlier. In this sense, this congress represented a turn in China's foreign policy orientation and created the principal bases for gradually settling and normalizing relations with the parties of the international communist movement. This circumstance also had a favorable impact on the further development and consolidation of the reform and opening policy.

Further Development of Reform and Opening Policy

The obvious successes achieved in the period of the "readjustment policy" and the approval won at the 12th congress of the CPC created advantageous conditions in China for the further development and consolidation of the reform and opening policy. In the following years this policy increasingly became a determining factor and main tendency of Chinese economic policy.

Organizational and legal foundations of the reform process

In May 1982, in the framework of "streamlining" and reorganizing the government organs and institutions operating under the direct control and supervision of the State Council, the State Commission for the Reform of the Economic System (henceforth: State Reform Commission, abbreviated SRC) was created. It relied on the reform bureau base of the state council system created in 1980, through its expansion and reorganization, and its chairman was the prime minister, i.e., the Chairman of the State Council. It follows that the SRC became the most important central control organ and the institution of highest rank of the theoretical and practical activities, research and experiments related to the preparation, introduction, and testing of economic reform. Elaboration of the comprehensive draft of the reform, as well as coordination of the various widespread activities related to the reform was entrusted to this commission. Thus, its scope of authority in questions related to reform and reform experiments exceeded that of the two most influential central economic management organs and institutions: the State Planning Commission (SPC) and the State Economic Commission (SEC), although its staff of less than 300 constituted only 1/4 that of the SPC and not even 1/5 that of the SEC.[12] Similar to the two functional management organs, the provincial and city-level organizations of the SRC were soon formed as well (with similarly small staffs) to directly guide and control the activities of the areas and enterprises selected for various reform experiments while maintaining close working relations with the SRC in Beijing. This was facilitated by the fact that about 1/3 of the staff of the SRC were usually travelling about the country to gather personal experience and to collect and impart information and give instructions.

At the end of November 1982, the fifth session of the 5th NPC was convened; it approved the sixth 5-year plan of the PRC for 1981-1985 and the new constitution of the PRC. Reviewing the tasks to be accomplished in the remaining 3 years of the sixth 5-year plan period, Prime Minister Zhao Ziyang underlined the following three in connection with economic reform:

1. In the state enterprises there should be a gradual transition from the delivery of profit to profit taxation, thus improving the relations between the state and the enterprises.

2. The central economic role of the cities was to be developed, thus resolving the contradictions deriving from the separation by area and by branches.

3. The system of trade and turnover should be reformed, thus promoting the development of commodity production and commodity trade.

In the approved document of the sixth 5-year plan the tasks related to the reform did not appear in separate form. (This happened only when the seventh 5-year plan was elaborated.)

The new constitution of the PRC, approved on December 4, 1982, already made reference to the reform and opening policy but, on the whole, it significantly lagged behind what was necessary for the wider implementation of this policy, and partly behind the codification requirements of the established practice as well. In the articles of the constitution defining the economic order of the PRC more resolute standpoints and constitutional gurantees were formulated - relative to the texts of earlier constitutions - above all in regard to the collective sector and its workers. The private economy as such remained outside the vision of those formulating the basic law. Article 11 mentioned only the individual undertakings of urban and rural workers provided for by law - as complements to the economy in socialist public ownership - and secured state protection for their legal rights and interests. The term "private capitalist" and such qualifications were avoided, even in connection with the direct capital investments allowed to foreign firms and other economic organizations. As a matter of fact, at the end of 1982, besides the 53 Chinese-foreign joint ventures (with joint capital investment and management), there were already 38 capitalist private enterprises in China with exclusively foreign capital, not to mention the mushrooming Chinese private ventures exceeding in size not only individual but even family undertakings.

The rules of the new constitution relating to land use were also in conflict with the established practice. Article 10 prescribed, for example, that "It is prohibited to occupy land for any organization or person, to buy and sell, lease or cede land in any illegal way to others."[13] The reality was that in some areas of China it had already become practice that a part of the land received for cultivation from the producing teams in the framework of the conctractual production responsibility system, or even all of it, was leased, or ceded against various services to other persons or families. This was necessitated partly by differences in the work load of individual families, and partly by the more advantageous working conditions offered by the rapid development of rural sideline occupations (particularly by the rural industries). In many places, leasing of the land for cultivation required only that those cultivating it (the lessee, tenant) fulfill the commitments undertaken by the family towards the state and the producing team instead of the family, and secure above it the centrally determined grain needs of the family, that is, produce and hand over to the leasing family the volume of grain corresponding to their per capita ration. Thus, some families had access to a greater cultivable land area and could arrange for specialized production, while others, besides carrying on some other gainful occupation, received the grain ration that secured their basic nutrition; both parties were satisfied, and neither the state nor the collective suffered any shortage.

Since the contracts for land use were at that time concluded between the families and the producing teams - for the sake of greater security and to stimulate investment - generally for 15 years, this system of land lease or cession between families spread even more in the next few years. Thus, the prohibitive articles of the 1982 constitution soon had to be repealed. (The relevant two articles of the constitution were modified in April 1988, at the first session of the 7th NPC: the category of "individual farm" was replaced by "private farm," and transfer of the right to land use was allowed according to legal prescriptions.)[14]

Rural economic reform

Early in 1983, the attention of those guiding the reform policy again turned toward the rural economy. It was recognized that the consolidation and further development of the results and successes there attained were the broadest and most stable economic and political foundations for the planned comprehensive economic reform. It also was clear that the consolidation and further development of the "contractual responsibility system linked to production" (in Chinese: lianchan chengbao zerenzhi), that had developed nationwide in earlier years but still showed varied success because of the mostly spontaneous local initiatives, required significant organizational changes and central measures.

Setting out from this situation, on January 2, 1983, the CPC sent out a voluminous document to the party organizations with the title: "On some questions of the present rural economic policy." For several months this was mentioned in China as the no. 1 document issued by the CC, CPC, in 1983.[15] In this document, previously discussed and approved by the PB, the most important tasks in rural economic development were summed up in 14 groups of questions:

1. Elaboration of own agricultural development plans and taking of effective measures on the basis of local resources and local economic and technical conditions in order to attain the strategic goal set by the party: "quadrupling" the combined gross output value of industrial and agricultural production by the year 2000.

2. Development of production patterns best corresponding to local conditions.

3. Consolidation and further development of the agricultural production responsibility system.

4. Development of diverse forms of cooperatives corresponding to the requirements of commodity production.

5. Reform of the rural people's commune system in two directions: on the one hand, generalizing the production responsibility system, particularly the contracting system linked with production and, on the other hand, separation of the public administration functions from the communes.

6. Expansion of the forms and possibilities for collective and individual ventures.

7. Enlivening of commodity trade, partly by adjusting and liberalizing the procurement policy and partly by developing cooperative trade.

8. Gradual technical reconstruction of agriculture with creation of the necessary technical, scientific, and educational background.

9. Expansion of financial resources to accelerate rural construction.

10. Establishment of commodity production bases in various regions of China in order to satisfy the demands of home and foreign trade.

11. Acceleration of development in the faraway mountainous regions and the areas inhabited by ethnic minorities.

12. The warding off of three imminent dangers: (a) reduction of forest area in consequence of excessive felling, (b) reduction of the cultivated land area because of irrational construction, and (c) overpopulation because of the nonobservance of demographic policy guidelines.

13. The building up of civilization in two ways (materially and spiritually).

14. Systematic training of cadres to improve their quality and to perfect and strengthen the leading role of the party.

As can be seen from this brief list, some of these tasks were linked only indirectly to the reform process that had started in the rural economy, yet to accomplish them the acceleration of rural economic reform was necessary.

Following the release of this party document, the State Council and the competent ministries issued a number of decrees in the interest of the quickest possible realization of the goals identified therein.[16] One of these, the joint circular issued by the CC, CPC, and the State Council in November 1983 was of outstanding importance. In this the local party and state organizations were called upon to smoothly implement the separation of rural administration from management functions, and to complete the creation of district governments (i.e., councils) nationwide by the end of 1984. In this context, the circular emphasized that the situation where "the party did not mind the affairs of the party and the government did not mind those of the government," and "the government and the enterprise were mingled" must be put to an end.[17] It also prescribed that the staff of the district governments to be set up must not exceed the size of the commune apparatuses until then fulfilling public administration functions, and that the district (commune) level cadres could be moved both upwards and downwards. In the course of implementing the measures not only were the public administration functions separated from the people's communes; the earlier, highly centralized, hierarchical, organizational and management order was also radically transformed in the earlier communes, and the former producing brigades were transformed into self-accounting units. Thus, by reorganizing the latter into enterprises, in place of the communes, "agroindustrial-commercial joint enterprises (in Chinese: nong-gong-shang lianhe qiye) were created.

These unions of enterprises operate as peak organs of the enterprises brought together in the union, with a not-too-large apparatus and, on commission by the member enterprises, mainly coordinate, protect interests and conduct representative and business activities. In consequence of the household contracting responsibility system that became generalized in agricultural production, the organizational setup of the agricultural "enterprises" and their work essentially differs from those of other enterprises in industry, construction, transport, and trade. In the former, namely, productive work is done mainly within a family (household) framework, in a decentralized way and independently. The agricultural enterprises operate in independent, specialized self-accounting units (groups), which mostly perform various service activities (conclusion of contracts, advising, seed supply, water supply, crop protection, veterinary service, lending of machines, etc.) in conformity with the needs of the independently managed peasant households.

Under the impact of the various reform measures the development of rural economy considerably accelerated in 1983 and 1984, so much so that the output of agriculture and the rural sideline activities achieved record results in almost every field. The total value of agricultural output increased (at constant prices) by 9.6% in 1983 and by 17.6% in 1984. Regarding the latter figure, crop production increased by 9.9%, animal husbandry by 13.4%, and the value of sideline activities by 47.9% in a single year. (With regard to rural sideline activities, the total value of rural industrial activities carried on in brigade-level enterprises increased in 1984 by 53%, and its share in the total value of agricultural production was already 17%.) In 1984, for the first time in the history of China, the annual output of grain exceeded 400 million tons, that of cotton 6 million tons; i.e., the former was higher by more than 100 million tons, the latter by more than 4 million tons, than 6 years earlier, in 1978. At the same time, even in this phase of agricultural upswing, the decline in complementary agricultural investments was perceptible (e.g., neglect of maintenance of irrigation equipment).

Reform of the turnover sphere

The upswing in agricultural and industrial production necessitated a reform of the earlier established commodity turnover system both in villages and in cities, as well as of the commodity exchange between villages and cities. The centralized system of state procurement and sales, established in China in the mid-1950s, later led to the decay and deformation of cooperative trade and to the almost complete liquidation of private retail trade. It became clear that this system was no longer capable of handling the sale of the increasingly decentralized agricultural and industrial production and of the more and more expanding and differentiating commodity production.

The fast growth of agricultural production and of rural sideline activities required, above all, the transformation and expansion of the rural system of commodity turnover. In order to better organize and more smoothly transact the rural commodity trade, efforts were made to expand the network of rural and provincial purchasing and selling cooperatives, and to adjust their activities to the demands of the membership. This required restoration of self-administration and mass organization to the cooperatives, democratization of management, and making economic activities more mobile and flexible. Beyond these, the network of rural markets and of market centers of district seats (rural towns) had to be expanded, so that peasants could exchange their products among themselves and procure the necessary industrial articles and means of production.

For a wider development of commodity exchange between villages and cities, the commercial centers, markets for means of production in large, medium-sized and small towns, and the wholesale markets for local industrial products and for the agricultural and sideline activity products of the surrounding areas were of great importance. At these places, namely, sellers and buyers could appear from any part of the country and from any sector of the economy and, on the basis of samples, also could conclude contracts for future business. A number of foreign trade firms also visited these markets, and thus some of the products offered there could even be exported. This provided the basis for horizontal economic cooperation, which increased in later years, between enterprises in different administrative areas or belonging to different branches and helped to form and strengthen the role of the cities in organizing production and turnover.

By the end of 1984, altogether 2248 commercial centers had been established in the cities and towns of China; 1254 of them transacted trade in manufactured goods, 753 in agricultural and sideline activity products, and 241 were trade centers of a more complex nature. In 1984 the first centers for transacting trade in the means of production were also set up, altogether 96, 69 of which were of a complex nature and 27 of which were centers of trade specializing in the means of production.[18]

In consequence of the powerful development of cooperative trade and the fast growth of private retail trade (again permitted), the percentual distribution of retail trade turnover by forms of ownership underwent significant change in these years (see Table 3):

Table 3. Distribution of retail trade by forms of ownership (in percent

	1978	1982	1983	1984
Total retail trade turnover	100.0	100.0	100.0	100.0
- State sector	90.5	76.6	72.1	45.6
- Cooperative sector	7.4	16.1	16.6	39.6
- Joint ventures	0.0	0.1	0.1	0.2
- Individual retailers	0.1	2.9	6.5	9.6
- Direct sales of peasants	2.0	4.3	4.7	5.0

Source: Zhongguo Tongqi Nianjian 1985. Beijing, 1985, p 465 (Statistical Yearbook of China)

The main direction of reform in foreign trade and external economic relations in these years was a closer linking of industry and trade and of technical progress and trade, as well as the separation of government functions from enterprise activities. On the one hand, this meant closer cooperation, relying on material interests, between productive enterprises and investors with the foreign trade firms transacting exports and imports, taking increasingly the form of commission business; on the other hand, it allowed for greater autonomy of the foreign trade companies and less dependence on the administrative organs of management. At the same time, more rights and greater autonomy were given in fostering and developing foreign trade to seven towns of province rank: Chongqing, Wuhan, Shenyang, Dalian, Heerbin, Guangzhou and Xian.

In the spring of 1984, in addition to the four special economic zones that had been created in 1980, a further 14 coastal towns[19] and the largest offshore island of the South China sea (Hainan) were opened to foreign investors. Shortly thereafter, the provinces of Shanxi and Shaanxi, rich in coal fields, were vested with similar rights, and in the autumn of 1984 24 large towns or provincial seats in the internal areas of the country were also allowed to accept foreign capital investments and to create various joint ventures. As a result of these measures the sum of direct capital investment by foreigners in 27 provinces of the PRC approximated US $1.4 billion at the end of 1984, and the number of joint ventures was 931. (Direct investments by Hong Kong firms approximated US $800 million of the total, and the number of their joint ventures was 741.)[20]

Attempts to develop economic regions centered around cities

From the point of view of reducing and gradually eliminating the anomalies deriving from the rigid limits to economic activities set by administrative areas and branches, the planners and leaders of the Chinese economic reform attributed great importance - particularly in the preparatory stage - to the exploitation of the production, cooperation, and sales organization possibilities deriving from the role of large towns and cities as economic and cultural centers. To this end, in the course of 1984 - through rearrangement of administrative frontiers and scopes of authority - the administrative area of cities (in Chinese: shi) was extended significantly (by annexing quite a few districts, in some cases even counties), and new criteria were established for qualifying rural settlements as small towns (rural towns, in Chinese: zhen). Afterwards, the population of these rural towns was included into the urban population. As a result, in 1984 there was a sudden change in the ratio of urban population to the total. (At the end of 1983 this ratio was still 23.5%, at the end of 1984 already 31.9%, and by the end of 1985 it had risen to 36.6%.)

Attempts at developing economic regions around cities and small towns were launched, as a matter of fact, as early as in 1982, immediately after establishment of the SRC. First two medium-size cities (with fewer than 500 000 inhabitants), Shasi in Hubei province and Changzhou in Jiangsu province, were earmarked for the purpose of "complex experiments related to the reform of the economic system."[21] The various reform experiments conducted there were directly guided by the SRC through the local reform committees. Early in 1983, the State Council selected also the seventh largest city of the PRC, Chongqing in

Sichuan province, as a theater for such complex experiments. To the city with 3 million inhabitants an area with about 10 million inhabitants was annexed - from its natural catchment area - and this administrative area with 13 million inhabitants constitutes the Chongqing economic region. In economic respects, this area was withdrawn from the administrative supervision and control of Sichuan province and was directly subordinated partly to the SRC and partly to the SEC. In these economic regions centered around cities (the number later increased to ten) the various reform measures were sooner introduced, and in some cases also parallel experiments were conducted with alternative solutions. These experiments were an important part of the preparation for the comprehensive economic reform and for working out individual concrete solutions.

Further broadening of entrepreneurial independence

During the preparatory stage of the comprehensive economic reform the conviction was strengthened among Chinese economic and political leaders that the key problem of the economic reform was to increase the viability and autonomy of enterprises. This meant a shifting in relations between the state and enterprises from direct management to indirect guidance through economic regulators. It was intended to approximate this goal gradually, and already in this period several measures were taken to facilitate the later introduction of the comprehensive reform.

Beginning on June 1983, more than 25 000 industrial state enterprises and about 51 000 commercial state enterprises shifted from the system of delivering profits completely to the state to the system of profit taxation. The rate of the profit tax was established uniformly at 55% of the net profit. The enterprises in question constituted 94.2% of the profitable enterprises in the state industry and 99.8% of those in trade. But it soon turned out that in Chinese industry and trade conditions had not yet developed, even in the state sector, which would allow a normative regulation of enterprise profit taxation. Thus, at the end of the year the leaders were compelled to introduce a kind of "regulating tax" (in Chinese: tiaojie shui), with rates differing according to the enterprise. (The justification for this tax was that, owing to the irrationality of the price system, the underdeveloped state of the market, the monopolistic position of several state enterprises, and the significant differences among enterprises in respect of technical equipment, supply with materials, labor and energy, the size of the actually realized profit depended only partly on the quality of management of the given enterprise and on the industry of those working there.) The rate of this "regulating tax" was in each case established by the supervisory organs <u>ex post facto</u> and individually, when the annual financial balance sheet of each enterprise was drawn up in final form. In addition, the territorial management organs could levy various local taxes on the enterprises under different titles. Thus, the part of profit left with the large and medium-sized state enterprises in 1984 rarely or only in exceptional cases exceeded 10%-12% of the realized net profit; in most cases it ranged between 5% and 10%.

In May 1984 the State Council issued a temporary decree about expanding the autonomy of state industrial enterprises which extended the scope of authority earlier possessed by enterprises in the following ten fields:[22]

1. Planning production and management
2. Sale of products
3. Determination of the price of products
4. Procurement of materials
5. Use of monetary assets
6. Disposal of property
7. Development of the organizational setup
8. Deciding on personnel and labor questions
9. Setting of wages and premiums
10. Creation of economic associations

This measure was closely related to the various arrangements being worked out and still to be introduced which affected the reform of the system of planning and materials management, the wage and price system, and the manpower management system - for all of which the legal regulations had already been drafted in 1984. For example, the Planning Commission published the document entitled "Some temporary measures related to the improvement of the planning system"[23] on August 31, 1984. On the one hand, it determined the notion and contents of the "mandatory plans" (in Chinese: zhiling xingde jihua) and of the newly introduced "guidance plans" (zhidao xingde jihua); on the other hand, it considerably reduced the number of mandatory plan indicators relating to production and commodity turnover.

The actual extent of enterprise independence was earlier and still is a function of several factors. It depends first of all on the size of the enterprise (large, medium, or small), secondly, on the forms of ownership (state, collective, or private), and thirdly, on its subordination (to central or territorial organs, or to ministries or local authorities). The large and medium-sized enterprises are usually state owned and operate under the control and management of the central ministries. In 1984, in the interest of making economic management more unified and flexible, more than 46 500 of the 58 000 small industrial state enterprises were placed under the enterprise collective for management, while the state property was left intact. They thus provided the bases for the later developed "contracting management responsibility system" (chengbao jingying zerenzhi). A further 5500 were transformed into collectively owned industrial enterprises, state ownership rights were also renounced in the similarly collectively owned small establishments which had been nationalized during the "cultural revolution."

At the same time it was decided that the small state-owned establishments (with fixed assets worth less than 3-5 million yuan and with profits less than 300-500 thousand yuan) should henceforth be controlled and managed by the district industrial inspectorates of the large cities - according to the prescriptions relating to the collectively owned establishments. The reorganization of enterprises was in many places used to create economic unions, i.e., common service enterprises for various purposes and in diverse forms. In more than 2900 industrial state enterprises the "manager responsibility system" (changzhang zerenzhi) was introduced experimentally in 1984. In its framework attempts were made to abolish the direct party guidance of enterprises and to prevent that the rights of the appointed or elected managers be expropriated by the secretaries of the party committees.[24]

Elaboration of the Complex Draft on Comprehensive Economic Reform

It has already been mentioned that the State Reform Commission, working beside the State Council under the direct control of the prime minister, was created in May 1982 with the purpose that it should elaborate as soon as possible the complex draft of the comprehensive economic reform; in this context, it was to guide and coordinate the theoretical research and practical experiments going on in different places and institutions.

In his opening address to the 12th congress of the CPC, Deng Xiaoping had pointed out that it was necessary "to integrate the universal truth of Marxism with the concrete realities of China, blaze a path of our own, and build socialism with Chinese characteristics - this is the basic conclusion we have reached in summing up our long, historical experience."[25] Afterwards, to "build socialism with Chinese characteristics" (jianshe zhongguo teside shehuizhuyi) became a political program and an ideological notion, and hundreds of articles and dozens of books were published about its interpretation. Almost every author agreed that the building of socialism with Chinese characteristics was inseparable from carrying out the "four modernizations," from the thorough reform of the existing economic and political system, as well as from raising the level of material and spiritual civilization and establishing a socialist democracy and legal order.

It was again Deng Xiaoping who expounded in one of his speeches that one of the important guarantees of success of the work related to the four modernizations was that the reform should permeate the whole process of the "four modernizations."

At the same time, he proposed that before individual steps were taken for reform, they should be weighed against the following three criteria: is the step conducive to (a) socialism with Chinese characteristics, (b) the thriving and development of the country, and (c) the welfare and prosperity of the people.[26] However general these criteria may seem for weighing concrete steps in a practical reform policy, in the course of the reform frequent references were made to them when certain measures were taken or delayed. (For example, the price reform has been delayed or suspended several times in recent years, with the justification that if it were consistently implemented, significant groups of workers would be pushed into a difficult situation by the rapid rise of living costs. A rapid rise in living costs occurred nevertheless - particularly in cities - even without the implementation of the comprehensive price reform.)

In his report about the work of the government to the first session of the 6th NPC, which convened in June 1983, Prime Minister Zhao Ziyang proposed that the following, more practical questions be considered before any step in the reform process was taken: (a) Is it favorable for the implementation of various tasks defined in the state plan? (b) Is it advantageous for the harmonious development of the national economy? (c) Is it favorable for various economic activities; will it result in relatively high socioeconomic efficiency? (d) Is it favorable for the simultaneous consideration of the interests of the state, the enterprise, and the individual; will it secure rational growth of the revenues of the state budget every year?[27] When the draft of the comprehensive reform was elaborated, rather the latter points were observed, but the more general principial political and ideological considerations were not forgotten.

The experts of the SRC, incorporating the work of experts from several institutions, started work on the complex draft of the comprehensive reform in the autumn of 1982. First they summed up the results of the theoretical debates and target-oriented research carried out in the preceding years related to the concept of the reform. Next they compiled a list of problems requiring further theoretical investigation or practical solutions. For the latter, a program of experiments was drafted, and these were carried out in cities selected for complex reform experiments; frequently more than one method was applied simultaneously. The collection and processing of domestic experience was complemented partly by reviewing the professional literature related to economic reforms in other socialist countries, and partly by study tours with the aim of becoming directly acquainted with foreign experiences. In addition, a rather large number of well-known experts in reform matters were invited, from both the East and the West, to hold lectures and consultations.[28] In becoming acquainted with international experiences and in establishing contacts with internationally known economic reformers, China received diversified and considerable help in this period from the World Bank and its experts.

In the course of elaborating the complex draft of the comprehensive economic reform, the leaders and experts of the SRC devoted special interest to the reform of the Hungarian system of economic control and management, and to studying the experiences and lessons of the new economic mechanism introduced in 1968. In view of the fact that the model of economic management selected as the target model for the Chinese economic reform - relying on the linking of plan regulation with market regulation and their simultaneous application - was most approximated by the Hungarian system, this attention and interest was completely justified.

The first delegation of experts from the SRC arrived in Hungary as guests of the Hungarian Academy of Sciences and "under the colors" of the CASS on May 26, 1983. It was headed by Professor Liao Jili, director of the research and analysis section of the SRC. They studied the questions contained in their plan of work, sent in advance, for 35 days. Their interest extended to almost every area of the economy and to all important questions of economic management reform. In the course of the consultations they acquainted themselves in detail with the concrete practice and armamentarium of Hungarian planning, regulation, and fiscal systems, with commodity turnover and circulation of money and with the system of enterprise management. From a professional point of view, the Chinese economists were extremely satisfied with the results of their visit and expressed their willingness to make working relations and mutual visits more regular between the Chinese and Hungarian organs and institutions responsible for the further development of economic reform.[29]

To return the invitation, the CASS and the SRC asked a delegation of Hungarian economists, both theoretical and practical experts, to come to China for a 3-week study tour in the autumn of 1983. The Hungarian delegation of ten experts visited in October-November 1983, headed by Rezső Nyers, chairman of the Trade Commission of the Hungarian National Assembly and scientific adviser of the Institute of Economics, HAS.[30] Nyers was known as "father of Hungarian reform." In addition to visiting the central organs of economic management in Beijing, the Hungarians were conducted to the economic regions of Chongqing and Changzhou where the complex reform experiments were carried out, to Shanghai and Guangzhou, which maintained close economic and trade relations with foreign countries, and to the special economic zone of Shenzhen, bordering on Hong Kong. In addition to acquainting themselves with the theory and practice, the problems and difficulties of Chinese economic reform, the Hungarian experts held lectures and consultations in these cities and zones for leading Chinese economists and experts about questions affecting the whole of Hungarian economic management or its various fields. In the course of the tour we saw for ourselves how thoroughly relatively wide groups of Chinese economists were acquainted - as a result of the reports about the study tours of 1979 and 1983 and from translations of various articles and books - with even the details of the practice and problems of the Hungarian system of planning and economic management.

In the autumn of 1983 - initiated by conservative forces, who were still represented in significant numbers in the Political Bureau of the CC, CPC, and in the party apparatus - a broad ideological campaign developed against the so-called spiritual pollution (in Chinese: jingshen wuran). This had taken root back in the spring of 1983, at ceremonies held on the 100th anniversary of Marx's death when some Chinese social scientists applied the Marxian notion of "alienation" to processes taking place in socialist societies. The dogmatic ideologues of the CPC attributed this to the "bourgeois" and "revisionist" ideological impact from abroad, and to "spiritual pollution," and proclaimed a fight against representatives of these and similar views. The targets of the campaign soon broadened to include several theoretical statements and conclusions of the reform economists. This is why, in the autumn of 1983, we witnessed a considerable slowdown in the process of formulating the complex draft of the comprehensive economic reform.[31]

It was in August 1984, after a break lasting more than a quarter of a century, that - from the five Central and Eastern European countries cooperating most closely with the Soviet Union on questions of foreign policy (Bulgaria, Czechoslovakia, Poland, Hungary, and the GDR) - a higher than ministerial-level visit was paid for the first time by the Hungarians. In conformity with the wishes of the Chinese party, deputy Prime Minister József Marjai selected the members of this delegation in such a manner that the professional questions related to the reform could be the thoroughly discussed on the occasion of this visit.[32] By the time of the visit the first draft of the comprehensive economic reform was already available and its discussion in the leading bodies of the Chinese party and government was under way. A greater consideration of Hungarian experiences was advocated, just as earlier, by Prime Minister Zhao Ziyang, chairman of the SRC. He took measures himself to see that the various pieces of information acquired by the different Chinese delegations to Hungary about the reform and improvement of the system of economic management were carefully collected and processed. It may thus be stated without any exaggeration that in the phase of elaborating the complex draft of the comprehensive economic reform the Chinese experts working on the draft had the closest and most immediate working contacts with the leading officials of the Hungarian economic management organs and with experts of the economic research institutes. Consequently, several new economic notions or technical terms related to economic reform were translated into Chinese and introduced with contents and meaning conforming to the Hungarian terminology.

Third Plenary Session of the 12th CC of the CPC: Resolution on Reform of the Economic System

After much preparatory work, the 3rd plenary session of the 12th CC, CPC, was convened on October 20, 1984, and it unanimously adopted the party document: "Decision of the Central Committee of the Communist Party of China on Reform of the Economic System."[33] Reviewing the substance of the resolution, the official communiqué issued about the session stated: "Relying on the principle that the basic tenets of Marxism have to be integrated with the Chinese realities, the resolution expounded the necessity and urgency of accelerating the reform of the system, considering the towns and cities to be centers of the whole economic system, determining the direction of reform, its character, tasks, basic principles, and the policy to be pursued in individual spheres. The resolution is a program-like document, authoritative for reforming the economic system of our country." The plenary session also adopted unanimously the "Resolution of the 3rd plenary session of the CC, CPC, about convening the national conference of party delegates" for September 1985. (The premilinary agenda of the party conference comprised two themes: (a) discussion and approval of the proposals related to the basic tasks of the seventh 5-year plan - for 1986-1990 - for the development of the national economy and society; (b) election of new members to the central committee of the party and to other leading bodies, and other organizational questions.) The plenary session was preceded by a preparatory consultation lasting 6 days.

Although the party conference that convened almost a year later also proved to be a significant event in the development of the reform process, the main theme of the 3rd plenary session of the 12th CC was discussion and approval of the resolution on the reform of the economic system. Later, this party resolution was also referred to in China as the one "on the reform of the urban economic system," since several earlier party resolutions about the reform of the rural economic system were in force. As regards its nature and importance, this resoulution may best be compared to the resolution of the CC of the Hungarian Socialist Workers' Party (HSWP) of May 1966 and to that of the CC of the Communist Party of the Soviet Union (CPSU) of July 1987 - with the difference that the resolution of the Chinese CC was less elaborate regarding details of the reform and its concrete modes of solution, but more resolute and forward-looking in questions of principle and theory. (In formulating the complex draft of the comprehensive economic reform, which was the main content of the CC resolution, the Chinese experts were obviously able to rely to a great extent on the positive and negative experiences of reforms going on or halted in other socialist countries. They were also able to take into account the experience gained with the partial reforms already implemented in the Chinese villages and still going on experimentally in the cities.) Although the Chinese CC resolution of 1984 dealt with almost every basic problem and task of the economic reform, and although it took mostly a correct, forward-looking and consistent standpoint on principial and theoretical problems, it was not yet in a position to formulate the goals of the comprehensive economic reform in a theoretically well-founded manner that would satisfy scientific standards. (This was done only 1.5-2 years later, after the positive and negative experiences of the period following the introduction of the comprehensive reform had been summarized, and a new, thorough analysis of the Hungarian economic reform process had been made.)

The resolution of the 3rd plenary session of the 12th CC, CPC, set out from the standpoint that besides asserting the directive of "opening to the outside world - and invigorating the domestic economy," the comprehensive and complex reform of the economic system was a pressing necessity for the socioeconomic development of China. Since the point of gravity of the economic system is the urban economy, the reform of the system should be implemented by concentrating on the cities. "Expediting reform is a prerequisite for the growth of the urban economy" appears in the first chapter of the resolution. Next, the resolution stated that "conditions are now ripe for all-round reform of the economic system."

Alone the title of the second chapter is telling: "Reform is aimed at establishing a dynamic socialist economic system." The main reason for the failure of the socialist system to attain superiority in China for several decades, after initally promising signs, beyond the historical, political and ideological reasons, was the ossified economic system which could not fulfill the requirements of the newly developed social forces of production. The reform consists in the self-improvement and development of the socialist system, called upon to bring the obsolete and inadequate elements of the relations of production and of the superstructure into harmony with the requirements raised by the forces of production. Whether it is advantageous for the development of the forces of production or not is "the most important criterion for assessing the success or failure of all reforms" - this is to be read in the last sentence of the second chapter of the resolution.

The title of chapter three states that "Invigorating enterprises is the key to reforming the national economy." It is also emphasized that "socialism with Chinese characteristics should, first and foremost, be able to instill vitality into the enterprises." To this end, a correct relationship has to be developed between the state and the enterprises in all-people's ownership on the one hand, and between the enterprises and their workers on the other hand, ensuring that the autonomy of enterprises be expanded and also that the workers be masters of their enterprise. The resolution attributes several past mistakes to the fact that the notion of all-people's ownership was mixed up with the direct management of enterprises by the state organs. "As Marxist theory and the practice of socialism have shown, ownership can be duly separated from the power of operation" (scope of administration). (The phrase in parentheses is an alternative translation of the Chinese term "jingyingquan", or a possible interpretation, not part of the original text.) In fact, practice up to now has shown that direct state management and administration unavoidably give birth to grave subjectivism and bureaucracy which stifles the mobility and vitality of enterprises. "In short, the enterprise should be truly made a relatively independent economic entity and should become a producer and operator of socialist commodity production that is independent and responsible for its own profit and loss and capable of transforming and developing itself, and that acts as a legal person with certain rights and duties." The source of the vitality of enterprises is the activity, knowledge, and creative power of its intellectual and manual workers. The reform has to bring about the conditions needed for their development. At the end of Chap. 3 the resolution repeatedly stresses: "Correct relations between the state and the enterprise and between an enterprise and its workers and staff are the essence and basic requirement of the reforming of the economy as a whole with focus on the cities. Fulfillment of this basic requirement inevitably calls for reform of every aspect of the entire economic structure. This involves a whole range of reforms, including planning, pricing, economic management by state institutions, and the labor and wage system." Also at the end of this chapter - hidden in a long sentence - is the CC's opinion that the reforms should be planned in a way that they can basically be accomplished in every field in about 5 years. (As it later turned out, this was a too optimistic goal.)

In further chapters of the resolution directives can be found regarding the most important tasks of the economic reform. The title of Chap. 4 states the goal: to "establish a planning system under which the law of value is consciously applied for developing a socialist commodity economy." "In the reform of the planning system, it is necessary, first of all, to discard the traditional idea of pitting the planned economy against the commodity economy. We should clearly understand that the socialist planned economy is a planned commodity economy based on public ownership, in which the law of value must be consciously followed and applied. The full development of a commodity economy is an indispensable stage in the economic growth of society and a prerequisite for our economic modernization." This is one of the most definite references to and indications of the theoretical bases of the reform in the resolution. It does not explicitly deduce the conclusion for the theory of social formations that going through the historical stage of developed and accomplished commodity production is an indispensable precondition for surpassing the capitalist mode of production; it stipulates resolutely, nevertheless, that full development of the commodity economy is an unavoidable stage of socioeconomic development. This chapter of the resolution goes on to explain that the difference between a socialist and a capitalist economy is not whether commodity economy exists in them, whether the law of value asserts itself in them, but that the forms of ownership are different. Also, the difference consists in whether an exploiter class exists, in whether the working people are masters of the country, in what goals of production serve the economy, in whether the law of value can be applied on a global social scale and also in that the frameworks for commodity relations are different. "Under our socialist conditions, neither labor power, nor land, mines, banks, railways and all other state-owned enterprises and resources are commodities." This is established in Chap. 4. At this point it is not difficult to detect the survival of the traditional notion of socialism in the consciousness of the leaders of the CPC, proven by the fact that 2 years later - for practical reasons - the theoretical thesis about the "noncommodity" nature of labor, land, mines, state enterprises, and other resources had to be revoked and a market for the factors of production had to be created. This chapter reviews in the end the main characteristic features of the planning system to be established through the reform, outlining the scope and role of plan regulation and market regulation, as well as - within plan regulation - the mode of application and development tendency of the mandatory and guidance plans. It states that the scope of mandatory plans will narrow, that of the guidance plans will expand, while the emphasis in planning will shift from annual plans to medium and long-term planning.

The title of Chap. 5 sets the goal "to establish a rational price system and pay full attention to the economic levers." The resolution justifies the necessity of a price reform by stating that, without it, it is impossible to correctly determine the actual performance of enterprises, ensure the smooth turnover of goods between cities and villages, and promote technical progress as well as modernization of the production and consumption patterns. Lack of a rational price system causes a huge waste of social labor and seriously prevents the assertion of the principle of distribution according to work done. In this part of the resolution it is pointed out that the success of economic reform, particularly of the planning and wage systems, greatly depends on the reform of the pricing system, because price is the most effective instrument of regulation. "Therefore, reform of the price system is the key to reform of the entire economic system" - so reads Chap. 5 of the resolution. Next, the principles of price reform are reviewed; it is stressed that the measures related to the price reform have to be planned and implemented in such a way that the real incomes of the urban and rural population should not diminish as a result. Parallel with the transformation of the price system, the taxation system has to be improved and the reform of the financial and banking systems has to be continued.

Chapter 6 discusses the correct direction that should be taken in separating government functions from those of enterprises, as well as how management functions of the government organs should develop. It reviews the main economic functions of the government agencies in detail and then points out: "After the functions of government and enterprises are separated, the central role of the cities must be brought into full play and open and interconnected economic zones of various sizes gradually formed with support from cities, the large and medium-sized cities in particular." As regards relations between enterprises, while the necessity of cooperation and mutual help is emphasized, the importance and unavoidability of competition are underlined. "Where there is commodity production, there is bound to be competition." In the interest of creating real competition as soon as possible, the normative legal regulation of economic activities should be accelerated. But the measure of success of enterprises still is the judgement which the consumer passes about them on the market, and under such conditions only the best enterprises can survive. In this part of the resolution the necessity of further organizational changes and of the reform of the political superstructure is also indicated. "The separation of the functions of government and enterprises as well as simpler and decentralized administration constitute a deep-going transformation of the socialist superstructure. When the structure changes, the organization and the style of thinking and work should also change." An end must be put to the practice of enterprises serving the leading organs instead of the other way around. Bureaucracy and overlapping between organizations and scopes of authority have to be eliminated, and the superfluous overstaffing of institutions has to be abolished.

The title of Chap. 7 is: "Establish various forms of economic responsibility system and conscientiously implement the principle of distribution according to work." This stems from the experience that the tested principles of the system of contracted responsibility in the rural areas can also be applied in the cities. These principles are the following: personal responsibility for the work performed; combination of authority and interests; harmonization of the interests of the state, the collective, and the individual; linking of the income of workers with performance. The manager responsibility system is an indispensable condition of up-to-date enterprise management. An end must be put to the former practice whereby the guidance of economic work was in the hands of the party organizations and thus it was actually the party secretaries who managed the enterprises. While restoring the manager responsibility system, it must also be ensured that employee representatives have a say in the more important decisions of management and can protect the legal rights and interests of the workers. Parallel with universal replacement of the delivery of profits by profit taxation, and with the various forms of economic responsibility being realized in enterprises, the socialist principle of distribution according to work will be better enforceable; "... egalitarian thinking is utterly incompatible with scientific, Marxist views on socialism. History has shown that egalitarian thinking is a serious obstacle to implementing the principle of distribution according to work, and if it is unchecked, the forces of production will inevitably be undermined" - so states Chap. 7 of the resolution. Yet, those drafting the resolution had not yet come to the conclusion that egalitarianism is also a kind of exploitation - organized by the state and implemented through the redistributing function of the budget (meaning that diligent workers are exploited by the lazy). "Only when some regions, enterprises, and individuals are allowed and encouraged to get better off first through diligent work can there be a strong attraction to the majority of the people." Care should also be taken to assert the principle whereby higher wages are due to those performing more complicated work or such as demands greater skills or which is more difficult. The resolution says that: "In particular, it is necessary to change the present remuneration for mental work, which is relatively low." At the same time, incomes can be raised only as a result of growing labor productivity and improved efficiency of management.

Chapter 8 of the resolution emphasizes in its title the necessity of developing diverse economic forms and continuing to expand foreign and domestic economic and technological exchanges. It points out that in the course of reforming the economic system rational proportions have to be developed between the different sectors of the national economy and between the economic units operating under different ownership relations. In this context, the qualifications and hierarchical orders laid down in the 1982 constitution are essentially repeated. The idea of equality in competition appears here only in that the resolution establishes: the consolidation and development of enterprises owned by the whole people should not be implemented to the detriment of other sectors and other forms of management, by restricting or excluding them. Instead: development of diversified and flexible forms of economic cooperation and association between state, collective and individual enterprises should be stimulated. A portion of the small enterprises owned by the whole people can be leased to collectives and individuals, but they can also be operated on a contractual basis. "It is our long-term policy and the need of socialist development to promote diversified economic forms and various methods of operation simultaneously." But those drafting the resolution felt it necessary to add immediately that: "This is not retrogression to the new-democratic economy of the early period of the People's Republic, when the socialist public ownership was not yet predominant in town and country." This chapter of the resolution presents the policy of "opening outward," together with the use of foreign capital as a long-term policy of the state. It provides for reforming the system of foreign trade and also forecasts further reform of the system of domestic commodity turnover. "As we open to the outside world, we shall open up even more between different areas within China itself." As a result, horizontal economic relations and forms of association will develop and, in the last resort, this will promote the development of a rational economic structure and a more balanced territorial distribution of the forces of production in China.

The ninth chapter of the resolution emphasizes the pressing need for educating the cadres required to implement the reform of the economic system. It points out that this demands the education and employment of a new generation of cadres capable of modern economic and enterprise management; "... we must respect knowledge and talented people. We must combat all ideas and practices that belittle science and technology, the cultivation of intellectual resources, and the role of intellectuals. We must take resolute action to redress cases of discrimination against intellectuals which still exist in many localities and to raise the social standing of intellectuals and improve their working and living conditions." The chapter ends with the important statement that, with the progress of the reform of the economic system, also the reform of science and technology as well as of the system of education become tasks of increasingly urgent strategic importance.

The tenth, concluding, chapter of the resolution emphasizes the importance of strengthening party guidance of the reform process and underlines that every step in the course of the reform should be tested in practice, since new experience can be acquired only in this way. The reform is an exploratory and innovative undertaking of the masses, but it is a very difficult and complicated venture. Mistakes can hardly be avoided, but everything has to be done to prevent major mistakes; those that are made nevertheless should be mended as soon as possible and should serve as lessons for the future. Should errors and deviations emerge in the course of the reform, a policy of persuasion, criticism, and education should be used towards those affected, and they must not be given political labels. Cadres and the masses must not be divided by calling a part of people "reformers" and others "conservatives". Those having doubts have to be convinced about the correctness and timeliness of the reform with practical results: "In citing the facts about reform, we should provide Party members and the masses with lively education in the theory and policies of the reform. This will help them realize that socialism with Chinese characteristics should be full of vitality, different from the rigid pattern of the past, and fundamentally different from the capitalist system. This will deepen their understanding of scientific socialism so that they will devote themselves to the reform."

This is a succinct summary of the most essential statements of the resolution, approved at the 3rd plenary session of the 12th CC of the CPC, on the guidelines and major tasks of the reform of the economic system. In reviewing its contents an effort was made to stick to the original formulations of the resolution, even where this was not separately indicated by quotation marks. In such basic questions the formulations themselves are of principial and political importance, since they reflect the political maturity of the body approving such a program-giving document, in a double sense. On the one hand, they indicate what recognitions the widest forum of the Chinese party leadership has reached in connection with the primary points of the economic reform; on the other hand, they expose the points where, in the interest of creating unity of thinking and action, various compromises have been made or backward steps have been taken.

This resolution of the plenary session about the reform of the economic system covers essentially every important field and question of the planned reform. Still, in its structure, and in setting down the various targets of reform, it does not clearly and logically determine the order of importance of the individual targets and tasks. The resolution thus does not satisfy the requirement of a <u>systems-approach</u> and exposition expectable and necessary in the case of such a program-presenting document dealing with complex problems, either. It does not follow from the document in which fields, in what order, and at what rate is it expedient to start the comprehensive reform of the economic system under the given Chinese circumstances. Nor does the document elucidate the key problems that must be solved, one by one or in a coordinated manner, if a planned commodity economy that is really sensitive to market impacts is to be created. This deficiency of the resolution soon became conspicuous. The "urban reform" was started with great impetus and released spontaneous processes and produced such "overheating" of the economy, that administrative measures contrary to the goal and spirit of the reform had to be resorted to. These "planned-economy reflexes" began to operate all the more easily as, beginning in 1983 - parallel to and simultaneous with the preparation for comprehensive economic reform - higher growth rates were forced again in some fields and preferential handling of big investment projects financed from the state budget was seen. This meant a departure from the equilibrium approach, proportionality, and quality requirements more strictly asserted in the years of the "readjustment policy."

Strengthening Extensive Growth Tendencies

Following the 12th congress of the CPC and the fifth session of the 5th NPC - i.e., after the strategic goal of economic construction ("quadrupling" output) had been set and the sixth 5-

-year plan had been approved - economic development gathered momentum in several branches of the Chinese national economy. Efforts were made to expand big state investment projects financed from central budget resources, and to use resources "in a more concentrated manner." These were manifest as follows:

1. The target of "quadrupling" the combined gross output value of industrial and agricultural production was interpreted by many to mean that the fastest possible rate of growth ought to be attained in every field. Some again talked about a "leap" and a general economic "upswing."

2. In 1983-1984 greater efforts were made by the central economic management organs to bring important investment projects aimed at the development of transport and communications as well as of energy and raw material production under their own direction and control again and, accordingly, to finance them from central budget lines. In addition to greatly increasing the demands made on the central budget, this led to oversize projects, protracted implementation, and higher costs, as well as to a situation whereby some imported equipment stood idle or was underutilized, or was even damaged or ruined in consequence of careless warehousing.

3. The increased demands on the central budget could, temporarily, be met only through increased collection and centralization of enterprise income and by stricter foreign exchange management. In spite of the fact that the rate of collected enterprise profits in 1984 again reached about 90% in state enterprises, and the rate of retainable foreign exchange fell below 30%, the growing state budget deficit was replaced by the issuing of banknotes in an amount far exceeding the needs of turnover. The quantity of money in circulation increased by only 20.6% in 1983 but by 49.5% in 1984 and the sum of additional issue in 1983 was 2.1 times, in 1984 6.1 times that of 1982. Inflation started in China in 1983, though the level of consumer prices rose, on a national average, by only 1.5% in that year.

4. Because the supply of building materials, machinery, and equipment needed for investments could not keep pace with the fast increase in demand, the planning organs prescribed for

these products mandatory production and sales indicators. At the same time, investment construction not figuring in the central investment plans was prohibited, and the use of enterprises' own development funds was made dependent on the payment of various surtaxes and dues (e.g., tax on the source of assets, investment dues). This amounted to even heavier taxation of enterprise incomes.

We may conclude from this that, during the preparation for comprehensive economic reform, some central organs of economic management - while working in theory and on paper to ease overcentralization and reduce the number of mandatory plan indicators - took steps in exactly the opposite direction in practice.

Later works analyzing the economic policy of this stage have pointed out that - beyond the "natural inclination" to revert to the "Soviet model" of central plan instructions another disturbing factor emerged. Namely, the spread of Western economic views which considered inflation to be a necessary concomitant of economic growth, or even its "engine", caused ever more serious troubles in the orientation of Chinese economists and practical experts. No lesser disturbance was caused by the view that price liberalization was the most effective instrument for creating a market economy. But when demand far exceeds supply, the "freeing" of prices generally entails incalculable and frequently catastrophic conseqences, releases "galloping" inflation, which can then be braked only with various administrative tools (price and wage ceilings, rationing, etc.). Thus, in the stage of reform, economic liberalism and planned economy exert on each other a strange impact. The rigid and bureaucratic planned economy enhances the wish for and efforts towards liberal economic management, while the negative phenomena produced by a liberal economic policy (inflation, rising prices, speculation, corruption, etc.) give rise to a nostalgic desire for administrative and bureaucratic "order" and to efforts at recentralization.

Reform of the traditional system of "socialist" planned economy can lead to substantial results only if it sets the goal of radically and consistently eliminating the system itself. To this end measures have to be taken, relatively early, which will put an end to chronic overspending and to absorbing the losses of state enterprises. In contrast, efficiently operating enterprises have to be supported - independent of their form of ownership, that is, by creating for them equal conditions in competition - in self-management with the risks and responsibilities this entails. Also important are basically administrative measures of the state economic management organs which try to forestall speculative exploitation of shortage situations via increased financial control and fines. However, this requires government officials of strict morals who are relatively well paid, and can thus resist the attempts of speculators to bribe them.

Footnotes to Chapter Four

1. Opening speech of Deng Xiaoping at the congress, The Twelfth National Congress of the CPC (September 1982), Foreign Language Press, Beijing 1982. Pp 1-2
2. Ibid., p 9
3. Ibid., pp 19-20
4. Ibid., pp 23-24
5. Ibid., pp 34-35
6. Ibid., p 28
7. Ibid., p 31
8. Ibid., p 32
9. Ibid., p 33
10. Ibid., pp 54-55
11. Ibid., p 59
12. In the apparatus of the State Planning Commission and the State Economic Commission more than 2000 people were employed (not including the attached background institutions). In June 1988 the two commissions were amalgamated in the framework of a new "streamlining" of the central organs supervised by the State Council, and also regrouped. In the course of this reorganization the number of departments

of the new State Planning Commission fell by 60% (relative to the earlier number for the two institutions), i.e., from 66 to 26, and the staff was reduced by 40%. See: <u>Renmin Ribao,</u> June 13, 1988, p 1.
13. ZJN 1983, Part II, p 27
14. <u>Renmin Ribao,</u> April 13, 1988, p 1
15. This document was published in abbreviated form only in April 1983; it could be read for the first time in <u>Renmin Ribao,</u> April 11, 1983. See   1983, P. II, pp 173-180
16. The decrees a covered the following matters:
    - Temporary decree about questions related to the reform of turnover in rural trade (Feb. 11, 1983)
    - Decree on some questions of agroindustrial-commercial united enterprises to be set up on virgin land (Feb. 17, 1983) - Joint resolution to actively support plant protion enterprises (May 23, 1983)
    - Circular about separating public administration functions from management in villages and about creating district governments
    - Decree on some questions of organization and development of the local processing of agricultural and complementary products (Feb. 25, 1984)
    - Circular about changing the name of commune- and brigade--level enterprises into rural and village enterprises (March 1, 1984)
17. Report of the New China Press Agency (Xinhua Shi) on Nov. 22, 1983 - <u>Renmin Ribao,</u> Nov. 23, 1983, p 1
18. ZJN, 1985, P. V/p 208
19. The 14 port towns were the following: Dalian, Tianjin, Qinhuangdao, Yantai, Qingdao, Lianyungang, Nandong, Shanghai, Ningbo, Wenzhou, Fuzhou, Guangzhou, Zhanjiang, and Beihai.
20. ZJN, 1985, P.V/p 208
21. The town of Shasi was earmarked for reform experiments by the State Council in October 1981. The reform experiments started early in 1982. Changzhou was earmarked half a year later, in March 1982, and the complex experiment began in

May. This was followed in February 1983 by the first large town, Chongqing, and not much later the entire Chongqing area was formed into an economic region for this purpose. See: Dangdai Zhongguo jingji tizhi gaige, Beijing 1984. pp 788, 791, and 795

22. ZJN, 1985, P.X/pp 21-22
23. Ibid., P.X/pp 5-8
24. Ibid., P.II/p 2
25. The Twelfth National Congress ... p 3.
26. Dangdai Zhongguo ... p 199
27. ZJN, 1984, P.II/p 10
28. Besides Yugoslavian and Hungarian social researchers and economists, several experts on Eastern Europe from American, West-European, and Japanese universities and research institutions were invited, among them Wlodimierz Brus and Ota Sik, who visited China in 1982-1983.
29. Afterwards, the experts of the SRC made study tours in Hungary on three further occasions: in the spring of 1985 on invitation by the Secretariat for International Economic Relations of the Council of Ministers; in May 1986 on invitation of the Ministry of Finance (and financed by the Soros Foundation); and in September 1988 on invitation by the Commission for Planned Economy of the Council of Ministers. On the first occasion the SRC delegation was again headed by Professor Liao Jili, but its members were recruited mostly from the Economic System Reform Institute of China (ESRIC). In May 1986, the delegation was headed by Gao Shangquan, deputy chairman of the SRC (this delegation also visited Yugoslavia). The delegation visiting Hungary in the autumn of 1986 was led by another deputy chairman of the SRC, Zhang Yanning. This delegation had previously visited the GDR, and this fact also indicated a change in the direction of interest of the Chinese leadership.
30. Members of the delegation of Hungarian economists, headed by Rezső Nyers, were: Gyula Csáki (Ministry of Finance), László Gelencsér (State Wage and Labor Office), László Horváth, (Manager Training Center), János Illés (Planning Office),

Iván Németh (CC, HSWP), Jolán Papp-Ritter (Price and Materials Office), Zoltán Pék, and the author (both from the Institute for Economic Planning).

31. Organizers and leaders of the campaign against "spiritual pollution" were, on the part of scientists, Hu Qiaomu, member of the PB of the CC, CPC, retired chairman of the CASS, and, on the part of the leading functionaries, Deng Liqun, member of the secretariat of the CC, CPC, and head of the agitation and propaganda section of the CC. As far as we know, the campaign was braked and suppressed only after the resolute intervention of Deng Xiaoping and Zhao Ziyang; it was channeled into the flow of scientific discussions in late 1983 and early 1984, since it would have seriously endangered the elaboration of the complex draft of the reform and the international respect for the Chinese leadership supporting reform.

32. József Marjai was accompanied by Ede Bakó (National Bank of Hungary), Tamás Beck (Chamber of Commerce), Béla Csendes (Planning Office), András Gábor (Ministry of Industry), László Iván, ambassador, Iván Németh (CC, HSWP), Ferenc Vissi (Office for Prices and Materials), and the author.

33. In: Liu Suinian and Wu Quangan: op. cit, pp 672-694. In the review of the resolution the source of quotation will not be repeated, and more precisely marked.

Chapter Five
PROBLEMS OF EQUILIBRIUM IN THE INTRODUCTORY STAGE OF COMPREHENSIVE ECONOMIC REFORM (1985-1986)

Preliminary Measures to Ease Introduction

In the interest of a smooth introduction of the comprehensive economic reform, with its emphasis on the urban economy, and particularly on reform of the management of state enterprises, the State Council and the central economic management organs issued a number of preliminary instructions, circulars, decrees, and legal rules. All of them were aimed at facilitating the start of the reform on January 1, 1985. Some of them have already been mentioned or reviewed in the preceding chapter (e.g., replacement of the delivery of profits by profit taxation, the further expansion of autonomy of state enterprises, some temporary measures to improve the planning system). We have not yet mentioned the preliminary measures affecting the reform of the financial and credit system, or the labor and wages system, which were in some form linked to the above measures or to the complex reform experiments carried on in the cities earmarked for the purpose. Nor have we mentioned the preliminary measures related to the planned comprehensive reform of the price system, necessitated partly by the reform of agriculture and the rural economy, partly by the reform of the turnover system, outlined above. In the context of the reform of the financial and credit system, separate mention should be made of the preliminary measures taken to reform the banking system, because some of these had an extremely negative impact on the financial equilibrium and the credit balance of the state banks that had developed by the time the comprehensive reform of the urban economy was to be introduced.

The purpose of the comprehensive reform of the banking system was to separate the functions of the bank of issue from those of the credit bank, and thus to bring about in China a two-tier banking system allowing the industrial and commercial credit banks handling the monetary assets of enterprises to carry on their activities on a business basis. The idea of a two-tier banking system in China was born after the return of the SRC delegation from their 5-week study tour in Hungary in early July 1983. They reported that in Hungary one of the main directions of the reform of economic management was the establishment of a monetary economy, and that a radical reform of the banking system was to be carried out in a few years, the first step of which would be the creation of a two-tier banking system. In the course of their visit the experts of the SRC paid close attention to the relevant Hungarian ideas. Frankly speaking, they did not quite understand why Hungary needed several years of preparation for this important reform step, and they indicated that they intended to take this step in China simultaneous with the introduction of the comprehensive economic reform. This meant that the two-tier banking system had to be created in barely one and a half years.

In a speech held in the summer of 1983, Deng Xiaoping pointed out that banks should be made, as soon as possible, into effective levers of economic development and technical innovation also in China, and to this end banks must become genuine banks. On September 17, 1983 the State Council passed a resolution prescribing that in the future the People's Bank of China (PBOC) was to fulfill the function of a central bank and that the Industrial and Commercial Bank of China (ICBC) was to be created, which would take over the enterprise accounts from the PBOC, together with the function of collecting deposits and granting credits.[1] In the spirit of this resolution, the two functions were actually separated as of January, 1984, and the national center of the ICBC was founded. By the end of 1984 - with active support from the branches of the PBOC - the national network of ICBC branches was established. At the same time, the earlier, highly centralized, system of credit judgement was modified and various value limits were set for the right of approval of government organs of different levels.

The two simultaneous steps proved to be hasty and not sufficiently founded. The local government organs approved the investment ideas and plans submitted to them mostly without any review and instructed the local branches of the banks to make payable the credits necessary to start construction. Another mistake was that - since the banking network was new - they told the leaders of the ICBC that the credit lines for 1985 would be determined at the end of the year on the basis of the credits actually placed in the course of 1984. Owing to the simultaneous impact of these two factors - decentralization of investment decision rights and the "basis-approach" in setting the credit line - beginning in the autumn of 1984 a credit-granting competition started between the local government organs and the territorial branches of the ICBC toward the enterprises in their area of authority. As a result, the sum of credits placed in 1984 increased over the preceding year by 28.9%, while the amount of credit issued in December was 48.4% of the total credit issued in that year.[2]

This hasty reform of the banking and credit system, also mistaken in its methods, produced grave imbalances in the domestic financial situation of the PRC by the time the comprehensive economic reform was introduced. In the economic organizations it produced such an "abundance of money" that the economy became "overheated" in a few months, giving rise to all those negative phenomena which are concomitant with such a state of the economy. (Sudden growth and fragmentation of investments, disruption of the balance of aggregated social demand and supply, accelerating inflation, etc.) While in the course of 1984 the sum of domestic deposits placed with the state banks increased by 62.9 billion yuan, the sum of credits placed rose by 98.9 billion yuan. As a result, the annual difference between the stock of deposits and the credit stock was 111.4 billion - in favor of the latter.[3] This deficit was covered partly by raising foreign loans, but mostly by increasing the amount of money in circulation, that is, by the classical method of deficit financing. This necessarily started an inflationary process that gathered momentum - something that had not been experienced in China for decades.

The issue of purchasing power without the backing of commodities soon produced growing and unsatisfied demand and - as a result - tensions on the markets of both investment goods and consumer articles. The enterprises spent a portion of the credits raised to start various investment projects, another portion on raising wages and paying substantial premiums. This liberal credit policy made its impact mostly in the following year - 1985 - when the value of national economic investments rose, at current prices, by 45% as against 25% in 1984. The wages of manual workers and white-collar employees increased in 1984 by 19% (by 38% in the last quarter). (It is characteristic of the accelerating growth of wage payments that in the second half of the year the monthly rise was 16.6% in July, 19.2% in August, 26.8% in September, 27.8% in October, 35.5% in November, and 54% in December.)[4]

In order to facilitate introduction of the comprehensive economic reform, on October 1, 1984 the temporary decree of the Ministry of Finance took effect, replacing the profit delivery of state enterprises with the profit tax and, as a second step, introducing a multichannel and differentiated system of profit taxation. While in the first step basically two kinds of tax were levied on enterprise profit, i.e., income tax and regulatory tax, in the second step these were complemented by the following types of tax (partly at the expense of the regulatory tax): tax on the source of assets, urban building-protection tax, tax on immovables, land use tax, and tax for the use of vehicles. The latter were levied and collected by the local tax offices and may thus be regarded as kinds of local taxes. As a result, almost 90% of the enterprise profit was again collected. In addition, in this step also the types of tax to be accounted as cost were differentiated: instead of the unified industrial and commercial tax, four kinds of tax were introduced. They were: product tax, value-added tax, salt tax (to be paid only by producers and exporters of salt), and business or transaction tax (in Chinese: yingye shui). These had to be paid by state enterprises engaged in trade, including trade in materials and means of production, transport and communications, construction and fitting work, banking and insurance, postal and communication services, communal services, publishing, entertaining, manufacturing and repair industries, as well as various service activities.[5]

In the interest of facilitating introduction of the comprehensive economic reform, the SRC organized a conference in Changzhou - one of the scenes of complex reform experiments - in April 1984, to summarize the results and experience gained up to that point with the experiments related to the reform of the urban economy. The most important findings of the conference were put in writing and sent to the central economic management organs. They were summed up under six points:

1. Steps related to the reform experiments of the urban economic system have to be accelerated

2. Government administration has to be simplified and the scopes of authority decentralized, thus invigorating the activity of enterprises

3. A new system of planning and control has to be elaborated for cities

4. Markets have to be opened, turnover invigorated

5. The new system under which counties are guided by cities has to be perfected

6. New towns have to be included in the reform experiments.[6]

One year later, in March 1985, the SRC organized a similar conference in Wuhan. The document drawn up there summed up the most important tasks in five points:[7]

1. Knowledge has to be unified, the guidelines of reform activities in the current year have to be clearly indicated
2. Simplification of government administration has to be continued, scopes of authority decentralized, thus invigorating the activities of enterprises, particularly of large and medium-sized ones
3. The gates of cities have to be opened, freeing the development of horizontal economic relations
4. The economic levers (regulators) have to be used in a complex manner, thus perfecting economic relations
5. The healthy development of the reform should be secured by carefully set guidelines.

At the 2nd session of the 6th NPC held in May 1984, Prime Minister Zhao Ziyang emphasized the need to abandon the egalitarian approach of "eating from the big common pot" as soon as possible, to ensure rapid urban economic reform as well as improvement of the management system of construction and investments, development of the multichannel system of commodity trade, expansion of economic and technological cooperation with foreign countries, and an enhanced appreciation of the intelligentsia and of knowledge in general.[8]

Circumstances of Introduction in 1985

The comprehensive, or urban, economic reform was introduced in China in the last year of the sixth 5-year plan period covering 1981-1985. By consistently following the "four-word directive" in this period, the Chinese economy attained outstanding achievements in every respect. The original goals of the sixth 5-year plan had already been reached in most areas by 1984. Thus, the task for 1985 was mainly to consolidate the achievements and create, on this basis, more propitious conditions for the seventh 5-year plan. The annual plan for 1985 noted "three big things" that should be simultaneously well performed as the main task of the economy in that year: (a) initiation of the price reform, (b) step-by-step implementation of the wage reform, and (c) fulfillment and overfulfillment of the sixth 5-year plan in every field, as well as adequate preparation for the seventh 5-year plan. In the context of the last task, particular attention was called to the fact that priority construction and technological reconstruction projects should be kept within the order of magnitude prescribed in the plan, i.e., they should not exceed it. Having learned from the experience of underplanning in preceding years, the annual plan for 1985 reckoned with 8% growth of the total value of industrial production and with 6% in that of agricultural production (including the output of rural industries).[9] An interesting feature of this plan proposal, submitted to and approved by the 3rd plenary session of the 6th NPC held in March 1985, was that it clearly identified also those tasks in macroeconomic control and management, the unsatisfactory solution of which led by the end of the year to acute imbalance and disproportions, signs of which could already be seen early in 1985. In this respect the plan proposal emphasized the following tasks: (a) firmer control of credit granting and restriction of the issue of money, (b) stronger control of the consumption fund, (c) a curb on the amount of fixed capital investment, (d) stricter control of foreign exchange management, and (e) stricter financial and management discipline.[10] It can be seen that the SPC clearly perceived all the problems and dangers that derived from the decentralization of economic management and from the expansion of territorial and enterprise autonomy, as well as from the reform of the planning system introduced on January 1, 1985. At the same time, the SPC was no longer - and not yet again - in a position (in the atmosphere of general reform developed after the 3rd plenary session of the 12th CC, CPC) to advocate firmer central control and management. This would no doubt have involved a wider use of administrative methods, all the more as at that time the armory of indirect economic and financial regulation was still rather deficient and underdeveloped. (Similar to the central planning organs of other countries with planned economies that had taken the road to reform, the SRC's position became delicate in the developmental stage of comprehensive economic reform. Every declaration or step which was aimed at firmer macroeconomic control and management was likely to be regarded by many - with or without reason - as an open or concealed attack against the reform efforts in defense of the earlier positions of the central planning organs.)

One of the most important steps in the introduction of comprehensive economic reform was no doubt the "perfection" of the planning and materials management system. The document entitled "Some temporary measures aimed at perfecting the planning system" was issued by the SPC on August 31, 1984, approved by the State Council on October 4, 1984, and took effect on January 1, 1985.[11] These rules prescribed in detail, for every field of national economic planning, what the mandatory plans still in use were to cover beginning with 1985 in respect of the production, procurement, distribution, transportation, and trade of which products and kinds of products, and also which other various economic activities should be comprised in them and to what extent. The prescriptions were so formulated that it should be clear from them which the spheres and fields of production and commodity trade were that would remain outside the scope of the mandatory plans, and in what manner and to what extent these would be divided between the so-called guidance plans and pure market regulation. (We will present a detailed review of the planning system developed in the wake of the reform in the chapter presenting and analyzing the system of goals of the economic reform.)

Following the taking effect of the above-quoted document, in 1985 the number of centrally prescribed mandatory plan indicators significantly diminished, as did the weight of production and commodity trade determined by them within the global social product and total turnover. According to official publications, the national economic plan for 1985 comprised mandatory plan indicators for only about 60 kinds of industrial products, as against 123 in 1984, and their value of output was merely about 20% of total industrial output in 1985, against their share of about 40% in the preceding year. But the ministries and territorial economic management organs were allowed to expand the scope of centrally prescribed mandatory plan indicators, regarding both their number and the quantitative prescriptions. This increased, according to some estimates, the proportion of total industrial output prescribed in central plans by about 10% already in 1985; thus it was actually around 30%. In agricultural production - under the impact of the record harvest of 1984 - the mandatory central prescription of sown acreage for the most important agricultural products was abolished and in the state procurement of these products there was a shift to the method of contracted production and procurement, instead of the state monopoly for purchase and marketing (in Chinese: tonggou - tongxiao) which had been in force for more than three decades. In the framework of the new procurement system the number of agricultural products and those from complementary activities, of which the state continued to purchase a definite quantity on the basis of mandatory plan indicators set for the procurement agencies (not for the producers!), fell from 29 in the 1984 plan to hardly ten by 1985, while direct trade in these products was also allowed on the rural and urban free markets. The scope of kinds of products purchased by the state for export fell from more than 70 in 1984 to 36 by 1985. As regards the procurement of foodstuffs and industrial consumer goods most important for the supply of the population, the number of plan indicators mandatorily prescribed for the state commercial organs diminished in the same time from 65 to 20. Last but not least, the number of types of materials and means of production centrally allocated in the framework of the state plan was reduced by the reform from 256 to 65. Of these, 30 kinds were directly allocated by the SPC, the remaining 35 by the State Administration of Supply.

The number of kinds of products covered by the mandatory plan indicators and the volume of production, procurement, and sales determined by them changed later from year to year - also by branches and areas. In the case of shortages or supply disturbances and tensions their scope is expanded and their volume increased; in the case of excess production or accumulation of unsaleable stocks it has even happened that at some places the mandatorily prescribed and produced amounts were not purchased by the state trade organs. In the next year such products were either deleted from the list of mandatory plan indicators, or the mandatorily prescribed amounts for the production and procurement of these products were set at a significantly lower level. This practice not infrequently produced serious dissatisfaction among producers, particularly peasants and other small producers.

The start of the price reform promised for 1985 did not take place. The reason was that the large-scale outflow of purchasing power that had begun late in 1984 and continued into early 1985 caused supply disturbances and tensions on the market, and the demand, far exceeding supply everywhere, produced spontaneous price rises. Since, as a result of the planning system's reform, essentially a three-level price system developed - frequently for the same product - this allowed manipulations and abuses with prices of products traded through various channels.

The supply of production carried on in the framework of mandatory plans took place, namely, at centrally fixed "state list prices" (in Chinese: guojia paijia) which did not even cover costs in several cases (they affected both the supply with materials and energy and the sale of products thus produced). For the production determined in the guidance plans the enterprises bought materials, energy, and means of production from the output of other enterprises similarly under the guidance plan regime and sold their products also in the framework of such direct interfirm agreements. In this case they were also free to agree on prices directly, with the knowledge and under the supervision of the price authority. Although there were certain central prescriptions for price formation in these cases, and it was a general requirement that these prices should exceed the level of state list prices by only about 15%-20%, in reality the difference was much higher.[12]

Finally, beyond the prices for products turned out and sold in the framework of mandatory and guidance plans, there were and still are free market prices for products produced and sold outside of the said plans; they adjust to supply and demand and their level is substantially higher than even that of the "agreed prices."[13] Thus, instead of the originally planned three-tier "fixed", "moving", and "free" prices, actually "state", "agreed," and "free" prices developed; the first and the last of these essentially correspond to each other, the middle one does not necessarily adjust to a predetermined lower and upper limit.

The basic target of the price reform was to gradually approximate to each other levels of prices belonging to the three price categories and to gradually abolish the budget subsidies granted to the "state list prices." In this respect, not even the first steps planned for 1985 could be taken, since the raising of the irrationally low "state list prices" for basic (raw) materials (grain, cotton, steel, cement, etc.) and primary energy (coal, crude oil) would have produced, through secondary effects, rises in the price level of manufactured goods that would have made inflation intolerable; it accelerated in any case in response to the rise of the "agreed" and "free" prices.

In consequence of the exaggerated outflow of purchasing power and the commodity shortage that occurred in its wake, the wage reform already begun in 1985 had to be interrupted as well. Only the salaries of pedagogues in primary and secondary schools were raised as of January 1, as well as those of employees in government institutions on July 1, when several wage supplements and other benefits were amalgamated with the basic salaries. In productive enterprises the wage rise could no longer be implemented, although modification of the earlier irrational relative wages had also been planned. In fact, the high premiums paid in late 1984 and early 1985 had to be radically reduced as well.

Nor could the national economic investments be kept within the limits set in the plan for 1985. Their value exceeded (at current prices) the level of the preceding year by nearly 45%. Attempts were made to satisfy the excess demand on both the investment and the consumer markets with imports. The rising demand was due to the slower growth of domestic supply and its inadequate commodity pattern. By the end of the year this produced a trade deficit of US $14.9 billion, amounting to almost 55% of the annual value of exports. Still, because of the increased tax revenues, the balance of public finances showed some surplus in 1985 - for the first time in 6 years.

Thus, the circumstances under which the comprehensive economic reform was introduced were rather controversial in 1985. The "overheating" of the economy and the concomitant abundance of money stimulated production and investments on the one hand, while on the other they produced a shortage, becoming chronic, on the markets of both investment goods and consumer articles. This started an inflationary process that has not yet been halted. Neither the production of basic materials and energy, nor the expansion of transport capacities could keep pace with the 18% annual growth of urban industrial production and with the almost 37% growth of rural industries. This produced serious disturbances and stops in both production and trade. The consumer price level rose - also according to official data - by 8.8% on a national level (by 12.2% in the cities). This reduced the increase of the per capita real incomes of peasants and of the per capita real wages of blue- and white-collar workers from 13.7% and 14.8% respectively in 1984 to 8.4% and 4.7% respectively in 1985. In spite of this, the volume of retail sales increased - at constant prices - by 13.6%. It is characteristic of the abundance of money that while the sum of domestic deposits placed with the state banks increased by 96.7 billion yuan over the preceding year, the sum of credits placed rose by 148.6 billion yuan, and thus the difference between deposits and credits granted increased by the end of the year to 163.2 billion yuan, in favor of the latter. The amount of money in circulation increased in 1985 by 24.7% as against the annual 12.5% growth of the GNP, and in absolute terms it approximated 100 billion yuan. The savings of the urban population placed in deposits exceeded this, reaching 105 billion yuan in 1985. The savings deposits of the peasant population in that year amounted to 56.5 billion yuan. Considering the total retail trade turnover of 430 billion yuan, the total savings deposits of more than 160 billion yuan meant a huge potential purchasing power in China.

Slowdown in Growth Rate of Agricultural Production

Abolition of the mandatory plan indicators and the shift to contracted production and procurement allowed the peasants essentially greater freedom, basically arranging for family management, both in the formation of the production pattern and in choosing the mode of earning an income. The sales difficulties and low procurement prices that resulted from the outstanding grain and cotton harvest of 1984 led some peasant families to think it would pay better to reduce the acreage devoted to these products in favor of other crops such as oil and sugar-beet or cane, fiber crops, or tobacco, or even to shift from crop cultivation to animal husbandry and/or various rural sideline activities (industry, construction, transport, trade). As a result, the annual grain harvest declined from 407 million tons in 1984 to 379 million tons in 1985 and - in spite of the fact that the area to be sown was again prescribed - it rose to only 391.5 million tons even in 1986. The decline in cotton was even greater: 6.26, 4.15, and 3.54 million tons in the respective 3 years.

The decline in the output of grain and cotton by 7.4% and 50.9% respectively in 1985 was only partially counterbalanced by the more than 30% increase in the quantities of oil and sugar crops produced, as well as of fibers and tobacco. In addition, the production growth halted in 1986, or even fell. Thus the share of crop production within the gross output value of agricultural production fell - at comparable prices - from 58% in 1984 to 49.8% in 1985 and to 45.3% in 1986.

The earlier method of statistical accounting also played a role in this large-scale decline of the share of plant production, in that the gross output value of the rural industries (in Chinese: cunban gongye) was also included in the gross output value of agricultural production. In these years, namely, the rural industries were the most dynamically growing branch of all rural economic activities: they showed a growth of 67.1% in 1985 and of 33.3% in 1986 over the preceding year, and their weight within the agricultural gross output value was already 24.8% in 1985, as against 17% in 1984, and reached 29.8% in 1986. As a consequence, animal husbandry - which increased its gross output value by 17.2% in 1985 and by 5.6% in 1986 over the preceding year - had only a 14.5% share against 14.2% in 1984, and in 1986 this share fell to 13.8% within the gross output value of agricultural production.

Within the rural industries only the "other" complementary activities and fishing increased their share - by a few tenths of a percent - within the agricultural total against 1984: the former from 5% to 5.3% and 5.7%, the latter from 1.7% to 1.8% and 2%. The share of forestry fell from 4.1% in 1984 to 3.8% in 1985 and to 3.3% in 1986. If we separate the rural industrial activities from the agricultural ones and add their gross output value to the industrial one - as has recently been done in Chinese statistics accounted at current prices - quite naturally, different percentual shares are obtained for the sub-branches of agricultural production (see Table 4).

Table 4. Distribution of the gross output value of agricultural production by sub-branches (in % and at current prices)

	1984	1985	1986	1987
- Crop cultivation	68.3	63.0	62.2	60.7
- Forestry	5.0	5.2	5.0	4.7
- Animal husbandry	18.2	22.0	21.8	22.8
- Sideline activities	5.8	6.3	6.9	7.0
- Fishing	2.7	3.5	4.1	4.8

Source: Zhongguo Tongqi Zhaiyao 1988, Beijing, 1988, p 23 (A Statistical Survey of China 1988)

As regards the annual growth rate of agricultural production - excluding rural industries - from 1985 it has shown significant decline over the preceding 5-6 years. While between 1979 and 1984 the gross output value of agricultural production increased, on annual average, by 7.8%, between 1985 and 1987 the increase was only 4.3%. (Actual growth in 1985 and 1986 was 3.5% and 3.4% respectively, while the gross output value of plant production diminished by 2.0% and increased by 0.9% respectively.) These data indicate, or at least allow us to conclude, that the factors brought to the surface by the rural economic reform that started in 1979 and which stimulated agricultural production significantly weakened by the mid-1980s. The reasons are manifold; one of them is no doubt to be found in the irrational relative prices of the prevailing price system, which is disadvantageous for the whole of agricultural production. According to a survey made in 1985, the agricultural price scissors regarding the two basic products, grain and cotton, opened twice as wide as would have been the case at world market prices. (The price of 1 kg of grain in 1985 was equal to the price of 4 kg of fertilizer on the world market, while in China less than 2 kg of fertilizer could be purchased for 1 kg of grain. On the world market the price of 1 kg of cotton was equal to the price of 4-5 m of cotton fabric, in China to less than 2.5 m. In Japan, to buy a 20 HP tractor 5.5 tons of rice had to be sold; in China 45.5 tons were necessary for a 28 HP tractor.[14] A further problem was the declining tendency of agricultural investments; this was partly a consequence of the curbing of state investments and their regrouping to other areas of the economy, partly a result of the slow growth of investments by the peasants themselves. The latter fact was closely related to the unclear legal problems of land ownership and land use, to the the appearance of various - frequently contradictory or even mutually exclusive - concepts of the reform of ownership, and last but not least, to the significant differences in established practices from one region or province to the next.

On the one hand, in recent years views have been published which do not exclude in principle that the land (or a part of it) should be privately owned (through sales), setting out from the idea that in a commodity economy all factors of production and means of production have to become commodities. On the other hand, it is not clear to date what is actually meant by the right of peasants to land use. (How long should the right to land use last? Should it necessarily relate to the same plot of land? Is it transferable, inheritable, and if so, under what conditions?) This has led to the situation whereby a considerable portion of the peasantry are not willing to make major investments on the contractually "leased" land area (soil improvement, irrigation projects); in fact, they think that the maintenance of the existing infrastructural establishments (irrigation channels, pumps, roads, etc.) is the duty of the "lessor".

As a consequence, by the mid-1980s in some agricultural areas of the country the quality of the soil had deteriorated, irrigation works were in a neglected state, and soil erosion had increased. This called a halt to the earlier rising tendency of yields per unit of land area, with almost every kind of crop in 1985-1986; with some products there was even a significant decline. In China, however, since the proportion of cultivable land area has always been low and continuously declines as land is used for other purposes, practically the only way to raise agricultural output is to increase yields.

Owing to the "liberalization" of prices, the production of vegetables and the development of animal husbandry and fishing accelerated in 1985-1986, the target being the big and medium--sized urban markets. An even faster development of animal husbandry was limited mainly by the shortage of fodder, though considerable results were attained in the production of milk and eggs. In spite of this, according to a representative survey made in different regions of the country, food consumption of the rural and urban population increased in these years at a rather low rate, while the significant difference in the food consumption level that had existed earlier between the rural and urban population hardly changed (see Table 5).

Table 5. Average per capita annual consumption by rural and urban populations of the most important foodstuffs (kg/head/year)

	1978 Rural	1981* Urban	1984 Rural	1984 Urban	1985 Rural	1985 Urban	1986 Rural	1986 Urban
Grain (cleaned)	123	145	209	142	209	135	212	138
Vegetables	142	152	140	149	131	144	134	148
Edible oil	2.0	4.8	4.0	7.1	4.0	5.8	4.2	6.2
Meat	5.8	18.6	10.6	19.8	11.0	19.3	11.8	21.6
Poultry	0.3	1.9	0.9	2.9	1.0	3.2	1.1	3.7
Eggs	0.8	5.2	1.8	7.6	2.1	6.8	2.1	7.1
Fish, crab	0.8	7.3	1.7	7.8	1.6	7.1	1.9	8.2
Sugar	0.7	2.9	1.3	2.9	1.5	2.5	1.6	2.6

Source: Zhongguo Tongji Nianjian 1987. Beijing, 1987, pp 693 and 696 (Statistical Yearbook of China 1987)

Note: * For urban food consumption data are available only from 1981 on

Because of the disturbances and difficulties in supply, in 1986 - contrary to original ideas - the rationing system had to be reintroduced for some so-called foodstuffs of secondary importance (e.g., pork, sugar). The prices of such foodstuffs remained centrally determined, and thus their price level was essentially lower than the free market prices for the same products.

National Conference of the CPC in 1985: First Manifestations of Differences in Views on Basic Reform Issues Among Highest Party Leaders

In September 1985 the national conference of the CPC was convened, hardly a year after the 3rd plenary session of the 12th CC. Such a conference (which has almost the same scope of authority as a congress), counts as a rare event in the history of the Chinese party. Since its foundation in 1921, party conferences had been held on only two occasions, in 1935 and 1955. The convening of the national party conference in the autumn of 1985, "halfway" between the 12th and 13th congresses, was justified on two counts. One was the need for preliminary discussion on the draft of the seventh 5-year plan proposal, to take effect on January 1, 1986; the other was the implementation of the personnel changes deemed necessary in the leading party bodies in the spirit of rejuvenation and increasing expertise.

The party conference was held at a time when, in addition to the undoubtedly great successes of the reform and opening policy, certain negative phenomena and "unhealthy" tendencies had also become perceptible. In spite of the preparation for and efforts made in the interest of the smooth introduction of the reform, in several fields of the economy equilibrium problems and tensions were growing.

These disquieting phenomena and tendencies were all the more obvious at the center of the party leadership, since this conference had to decide not only on the expedient rate of development of the national economy and society, the main proportions and basic directions for the next 5 years, but also on the rate of implementation of the planned comprehensive economic reform and its "time schedule."

Related to the first point on the agenda of the party conference, a lengthy document was published with the title: "Draft proposal of the CC of the CPC for the seventh 5-year plan for national economic and social development." In seven chapters and 70 points, the ideas of party and government leaders are expounded in connection with the elaboration of the seventh 5-year plan and the development of the comprehensive reform. The documents of the party conference were at that time also published in English,[15] we will here briefly review and evaluate the standpoints and opinions related to the subject of this book by following the English version.

The first chapter of the proposal, comprising six points, is entitled: "Basic principles and main strategic goals." It first of all points out that the initial conditions are propitious for starting the seventh 5-year plan. The economy is in a stage of dynamic, continuous, stable, and balanced growth, and perspectives are opening up for a positive growth cycle. Deep reform processes are also taking place in the organizational and operational structure of the economy. The seventh 5-year plan, to start in 1986, will be of great importance in providing the foundations for a more efficient and dynamic economic and social development in the 1990s. The document examines the results of economic growth and structural changes attained in the first half of the 1980s and states that the favorable change set as a goal for the economic and financial sector has been achieved in the past 5 years. Although beginning in the autumn of 1984, various tensions and problems arose in consequence of (a) too fast growth of industry, (b) oversized fixed capital investments and their fragmentation, (c) inconsiderate expansion of credit sources and of the consumption fund, (d) a fast rise in the prices of certain products, and (e) diminishing foreign exchange reserves of the state, with proper guidance and enhanced macro-level control these can be eliminated in 1 or 2 years.

As regards the basic principles to be observed during the seventh 5-year plan period in developing the economy and society, the document underlines the following:

- Reform must be given first priority; reform and development should be adapted to and should promote each other.
- Aggregated social demand and supply have to be balanced on the whole; adequate proportions have to be maintained between accumulation and consumption.
- Particular attention should be paid to the relationship between quality and quantity, as well as to that between the growth rate and economic efficiency, with emphasis on quality and efficiency.
- Together with material civilization, also ideological civilization has to be enhanced, since, if the latter is neglected, the former might lose its socialist character.
- It should not be forgotten that the four modernizations aimed at are of a socialist character, and that the purpose of the policy aimed at reform, at opening to the outside world, and at revitalizing the economy is to build socialism with Chinese characteristics.

The questions of economic reform are dealt with in Chap. 5 of the document, entitled: "Economic structure and means of regulation," in altogether ten sections (points 48-57). The first goal is "... in the next 5 years or more to lay the foundation for a vigorous socialist economic structure with Chinese characteristics."[16] To this end, the plan proposal sets the accomplishment of the following, closely related, tasks as the primary requirement: (a) All enterprises, especially the large and medium-sized ones owned by the whole people have to be further stimulated, so that they will work efficiently as socialist producers and distributors of commodities, each enjoying autonomy and independence, bearing responsibility for profits and losses; (b) socialist planned commodity markets have to be further expanded, gradually improving the full-scope market network; (c) in the state management of enterprises there should be a gradual shift from direct to indirect control, mainly by economic and legal measures and, if necessary, by administrative ones as well. While efforts were to be focused on these three main fields, various complementary reform measures were also provided for in several other fields. These affected the system of planning, the price system, manpower management, and the wage system and were aimed at creating a new, comprehensive economic system in which planning and market, microlevel invigoration and macrolevel control are organically integrated. The proposal states: "Accomplishing this will lead to a satisfactory handling of various economic relations, making it possible to harmonize the interests of the state, the collectives and the individuals, to achieve greater uniformity in the speed, proportions and efficiency of economic development and to bring about self-sustained growth in our national economy as a whole."[17]

The document identifies the invigoration of enterprise activity as the central link of the economic reform focused on the cities. It is believed that this can be achieved with the following methods:

1. By streamlining administration and by further delegation of power to lower levels

2. By gradually and rationally reducing the burdens on big and medium-sized enterprises deriving from the regulatory tax, and with urban collective (cooperative) enterprises and individual ventures by improving management policies and the taxation system, so that all enterprises compete under roughly the same conditions

3. By gradually reducing the scope of mandatory planning and giving enterprises greater autonomy in production, procurement, and sales, as well as in management of money, materials, and manpower

4. By maintaining a balance between aggregated social demand and supply, which should force enterprises to compete on the real market and thus also to improve the quality of management and efficiency

5. By establishing various responsibility systems within the enterprises, reforming the personnel system, democratically selecting leaders, and adequately remunerating good performance

6. By turning over a portion of the smaller state enterprises to collectives or individuals, by contract or lease, for management.

In order to invigorate enterprises the document deemed it necessary to do away with the rigid barriers and limits between enterprises by branches, areas, forms of ownership, and administrative levels. This should remove the obstacles to direct commodity exchange and cooperative relations, and should make it possible to establish horizontal economic unions.

According to the document, the key to the gradual establishment and perfection of the market system is reform of the pricing and the price-control systems. In a detailed explanation, the docement essentially repeats the principles and arguments already found in the resolution of the CC of October 1984, but on this conference the emphasis on prudence and gradualness was even greater.

Not many new elements can be found in the points dealing with the reform of the financial system, either. Here too, the importance of maintaining stability is emphasized. Under the given conditions, it was not believed expedient to increase the part of profit retainable by the enterprises, as it would stimulate new investments by them. Instead, a further diversification of the system of budget levies was envisaged. In the development and further reform of the banking system, expansion of the scope of activity of the specialized banks and putting banking activities on a business basis were provided for. At the same time, the leaders wished to strengthen the controlling and supervisory role of the People's Bank of China, as the bank of issue, in monetary and credit turnover and, particularly, in foreign exchange management.

Summing up the experiences of past years, the document stipulates that in the following stage of the reform a correct relationship should be maintained between demolition of the old system and introduction of the new one, between "destruction and construction," with a careful watch on the following:

1. The state's _indirect_ control and management should be strengthened in all fields of economic activity, since _direct_ interference in microeconomic activities can be reduced only in direct proportion to the increase of the former (i.e. indirect control).

2. Though the basic direction of reform is toward suppressing administrative instruments, some instruments are indispensable, both now and in the future. In fact, it is precisely the future suppression of administrative instruments that justifies at the time of transition from the old system to the new one - in the interest of the smooth introduction of the reform - a certain strengthening of the absolutely necessary administrative interference.

3. Since the law is an important instrument for the regulation of economic relations and economic activities, efforts should be made - wherever possible - to regulate requirements, forms of procedure, and behavior in a normative, legal way, prescribed in laws and decrees.

4. Cadres have to be made aware of the fact that the reform of the economic system is a difficult and complicated process, in the course of which many new problems and difficulties may arise, which can be solved and fought only step by step and through a complex approach.

In foreign reports and analyses published about the 1985 national party conference of the CPC, much space was devoted to the differences in emphasis and approach of the contributions made by Chinese leaders at the conference. To a certain extent this is understandable, as at this conference all five members of the Standing Commission of the PB made contributions, and in their speeches they touched upon both questions on the agenda. These speeches differed in nature and volume and, beyond the undoubtedly perceptible differences in approach, they also reflected the individual, particular features and style of the leader in question, deriving from his function and role in the party and state hierarchy and, last but not least, from his personality.

The task of opening the party conference and giving a comprehensive introductory speech devolved on General Secretary Hu Yaobang. Immediately following him, the floor was taken by Prime Minister Zhao Ziyang, responsible for the elaboration of the plan proposal, the written document of the first point on the agenda. In his report, about double the volume of the opening speech, he dealt with almost every important point of the CC proposal for the elaboration of the seventh 5-year plan. From both a professional and a political viewpoint, this speech testified to a high standard, an imposingly firm approach, and a resolute stand, and regarding economic policy , it put the emphasis on the development of the economic reform and its consistent implementation. Interestingly, despite its smaller volume (or precisely on this account), the basic principles and priorities of the Chinese economic policy intended to be pursued during the seventh 5-year plan can be seen and traced much more clearly in this document than in the 70-point plan proposal, five times the length of the speech. The speeches of Deng Xiaoping and Chen Yun, as well as the closing address of State President Li Xiannian, were read on the last day of the party conference - September 23 - and, since their texts were published in full the next day by the dailies, the general public was able to become acquainted with them 2 days earlier than with the "Draft proposal" of the CC and the "Explanations" attached to it by Zhao Ziyang.

The speeches of the three "great old men" were utterly different in nature and length. The speech of Deng Xiaoping - longer than the opening address of Hu Yuobang but shorter than that of Zhao Ziyang - grouped his concise message around four questions. Speaking "about the situation and the reform," he established that since the 3rd plenary session of the 11th CC, that is, in 7 years, two important tasks had succesfully been solved: correction of the bad things and the starting of the reform. Within the reform he stressed two basic principles: the priority of the socialist public sector of the economy and common prosperity. In the latter context he pointed out that: "It is precisely for the purpose of spurring more and more people to become prosperous until all are prosperous that some areas and some people are encouraged to do so first."[18] About the seventh 5-year plan Deng Xiaoping said little; he only indicated that the targets were realistic and pointed out the domestic and international importance of implementing the plan. He said much more "about socialist civilization with advanced culture and ideology." In this context he emphasized the importance of fighting against greediness, corruption, and injustice, of ideological and political work, of fighting against the pernicious influence of capitalism and feudalism, and against behavior not becoming communists. He also spoke at length "about the succession of new cadres to old and theoretical study." In the latter context he pointed to the necessity of constantly studying Marxist theory. As chairman of the Central Advisory Commission of the CPC he believed that this was indispensable in order to give correct answers to the new theoretical questions raised by practice.

The speech of Chen Yun, first secretary (that is, chairman) of the Central Commission for Discipline Inspection, which caused rather a great sensation and echo, summed up six groups of question. He dealt relatively briefly with the fact that there must be an orderly system of succession for cadres, so that a stepwise age structure be preserved. He emphasized that "we must continue to pay attention to grain production" and exercised sharp ciriticism of the views and tendencies underestimating this requirement. He confronted the slogan: "no prosperity without engaging in industry" - under the influence of which a growing portion of the peasantry showed indifference towards grain production and, in general, towards agricultural activity, and, in the hope of becoming rich quickly, only wanted to engage in industry and commerce - with the thesis "no economic stability without agricultural development." He castigated the mass media for exaggerated propagation of "10 000-yuan households," as there were actually not many of them in the country. This meant that the mass propaganda was divorced from reality. He underlined that "the socialist economy must be developed proportionately and in a planned way," and warned that the viewpoint and guiding principle that "the planned economy's primacy and the subordinated role of market regulation are still necessary" had not lost their topicality. He identified macroeconomic control as the substance of planning which is an indispensable condition of the dynamic but not chaotic development of the microeconomy; "... guidance planning is not the same as market regulation. Market regulation involves no planning, blindly allowing supply and demand to determine production."[19] He warned against the drive for high growth rates and quick results as it would lead, in the end, to deceleration of growth and to setbacks. He quoted the Confucian adage, well known in China: "More haste, less speed." Chen Yun used sharp words against the "unhealthy phenomenon" that had been spreading since the start of the reform, listing almost every manifestation of it (selfish gain, speculation, swindle, graft, corruption, kowtowing to foreigners in the hope of gifts, etc.). He related all these phenomena to looseness in ideological and political education, party discipline and public discipline. In conclusion, he called attention to adherence to democratic centralism as laid down in the party constitution.

No doubt, in content and style Chen Yun's speech differed from those of the party leaders who took the floor before him, since he put much greater emphasis on the critique of negative phenomena and on the importance of eliminating them. Later, this provided an opportunity and a base of reference for the anti-reform actions and attacks of conservative forces, to be found on almost every level in the ranks of the CPC, although this was not necessarily the purpose and intention of the old, experienced leader, who was particularly well versed in questions of macroeconomic management.

The closing address of State President Li Xiannian did not contain many new elements relative to those speaking before him. His was the shortest speech. Although - in view of the summarizing and evaluative nature of the speech - Li Xiannian aimed in problems of content at balance and at underlining the most important points, in style and tone it was nearer to the speech of Chen Yun than to those of the former three leaders. He, too, emphasized the importance of planned and proportionate development and warned against propaganda blowing up the results. He underlined the necessity of strengthening ideological and political education, with a view to the policy of "opening outward."

In the final analysis, the 1985 party conference of the CPC resulted in a strengthening and consolidation of reform and of the policy of opening. And this happened at a time when, because of the various difficulties and negative phenomena accompanying the development of urban reform, some leaders and party members felt a certain hesitation. This was caused, to a considerable extent, by the large-scale "rejuvenation" of the leading party bodies, affecting about half of the members of the Political Bureau and about one third of the Central Committee. The Central Advisory Commission and the Central Commission for Discipline Inspection were somewhat less affected by the personnel changes. Through these changes mainly middle-aged or not very old cadres, mostly committed to the economic and political reforms, entered the leading bodies. In spite of this, a sufficiently large number of aged cadres remained in these bodies for on the whole identical power relations to develop between those wanting faster and more resolute reform and those wanting to make slower and more cautious progress. Among the latter there were, of course, also those who did not openly raise their voice against the reforms, but who were nevertheless conservative and dogmatic cadres who were averse to or expressly feared them.

1986: Attempts to Establish Macroeconomic Equilibrium and to Increase Independence of Enterprises

The events of the year following the introduction of the comprehensive economic reform made the Chinese political and economic leaders in early 1986 circumspect and cautious. There was no doubt that the reform had produced results, but disquieting phenomena and tendencies were also surfacing. Some were traced by the Chinese leadership to the controversial, so-called double-track (in Chinese: shuangguidao) management system, a system of control and management in which the constitutent elements of the old and the new economic system exist side by side and frequently work against each other or weaken each other. Beside introducing several incalculable elements of uncertainty into both the macro- and the microlevel economy, this situation provides the opportunity for many enterprises to evade central prescriptions and orders, to look for various loopholes and back doors in legally unregulated areas. Such a situation is unfavorable for the majority of enterprises, however, because - particularly in the case of state enterprises - this makes the extent and impact of state interference incalculable and thus strengthens a preference for short-term interests and the tendency to live from one day to the next. In the final account, this harms the consumer, since, with growing speculation and exploitation of shortages, enterprises unambiguously aim at raising their prices; in most cases they succeed where demand far exceeds supply.

From the controverersial development of the reform process in 1985 the Chinese economic and political leaders deduced the following lessons:

1. The reform ought to be more consistently developed in the direction of planned commodity economy. This means that in practice, in choosing models and making decisions, the intention to create an economic system based on an organic linking of planned economy with market mechanisms should be more resolutely asserted.

2. The relationship between opening and invigorating the microeconomy and firmly handling the macroeconomy should be carefully controlled. The microeconomy must not be allowed to run quite free. In a modern economy microeconomic activity is always carried on in a definite macroeconomic environment, with adequate macroeconomic control. The economic and financial regulatory instruments of this macroeconomic control (e.g., taxes, interest, and exchange rates) are still being established in China, and thus, for a time, the instruments of administrative regulation also have to be used.

3. While insisting on the principle of a harmonious, complex, and methodically implemented reform, care should be taken that the initiative spirit, responsibility and creative talents of the masses in various fields and branches can develop. But there is no place for impatience and haste, for accomplishing the difficult and complicated tasks "at one stroke." Reform guidelines must adjust flexibly to local conditions and customs in order to find the most expedient solutions.

4. To enhance understanding of and support for the reform on the part of cadres and the masses, ideological and political education have to be strengthened, because reform of the economic system requires not only the transformation of the old system, no longer conforming to the development needs of the forces of production, but also a change in the people's way of thinking and way of life. This is not at all an easy process that is free from conflicts. This is why the cadres dealing with economic reform can not simply immerse themselves in their work; they have to continuously explain to the masses and cadres the guidelines for reform, the problems and difficulties that arise and how they plan to solve them. In the meantime, the reaction of cadres and the masses has to be watched, and in elaborating the individual reform steps the receptivity and tolerance of society have to be considered.

Thus, based on these considerations, the Chinese party and government leaders issued another "four-word directive" in early 1986 for the following 1-2 years, concretely formulated as "consolidation, digestion, completion, and correction" (in Chinese: gonggu, xiaohua, buchong, gaishan). In practice, this also expressed an intention to slow down the reform process, since - from the experiences of the preceding years - many within the leadership concluded that "consolidation" of the results already attained could take place only if the economic units and the cadres and masses had sufficient time to "digest" the effects and consequences of the reform steps already taken. In addition, they believed it was necessary to "complete" certain reform steps adequately, and to "correct" the hasty, insufficiently founded, or mistaken measures. This idea was basically correct. However, the formulation and setting of this new four-word directive was at the same time the result of a compromise between the "radical," the "moderate," and the "conservative" forces within the CPC leadership. This circumstance - which will be handled later in more detail - created a chance for the adversaries of reform of all ranks to activate themselves to a greater extent than ever, and in some places or in some questions they were even able to hinder or sabotage reform measures already taken.[20]

Nevertheless, 1986 was the year when the seventh 5-year plan of the PRC for the development of the national economy and society was successfully started and when the urban-centered comprehensive reform was further founded and deepened. The 4th session of the 6th NPC was held between March 25 and April 12, 1986, and at this session the final version of the seventh 5-year plan was debated and adopted. In the course of the discussions it was also pointed out that during this plan period the reform of the economic system - closely linked to the general objective of a planned commodity economy to be developed on the basis of the socialist public ownership system - had to concentrate on the following three main tasks: (a) to increase the viability of enterprises, (b) to perfect the market system, and (c) to make the macroeconomic management system more efficient.

In accordance with the four-word directive of "consolidation, digestion, completion, and correction," the concrete measures and experimental steps to be taken in urban reform in 1986 were formulated as follows:

1. To reform the management system of enterprises; to explore the most expedient ways in which the rights of ownership can be separated from those of management

2. To create new forms of enterprise organization by developing various horizontal economic unions on a broad scope, as well as by further eliminating the restrictions between areas and branches

3. To expand reform of the financial system by creating money markets granting short-term credits

4. To invigorate enterprise activity by gradually expanding the market for the means of production

5. To promote fundamental changes in the economic function of government control by gradually starting urban structural reform experiments

6. To provide effective legal guarantees and support the reform by continuing the creation of a socialist legal economic system

The most important reform measures introduced during 1986 are presented below as they relate to these six tasks, and their impact on management relations is discussed.

Ad 1. Invigoration of enterprises is a central link in the reform of the economic system and, at the same time, the starting point and base of urban reform. In 1986 the emphasis shifted increasingly from extraenterprise factors (e.g., delegation of certain decision-making rights by economic management organs to the enterprises in order to increase their independence) to those within the enterprise. Among these, the general introduction of <u>the manager responsibility system</u> in state enterprises was of outstanding importance. It had been tried experimentally and with rather good results for 2 years in more than 23 000 large and medium-sized so-called key enterprises. In September 1986 the Central Committee of the CPC and the State Council of the PRC issued three joint decrees about the scope of authority and rights of the managers, party organizations, and delegate--meetings of blue- and white-collar employees of state enterprises. In these, the duties of the three enterprise institutions were clearly separated, and it was stipulated that the manager is the exclusive representative of the enterprise as a legal entity and is responsible for its activities in every respect. At the same time, a system was introduced under which managers are appointed or elected for a definite period. The practical implementation of these decrees was not smooth, mainly because of the resistance of the local party organizations, which thought that the expansion of the scope of authority and responsibility of the managers encroached on their own rights and restricted their power and influence. They particularly objected to those parts of the decree on the rights and duties of managers which allow managers to select and appoint their deputies and other executives themselves, independently of the opinion of party organizations. This gave rise to serious conflicts in several enterprises, and quite a few managers soon offered their resignation because - since they had relieved unsuited executives - the local party organizations and committees persecuted them.

Another important reform measure of 1986 was the revival of <u>the managerial responsibility system of enterprises</u> in diverse forms. Some large and medium-sized enterprises shifted to an enterpreneurial type of management, with the leaders and workers of enterprises undertaking responsibility - mostly also broken down into smaller units within the enterprise - for a definite volume of production or investment against a predetermined amount (observing, of course, the prescribed requirements as to quality), and committing themselves to surrender a definite amount of profit or to increase profit to a stipulated extent. In the latter case, the higher economic management organs waived the normative taxation of profit and the individual levying of the so-called leveling or regulatory tax (in Chinese: tiaojie shui). In small and some - mostly loss-taking - medium-sized enterprises in state-owned industry and trade the method of leasing and operation under contract was widely used. By the end of 1986, all over the country some of the reform methods of "transformation, cession, leasing, sale" were implemented with almost 6700 small state commercial enterprises. It was the leasing method that spread the fastest; the number of leased commercial enterprises increased in 1 year by 55%.

Reform of the employment and wage systems within the enterprises also received new impetus. For new employees, contracts concluded for a definite period were uniformly used, and efforts were made to abolish the earlier system of "recruiting from within the enterprise," whereby the children of retiring blue- and white-collar employees were employed. The social insurance system for "those waiting for work" (the euphemistic term for the unemployed in China) was introduced in the form of unemployment benefit paid under definite conditions, and the managers were authorized to dismiss, through disciplinary procedure, workers who grossly violated work discipline. Managers were given a freer hand to establish differentiated forms of wage payment and premiums, in order to suppress the leveling method of "eating from the same big pot." In more than 300 cities and counties the pension system was also reformed in 1986 within the broader framework of a comprehensive reform of the social insurance system.

Ad 2. Enterprises were also invigorated by the rapid spread of horizontal economic unions of various types, which meant new organizational forms for enterprises, breaking down the walls separating areas and branches from each other. It was in March 1986 that the State Council issued the organizational guidelines for these unions. In the course of the year they began to mushroom, and by the end of the year their network already covered the whole country, with more than 32 000 horizontal economic unions operating; more than 7000 of them were "associations of enterprises" (in Chinese: quiyequnti) and "groups of enterprises" (quiyejituan) of a new type, which developed around diverse large and medium-sized key enterprises. Already 24 such networks of economic unions were operating all over the country, several of which figured as independent units (addressees) when the state plans were broken down to enterprises, and they organized the implementation of the plan tasks themselves.

Ad 3. Parallel with the development of a commodity economy, significant steps were taken to reform the financial and credit system. In January 1986, the State Council issued a decree entitled: "Temporary rules for bank control in the PRC," which allowed specialized banks to regroup monetary assets between themselves, in the framework of short-term agreements. Those granting and raising the loans were free to agree on rates of interest and other terms of repayment. Next, in July, an experiment was begun in five large cities (Canton, Chungking, Wuhan, Shenyang, and Changzhou), with the participation of the banking branches of 11 cities, to create money markets with nationwide authority; these transacted short-term credits totaling approximately 30 billion yuan by the end of the year. The creation of these money markets greatly eased the money shortage that had developed in the wake of the credit-squeezing measures of the PBC early that year. Simultaneous with strengthening the macro-level control function of the central bank, and by operating the local branches of the various specialized banks on a business basis, banking activities were made more flexible and profitable, and several new forms of collecting deposits, granting credit and capital formation were introduced (e.g., deposit certificates, bonds, shares, and the issue, sale, purchase, and discounting of bills of exchange).

Ad 4. In consequence of the growing autonomy and viability of enterprises and the narrowing scope of mandatory state plan instructions, the range and volume of centrally procured and allocated products narrowed significantly. In the wake of the increase in the volume and range of materials and means of production drawn into the scope of market turnover, <u>markets for means of production</u> developed all over the country, where such raw materials of fundamental importance appeared as rolled steel, cement, wood, and coal. These products were produced either under the so-called guidance plans or above the plan targets, and for these the rules allow sales on the markets for producer goods, at prices agreed on between sellers and buyers. In order to diminish opportunities for abuse, in February 1986 the CC of the CPC and the State Council issued ten joint decrees which prohibited the government control and party organizations and leading cadres from setting up and operating various industrial, commercial, and other service companies in order to "invigorate the economy and commodity turnover" or for the purpose of "self-financing official activity." These enterprises had become hotbeds of corruption and profiteering, as well as of abuse of office and power. Such "companies" were headed mostly by leading party and government functionaries who used their authority and influence to lobby for permits and favors, procuring and selling shortage goods, thus gaining unjustified financial advantages for themselves. The practical enforcement of these decrees met with extremely great difficulty and opposition, also shown by the multitude of unmasked abuses in the years that followed.

Ad 5. Following the expansion and deepening of urban economic reform, the reform process gradually spread from the economic basis to the superstructure. <u>The reforms affecting the operational principles and methods of the urban government organs</u> may also be conceived as reform of the system of economic management and of the political system. In the course of 1986, relying on the guidelines issued by the leaders of the State Council, the SRC and the Ministry of Labor and Personnel Affairs implemented some experimental reform measures affecting the organizational setup and work of the government organs in 16 cities of China. On the one hand, these simplified administrative work; on the other, they made it possible to reduce the staff of urban government organs to about one third. The principle followed was: "First decentralize scopes of authority, then shift to the new path, and finally, simplify administration and reduce the staff of the apparatus."

These measures significantly promoted adjustment of the economic control and management functions of the urban government organs to the reform requirements. The changes also affected the work of the central economic management organs (Planning Commission, ministries, bureaus with nationwide authority), and they simplified the work and reduced the staff of urban and territorial committees, directorates, and bureaus.

Ad 6. In 1986 substantial progress was made in economic legislation and in creating legal support for the various reform measures. In the course of the year the Standing Committee of the 6th NPC approved 11 laws and the State Council issued 59 legal decrees, mostly on questions affecting the economy. Beyond the laws and decrees already mentioned, these included a decree of 22 articles, issued in October 1986 by the State Council, on facilitating capital investment and the founding of enterprises by foreign firms in China. This one provided for further favors and accelerated administrative procedures in addition to those contained in "Law no. 39 on enterprises with foreign capital investment in China," promulgated in April 1986.

In spite of the many-sided reform measures taken in several directions, the second main objective set for 1986, i.e., the restoration of macroeconomic equilibrium, was only partially attained. Although the "overheating" of the economy somewhat diminished in the first part of the year - under the impact of various administrative measures and financial restrictions introduced at the beginning of the year, in the second half of the year the investment wave took a new upswing, and the tensions in material and energy supply could not be eased significantly, either. In the course 1986 - computed at unchanged prices and relative to the preceding year - both the total social product and the gross national product increased by 9.8%, national income by 7.8%. The annual growth rate of the gross output value of industrial production reached 11.7% (as against the planned 8%), while that of agricultural production remained 0.6 percentge points below the 4% planned (i.e., 3.4%). Investments increased at current prices by 18.7% in 1986, and the retail trade turnover - similarly at current prices - increased by 15%. The price level of consumer goods rose by only 6% in 1986 as against 8.8% in the preceding year, but the living costs of the urban population grew by 7%. Essentially less success was attained in that year in reducing the trade deficit; from US $14.9 billion in 1985 it diminished to US $12 billion by 1986. The balance of the state budget showed a deficit of more than 7 billion yuan, as against a surplus of 2.2 billion yuan in 1985. The method of deficit financing was again used: the quantity of money in circulation grew in the course of the year by 23.3%, and its amount in absolute terms exceeded 120 billion yuan at the end of the year. Foreign money sources were increasingly used. While in 1985 US $4.7 billion in foreign monetary resources were used (US $2.7 billion in the form of loans and US $2 billion in direct capital investment), in 1986 the sum of foreign loans and direct capital investments was US $7.3 billion, (of which 5 billion were loans and 2.3 billion direct investment). But the number of new investment agreements with foreign firms fell in 1986 to half of the number in 1985 and also the amounts invested through them fell to almost the same extent (from US $6.3 billion to 3.3 billion).

The difficulties and failures experienced in the restoration of macroeconomic equilibrium shook the trust of a considerable number of the leading party and government cadres in the possibility and success of management with economic and financial methods. This came at the most opportune time for the cadres who were opposed to the reforms, mainly for political and ideological reasons and on existential considerations, and they launched a new attack on the reform and opening policy.

Footnotes to Chapter Five

1. Jingji Tizhi Gaige Shouce (Handbook of the reform of the economic system). Wang Zhiye, Zhu Yuanzhen (eds) "Jingji Ribao" Chubanshi (Economic Daily Publishing House, Beijing 1987 (Henceforth: JTGS) pp 304-305
2. ZJN 1985, P. IV/p 37
3. Zhongguo Tongji Nianjian (henceforth: ZTN), Beijing 1985 (Statistical Yearbook of China) p 526
4. ZJN 1985, P. IV/p 37
5. JTGS, pp 319-324
6. Ibid., pp 15-19
7. Ibid., pp 20-22
8. ZJN 1984, P.O/p 3 - O/p 8
9. ZJN 1985, P.I/p 38
10. Ibid., P. I/pp 41-42
11. Ibid., P. X/pp 5-8
12. For example, the "plan price" for rolled steel sections was 600 yuan/ton in 1986. At the same time, the "agreed price" ranged from 1100 to 1200 yuan/ton.
13. The "free price" of rolled steel sections, quoted in the above example, was 1600-1700 yuan/ton in 1986. The steel works supplied steel sections to the rural and urban collective enterprises and private ones at this price, - in restricted quantities.
14. Problemi upravlenyija selskim khozjajstvom Kitaja. Moscow, 1985. p 111
15. See: <u>Beijing Review</u> (henceforth: BR), vol. 28, nos. 39, 40, 41
16. BR, vol. 28, no. 40, p 18
17. Ibid, p 19
18. BR, vol. 28, n. 39, p 16
19. Ibid. p 19
20. From that time on, negative references to the Hungarian and Yugoslav examples were to be found with increasing frequency also among those opposing the introduction of a market economy, that is, as "deterrent" examples. At the same time,

the "moderate reform" and conservative factions of Chinese leadership showed increasing interest in the system of economic management in the "most successful socialist country," the GDR, and in various ideas about the reform of the Soviet economic system. This was manifest in the "changes in the travel route" of Chinese expert delegations.

Chapter Six
SLOWDOWN OF THE REFORM PROCESS (1987-1988)

Hidden Attack on the Reform and Opening Policy Under the Pretext of Struggle Against "Bourgeois Liberalization"

Orthodox and conservative forces launched open or concealed ideological and political onslaughts against almost every phase of the reform policy. While the reform policies were taking shape, these attacks and manifestations presented no serious obstacles and appeared to be merely caviling by cadres who could not rid themselves of the old ways of thinking and the command methods they had become accustomed to. The main reason for their insignificance was that in the wake of palpable success (e.g., improving market supply, growing earnings, rising living standards) the reform policy enjoyed ever greater support from the masses. At the same time, the earlier extreme-left politics became increasingly discredited, even among the cadres, as freedom of speech expanded and the horrors of the "cultural revolution" were exposed in the press. Serious disturbances and a certain halt were caused only by the excessive ideological campaign launched in the autumn of 1983 against the "intellectual pollution." However, in early 1984 the party leadership succeeded in braking this campaign and in channeling it into a narrower framework.

After the party conference of 1985 the critics of the reform and opening policy again became active and unambiguously ascribed the various negative phenomena and disorders to it. They particularly castigated the desire to accumulate money and property, which was growing among certain groups of the population, and the various abuses in the economy that had also been unmasked by the press (which were committed mostly by leading cadres on different levels or by their children). Some of them made attempts to ascribe these phenomena to "harmful external effects" (foreign films, books, magazines, television, the behavior of foreign tourists and businessmen, etc.) and attributed them, in the last resort, to the "opening outward." Perhaps the most effective answer to such charges was given by Deng Xiaoping, when he declared at the end of 1985: "There are those who say we should not open our windows, because open windows let in flies and other insects. They want the windows to stay closed, so we all expire from lack of air. But we say 'Open the windows, breathe the fresh air and at the same time fight the flies and insects.'"[1]

In the second half of 1986 the pressure of conservative forces wishing to slow down the reform and to restore macroeconomic equilibrium, mainly by strengthening central control and management but also with administrative measures, again became palpable. They could be found at every level of management, but their bases were above all the central economic management organs, some departments of the CC, CPC, and the provincial and urban party and government organs intertwined with each other. Their objection to the introduction of the "manager responsibility system" was already mentioned in the preceding chapter, but we could equally have mentioned their violent attacks against the approval and application of the "bankruptcy law". For these conservative and antireform groups within the party and government leadership, the student movement taking place in some large cities of China at the end of 1986 was a godsend. First, it manifested itself merely in objections to the miserable conditions prevailing at the universities and other institutions of higher education (crowdedness, low scholarships, poor food) and took the form of newspapers with big characters ("tatsepao"), sit-down strikes, demonstrations and marches, but later - parallel to demanding autonomy for the universities - they increasingly took on the character of political demonstrations. The students' demands included the radical reform of the system of political institutions and its democratization, full democratic rights for young people starting on their career (e.g., free choice of place of work, filling posts by competition). During their demonstrations slogans appeared on their posters, such as: "No economic reform without political reforms", or "Only free people can perform genuine creative work." Also the local party committees were condemned for treating their "subjects" as "feudal lords" did, and for striving to preserve their privileges.

Analyzing the situation in early 1987, the Political Bureau of the CC, CPC, made Secretary General Hu Yaobang responsible for the "bourgeois liberal" ideas spreading among a part of the intelligentsia, as he had been too lenient with the representatives and propagators of these ideas. At the extended session of the PB, held on January 16, 1987, a resolution was adopted according to which "Hu Yaobang's request to be relieved from the function of secretary general of the CC, CPC, was unanimously accepted" and Prime Minister Zhao Ziyang was charged to fulfill this function as "acting secretary general."

The relieving of Hu Yaobang from his post as secretary general was - in spite of the "promotion" of Zhao Ziyang - a heavy blow, or at least a serious warning to the "reform wing" of the CPC leadership, and it could not fail to have an impact on the power relations in domestic politics. It affected the compromise and balance that had come about at the national party conference, in the autumn of 1985, between the forces committed to the reform and opening policy and making efforts to consistently implement it, and both the "moderate reformers", who agreed with this policy only with reservations, and the "antireformers" who rejected it. After the PB session in January, some leading intellectual cadres "infected by bourgeois liberalism" were soon expelled from the party (university professors, leaders of research institutes, writers, artists) and, related to this, a campaign was launched within the party against "bourgeois liberalism." Although, having learned from the fight against "intellectual pollution" 2 and a half years earlier, the leaders made an effort to restrict this campaign to the ideological and cultural sphere, its impact was also felt for a few months in the field of economic reform and in the development of China's external economic relations.

In addition, the fight against "bourgeois liberalism" unfolded in those months (February, March, April) when the party leadership was preparing for the 13th national congress to be convened in the autumn of 1987. The main preliminary point on the agenda was the elaboration and approval of guidelines related to the reform of the political system. Although the expansion of the ideological fight against "bourgeois liberalism" into a mass movement was prevented - thanks to the firm stand taken by Deng Xiaoping and Zhao Ziyang - still, the committed advocates of the reform and opening policy were rather pushed into the background in the mass media in the first 5 months of 1987 and had to take a defensive position. It was only beginning in June that the continuation of reform and opening became more powerful and emphasis could be put on the necessity of completing the economic reforms with political ones. Still, even in early August five well-known scientists were relieved of their leading posts (and four of them were expelled from the party as well), precisely because of their "liberal" views about the political reforms. (Among them was professor Su Shaozhi, already mentioned in an earlier chapter, who had visited Hungary twice, and who was now relieved as director of the Institute for Marxism-Leninism-Mao Zedong Thought of the CASS but not expelled from the party.)

In this precarious political situation even the leaders most committed to reform were compelled to exhibit more cautious behavior towards the economic reforms decided on earlier and to emphasize the importance of creating stability. The editorial of Renmin Ribao that appeared on January 1, 1987, identified insistence on the "four basic principles" as the main guarantee for correct application of the policy of opening and reform. It was on the same day that the "Land management law of the PRC" took effect. It laid down that "in the PRC the socialist public ownership of land is realized; no unit or person may occupy it, buy or sell it, lease it or cede it in any form in an illegal way." (This law was modified 1 year later.) The price reform was repeatedly suspended and the importance of strengthening price control and basically preserving the stability of market prices was underlined. In this report on the work of the government to the 5th session of the 6th NPC, which convened in March 1987, Prime Minister Zhao Ziyang summed up the main tasks in continuing the economic reform in the following five points:

1. To deepen the enterprise reform; to create and perfect an enterprise management system based on the mutual interrelations of responsibility, scope of authority, and interests

2. To further develop the various horizontal economic unions, stimulating the creation of associations of enterprises and groups of enterprises; to deepen the reform of the financial system, thus promoting the flexible use and mobility of different forms of social capital

3. To further expand the market of the means of production in the interest of bringing about conditions propitious for enhancing the vitality of firms

4. To reform the employment and wage system of enterprises, gradually improving the distribution relations in firms

5. To improve the method of managing fixed capital investments, further increasing economic efficiency.

It may be seen from the above list that for 1987, the Chinese leadership essentially provided for the continuation of reforms begun in former years, without setting new tasks. In practice this meant a break in the momentum of the comprehensive economic reform - the so-called urban reform - started in 1985-1986, and it resulted in a slowdown of the entire reform process.

Serious difficulties were also met with in implementing the second step of the rural economic reform, since the goals set for increasing agricultural output in the national economic plan could not be attained in 1986 with respect to most agricultural products. Although the output of grain rose from 379.1 million tons in 1985 to 391.5 million tons by 1986, a considerable decline was seen in cotton, in oil and sugar crops, and in fiber plants. The interest and production zeal of peasants continued to be directed toward industrial and commercial activities, which increased at a fast rate in both 1986 and 1987.

The growth rate of investments, at current prices, again showed a rising tendency: from 18.7% in the preceding year to 20.6% in 1986. Nor did efficiency improve; rather it deteriorated somewhat. The 14.1% annual growth of the social product was accompanied by a 10.6% increase in the GNP and by a 10.5% increase in the national income. There were indications of excess employment in both industry and agriculture, and the unmistakable signs of latent unemployment began to appear. The gross value of industrial output increased in 1987 by 17.7% (that of rural industries by 34.3%!) and that of agricultural production by 5.8% (that of crop production by 5.8%). The annual output of grain was 404.7 million tons, still 2.6 million below the record harvest of 407.3 million tons in 1984. The output of the other more important products approximated the average level of the preceding years.

The value of retail sales - at current prices - was 17.6% higher than in the preceding year, while the consumer price level rose - on account of accelerating inflation - by 7.3%. The price rise was essentially higher in the cities (15%-20% on the free markets) and, as a consequence, the living costs of blue- and white-collar workers increased by 9%-10%, with which the 9.8% rise of average wages and salaries just kept pace. By strongly curbing imports, keeping them at the level of the preceding year, and by increasing exports by 27.6%, the trade deficit of the country was reduced in 1987 to US $3.8 billion - down from US $12 billion in 1986. As a result, the foreign exchange reserves of the PRC increased in 1 year from US $10.5 billion to US $15.2 billion. In spite of having attracted foreign monetary resources in the amount of nearly US $8.5 billion, of which direct capital investment by foreign firms amounted to US $2.6 billion, the balance of public finances was not restored; the budget closed in 1987 with a deficit of 8 billion yuan. (This was merely 3.4% of the budget revenues.) The quantity of money in circulation increased in the course of the year by only 19.4% and in absolute terms it amounted to somewhat more than 145 billion yuan. The accumulated amount of savings deposits of the population with banks and saving cooperatives of the country reached nearly 270 billion yuan by the end of 1987, meaning an additional potential purchasing power of 46% relative to the annual retail sales turnover of 582 billion yuan. Under such conditions stability on the domestic market could not be attained; with demand far exceeding supply, an increase in inflation had to be expected. Beginning in 1987, this became one of the gravest concerns of the Chinese economic leaders, one which had to be increasingly reckoned with in the further planning and implementation of the reform process.

Strengthening of Reform and Opening Policy at the 13th National Congress of the CPC

In spite of the criticism and concealed attacks on the reform and opening policy, beginning in June 1987 the leaders of reform in the CPC and the PRC again took the initiative. They launched a genuine ideological offensive in the Chinese press and other mass media in order to provide theoretical foundations for the reform and opening policy and for their consolidation from ideological and political aspects. Reform economists had already published a number of high-standard theoretical articles and reports of practical experiences in the dailies and the professional press in order to support and deepen the concept of the comprehensive economic reform. Beginning in June, the economic analyses were complemented by ideological articles and analyses. In harmony with the concept then spreading in the Soviet Union as well, the "revolutionary" character of the reforms and the necessity of total "change of model" were more and more frequently emphasized. The reforms that had developed in China since 1979 were called the "second revolution," without the consistent implementation of which the "socialist modernization" of the country could not be realized. Comprehensive analyses were published about the outstanding results of the reforms implemented through 8 years in all fields of economic and social life and, besides urging continuation of the reforms, the demand for a radical reform of the existing political system was also given greater emphasis. To support it, the first theoretical writings were published in August and September of 1987; they interpreted the earlier statement that the development of Chinese society was "in the initial stage of socialism" that may last even 60-70 years, depending on when the huge historical task of the socialist modernization of the country will have been solved. According to these interpretations, in this "initial stage" the main task was to develop the forces of production and, accordingly, to establish ownership and distribution relations as well as to create a political superstructure which would promote a fast and harmonious development of the forces of production of Chinese society, the socialist modernization of the country and society, and accomplishment of the material and intellectual civilization. All these ideas were basic to the preparation for the 13th national congress of the CPC, which was held in Beijing between October 25 and November 1, 1987.

According to the organizational rules of the CPC, the 13th national congress of the party was convened 5 years after the 12th congress. It took place when some of the problems that had emerged in the meantime had already been solved by the national party conference held in the autumn of 1985, or at least the road to be followed was marked and the main guidelines were set for general policies. However, the compromise established there proved to be fragile in many respects during the 1-1.5 years following the party conference and seemed to break up. This is why one of the most important tasks of the 13th congress was to restore the unity and striking power of the party, if in no other way than by forming a new compromise based on new principles.

Because of the reshuffle among the highest party leaders, real preparations for the 13th congress began only in February 1987. Although the questions to figure on the agenda of the next congress had been decided at the 6th plenary session of the 12th CC, held in October 1987, the actual work of the teams engaged in preparing the documents to be submitted began only 4 months later. It was long debated whether the congress should approve a separate resolution on the reform of the political system, or whether the subject should be included in the report of the CC and be approved in this manner. Finally, in August 1987, the latter solution was chosen, mainly because most of the CC members believed that the draft resolution worked out in connection with the reform of the political system was too radical. (It was at that time that the five social scientists were relieved and four of them expelled from the party, because they had participated directly in the elaboration of the draft resolution.)

The report of the CC to the congress was completed after extremely lively and fierce debates. The outlines were debated for 2 months (March-April) and the draft of the text for a further 5 months (from May till October). Altogether, seven versions were drafted, and it is characteristic of the hard fights that even at the CC session immediately preceding the opening of the congress, 150 diverse corrections were made in the text - the sixth one - there submitted. The drafting of the report of the Central Commission for Discipline Inspection was accompanied by similarly hot debates. At the congress itself - in addition to these two reports - the report of the Central Advisory Commission and the proposal for modification of the Party Constitution were also read and approved. Next, the members of the leading party bodies were elected, and in this framework new and important personnel changes took place as a way of rejuvenating and enhancing expertise.

As distinct from the preceding four congresses, the 13th congress of the CPC received wide publicity. In addition to the more than 1900 delegates, several hundred invited personalities and more than 400 representatives of the Chinese and international press participated at the plenary sessions. Chinese television reported live on the events several times a day and also transmitted interviews with the participants about their impressions and opinions. Foreign party delegations did not participate at the Chinese party congress this time either, but most of the "brotherly parties" - among them the Hungarian Socialist Workers' Party - greeted the 13th congress in telegrams. (By the summer of 1987, the CPC had restored relations broken or "suspended" in preceding decades with all Eastern-European communist and workers' parties - with the exception of the CPSU and the Albanian Workers' Party.)

At the first plenary session of the congress, opened on October 25, 1987, following a few introductory words by Deng Xiaoping, it was acting General Secretary Zhao Ziyang who read the report of the CC, which consisted of 35 000 characters i.e., about 70 typewritten pages). The report was published in the Chinese press under the title: "Advance along the road of socialism with Chinese characteristics."[2] The report consisted of seven main parts with the following titles:

   I Historic achievements and the tasks of the current congress
  II The primary stage of socialism and the basic line of the party
 III The strategy for economic development
  IV Reforming the economy
   V Reforming the political system
  VI Strengthening party building while carrying out reform and the open policy
 VII Striving to win new victories for Marxism in China

The most conspicuous feature of the report to the congress was the effort it made to provide stable theoretical bases - that are flexible in the long run but can also be defended from the ideological aspect - for social progress and economic construction, the fundamental objective of which is to develop and modernize the forces of production of society faster and more efficiently than before. In fact, every planned measure - the multiphase strategy of economic development, reform of the economic and political systems, strengthening party building, development of the theory of Marxism, continuation of the policy of opening - was subordinated to this basic objective. At the same time, this is the decisive criterion by which it was intended to measure the success and efficiency of the policy worked out by the party in the future.

There can be no doubt that the greatest result of the 13th congress of the CPC was the fact that it repeatedly confirmed the political guideline followed since the 3rd plenary session of the 11th CC: the policy of reform and opening. This was achieved although the policy was being criticized and attacked from many sides, and it testifies to the sound tactical acumen of the "reformist" leaders. From the point of view of emphasis on results it proved to be advantageous that in the first part of the report the most important achievements, not only those of the 5 years between the two congresses but also those of the preceding 9 years, were summed up, and it was attempted to draw conclusions for the future from them. It was important that next the report identified acceleration and deepening of the reform as the "central task" of the congress.

From the theoretical aspect, the most significant part of the report is Chapter Two, which expounds, in the context of the main guideline of the party, the concept of "the primary stage of socialism." The following introductory sentences are quoted here:

"A correct understanding of the present historical stage of Chinese society is of prime importance for building socialism with Chinese characteristics, and it is the essential basis on which to formulate and implement a correct line and correct policies.

Our Party has already made a clear and definite statement on this question: China is now in the primary stage of socialism. There are two aspects to this thesis. First, the Chinese society is already a socialist society. We must persevere in socialism and never deviate from it. Second, China's society is still in its primary stage. We must proceed from this reality and not jump over this stage. Under the specific historical conditions of contemporary China, to believe that the Chinese people cannot take the socialist road without going through the stage of fully developed capitalism is to take a mechanistic position on the question of the development of revolution, and that is the major cognitive root of Right mistakes. On the other hand, to believe that it is possible to jump over the primary stage of socialism, in which the productive forces are to be highly developed, is to take a utopian position on this question, and that is the major cognitive root of Left mistakes."[3]

With this formulation - independent of its scientific foundation and validity (which we will evaluate in one of the theoretical chapters to follow) - the Chinese reform leaders maneuvered themselves into the position of a "party center" carrying on a "fight on two fronts." This involved fighting against both the "Right deviationists," who questioned the policy of reform and opening and the justification for the existence of a "socialist road" for Chinese social development and wished to guide it to a "capitalist road," and the "Left deviationists," who opposed the reform and opening policy by branding it "Right deviation." Then, summing up the historical lessons of development in the past decades, the report explains the main characteristics of the primary stage of Chinese socialism in detail, together with the guidelines for deriving lessons from the realities of this stage for the future development of society. The following key sentence refers to the main guideline of the party:

"The basic line of our Party in building socialism with Chinese characteristics during the primary stage of socialism is as follows: to lead the people of all our nationalities in a united, self-reliant, intensive and pioneering effort to turn China into a prosperous, strong, democratic, culturally advanced and modern socialist country by making economic development our central task while adhering to the four cardinal principles and persevering in reform and the opening policy."[4]

In the interpretation of the "four cardinal principles" as well as the relationship between them and the reform and opening policy, we again encounter the emphasis on a dialectical approach and on the necessity of a "two-front fight":

"The two basic points - adherence to the four cardinal principles and adherence to the reform and opening policy - are interrelated and mutually dependent, and they are integrated in the practice of building socialism with Chinese characteristics. We must not interpret the four cardinal principles as something rigid, lest we come to doubt or even reject the general principle of reform and opening to the outside world. Neither can we interpret reform and the open policy as something bourgeois liberal, lest we deviate from the path of socialism."[5]

But the following two sentences are also deserving of attention: "The struggle to eliminate the interference and influence of the two erroneous tendencies - hidebound thinking and liberalization - will last through the primary stage of socialism. Since the old Left habits of thought are deep-rooted and since they are the main source of the obstacles to reform and the open policy, the major task for quite a long time will be to overcome the hidebound thinking."[6] This is clear speech and testifies to a profound knowledge of the actual situation.

The following, third and fourth, chapters of the report discussing the strategy of economic development and the reform of the economic system do not reveal much novelty relative to the earlier published documents. The former repeats the principles and tasks laid down in the seventh 5-year plan, the latter those formulated at the last session of the 6th NPC. This is well indicated by the titles of the subsections listing the further tasks related to the reform of the economic system.[7] The longest part of the report is the fifth chapter, dealing with the reform of the political system. Its contents will be reviewed in a separate chapter of this book. Also the seventh, concluding chapter of the report is worthy of attention: it is here that we first meet with theses and views, drafted in single sentences, by the leaders of the CPC, who felt that by formulating them they had contributed in a creative manner to the development of Marxist philosophy, the political economy, and the theory of scientific socialism, outlining at the same time the theory of building socialism with Chinese characteristics.[8]

The results of the elections to the leading posts, held on the last day of the congress, did not basically change the earlier established power relations in the leading bodies of the CPC, in spite of the rather considerable number of personnel changes. "Withdrawal" of the old leaders (Deng Xiaoping, Chen Yun, and Li Xiannian) and the earlier leaving of Hu Yaobang almost completely changed the composition of the five-member Standing Committee of the PB. Besides the post of secretary general for Zhao Ziyang, places were given to Li Peng (then acting prime minister, aged 58), Qiao Shi (member of the Secretariat, first secretary of the Central Commission for Discipline Inspection, 63), Hu Qili (leader of the Secretariat, 58), and Yao Yilin (deputy prime minister, chairman of the State Planning Commission, 70). From the earlier PB of 22 ordinary and two alternate members, ten ordinary members and one alternate member were left. The newly elected PB has only 17 ordinary members and one alternate. It is worth noting that Hu Yaobang, the general secretary relieved in January at 72 years of age, remained a member of the new PB. The new Central Committee has 175 ordinary and 110 alternate members, that is, their number has been reduced in both categories by 30. Considering also the changes implemented at the party conference of 1985, merely one third of the membership of the 13th CC were also members of the 12th CC, elected in 1982. Chen Yun, then 82, (first secretary of the Central Commission for Discipline Inspection) was elected chairman of the 200-member Central Advisory Commission, replacing Deng Xiaoping in this post. (At that time, Deng Xiaoping assumed only the chairmanship of the Military Commission of the CC for a few years.) The membership of the Central Commission for Discipline Inspection was reduced to exactly half - from 138 to 69 - and, as has been mentioned, at its head Chen Yun was replaced by Qiao Shi, one of the CC secretaries.

Thus, the 13th congress of the CPC again succeeded in achieving a compromise in the renewed leading party bodies to demonstrate unity between the representatives of the various trends (reformists, moderates, conservatives). The composition by persons changed, but the proportions were on the whole the same. The unity was the result of a compromise which affected above all the rate, depth, and breadth of the realization of planned reforms. Although the resolutions of the congress confirmed the reform and opening policy, it was clear that, in continuing the policy during the next few years, rather slow progress, interspersed with cautious forward steps and retreats, was to be reckoned with rather than grand, spectacular radical reform steps and reform measures.

1988: The "Critical" Year of the Reform

1988 was the tenth year of implementing the reform and opening policy. According to the traditional lunar calendar, consisting of 12-year cycles and adopted in China and throughout the Far East, that year was "the year of the dragon" and, according to tradition, it was supposed to bring people joy, happiness, flowering, and good luck. It was the second time that this prophecy did not come true in China, however. In the preceding "year of the dragon," 1976, there was a devastating earthquake in the vicinity of Beijing and Tientsin (with its epicentre in Tangshan) which caused the death of several hundred thousand people. In that year the three best-known Chinese leaders died: Zhou Enlai, Zhu De, and Mao Zedong, and the economy of the country moved "to the brink of collapse." In early 1988, again, grave economic troubles were foreshadowed: inflation accelerated, because of supply difficulties rationing of sugar, pork, and later even of eggs had to be reintroduced in cities. Thus, the tenth year of the reform had become a critical year of the reform process.

In the first half of the year the reformist leaders of the CPC were still optimistic and made efforts to translate the theoretical guidelines confirmed by the 13th congress into practice. The New Year editorial in Renmin Ribao, entitled: "We greet the tenth year of the reform," stated that the reform had entered a new stage, in the course of which the main tasks were to deepen reform on the one hand and to stabilize the economy on the other. In his speech greeting the new year, acting Prime Minister Li Peng also said that in 1988 steps would be accelerated in several fields of the reform of the economic system. At the same time, he called attention to the dangers arising from the overheating of the economy, from demand far exceeding supply, from looseness in economic discipline, which - if not overcome - could disadvantageously affect the whole reform process.

In the course of the first quarter, General Secretary Zhao Ziyang several times confirmed the resoluteness of the party leaders to continue the reform and judged the economic situation favorable for it, although he, too, pointed to the necessity and importance of braking inflation. He dealt intensively with the strategic problem of developing the economy in the "coastal areas" of key importance for the opening policy. He urged the quickest possible elaboration of the "enterprise act" and its approval, comprehensive reform of the commercial system, and continuation of the reform of the price system, and he also envisaged a new phase in the reform of the wage system. These declarations of the general secretary did not evoke unanimous enthusiasm and support in the higher circles of the party and government leadership, although Deng Xiaoping himself threw in his authority to support the guideline of Zhao Ziyang. At the 2nd plenary session of the 13th CC, held in March 1988, several older leaders voiced their anxiety in connection with the consequences of a too radiply growing economy and accelerating inflation.

The first session of the newly elected 7th NPC was held on March 25, 1988. Li Peng, acting prime minister, reported on the work of the government, and at this session he was formally elected president of the State Council. In his speech he summed up the results of the preceding 5 years in socialist construction and reform, together with the problems emerging, he reviewed the tasks of the government related to the economic, political, and social development in the coming 5 years, and he discussed in detail the foreign policy tasks of the PRC.

Speaking about the problems, he mentioned above all the unjustifiably fast and steep price rises, which had prevented a rise in the living standards of the population during the past few years; some groups of the urban population had even experienced a decline in living standards. He analyzed the causes of rising prices in detail, the factors producing a demand exceeding supply, and declared that, in spite of the emerging difficulties, the government would not abandon its ideas related to the consistent implementation of the price reform, but it would make efforts to proceed more circumspectly in the future and take proper measures to see that the living standards of the population did not decline as a consequence of the unavoidable price rises.[9] The head of the government criticized the trend to striving for unjustifiably rapid and spectacular economic development. (Many of the foreign observers deemed to discover in this a critique of the economic development trend represented by Zhao Ziyang.) He promised severe retaliation against those committing various economic abuses and unlawful actions, and proclaimed a consistent fight against every form of bureaucracy in the work of government organs and institutions.

Li Peng was of the opinion that the average economic growth rate planned for the 5-year period between 1988 and 1992 was optimal, as it would help to safely attain the objectives of economic and social development set earlier: quadrupling the combined output of industry and agriculture by the turn of the millenium and ensuring that the population of the country - more than 1.2 billion by that time - should live then under conditions of a "moderate welfare" (in Chinese: xiao kang). But it was an essential condition that the government should make every effort to consistently and vigorously implement the policy worked out at the 13th congress of the CPC. That is, under the conditions of the primary stage of socialism, insistence on the "four basic principles" and adherence to the reform and opening policy was necessary.

More than half of the government report was a detailed exposition of the objectives, principles, and tasks related to economic development in the next 5 years and to the reform, grouped around ten major tasks.[10] Since they do not comprise new elements relative to the goals set in the seventh 5-year plan and at the 13th party congress, we will not review them here. Li Peng emphasized that in order to implement these tasks the reforms had to be at the center of China's economic, political, and social life and activities, and the primary task ought to be the uninterrupted development of the forces of production. At the same time, with the deepening and acceleration of economic reform also the implementation of the reform of the political system had to be accelerated, above all in the direction of developing a socialist democracy.

The government report submitted to the first session of the Chinese parliament dealt with the foreign policy of the country in unusual length and detail. It qualified the policy pursued as successful and expedient and stated that the adjustments and modifications in this field were correct. It dealt with the development of Sino-American and Sino-Soviet relations and, as regards the latter, it expressed satisfaction with the expansion and improvement of relations, mentioning at the same time that the well-known obstacles to complete normalization of these relations had not yet been removed. Speaking about the relations between China and Eastern Europe, Li Peng said that these relations had developed spectacularly in the past few years. The PRC had normalized its relations with Poland, the GDR, Czechoslovakia, Hungary, and Bulgaria. China was ready to exchange with these countries the experiences of socialist construction and the reform, to develop fraternal relations in every field on the basis of mutual esteem, full equality of rights, and mutual advantages.

The first session of the 7th NPC took place under conditions of unusually wide publicity and in a rather democratic atmosphere. It was the first time that the population and representatives of the foreign press had an opportunity to gain insight - through television transmissions and direct interviews - into the work and debates of the various parliamentary committees. On such occasions also opposing opinions were heard, and when votes were taken, also votes against and abstentions occurred. At this session, in addition to discussion and acceptance of the government report, articles 10 and 11 of the constitution of the PRC were also modified, in the course of which the right to land use was allowed to be transferred "according to legal prescriptions," and the part relating to private ventures was complemented with the following sentences: "The state allows the existence and development of private ventures in the framework defined by law. The private venture is a complement to the economy in socialist public ownership. The state protects the legal rights and interests of private ventures, and directs, supervises and controls the private ventures."[11]

At this session also the draft of the law on state enterprises was discussed and further modifications were implemented. Related to this law, there were fierce debates about the mode of application of the earlier enacted "bankruptcy law". The decision on the further "streamlining" of government organs was another important event of the spring session of parliament, in the spirit of which 14 ministries and government commissions were amalgamated and/or reorganized within 2 months. As a result, the number of ministries and state commissions working under the direct control of the State Council was reduced from 45 to 41. The Ministries for Energy and Water Management as well as of Labor and Personnel Affairs were divided into two, while some industrial ministries were amalgamated. The earlier State Economic Commission was merged with the State Planning Commission, while the staffs of both institutions were substantially reduced. Several ministries received new heads (e.g., the Ministry for Foreign Affairs, the Ministry for Defense), as did the Planning Commission and the People's Bank of China. In place of State President Li Xiannian, who retired because of his age, the earlier minister of defense, Marshall Yang Shangkun, and in place of Peng Zhen as chairman of the parliament, deputy prime minister Wan Li was elected. Yao Yilin, member of the Standing Committee of the PB of the CC, an advocate of the "primacy of plan-control" and of "moderate reforms," became chairman of the Planning Commission. The new minister of foreign affairs, Qian Qichen had spent years in the Soviet Union - similar to Prime Minister Li Peng - and beginning in 1982 he had led the Sino-Soviet negotations on the deputy foreign ministerial level on the part of China.

Despite the optimistic atmosphere of the parliamentary session, beginning in April 1988 disquieting phenomena became increasingly frequent and also the debates about the expedient direction and rate of the reform were renewed. The overwhelming majority of the party and state leaders were particularly anxious about the continued fast growth of industrial production (particularly in rural industries) and the acceleration of price rises. Among economists, a vivid and in some places very sharp debate evolved about the causes and components of accelerating inflation, and various - in some cases diametrically opposed - proposals were made to properly handle the problem. Some proposed curbing the economic growth rate - if necessary, by means of administrative and financial restrictions - while others believed the way out lay in further liberalization of commodity trade and prices, that is, in developing a genuine market competition. Others, again, emphasized the need for a radical reform of the system of state ownership, bound by bureaucratic rules, for leasing state enterprises, for transforming them into joint stock companies and other forms of enterprise. Professor Li Yining, professor at the Beijing University and member of the Standing Committee of the NPC, known for his radical views, warned in one of his articles in May 1988 that the ever more chaotic economic relations might provide opportunity for the advocates of centralization to stop the reforms under the pretext of restoring stability, and to start "backward rearrangement." He explained that under the present Chinese management relations the price reform could not bring the desired results; in a shortage economy prices could not become genuine regulators. At the same time, the price reform involved a very high risk for the whole reform process. He also called attention to the danger that - because of the huge stock of savings deposits placed by the population - an inflation exceeding 10% might produce in China a "buying wave" and hysteria (this actually occurred in the autumn of 1988). Therefore, the issue of money and budgetary management had to be controlled more strictly. But his final conclusion was that "since we cannot improve the system taken over from the Soviet Union we must get rid of it." Li Yining believed that the most important tasks were to link the enterprise reforms with those of the ownership system and, in this context, to place stricter requirements on enterprise management as regards efficiency, to reorganize, and to close down nonviable enterprises.

In the middle of the year articles in a dramatic tone were published about the fact that in China about one third of the blue- and white-collar workers had no regular employment in the state sector. At some places of work the redundant "workers" played cards, watched television or "worked on their own." More than one fifth of the state enterprises produced lasting losses and should have been closed down long ago. But, for reasons of prestige and for fear of unemployment the leaders were "keeping them alive" to the detriment and at the expense of well-functioning enterprises. Because of the increasing energy shortage, well-equipped plants were forced to work at reduced capacity, while the mushrooming small plants "devoured" huge quantities of energy as a result of their obsolete and energy-intensive equipment.

The debates about reform continued throughout the summer and, at the end of July, even the usual summer conference of the Chinese party and government leaders in Beidaihe became the scene of sharp debates and arguments. Finally, the conference was interrupted because most of the leaders refused to accept the opinion of economists of the SRC that the price reform could not bring adequate results without a radical transformation of the system of state ownership. Allegedly, Zhao Ziyang proposed a 50% devaluation of the currency and a 20% rise in wages, which were not accepted. Finally, in August an 8% average wage increase was implemented in the state sector, to which urban blue- and white--collar workers received a "wage complement" of 30 yuan to counterbalance the rise in living costs. The situation of the decision makers was made difficult by the fact that they had to choose from five or six different proposals, worked out on the basis of different ideas, behind which at least ten "theoretical schools" could be found. Since even the "reformers" themselves could not agree on the direction and order of the concrete steps and measures of economic policy to be taken, the advocates of "law and order" were put into a more advantageous position.

The 3rd plenary session of the 13th CC was held in Beijing between September 26 and 30, the members listened to the report of Secretary General Zhao Ziyang on behalf of the PB. The session approved - after hard debates - the "guideline and policy aimed at improving the economic environment and rectifying the economic order" and, in principle, also adopted the "preliminary draft of the price and wage reform" as well as "the circular of the CC, CPC, about strengthening and improving ideological and political work within the enterprises." The document appeared in the press on October 1, 1988 - the national holiday of the PRC - with a heading in red characters, and the review of the questions on the agenda of the plenary session and the decisions made was carefully worded. Still, it became clear to readers that on this occasion the reform process had not simply been "adjusted"; it had been significantly braked, in some places completely stopped or "suspended," while central management and the administrative methods of control were restored. With this, indeed, a new stage began in the Chinese reform process, that of restrained and centrally managed reforms.

Slowing Down of the Reform Process Beginning in the Autumn of 1988

At the end of September 1988 the 3rd plenary session of the 13th CC decided "to shift the emphasis of reform and construction in the next 2 years to improving the economic environment and rectifying the economic order." In the interest of curbing price rises they believed it was necessary - while insisting on reform and the general guideline of opening - to take measures with which aggregated social demand could be curbed, inflation braked, and economic life consolidated - above all in the turnover sphere where a chaotic situation had developed. Bringing the economic environment under control and restoration of economic order demanded - in the judgement of the plenum - that the old economic system be replaced by a new one, that macroeconomic control be strengthened and improved and that the efficient production and a growing supply of agricultural and rural sideline products, of light industrial and textile products in demand, of primary energy, and of basic raw materials be attained. Every method and instrument should be used to ensure that the rate of price rises be lower in 1989 than in 1988; in the next year everything had to be subordinated to this goal.

The plenum pointed out that the comprehensive reform had to be continued in a coordinated, directed, and orderly manner because, if prices could not be contained and inflation curbed, the actual creation of the basis of the new economic system was out of the question. Clearly, the deepening of the reform process was not a question simply of price reform, but of many-sided, complex reforms. For the moment, the main task was to strengthen the reform of enterprises, particularly of large and medium-sized enterprises, and efforts in the next year were to be concentrated on this task. In this field further separation of government functions from those of enterprises and actual openness of enterprise management were needed on the one hand, and perfection of the contractual management system, experimental introduction of the joint stock company system, and further development of experiments with "groups of enterprises" on the other hand - with the dominance of the system of public ownership. Only enterprise autonomy, self-financing ability and a mechanism of self-restraint with the macrolevel control of the state can increase the efficiency of management and stem arbitrary price rises.

In the spirit of recentralization, among other things, the following concrete measures were decided on:

- The plans to lift the central control of prices for steel, cement, wood, and other basic materials were put aside, and the central (official) price control was reintroduced for a relatively wide range of consumer articles. Limitation of the price of grain to be sold on the free market was envisaged. In the case of products whose prices had been set by speculators and corrupt officials - e.g., fertilizers sold to peasants, crude oil, and pesticides - price regulation was introduced. By drawing in a wide circle of the population and authorities in charge of public order, "price control troops" were organized nationwide in order to closely watch market activities.

- With the exception of investments defined in the central plan, bank credits made available for industrial investments, for various construction projects and for loss-making enterprises were to be frozen. (The measure did not affect joint ventures with the participation of foreign capital.) The government was to thoroughly scrutinize the activities of those financing companies - until then little controlled - which had proliferated in the past several years and had become sources of unscrupulous lending (many of them were actually liquidated).[12] -

- With the exception of construction projects already approved by the State Planning Commission, the building of office buildings, congress halls, and hotels was to be stopped and no new ones were allowed to be started for 2-3 years.

- The State Council increased the number of "luxury articles," which the public offices could buy only with the permission of higher authorities, from 19 to 23. The list included cars, air-conditioning equipment, and video recorders. Offices buying imported cars, color television sets, or video recorders had to pay a 40% "luxury tax," and on public dinners financed with public money a 20% surtax was levied. Employees of government organs were prohibited from staying at higher-category hotels during their official travels at home or abroad.

- The government created 27 special groups to start a nationwide campaign for 4 months against various kinds of cheating (e.g., tax evasion, profiteering, the payment of unjustified premiums) and to organize the exposure, investigation, and appropriate punishment of such activities in various large cities and provincial centers.

However, all these measures proved to be too late to have any substantial influence on the disadvantageous tendency that appeared in 1988, manifesting itself in the further growth and sharpening of disproportions, tensions, and contradictions that had already begun in preceding years.

Despite every effort, the "overheating" of the economy was not successfully "cooled" in 1988. At unchanged prices, in that year the GNP increased by 11.2% and the national income by 11.4%. The gross output value of industrial production rose by 20.7%, within it that of rural industries by 35%. Fixed capital investment exceeded (at current prices) the level of the preceding year by 18.5% and, even considering rising prices, this indicates a rising volume of investments.

Among manufactured goods, growth was most rapid in household refrigerators (7.4 million, an increase of 84.4%), color televisions (10.3 million sets, 52,8%), tractors (52.1 thousand, 40.4%), cars (646.7 thousand, 37.1%), and pesticides (194.6 thousand tons, 20.7%). Still, there was a chronic shortage of these and many other products on the domestic market, so that even a partial satisfaction of demand required substantial imports.

Although the gross output value of agriculture production increased in 1988 by 3.2% - at constant prices - within it the value of crop production diminished by 0.5%. The grain harvest fell from nearly 405 million tons in the preceding year to 394 million tons (-2.2%). Significant increases were recorded only for sugar cane (+63.2%) and tobacco (+42.4%), while a major decline was seen in oil-bearing plants (-13.6%). The sugar supply faltered throughout, in spite of imports of 1.5 million tons (this is why, in the spring of 1988, the rationing of sugar was reintroduced in cities). The price of tobacco products was raised by 40%. It may be considered an achievement that, in consequence of the "liberalized" prices of the preceding year, pork output rose by more than 10%, but precisely because of the excessively high free market prices, in the cities pork had to be rationed in order to assure 1-1.5 kg per capita at relatively low prices. A general dissatisfaction of the urban population was caused by the 30%-40% rise in the prices of vegetables, highly important for the nutrition of the Chinese people; rationing could not be implemented in this respect. This all indicates that the lag of agricultural output behind the demand of the population for food could not be made up for in 1988, and the supply situation expressly deteriorated.

Retail turnover at current prices was 744 billion yuan in 1988, a nominal increase of 27.8%. Because of the rising prices, however, this was only 7.9% in real terms. It may be considered a positive phenomenon that the nominal value of purchases by public agencies increased at a somewhat slower rate, by slightly more than 20% over the preceding year. But the rate of increase of the consumer price level could not be braked; on a national level the rise was 18.5% (by December it was already 26.7% relative to the same month in the preceding year). Within that, average growth was 17.1% in villages and 21.3% in cities. The prices of foodstuffs increased by 23% (within it of grain by 14.1%, of meat and eggs by 36.8%, of fresh vegetables by 31.7%, of fish products by 31.1%) those of clothing articles by 12.7%, those of daily necessities by 12.2%, those of fuels by 16.1%, and those of medicaments by 24.8%. Against this, the nominal per capita increase of the annual income of the urban population increased in 1988 by 22.2% on a national average and approximated 1120 yuan - meaning in real terms only 1.2%. According to a representative survey made in 13 cities, because of the inflation, for almost 35% of urban families the per capita real income diminished. In the case of the rural population the per capita annual net income reached, on a national average, 545 yuan - meaning a nominal increase of 17.7% and in real terms one of 6.3% relative to 1987. But more than 10% of the rural population did not earn half of the average per capita net income, i.e., they earned below the minimum of 250 yuan regarded as the subsistence level.

The extraction of primary energy increased in 1988 by 4.2% and in terms of a coal equivalent this was 951 million tons (in natural units of measurement, coal output was 970 million tons, crude oil 137 million tons), and 543 billion kWh of electric energy were produced in the country. Still, there were troubles and tensions in energy supply, and in large cities restrictions of electricity supply were an everyday occurrence, causing capacity utilization in some factories to fall to 60%-70%. Despite steel output reaching nearly 60 million tons and that of rolled steel 47 million tons, meeting the demands of engineering, construction, and transportation for steel was a constant headache, let alone agriculture and rural industry, whose "hunger for steel" caused the official average prices of around 1000 yuan/ton to double or treble on the "free market." A similar situation developed in the sales of cement, wood, and fertilizers, despite the corresponding output levels of 203 million tons, 63 million m^3 and 17.7 millions tons. Thus, the "bottlenecks" of Chinese production could not be "expanded" in 1988 either.

The ineffectiveness of various "calls" and measures taken to tighten financial discipline considerably contributed to the "overheating" of the economy and to accelerating inflation. The basic reason is to be found in the duplicity of the functioning of the economic and political systems. These were no longer systems of plan instructions and command in the old sense, but neither were they systems of market economy and specialized management: they were unfortunate mixes of the two. Increased local autonomy favors increased assertion of particular interests and the evasion or beating off of central efforts and instructions, while responsibility for the success or failure of local management is not asserted. The local branches of banks and commercial organizations depend mainly on the local party and government leadership and carry out their orders. This is why the measures of the People's Bank of China aimed at narrowing credit and money supply not only proved to be ineffective, but produced the opposite results. Lacking money in the autumn of 1988, the state procurement agencies were unable for weeks and months to pay the peasants for their agricultural products (a phenomenon not quite unknown to Hungarian readers). At the same time, local office buildings, educational centers, hotels, and guest houses continued to be built, and the "commercial and financial centers" created by various offices received enough circulating funds. The end result was that the quantity of money in circulation increased in 1988 to an extent exceeding every former year - by 46.7% - and in absolute terms it reached 213 bilion yuan. This was an increment of 68 billion yuan, three times the additional issue of 23 billion in the preceding year. In spite of this, the deficit of the budget was 8 billion yuan, not including the foreign loans raised by the state (13 billion yuan) and the state bonds issued at home (also 13 billion yuan). At the end of 1988 the foreign debt of the PRC exceeded US $35 billion.

In 1988 more than 40 000 new investment projects were started in China. In the course of the year 14 000 of these were stopped or "suspended" and thus 44.2 billion yuan "was saved." The amount spent on investments still exceeded 430 billion yuan, which was more than 130 billion above the planned figure.

The foreign trade turnover of China exceeded in 1988 for the first time US $100 billion. The value of bilateral trade was US $102.8 billion at current prices, of which exports amounted to 47.5 (+20.6%) and imports to 55.3 billion dollars (+27.9%). The deficit of trade was thus US $7.8 billion, but the statistical data showed only US $3.1 billion, as the value of commercial credits granted by foreign firms and of commodities imported by them for processing or direct investments are not included in the statistics. The direct investment by foreign firms totaled US $2.6 billion in 1988, i.e., 13.1% more than in the preceding year.

The natural population increase was 14.2% in 1988, meaning a net increment of more than 15.4 million people. As a result, by the end of the year the population of China approximated 1.1 billion. But doubts about the reliability of demographic statistics have become stronger within China itself. In some areas of the country peasant families do not register the birth of girls. This may be concluded from the fact that in these areas the number of boys born has for years exceeded that of girls according to demographic statistics by 14%-17%, while this "male surplus" was only 5%-6% earlier. [13]

Footnotes to Chapter Six

1. <u>TIME</u> (USA), January 6th, 1986, p 14
2. <u>Renmin Ribao,</u> Nov. 4th, 1984
3. "Advance Along the Road of Socialism with Chinese Characteristics" - Report delivered at the 13th national congress of the CPC on October 25, 1987, <u>Beijing Review,</u> vol 30, no 45, Nov. 9-15, 1987 (Centerfold) pp III-IV
4. Ibid., p VI
5. Ibid., p VI
6. Ibid., p VI
7. These subsections and tasks are as follows:
   1. Invigorating enterprises owned by the whole people by separating ownership from managerial authority
   2. Promoting horizontal ties
   3. Speeding up the establishment and improvement of a socialist market system
   4. Gradually improving the macroeconomic control system based mainly on indirect control of enterprises
   5. Developing an economy with different types of ownership, with public ownership remaining predominant

6. Adopting diverse forms of distribution, with distribution according to work remaining predominant, and determining a correct policy in this regard (Ibid., pp XII-XIV)

8. These theses and views are the following:
   - "It is necessary to emancipate the mind, seek truth from facts and take practice as the sole criterion of truth."
   - "People must take their own road in building socialism in the light of the specific conditions of their own countries."
   - "There must be a very long primary stage in the building of socialism in a country that is backward economically and culturally."
   - "The fundamental task for a socialist society is to develop its productive forces and concentrate on a drive for modernization."
   - "The socialist economy is a planned commodity economy."
   - "Reform is an important motivating force for the development of a socialist society, and opening to the outside world is indispensable for the realization of socialist modernization."
   - "Socialist democracy and advanced socialist culture and ideology are essential characteristics of a socialist society."
   - "The two basic points - adherence to the four cardinal principles and adherence to the general policy of reform and opening to the outside world - are interrelated and neither can be dispensed with."
   - "The reunification of the motherland should be achieved by applying the principle of 'one country, two systems'."
   - "A good work style is vital to the very existence of a party in power."
   - "Relations with the Communist Parties and other parties in other countries should be developed on the basis of the principles of independence, complete equality, mutual respect and noninterference in each other's internal affairs."

- "Peace and development are the outstanding issues in the world today." (Ibid., p XXV)
9. According to the report of the government, in order to put a brake on price rises and diminish their negative impact on living standards, the State Council planned the following measures:

"1. We shall continue to reform the irrational pricing system step by step according to plan, readjust prices of agricultural and sideline products and straighten out the price parities among these products and between them and industrial products, so as to promote production.

2. Starting by increasing supply and restricting demand, we shall control the extent of price rises and keep the overall price level relatively stable, preventing the rises from going beyond the endurance of various sectors.

3. The various localities will give appropriate subsidies to workers and office staff for the rationed part of the principal foodstuffs, in accordance with local price rises.

4. We shall work hard to expand the market for means of production and shall fix price ceilings for the major items in that category.

5. We shall tighten control over commodity prices, tighten industrial and commercial administration, build and improve the system of supervision by the masses. We shall call to account and punish according to law any individual or organization that engages in speculation and profiteering or violates the price control regulations."
(Beijing Review, April 25 - May 1, 1988., p 22)

10. Ibid., pp 24-39
11. Xinhua Banyuekan, no. 4, 1988, p 37
12. Related to this measure, several hundreds of state-owned commercial and investment companies were liquidated because of illegal financial maneuvers and transactions serving profiteering and speculation. (It caused some stir in China when the fast-developing and expanding Kang Hua Investment

Company - closely related to Deng Xiaoping's son, Deng Pufang, a handicapped person - was deprived of its commercial and taxation privileges.)
13. <u>Far Eastern Economic Review,</u> March 2, 1989, p 64

Chapter Seven
THE REFORM PROCESS COMES TO A SUDDEN HALT (1989)

Situation in China, Spring, 1989

Half a year after the introduction of the "restrictive measures" in October 1988 (i.e., in March 1989) it became clear that the restrictive policy aimed at "control of the economic environment and restoration of economic order" (henceforth: controlling and putting in order) had not brought the desired result in the short run. Not only did the centralized measures squeezing the supply of money and credit cause difficulties in the first quarter of 1989 in the procurement of agricultural products; they also significantly disorganized industrial production and the whole domestic commodity turnover. Since the measures affected mainly that state enterprises, a growing number of these became insolvent. This insolvency showed not only, and not even mainly, in the cooperative deliveries among firms (since in these cases mutual settlement without cash, through bank accounts, and by issuing bills of exchange was still possible), but also in the procurement of basic agricultural and raw materials, as well as with the payment of wages and premiums. Not infrequently, this entailed the stopping of production or even of work, and this quite naturally resulted in new shortages on the markets. This is why the PBC finally had to relax the restrictions and instruct the industrial, commercial, and other specialized banks to make available the credits on circulating assets needed for continuous purchase of materials and for production.

These chaotic phenomena strengthened the impression or conviction of the leaders of central economic management organs - also felt earlier - that the basic problem was a too rapid decentralization with the introduction of the comprehensive economic reform, and the extensive autonomy given to local organs and enterprises. It followed that these cadres found the way out of the mess in a return - at least temporarily - to the earlier tested methods of central economic control and management, that is, in starting a <u>strong recentralization process.</u>

This effort of the economic leaders, which also had the consent and support of the moderate reformist and conservative wings of the party leadership, renewed the theoretical and ideological debates about the expedient direction and rate of the Chinese economic and political reforms; this had been discussed earlier, but no satisfactory conclusion had been reached. In these debates a new color was introduced by the appearance of a "new authoritarianism" among the Chinese economists and social scientists. With reference to several earlier and current foreign examples, they alleged that a country wishing to catch up and modernize at a fast rate needed not democratic institutions and a decentralized market economy, but above all a strong government and leaders with a large measure of authority, as well as economic growth and modernization directed through plans by the state, and firmly managed and adequately supported centrally. This group did not negate the need for and importance of professional skills and rejuvenation. In the formation of the authoritarian control it even wanted to give a pioneering role to the young, well-trained intelligentsia, preferably those with personal foreign experience. In the last resort, this group wanted to give political power and control - through a necessary change of generations - to a technocratic bureaucracy instead of to the party bureaucracy. Of course, this was not so openly and starkly formulated; in fact, they wanted the leaders in power to think that they were working to protect and consolidate their position.

The advocates of market-oriented and pluralistic economic and political reforms were, of course, against this trend emerging in academic and university circles. They made efforts also using historical and current examples, to prove that an authoritarian and centralized economic and social management could achieve successes only in exceptional cases and mostly for only a short time, while it entailed huge dangers and pitfalls. China had suffered enough for thousands of years from the authoritarian exercise of power, and even its current socioeconomic backwardness was mostly a consequence of it. But for negative experience in this field China need not look to the historical past; it was enough to consider the social development over the past 40--60 years. The Chinese people wanted to live at last liberated, in a free and democratic society, where everyone could prosper according to his own diligence, knowledge, and abilities, and there was no need for new "utopians" and "great helmsmen."

Although this debate was initially conducted with the exclusion of the public, mainly in academic and university circles, in special periodicals, and in newspapers read by the intelligentsia, it could not fail to have an impact on political decision-makers and on the more radical groups of the intelligentsia, demanding economic and political reforms.

The conservative wing of the party and government leadership, which saw new arguments and impetus for counter measures in every new deterioration of the economic and political situation, was satisfied to find that the "clever and learned intellectuals" were not able to take a uniform standpoint in respect of the policy to be pursued in the acute situation and, in fact, proposed diametrically opposed solutions. On the other hand, they were also satisfied and somewhat even comforted to see that some of the representatives of scientific life proposed the strengthening of central control and management, restoration of the authority of the political leadership, and firm, centralized handling of economic and social processes, as in these they saw the "theoretical" support for their own efforts at recentralization. At the same time, they watched and accepted with growing antipathy and anger the ever more radical manifestations of some intellectuals and students, which they attributed completely to the ideological spread of "bourgeois liberalization."

Some of the intelligentsia and the students - seeing the efforts at braking, halting, and even reversing the economic and political reform processes, the harried situation, and the diminishing support for the reform wing within the leadership of the CPC - demanded a resolute continuation and further development of the economic and political reforms and, in this context, put forward ever more radical demands.

On February 16, 1989, in a letter addressed to the Standing Commission of the NPC and the CC of the CPC, 33 leading intellectuals demanded the declaration of amnesty for and the freeing of political prisoners. In early March, in some Beijing universities, calls for overthrowing "authoritarian rule" and the "dictatorship" were posted and independent student organizations were set up to fight for "democracy, freedom and human rights." They declared that Chinese youth wanted to commemorate the 70th anniversary of the "May 4th movement" of 1919 in the spirit of the slogans: "democracy, freedom, human dignity and legal order."

The second session of the 7th NPC opened in Beijing on March 20, 1989, and this time it was in session for 16 days, until April 4. The opening of the session was preceded by calls to support national unity and the government, and these received a particular emphasis at the March 19th session of the CPPCC (the Chinese equivalent of the Patriotic People's Front of other socialist countries). The sessions of this body are usually begun 1 day before the opening of the NPC and are held parallel to those of the NPC. The agenda of the second session of the 7th NPC comprised - in addition to the report of Prime Minister Li Peng on the work of the government in the preceding year - reports on plan fulfillment in 1988, on the annual plan for 1989 for economic and social development, as well as on the implementation of the 1988 budget and on the estimates of the budget for 1989. An act on civil rights was also discussed and accepted, with some modifications, together with another act allowing local authorities in the special economic zone of Shenzhen to pass the necessary regulatory measures in their own area themselves.

The publicity and propaganda of the 1989 parliamentary session were much more reticent than in the preceding year. It was conspicuous that Deng Xiaoping did not appear even once at the sessions, although he was in Beijing and received several foreign guests while they were being held. He himselt felt it necessary to counter conjectures and to justify his absence a few days later with the following words: "I took leave, I wish to protect my health. And what is more important: I will completely withdraw from the scene, let others do the work; this has been my goal for several years already. At the 13th congress new leaders were elected and I am also among the aged leaders who left the PB and its Standing Committee. A new PB was constituted and there is no need, nor would it be good, if the new leaders felt that some power still exercises tutelage above them. In this respect we, the old people, have to possess adequate consciousness."[1]

The report of Prime Minister Li Peng on the work of the government did not contain many new elements. He concentrated on the goal set at the 3rd plenary session of the 13th CC: control of the economic environment and restoration of economic order, and all measures provided for were meant to support the implementation of this central task. Besides, in the report and in the speeches and contributions following it, the importance of social and political stability was repeatedly stressed, so much so that foreign reporters and observers denoted stability as the key word of the session. This frequent underlining of the importance of stability indeed forecast the mass movements of the following 2 months, although the signs were not yet perceptible for external observers.

The report of Li Peng was not devoid of elements of self-criticism. He confessed that in the spring of 1988 the government had been too optimistic in its judgement of the economic performance in 1987, and that in the practical implementation of the price reform it had not sufficiently reckoned with the different interests and possibilities of the enterprises and of the state, nor with the tolerance of the masses. Instead of having responded in time - by consolidating financial discipline and stabilizing prices - to the perceptible and accelerating inflation, it had further relaxed control and initiated further price adjustments. This accelerated inflation even more, which then led to buying fever and to the development of an atmosphere of panic among the population, and finally to a drastic drop in the stock of personal savings deposits. All this had produced a great unrest among the population, shook the stability of society, and diminished political trust in the reform. "If we do not take resolute measures to brake inflation, stabilization of the economy, its development and deepening of the reform are out of the question," concluded the prime minister. Li Peng also warned that "an atmosphere of unrest and uncertainty may fall out for the worse." This latter declaration proved to be prophetic, although no one could then have conceived of the bad things that in the end actually occurred.

As regards the most urgent tasks, the government report stressed above all restoration of the authority of the party and government leadership, of central power, implementation of central instructions without any contradiction, and consolidation of government discipline. It underlined that local interests should everywhere be strictly subordinated to national ones; otherwise, the whole program for control and order would remain merely a piece of paper. Thus, the government report unambiguously and resolutely <u>denoted recentralization as the main guarantee of the measures aimed at stabilization.</u> This contradicted the whole philosophy and practice of the reform up to that point.

As regards the concrete restrictive measures, the government report envisaged about a 20% reduction of investment estimates, a powerful curbing of budget expenditures, and strict control of wage management. The gravest blow was dealt to the collectively owned, individual and private enterprises and productive units, although these had become the most dynamically developing sectors of the Chinese economy since the introduction of the reforms. In 1989 these firms had no access to additional bank loans; many of them were closed down by official order, thus securing raw materials and energy for the state enterprises in industry. At the same time, the taxes on private economic units were raised and, beginning in August, strict financial auditing of every private enterpreneur was envisaged for 2 months, to reveal tax evasion and levy punitive taxes on concealed incomes. It was hoped and expected that the growth rate of gross industrial output and the rate of inflation could be pressed well below the 1989 level with these measures. (In the former respect, the annual plan provided for an 8% growth at constant prices; for the latter no concrete figure was included.)

The reports delivered by Prime Minister Li Peng, Deputy Prime Minister and Chairman of the Planning Commission Yao Yilin, and Minister of Finance Wang Bingqian were critically received by a considerable number of the deputies to the NPC, some of whom were not satisfied with the "collective self-criticism" exercised by the head of the government and demanded the names of those responsible for the mistakes made. This was a quite unusual tone in the Chinese parliament and provoked the displeasure of many of the "old guard," Li Peng evaded the demand partly by emphasizing his own personal responsibility and partly by stating that, because of the collective nature of leadership, nobody could be made personally responsible for past mistakes. (This principle was discarded a few months later when Zhao Ziyang was personally called to account for the explosion of the "counter-revolutionary turmoils" of April and May.) But most of the criticism was addressed at the bureaucratic working style of the government leaders, their propensity for finding administrative solutions and for "burying themselves" in petty, partial problems. There were also some who openly declared that "with tiny balancing steps" and various restrictions the difficulties could hardly be overcome. Many pointed out that the promised political reforms and particularly democratic consultations and dialogues with the masses were missing.

Following the second session of the 7th NPC, the State Council approved an economic reform proposal of 22 points, worked out for 1989 by the SRC. These proposals can be grouped around the five main goals formulated below:

1. Deepening of the reform and increasing economic efficiency have to be considered as prime tasks.

2. A macroeconomic regulatory system advantageous for global equilibrium and structural improvements has to be brought about gradually.

3. By controlling and directing consumption, by alleviating injustices in distribution, the transformation of the allocation mechanism has to be promoted.

4. By restoring market order, the development of the market has to be promoted.

5. Research related to the medium-range program of the reform and the work of elaboration has to be strengthened, the complex reform experiments have to be kept firmly in hand.

This document, however - drafted still in the basic spirit of the resolution of the 13th congress of the CPC and published in the dailies on April 11, 1989 - was destined to become the swan song of the SRC, advocating "liberal" and radical reform ideas. Afterwards, events in China unexpectedly accelerated and took an unusual turn. The streets and squares of Beijing - particularly the famous, and today rather notorious, Tienanmen square - became scenes of ever greater mass demonstrations and, not much later, similar manifestations occurred in several other large cities of the country.

What had actually happened in China in these feverish weeks? What was it that released the students' movement and turmoil in Beijing in late April? What demands were raised towards the government and party leadership? Was the brutal suppression of the "counter-revolutionary turmoils" in the night from June 3 to 4 in Beijing indeed unavoidable? Whom did the "hard core" of the Chinese leadership, actually wielding power, want to "reprimand" and intimidate? What can be expected after this turn in politics for the reform and opening policy? Can this be considered the end of the reform policy until now pursued and the beginning of a lasting "backward rearrangement process"? Concluding the chronological part of this study, which presented the development of the Chinese reform process by stages, we shall make efforts to answer these questions, relying on the scanty pieces of information available in Hungary as of September 1989. The answer will necessarily be deficient, as the author can use only the news and declarations published in the Chinese press during and after the events, as well as the written and illustrated reports of foreign reporters and witnesses. We cannot know what actually happened behind the scene, offstage, among the decision makers. We may draw conclusions about the events that took place there -no less dramatic in nature - only from later official publications. We cannot know when, if ever, the complete truth will come to light. But we know only too well, from the experience of our own country and many others, that frequently several decades have to pass before an objective judgement of such events can be made.

Sudden Halt in the Summer of 1989

In the summer of 1989, unexpected and exceptional events occurred in China which <u>forced the reform process to stop suddenly</u>. The reform had started with a great impulse 10 years earlier but, having met with more and more objective difficulties and ever starker subjective opposition in the last several years, it had decelerated. This sudden stop initiated a process of retreat in most areas - also manifest in several concrete steps and measures - which at present seem to be long--lasting, for various reasons. This raises the question whether the reform process that started in 1979 and encompassed the whole national economy in 1984 could have been continued at all according to the original ideas and theoretical conception.

This process of withdrawal - which had already begun in certain fields in the autumn of 1988 - was speeded up and supported in the summer of 1989 by a sharp political turn which was based on the traditional (Stalinist-Maoist) monopolistic conception and ideology of exercising power and the "building of socialism" as well as on the party state and "state party" system. Nevertheless, it is well known that this ideology is in flat contradiction with the ideology of the economic and political reforms, that set as an aim the radical transformation of the socioeconomic and political system. Consequently, the situation that developed in the summer of 1989 can also be interpreted as the encounter of an old with a new ideology in China, both testing their strength against a background of ever sharpening political contradictions and internal power fights. In the course of this fight the political forces representing the new ideology proved to be weaker than those insisting on the old one, which represented a guarantee of their position of power.

In the following subsections of this subchapter written at the end of September 1989 - that is, 5 months after the other chapter and subchapters of the book had already been completed - it was not possible to undertake a chronological review and analysis of the rapid and dramatic, even tragic, events taking place in China. This would have been beyond the structure and framework of this book. Thus, I will indicate the major points and deeper interrelations, relying on the events well known from the reports of the mass media. At the same time, this subsection serves as a transition to the further chapters of the book, which discuss mainly problems of principle and theory.

The events that took place in China between April and June 1989 - the process itself and its background, as well as the consequences to be expected, which we wish to present briefly in this section - seem to justify the opinion, even from the distance of some months, that in this case the substance was not simply the short breath of the reform and the sudden halt to it, but was above all <u>a very desperate and violent political fight and power struggle at the highest level of the party and state leadership.</u> It seems that members adhering to the traditional socialist ideology and power structure of the political leadership found the spring and the summer of 1989 the most appropriate moment to finish, for a longer period, with the forces which pressed for and insisted on sweeping changes and radical reforms that would endanger their power monopolies. Similar to the student demonstrations at the end of 1986 - which also demanded that the economic reforms be supplemented with political ones and, consequently, served as a good pretext for the replacement of Hu Yaobang, general secretary of the party at that time - this time the mass demonstrations by millions following student demonstrations and hunger strikes again provided an opportunity for the conservative kernel of the party and state leadership to hold one of the most consistent and influential representatives of the reform trend, General Secretary Zhao Ziyang, most responsible for "the counter-revolutionary rebellion." (The charges brought against the former general secretary are also incontrovertible evidence for the fact that the contradictions and breach within the leadership were not essentially of an economic-political, but mainly of an ideological nature, the chief issue being the support of "bourgeois liberalization" endeavors.)

The brutal reckoning with forces urging radical economic and political reforms in the summer of 1989 was, without any doubt, facilitated for the conservative kernel of the Chinese leadership by the circumstance that, from the middle of 1988 on, ever greater imbalances and functional disturbances appeared in the economy, which gave rise to certain social tensions as well. As a result of the breakdown of the traditional system of planned economy and the unstable position of the planned market economy, the state of "neither plan nor market" did not make it possible to "cool," with efficient macroeconomic regulation, the "overheating" that the economy had experienced for several years. Consequently, the aggregate social demand continually exceeded the aggregate social supply. This was also aggravated by the wasteful fiscal policy of the state. Thus, in 1988 the rate of inflation reached 30%. This was accompanied by a considerable decrease in the standard of living for significant strata of workers and white-collar employees living on wages and salaries, which shook their faith in the reforms. In agriculture - following spectacular development in the first half of the 1980s - from 1985 on crop cultivation showed no progress and it was not possible to surpass the harvest of 1984. The decisive role was played by the conservative agricultural price policy and the ever widening gap between prices of agricultural and industrial products. All the same, the mass demonstrations in April and May of 1989 were not occasioned by the deteriorating economic situation, but by the dissatisfaction because of the nonrealization of the promised political reforms and by the indifference of the leadership to democratic liberties of the masses, as well as by its prejudicial and arrogant behavior. Unwilling to discuss or agree, they regarded these manifestations from the very beginning as "turmoils against the party and socialism." With this behavior the conservative leadership of the CPC addressed a challenge to the people, provoking first the introduction of "martial law" in certain districts of Beijing, and 2 weeks later - after replacing Zhao Ziyang - the bloody reckoning with the demonstrators at Tienanmen Square and in its vicinity. Since then, in hundreds of articles and dozens of reports, "witnesses" have claimed that "the evolution of turmoils into a counter-revolutionary rebellion" forced the leadership to deploy armed forces. But it is a rather ineffective and useless claim, since the reports and news of that time in the press and television - in May, still in the hands of the supporters of the reforms and democratization - delivered strong and convincing evidence of the peaceful and democratic character of these movements and demonstrations.

Following this short introduction, let us look more closely at what really happened in China in April and May 1989, which led at last, in the night of June 3rd, to the nightmarish "military pacification" and at what impact it had on the Chinese reform process that developed 10 years earlier.

The character of the student demonstrations in April and May

From the middle of April on, a democratic revolutionary mass movement supported by a relatively narrow social stratum, and within it by those in the younger age-groups, developed in China. The main constituents of this movement were university and college students, teachers, employees of scientific institutions, journalists, and artists. In the culminating phases of demonstrations and manifestations other social strata joined them, mainly officials from government institutions, workers from industrial enterprises, and passersby. The center of the movement was the capital, Beijing, and it spread only to the larger provincial cities. It was a typical intellectual mass movement, with special features characteristic of the Chinese intelligentsia (faith in the superiority of morals and spirit, naive enthusiasm, missionary zeal in saving the nation, etc.). The aim of this revolutionary movement was to transform, radically but peacefully, the social system established in China after 1953 by means of political struggle, supporting from without the radical reformers who were equally to be found in the leadership and in the ranks of the CPC.

In contrast, the official document (which may even be considered a kind of Chinese white book) entitled <u>Report on checking the turmoil and quelling the counter-revolutionary rebellion</u> and put before the NPC Standing Committee on June 30 by Chen Xitong, mayor of Beijing and concurrently a state councillor,[2] characterized this movement as follows:

"During late spring and early summer, namely from mid-April to early June 1989, a tiny handful of people exploited student unrest to launch a planned, organized and premeditated political turmoil, which later developed into a counter-revolutionary rebellion in Beijing, the capital."[3] "We were confronted not with student unrest in its normal sense but with a planned, organized and premeditated political turmoil designed to negate the Communist Party's leadership and the socialist system."[4]

Between these two - seemingly radically different - characterizations of the events there is only an apparent contradiction. From a certain point of view both descriptions are true. The evaluation and qualification of similar events - for example, the Polish, Hungarian, and Czechoslovakian "events" of the past 33 years - was in each case a question of the established political power relations and opinions and standpoints reflecting them, which can be modified through changes in power relations or even turn into the opposite. Events that took place in China from mid-April to early June of 1989 can be placed - considering their character and nature - in the same category as the Polish and Hungarian revolutions of 1956, the Czechoslovakian one of 1968 and the Polish unrest in 1970, 1976, and 1980-1981. In fact, each case reflects the functional troubles and acute crisis of the same social system, established on the basis of mostly similar ideological preconceptions and by force of power. The aim of all such movements was to change and radically transform this system, even when the participating masses were not always and not fully conscious of the fact. The masses striking or demonstrating in the streets and at the squares wanted, in every case, to persuade or force by peaceful means the occasionally corrupt and uninhibited party and state leaders, who possessed the power monopoly of the party state and enjoyed different privileges, to share their power with other political forces and to replace the totalitarian power of the party state with the controlled system of institutions of a democratic constitutional state. Consequently, this movement was a <u>peaceful revolution</u> from the point of view of masses elbowed out of possessing and exercising power, while from the point of view of the party leaders sticking to the monopoly of power it was a <u>counter-revolution,</u> the more so because, according to Marxist--Leninist ideology, the communist party is the single and exclusive depositary of the revolution.

Factors giving rise to the student demonstrations

The fact that such a large-scale student movement came about in China precisely in April, 1989, is due to the simultaneous appearance and the mutually strengthening interactions of several objective and subjective, internal and external, regular and occasional factors and events.

First, in the spring of 1989 it became rather clear in China - at least to a significant part of the intelligentsia - that the political reforms promised in the autumn of 1987 would not be realized, and a strong retreat was experienced even in the economic reforms. Consequently, the great masses of the intelligentsia became exasperated, as they had expected a rise in their social position and rank from these reforms. This had an especially oppressive effect on the students and teachers of higher educational institutions, who had a broader view of political processes and an increasing awareness of knowledge in other parts of the world, while they were learning and teaching under miserable conditions. It is not by chance that also at the end of 1986 it was the university youth who showed dissatisfaction with the conditions prevailing at the universities and in the society. There can be no doubt that the dissatisfaction of the university students and teachers was intensified by reports of students and young experts returning from their foreign study tours or their university and postgraduate training about the conditions at universities in America, Japan, or Western Europe, as well as about employment possibilities for young experts in those countries.

Second, the majority of students, researchers, and teachers at faculties of social and economic sciences and at research institutes were rather well informed about accomplished political reforms and development tendencies in Hungary, Poland, Yugoslavia and, in particular, in the Soviet Union in recent years. They wanted the political reforms in China to take a similar direction, and they wanted the omnipotence of the party and its direct intervention in the work and internal life of universities and research institutes to be diminished. It is no accident that a majority of the demands by students were focused on assuring autonomy and the freedom of education and research at the universities and in the research institutes.

Third, the studens planned a wider political demonstration throughout the country, but especially in Beijing, for May 4, the 70th anniversary of the "4th of May Movement" of 1919. Since both the official organs and the youth organizations intended to commemorate it (the former according to the traditional and conventional patterns), a group of young people established - under various names - independent youth organizations, clubs, and discussion circles at the universities and other institutions of higher education. They invited personalities as lecturers and discussion leaders who were best known for their radical reform views - those from the "opposition" one may say, given Chinese circumstances - and with their help they tried to create an up--to-date political platform "worthy of the spirit of the 4th of May." These autonomous student organizations and discussion circles became the chief organizers and leaders of the demonstrations in April and May.

Finally, the direct cause of the student demonstrations was an unexpected event on April 15: the sudden death under tragic circumstances - as it is generally said - of the previous party secretary, Hu Yaobang. (Hu Yaobang suffered a heart attack at the session of the Political Bureau and died after being transported to the hospital.) The movement of students was triggered not simply by the fact of the death of the party leader (who was

74 and had been shelved for more than 2 years), but much more by the circumstances of his death and, especially, by the manner in which the top leaders of the CPC reacted to it. As regards the circumstances: in this respect the unrest was produced by the uncontrolled news spreading about in the capital the following day, according to which the former general secretary had suffered a heart attack while hotly debating with Prime Minister Li Peng; i.e., "Li Peng nagged Hu Yaobang to death." The official reports refuted and qualified this gossip as a false rumor. As regards the attitude of the leadership of the CPC to the death of the previous general secretary, the youth found it strange that the old party leader - slandered and shamed in the last years of his life - was buried with the ceremony due to an actual general secretary or head of state (1 week of mourning with several local commemorations; an abundance of articles praising his merits; lying in state in the building of the NPC with tens of thousands of people paying the tribute of respect; an official funeral service of enormous dimensions with more than 4000 people invited). At the same time, in the obituary published 1 day after his death and in the lengthy funeral address delivered by Zhao Ziyang on April 22, there was no mention of why he had been relieved of the general secretary's office in January 1987.

Consequently, the students of Beijing trooped to Tienanmen Square on April 19, on the one hand, to bow, before the memory of their previous supporter, who had been relieved of his office before his mandate expired, because he had "behaved in a tolerant and irresponsible way" toward the student demonstrations of that time and had disregarded the danger of the "bourgeois liberalization." On the other hand, they demanded open rehabilitation for Hu Yaobang, his acquittal from the previous accusations, which would be equivalent to public disapproval of the campaign against "bourgeois liberalization" that started immediately after his dismissal and lasted for several months. As it turned out later, the students did not correctly assess the real power relations in this respect, and they thought that the leaders of the CPC could be forced through demonstrations and mass movements to retreat and amend their previous judgement. The prime mover of the "student turmoils" was this demonstration on April 19, more precisely, the manner in which the party and state leadership reacted to the demands of the students in Beijing in the first days and weeks, rigidly refusing any kind of contact and dialogue with their representatives, qualifying their movements as "turmoils against the party and socialism."

In connection with factors giving rise to these events, it is worth mentioning the opinion expressed by Deng Xiaoping in his speech on June 9, 1989, addressed to commanders of the military units taking part in the suppression of the "counter-revolutionary riot": "This storm was bound to happen sooner or later. As conditioned by the international and domestic climate, it was bound to happen and was independent of man's will. It was just a matter of time and scale. It has turned out in our favor, for we still have a large group of veterans who experienced many storms and have a thorough understanding of things. They were for taking resolute action to counter the turmoil. Although some comrades may not understand this now, they will understand eventually and will support the decision of the Central Committee."[5] It will be the task of history to decide how favorable or unfavorable for the Chinese people "the presence of a large group of veterans" was. But one thing is sure: it will not be difficult to give the names of persons responsible for mopping up the peaceful demonstration of the students. The overwhelming majority belong to the group of veterans of the party leadership and are such well-known persons as Deng Xiaoping, Li Xiannian, Chen Yun, Peng Zhen, and the present State President: Yang Shangkun. But when China itself at last decides to find the persons responsible for suppressing and revenging the democratic mass movement of 1989, these "old comrades" are not likely to be among the living, considering their very advanced age.

Students' demands

At the beginning of the demonstrations, the students put their demands in writing and wished to hand them over personally to the prime minister, Li Peng, in the form of a petition. These demands - as far as we know - were published by the Chinese press neither then nor later, but it was possible to get a rather clear picture of their contents on the basis of foreign correspondents' reports. Between the 19th and 22nd of April several petitions were drafted; the news and reports made mention of a list of demands including sometimes seven, sometimes nine or ten items. In first and second place were the demands to hear the truth about the merits and faults of Hu Yaobang, on the one hand, and to condemn subsequently the campaign started against "the bourgeois liberalization" in the spring of 1987, and to rehabilitate the denounced and shelved persons in the course of the campaign, on the other hand. Moreover, they called for university autonomy, for recognition of the independent student organizations, for consideration of their opinions on educational reform, for higher scholarships, and for getting places on study tours and jobs through competition. But the petition also included demands of a political character, such as the speeding up of political reforms, struggle against bureaucracy and corruption, abolition of privileges for leaders, and ensuring the democratic civic liberties laid down in the constitution.

When the attempts to deliver the petition failed, one after the other, the most important demand of the student organizations was that their representatives be received by the responsible leaders of the government and the party. The students were greatly shocked on reading the editorial in Renmin Ribao of April 26, 1989, entitled "Take a firm stand against public disturbances", which qualified the student demonstrations as movements opposed to the party and socialism and urged a firm attitude of party leaders and masses against them. On April 27, in reply to the editorial, the students of Beijing organized a much larger demonstration than before. Primary among their demands was that the party leadership withdraw the unjust and insulting qualification given on the character of their movement in the editorial of the day before, since they wanted only that the party completely enforce its reform policy and correct the faults of the socialist system. At this demonstration not only were the slogans disapproving corruption and autocracy carried and chanted, but - in reply to the charges occurring in the editorial - signs appeared with the inscriptions "We support the communist party!" and "We support socialism!", and the young people sang the International and the Chinese national anthem.

After this demonstration the spokesman of the government declared that the government was ready to have talks with the representatives of the striking students, but exclusively in an official way, that is, through the university channels and "in a proper atmosphere."

During the last days of April the demonstrations became a little calmer, but on May 4 they continued with renewed power and insistence on ever more explicit political demands. As the spokesman of the government refused to recognize the independent student organizations on May 3rd, the students decided to hold the "historical march" under the slogan "For a freer China" the following day, independent of the official celebrations, and to commemorate in this way the 70th anniversary of the first large-scale political student demonstrations. Prior to it, they forwarded to the government a new petition, in which they asked the government to take a position, within 24 hours, on the question of whether it was ready to carry on televised round-table talks before the public with representatives of the students on press liberty, corruption, bureaucracy, the rehabilitation of Hu Yaobang, and the punishment of persons responsible for the country's economic crisis. The government spokesman also refused this "ultimatum" in his declaration on May 3rd. The situation was even more aggravated by the fact that the journalists were also about to organize themselves and raised objections to censorship, as well as to the restrictions and repression affecting the press. They demanded to be allowed to give information about the student demonstrations and questions drafted by students in conformity with the facts.

On the 3rd and 4th of May, Zhao Ziyang, having arrived in the meantime from the Korean People's Democratic Republic, tried to calm the agitated students. On the one hand, he analyzed in his commemorative speech in a dramatic way what it meant for China that in the 150 years since 1840, there had not been more than

20 years when order and stability prevailed in the country; he theorized about what circumstances would be brought about if the state of disorder and chaos were to dominate the country after 10 years of tranquility. On the other hand, in the course of his talks with the leaders of the delegations arriving to the annual meeting of the Asiatic Development Bank in Beijing, he set forth that - in his opinion - "no great turmoil can take place in China" (he obviously wanted to calm the foreign bankers intending to make investments in China) and "the students are not opposed, in effect, to our system, but they want us to correct faults in our work." (Both of his declarations are evaluated later as opinions being in flat contradiction to the previous resolution of the Standing Committee of the Political Bureau and to the spirit of the Renmin Ribao editorial of April 26, and it is stated that the former general secretary, publishing the differences in opinions at a high level of leadership in such a way, took the students' part and, consequently, gave new impetus to the turmoils.)

The student demonstrations in Beijing took a dramatic new turn when - because of the repeated refusal of their demands - a thousand students began a hunger strike at Tienanmen Square on May 13. The number of those participating in the hunger strike had grown to more than 2000 by May 15, the day of Gorbachev's arrival in Beijing and tens of thousands of students, sympathizing and declaring their solidarity with them, nearly filled Tienanmen Square. (This is why Gorbachev - contrary to custom - was given a ceremonial reception only at the airport and was able to enter the parliament building only through one of the back doors.) From this moment on, the main demand of the students was to have direct talks and establish a dialogue between the government and representatives of the striking students; however, this came about only on the sixth day of the hunger strike, on May 18, and the hospitals in Beijing were already filled with students who had grown weak and become unconscious in consequence of their fasting. The talks with Prime Minister Li Peng were broadcast on television as well, and the text of the memorandum made of them was published in the next day's press; they ended in complete failure, as the prime minister made no concessions and gave them the hope that he would deal with "their requests" only if they gave up the hunger strike and the demonstrations. At that time millions of people were already flooding the streets and squares of Beijing, and in other large cities as well, hundreds of thousands of people were marching in the streets to express their solidarity with the students of Beijing. On the same day - the 18th of May - the four members of the Standing Committee of the Political Bureau, Zhao Ziyang, Li Peng, Qiao Shi, and Hu Qili, visited the hunger strikers in weak health in a hospital. But their demands were not fulfilled even after this visit; moreover, 2 days later - on the 20th of May - martial law was declared in Beijing and preparations were made for mopping up the student demonstrations by military force. Zhao Ziyang was beaten in the political struggle with the "hardliners" of the party. His last public activity was to visit the students, who had already been striking for 7 days at Tienanmen Square. Tired, in a broken voice, he seemed to implore the students to give up their hunger strike and warned them that the situation was extremely serious and could get worse if the demonstrations went on. He already knew what would come to pass within some days, or more precisely within 2 weeks, but he could do no more than return to his office, take a sick leave of 3 days, and hand in his resignation. Some days later he was placed under house arrest, and his lot has been fully unknown to the world ever since that time. However, official declarations make him responsible within the leadership for the protection of the students' demonstrations and their "degenerating" into a "counter-revolutionary rebellion."

Organizers and supporters of the student demonstrations

The Chinese **White Book** holds about two dozen scientists in leading positions and intellectual cadres who had connections with foreign universities, periodicals, and various kinds of political organizations responsible for preparing and organizing the student demonstrations of April and May. Reviewing the events and their activities, it also gives their names, indicates their places of work. The two best-known persons - even abroad - among them are: Fang Lizhi, astrophisicist (who asked for asylum, which was extended to him and his wife as well, at the Embassy of the United States in Beijing on June 4, 1989) and Su Shaozhi, former director in the Institute of Marxism-Leninism-Mao Zedong's Thought of the Chinese Academy of Social Sciences. Among them are also: Bao Tong, former secretary to Zhao Ziyang; Chen Yizi, director of the Economic Structural Reform Institute; Chen Ziming, director of the Beijing Institute of Social and Economic Sciences; Yan Jiaqi, senior research fellow of the Institute of Political Sciences under the CASS; as well as chief editors and editors of several dailies, weeklies, and periodicals. The list also includes the Beijing correspondents of several Hong Kong journals and researchers of several institutes of the CASS. As regards the foreign organizers, in this respect only the editors of some Hong Kong journals and members of an organization named "Chinese Alliance for Democracy" were mentioned. However, we are aware of the fact that Deng Xiaoping, speaking about the factors giving rise to "turmoils" in China, indicated the impact of the "international macroclimate" as one of them. That is, he also mentioned - apart from the capitalist endeavors aimed at changing the internal social order of the socialist countries - the dangerous ideological impacts issuing from certain socialist countries, concretely referring to the impact of changes accomplished in Hungary, Poland, Yugoslavia, and in the USSR.

The organization and guidance of the student demonstrations were accomplished by leaders and members of the newly established student organizations. These demonstrations were run to the very last with an impressive organization and discipline. Disturbing actions occurred only in some country towns (Changsha, Xi'an) and in Shanghai (in this last one only when the driver of a train transporting soldiers drove - under constraint - among the demonstrators occupying the rails and crushed some people to death). The civilian population - despite the traffic jams - showed patience and sympathy for the demonstrators; many joined them and supplied them with food and drink. The railwaymen transported young people leaving for Beijing from the country towns without any tickets. Leaders of certain enterprises placed vehicles, amplifying systems, and decorative materials at the disposal of the student organizations.

Supporters were to be found in almost every state institution in rather great numbers. From the middle of May they took part in the movements as well. This support inspired the youth and moved them to stand fast considering themselves, indeed, national heroes. They made proud and self-conscious statements before the cameras of foreign television companies (who had come to China in great numbers, taking Gorbachev's visit into consideration, and subsequently stayed there to the end). This proved to be unfortunate, since many of the young demonstrators were identified and arrested on the basis of these very video tapes after June 4. From mid-May on, the Chinese state television also transmitted regular information and news on the events, but those taking part in the events were only very rarely questioned during these broadcasts.

Could the bloodshed have been avoided?

During the 6 weeks of student demonstrations there were at least three moments or periods when the "turmoils" might have been ended, with some good intention and indulgence without any difficulties and bloodshed.

The first such moment was April 23 and 24, if the leaders of the CPC had been ready to examine at least a part of the students' demands and to enter into talks on them before May 4. With some concessions - e.g., invitation of leaders of the newly established student organizations to the official ceremonies, assurance of a few minutes for them to make speeches at these ceremonies, and a promise to continue the dialogue - the unrest could probably have been calmed. Nevertheless, the top-level leaders who convened in the absence of Zhao Ziyang - as it was seen - took precisely the opposite measures: they qualified the youth demonstrations as a movement opposed to the party and socialism, and they invited the party organizations to carry on a political struggle against them. This was a very serious error which not even Zhao Ziyang was able to rectify after his arriving home, all the more as by this time he had to face Deng Xiaoping and the three members of the Standing Committee of the five-member Political Bureau (Li Peng, Qiao Shi, and Yao Yilin), and he could rely only on Hu Qili.

The second occasion presented itself on the week after May 4, when the "difference in opinion" of Zhao Ziyang and his readiness for dialogue set peoples' minds somehow at rest. However, Renmin Ribao, as well as the Chinese radio and television continued to scourge the students in the spirit of the editorial of April 26. In the opinion of many people, even on May 13 it would have been possible to close and clear Tienanmen Square of the students who were beginning their hunger strike that time, by putting greater police squads into action and resorting to force without any arms, taking into consideration the coming visit of Gorbachev. This might have been accompanied by smaller fights, but it would probably not have been too difficult to convey both to the Chinese people and to the outside world that demonstrations and hunger strikes should not necessarily be organized at the greatest square of the capital and before the Parliament building.

Finally, the introduction of martial law, if already decided on May 19 - even at the price of the resignation of Zhao Ziyang - should have been enforced only when all conditions were assured for its strict observance, including the curfew at night and the closing of roads leading to Tienanmen Square. Without supplies of food and water the some 20 thousand people at the square would have drifted away and the weakened hunger strikers could have been carried away by medical units of the army.

Indeed, by the end of May the student demonstrations had already run out of breath. In the course of the day there were no more than 10 or 15 thousand people at Tienanmen Square. In the evening the number of people going to the square grew, as many went after work to "see" - as if it were a kind of spectacle - what the students were doing. This was the case on the evening of June 3rd, and in the late hours of the evening there were somewhat more people in the square only because it was Saturday, and the following day people did not have to go to work.

What happened at Tienanmen Square?

The official and unofficial statements give radically different accounts. The official reports state that at early dawn on June 4, and without shedding one drop of blood, the dispatched forces "cleared" the square of demonstrators, who - obeying the warnings repeated many times - marched away through an "opening" at the southeast corner of the square, in close order. In contrast, the unofficial reports - referring to accounts of witnesses and some videotapes - stated that in the small hours of June 4, "at least 1300 people, mainly unarmed civilians, lost their lives when the army attacked the masses who had been demonstrating at Tienanmen Square for nearly 2 months with tanks and automatic weapons."[6] The official Chinese declarations qualified all foreign reports and accounts about "the massacres at Tienanmen Square" as "barefaced lies" and "malicious slander." However, they gave very dramatic and detailed accounts of events in the Xidan District of Beijing and on West Changan Avenue, were at dawn on June 4th "the mob", instigated by "evil-minded elements," attacked and set fire to the vehicles and armored cars left behind by the army sent to the square, and killed, in a bestial way, some of the soldiers commissioned to watch these and committed outrages on others of them. This "counter-revolutionary rebellion" continued - according to the official reports - even into June 5th and, in consequence of it, more than 6000 soldiers were wounded and several dozen lost their lives. As indicated in the report, the losses on the side of the civilians were 3000 wounded and more than 200 dead, but of the latter - it was stated - only 36 persons were university or college students.

It is not in our power to do so, and we do not intend to "hunt out the truth" on the basis of the insufficient information and contradictory reports at our disposal. This will someday be the task of Chinese historians. Since the suppression of the "counter-revolutionary rebellion" relates directly and indirectly to the issue treated by us, i.e., the economic reforms and the political reform endeavors, as well as their lot and future, let us - in possession of the known facts - put some questions and try to draw some lessons from them.[7]

1. If "nobody was injured" at Tienanmen Square, where did they come from, the large number of wounded, whose removal was shot - at the very beginning of East Changan Avenue - by foreign television teams on video tape at the East entrance to the square in the dawn hours?

2. Why did only several dozen or at most several hundred soldiers keep watch over the military vehicles transporting the troops near Tienanmen Square, and why were immediate and firm measures not taken to curb "the mob" when news was received of firing and lynching? (On the video tapes some hundred people can be seen firing, in perfect tranquility, at the standing vehicles and beating the soldiers in them, while troops in armored cars are passing by without trying to give any help to their fellow soldiers.) This is queer and provides food for thought.

3. From the official reports and accounts it is unambiguously clear that the students demonstrating at Tienanmen Square had nothing to do with the atrocities of Sunday and Monday. These were really the work of fringe elements and hooligans, which is also proven by vide tapes prepared on the interrogation of persons arrested by organs of public security. Why is it necessary, then, to assume or create an interrelation between the organized and disciplined movements of the students and the vandalism and cruelties of the "mob" - which fill any decent person with fear and disgust - using the "weak points" of the military actions under "martial law" for lynching and ravaging. These youngsters and hooligans were not, indeed "counter-revolutionaries" but such lumpen creatures who can be found, in rather great numbers, in any society and in any large city and who take every opportunity to ravage, to spread desolation, to kill people, or to give full vent to their aggressive instincts. This is especially the case when they can live out these instincts with apparent

impunity and in groups, in a mass turmoil. In Hungary too, in 1956, the majority of the lynchers and "revolutionaries" who took justice into their own hands were recruited practically out of these layers of society.

4. Thus we come to the major lesson. In each social system, but especially in a system that calls itself a socialist one, the essential task of military forces responsible for ensuring public security is not to suppress, by force of arms, the demonstrations and movements of a political character, but to curb the trouble-makers and the rowdyish and lumpen elements who wish to ravage and kill, using force if it cannot otherwise be accomplished. At the same time, the organizers of mass demonstrations of political character also have to be fully aware of the limit to which they are capable of controlling these demonstrations. They must make it impossible for the violent elements to penetrate their ranks; otherwise, the whole movement can become inconsistent with their aims and can be diverted towards a state of confusion and chaos. In the latter case, however, the organizers of demonstrations are responsible for any breach of order that takes place. The question is whether such a breach of order indeed happened in China during the first days of June, or whether the disturbing actions and the ravages took place independent of the student movements, perhaps owing to provocative actions.

Prospect for the Reform Process on the Eve of the 40th Anniversary of the Establishment of the PRC

After putting down the "counter-revolutionary rebellion," the Chinese leaders immediately tried to calm both the population of the country and international public opinion, as well as to assure that the policy of reform and opening would continue and would be characterized only - according to the objective situation and requirements - by smaller readjustments. They emphasized their unchanged foreign economic policy and their interest in the further development of international economic, technico-scientific, commercial and financial cooperation. Accordingly, further preferences were promised for those foreign firms which were ready, in spite of the events, to introduce and invest capital in China in the future as well. This was a response to the behavior of developed capitalist countries' governments; they condemned the "demonstration of power" and the brutal action of the Chinese leadership at the beginning of June, on the one hand, they introduced various economic, commercial and especially financial sanctions, on the other. Indeed, the reactions of the Beijing government to these sanctions were rather nervous and exasperated: it was emphasized that nobody is allowed to have a say in and interfere with the internal matters of China, as "it is unacceptable for the Chinese government and people." "The Chinese people cannot be reduced to obedience with any kind of sanctions."

Export limitations and restrictions on credit granting, introduced by governments of developed capitalist countries and certain international financial organizations were not of particularly great importance for the functioning of the Chinese economy. Incidentally, these kinds of sanctions - as the experience of several other countries has proven in the past - are only temporary. Business life does not tolerate any political intervention in the normal transactions for longer periods. Nevertheless, the Chinese economy was hit much harder by the stopping of tourism which had shown signs of rapid development in the preceding years. In consequence of this decline, in 1989 China stood to lose foreign exchange revenues amounting to at least US $1 billion, on the one hand. The broken faith of the Chinese living in Hong Kong in the former promises of the Beijing government, on the other hand, will entail a significant reduction in the number of transactions, as well as the "flight" of Hong Kong's capital to other countries and continents.

The overwhelming majority of developing countries not in the direct vicinity of China somehow ignored the events happening in China in the summer of 1989. Moreover, some of them expressly tried to take advantage of this situation to develop their own economic and political relations, sending high-level delegations to China after the events. The same method was followed, with the same intention, even by leaders of some East-European socialist countries who had previously greeted the leaders of the CPC and the PRC and assured them of their support concerning their firm attitude against the "counter-revolutionary danger." Among the Eastern European governments and politicians it was the Hungarian government and the then Minister of Foreign Affairs alone who officially condemned the brutal intervention by the Chinese leadership and protested against the gross violation of human and political rights, thus evoking deep indignation of the Chinese leaders.

The moderate and "neutral" attitude of the Soviet leaders made a favorable impression on the Chinese leaders, and this found expression in the fact that - in spite of their internal problems - they sent a large economic delegation to the Soviet Union in June 1989, to the 4th session of the Chinese-Soviet economic and commercial intergovernmental joint commission, headed by Deputy Prime Minister Tian Jiyun.

Thus, there is every indication that the Chinese leadership wishes to continue the policy of "opening outwards" and the economic, commercial and technico-scientific cooperation with foreign countries. As regards financial cooperation and credit relations, in this field there have been some modifications in the policy during the past year compared with the preceding period. China has already made allusions to the fact that she intends to proceed more carefully in the future when taking foreign credits, in order to get rid of too large burdens. Consequently, it gives preference to raising long-term investment credit with lower rates of interest offered by international financial organizations, and to direct capital investments; that is, it prefers the import of working capital. As a result of a perceptible decline in its export capacity, however, China is forced to reduce imports significantly in order to avoid an increase of its foreign trade deficit above US $10 billion again. (According to the customs statistics, in the first half of 1989 the foreign trade deficit of the PRC amounted to US $5.8 billion!)

However, the most important question is what will happen to the economic reforms launched in the preceding years and to the political reforms, which were generally more promised than realized. The prospects were not favorable at the end of September 1989, though promises to continue the reforms were not lacking.

In any case, it was declared that in the coming 2 years further "modernizations" were to be carried out in the economy in order to achieve the aim of "improving the economic environment and restoring the economic order," set in the autumn of 1988. In order to realize this, the price reform has been suspended and strict price controls have been introduced. Reform attempts aimed at transforming the property (ownership) forms have also been stopped, and ideological attacks have been launched against reform economists giving preference to joint stock company and leasing forms. The leadership wishes to achieve first of all restoration of the economic order by strengthening control of the state enterprises' central management, by "consolidating" collective enterprises, by strict financial control of private undertakings (by uncovering tax evasion), and by increasing the tax burdens.

It is planned to liquidate approximately 10% of the industrial enterprises, mainly those owned by families or collectives of small groups, and to significantly tighten the scope of activity of private enterprises. Moreover, thousands of enterprises in possession of independent foreign trade rights will shortly be deprived of their export-import license, and these enterprises will be able to accomplish their export and import transactions in the future only through the state foreign trade companies.

In the middle of August, 1989, Prime Minister Li Peng declared during his consultations with an American banker: "It is absolutely unfeasible for the Chinese economy to function exclusively on the basis of market principles. Our strategic aim is to establish a planned economy regulated with market instruments. In a Chinese market economy inflation would be speeded up, the economic situation would become unstable." "The market cannot be overemphasized in our country," he said, "since there is a shortage of goods in China." He considered the excess inflow of capital and excess household consumption dangerous, since they would result only in a superficial, but not a durable welfare.[8]

It is not so much the different manifestations of certain Chinese leaders - intended for "external consumption" as well - as it is the general atmosphere of the last months of 1989, the steps aimed at restoring "the monolithic unity," the control covering all fields of the party, and the witch-hunts recalling the period of the "cultural revolution" directed against the intelligentsia charged with "bourgeois liberalism" that give cause for alarm as regards the lot of the Chinese reform process in the future. <u>The sudden stop of this reform process in the summer of 1989 promises to be long-lasting,</u> - according to all signs - <u>and blockage and retreat are to be expected in many fields.</u> This relates, to an increased degree, to the political reforms, and within them to the most important element, to the key issue: separating the party from the state. At present, the institutional restoration of the power-wielding system of the party-state is going on in every field and in every respect.

The direction of work has everywhere been taken over by the party committees, and loyalty to the guideline of the party leadership has become a standpoint of vital importance in the political screening of cadres.

Taking all this into consideration 40 years after the establishment of the PRC, <u>the prospects are not too hopeful for the reform process to return into its previous channel and to continue according to the original concept. Nevertheless, it goes without saying that the reform steps made in China in the past decade cannot be ignored as if nothing had happened.</u> The Chinese people have already awoken to the profound consciousness of the necessity and unavoidability of political reforms; moreover, they have also been convinced of their beneficial results in practice. <u>Therefore, it is merely a question of time when and how the reform attempts will forge a way in the most populated country of the world.</u>

Consequently, the political turn that took place in the summer of 1989 can be regarded - in any case - as a sharp break in the 10-year development of the Chinese economic and political reforms. Only the future will show what remains of these reforms and reform attempts in the coming years, and when and how they will further develop.

Footnotes to Chapter Seven

1. See Renmin Ribao, March 24, 1989, p 1
2. See Annex to the July 11, 1989 issue of Renmin Ribao or Documents of Beijing Review, no. 29, July 17-23, 1989
3. Beijing Review, no. 29, July 17-23, 1989, Documents, p I
4. Ibid., Documents p VI.
5. Beijing Review, no. 28, July 10-16, 1989, p 14
6. See the report of Amnesty International, the international organization for civil rights, with its seat in London, on the events that took place in China in the summer of 1989 and the suppressive actions of the Chinese government.
7. It should be noted here that the author of this book had the opportunity, in August 1989, to see a six-part video made by the information organs of the PRC "On the suppressing of the counter-revolutionary rebellion" and to compare it with previous tapes taken by foreign camera teams.
8. Cites the August 24, 1989, issue of the Hungarian economic daily "Világgazdaság" (World Economy) p 2

PART TWO

Chapter Eight
THEORETICAL BASES OF CHINESE ECONOMIC REFORM

Choice of the Target Model

The necessity and inevitability of a radical change and reform of the traditional system of command planning, which was established in the mid-1950s and became distorted in the late 1950s in consequence of the willful policy of the "Great Leap," was recognized by the best economists and policy makers of the People's Republic of China in the early 1960s.[1] In the prevailing ideological and political atmosphere this recognition was not able to spread generally; in fact, representatives of this standpoint were soon branded as "right-wing deviationists" and "revisionists," and they were removed from the positions of leadership that they held in various institutions. It was only after the "Cultural Revolution" and with rehabilitation of the economists and social scientists who had been branded "rightist" or "revisionist" that these views could be expounded and published on a wider scope. Thus, there was a gap of one and a half decades between the appearance and the spread of reform concepts, which caused immeasureable losses and a needless detour in the socioeconomic as well as the ideological and political development of the PRC.

Immediately after organization of the Chinese Academy of Social Sciences in 1977, the rehabilitated researchers in its various institutes began intensive research and comparative analyses of the functional deficiencies of their economic system in order to select the "target model" that seemed most suitable for reforming this system under the conditions particular to China. They attempted to scientifically process and theoretically generalize previous efforts to achieve social progress and economic development in their own and other countries. They tried to study - on the spot where possible - the economic control and management systems of some Eastern European countries,[2] their functional mechanisms, as well as the various reform measures taken to update them, including their impact, achievements, or the causes of their failure. They were engaged in the problem of defining "stages" - on the basis of objective criteria - of socialist social progress and the historical transition to socialism, in order to learn and exactly define what steps were required at each individual stage. The results of this research and analysis appeared in a growing number of publications beginning in the spring of 1979, in the spirit of the slogan, released not much earlier, which set as the aim the liberation of thinking and denoted facts as the starting point of the search for truth, and practice as the sole criterion of truth.

As a result of their many-sided investigations, and based on international experience and examples, the Chinese economists and social science researchers explored and distinguished five different functional models of economic control and management that had been followed in the course of socioeconomic development toward socialism up to that point in history:

1. The economic model of War Communism
2. The traditional model of a centralized planned economy
3. The reformed model of a centralized planned economy
4. The economic model based on linking planned regulation with market regulation
5. The economic model of a decentralized socialist market economy or "market socialism".

For the first model the economic management model of the Soviet Union between 1918 and 1920 was quoted as an example, as was the management system working in China before 1949, in the so-called liberated areas, although they could similarly have referred to the economic systems of the Korean People's Democratic Republic, Vietnam, or Cuba. For the second model the examples mentioned were the economic management systems in the Soviet Union between 1928 and 1965, in China between 1953 and 1978, and in the Eastern European countries from the late 1940s till the late 1960s (with the exception of Yugoslavia). Also the then prevailing economic systems of Romania and Albania were listed here. The third model identified was the economic system prevailing in the late 1970s in the Soviet Union, the GDR, Czechoslovakia, Poland and Bulgaria. For the fourth model the new system of economic management introduced in Hungary in 1968 was mentioned as an example, and thus it was frequently called the "Hungarian model." For the fifth model the Yugoslavian system was quoted as an example, and it was named by some authors the "Yugoslav model." From the above list they drew the conclusion that progress from the first model toward the fifth - that is, gradual decentralization of the various rights of decision-making and gradual expansion of the autonomy of economic units was a basic and natural direction to take in reforming the socialist management system. In its course the instruments of economic management also change and direct management through plan indicators and instructions and based on central allocation is replaced by control through economic and financial regulators and reliance on the market mechanism. But they were of the opinion that it was necessary to clarify how this decentralization and growing autonomy of enterprises should be implemented (in what form, with what methods, and with the aid of what kind of intermediary institutions), how much time it should take, and, above all, how far it should extend and what it should cover.

By the early 1980s it was decided, also at the level of Chinese economic and political leadership, that the most expedient "target model" for the reform of the existing economic system should be, given the current stage of Chinese society, the one listed as fourth above: the system of economic management based on linking planned regulation with market regulation, i.e., the "Hungarian model." (Hence the intense interest from the first half of the 1980s on the part of the Chinese leaders in the experiences of the Hungarian economic reform and the operation of the Hungarian system of economic management.) However, no uniform standpoint has emerged to this very day as regards what concrete forms this linking should take, what methods should be employed and, mainly, in what proportions the two kinds of regulation - of different nature and principles - should be "mixed."

As we have seen, there are experts who emphasize "the primary role of plan regulation and the complementary one of market regulation" and try to restrict the latter to the less important economic processes. Others consider the two methods to be of completely equal rank and regard them as methods that can functionally be fitted together, and they believe that the most important task is proper selection and clear delimitation of the two spheres of regulation. Still others denoted the main task of reform to be restriction of plan regulation to the macroeconomic sphere and definition of the "rules of the game" of the emerging competitive market; accordingly, they wanted to trust the regulation of the complete microeconomic sphere to the operation of the market.

The CC resolution adopted in October, 1984, seemed to confirm the second standpoint, that of the national party conference held in October, 1985, the first one, and that of the 13th party congress in October, 1987, the third one. ("The state regulates the market, the market orients the enterprises.") However, the guideline and policy adopted at the 3rd plenary session of the 13th CC of the CPC, held in September, 1988, on "controlling the economic environment, restoring economic order and a diversified deepening of the reform" again brought the first standpoint to the foreground, and this was supported by the recentralization efforts that began in the spring of 1989.

All this shows that selection of the target model does not, in itself, solve every theoretical and practical problem of economic reform, and that the concrete progress of the reform process decisively depends on the actual economic situation and on the power relations within the leadership. At the same time, the target model is an important tool of orientation, as is a lighthouse for sailors; it indicates the direction in which the reform process has to proceed if it wishes to reach its final goal. Finally, it must be added that since the mid-1980s, this target model of the reform has no longer been called the "Hungarian model" by the Chinese reformers. In the meantime, namely, they have recognized that the economic management system based on linking plan regulation with market regulation was, also in Hungary, rather a "target model" than an actually working system. For the same reason, the decentralized model of socialist market economy is no longer called the "Yugoslav model" either. It was not discarded for reasons of principle, but rather for practical and political reasons, as it was held to be unsuitable as a target model for the reform of their huge and unevenly developed country.

Theoretical Basis

The principal starting point for elaboration of the basic concept of Chinese economic reform and the practical steps serving its implementation was the theoretical recognition that the most important goal and most general task of socialist economic construction for countries lagging behind in socioeconomic development was uninterrupted development of the forces of production. This helps, namely, to modernize the economy and society, to overcome backwardness and handicaps of civilization, and it better satisfies the growing material and cultural demands of the population in the best possible manner. In the interest of asserting this recognition the "extreme-left" policies of earlier decades had to be abandoned, as they emphasized the primacy of the class struggle and made efforts to accelerate socialist construction mainly with ideological tools (by affecting consciousness), by organizing political and production mass movements and through the direct party guidance and centralized command of every kind of productive and nonproductive social activity. Therefore, most of the Chinese reform economists and social scientists found the substance of the reform process, from the outset, in a gradual and continuous adjustment of production relations and the whole social superstructure to the requirements raised by development of the forces of production, i.e., in well-considered backward steps, where in earlier decades they had "run ahead" or - relying on erroneous theoretical assumptions - mistaken measures had been taken, but in bold forward steps and a search for new solutions wherever these were required and justified by the development of the forces of production.

Another cardinal starting point of the concept related to comprehensive reform of the Chinese economic system was the theoretical recognition that Chinese society, having underdeveloped forces of production and undeveloped commodity and monetary relations cannot avoid or skip the stage of developed and accomplished commodity production and universal commodity exchange, even choosing the socialist road to development and modernization, since this stage is a necessary and unavoidable concomitant of the civilization of human society and plays a definite historical role in this development. The most important characteristics of this commodity economy and of a commodity-producing society are summed up in the various Chinese documents in the following points:

1. A commodity economy relies fundamentally on diversified forms of public ownership, allowing at the same time a certain development of economic ventures in individual and private capitalist ownership.

2. In a commodity economy, planned development is realized first of all through the conscious use of the law of value and regulation of the market. ("The state regulates the market and the market orients the enterprises.")

3. The economic units (including state-owned enterprises) posses relatively great autonomy and self-financing ability. ("The enterprises manage truly independently; they answer for profit and loss themselves.")

4. The exchange relations among economic units are realized in the framework of a full-scope market system, extending to every factor of production, and in which the market subjects appear in an actual competitive position with equal chances.

5. In a commodity-producing society the functions of party and state, as well as those of the government agencies and enterprises, are separated from each other, as are the ownership functions and management functions and spheres of authority within the state economic sector.

The economic and political reforms as well as the policy serving their implementation ("the policy of reform and opening") received primary theoretical support from the 13th congress of the CPC. The report of the CC, serving as a basis for the resolution and as the basic guideline of the party, denoted the theoretical thesis about the "initial stage of socialism" as a central problem of prime importance and as a starting point. Accordingly, Chinese society is at present (and will presumably be for more than six decades) in the initial stage of socialism, which means - as we have seen - that: (a) China's society already is a socialist one, and (b) this socialism is, however, a rudimentary one. This initial stage differs from the "period of transition" when the "foundations of socialism" had not yet been laid, but neither is it identical with the stage into which Chinese society will enter after implementation of "socialist modernization." The main task in the initial stage is to gradually eliminate poverty and backwardness, to modernize the economy and society. As a result, China will move from being an agricultural country to being an industrial one, and the society, now mostly engaged in a natural economy, will turn into a society with advanced commodity production. The main contradiction in the initial stage, to be faced every day, is found between the ever growing material and cultural demands of the population and the backward forces of production, incapable of satisfying them. The class struggle will continue for a long time - within certain limits - but it no longer constitutes the main contradiction. In order to eliminate the main contradiction the commodity economy has to be vigorously developed and labor productivity increased. Modernization of industry, agriculture, and defense, as well as of science and technology, has to be gradually implemented (these being the so-called four modernizations), and to this end production relations have to undergo reform, together with those elements of the superstructure which do not answer the requirements of development of the forces of production. Reform is the self-improving and self-perfecting method of socialist society, socialist production relations, and the socialist superstructure, the main propelling force of social progress on a socialist basis.

There can be no doubt that, considering the political power relations and ideological situation in the PRC, the thesis worked out about the "initial stage of socialism" can do good tactical service for the cause of reform and opening. The importance of this thesis from a tactical viewpoint is that it makes it seem easier to isolate the "leftist" and rightist opponents of the present guideline. Namely, those who do not accept that the "initial stage", lasting almost a century, is a historical necessity in China and who continue to emphasize the willful thesis of "transition into communism while being poor" can thus be branded "leftist" opportunist deviationists, while those who, considering Chinese society immature even for socialism, propose to first follow the path of capitalist development may be branded "rightist" opportunists. The "two-front fight" was emphasized at the last - 13th - party congress, where the close interrelations between the "four principles" and the policy of reform and opening and their inseparable link were underlined.

Nevertheless, the thesis about "the initial stage of socialism" leaves much to be desired from the theoretical point of view and raises many questions. It can in no way be brought into harmony with the Marxian theory of social formations, the theory of development of these formations. We cannot undertake to expound this subject in detail here. I have produced several publications in the past 6-7 years about the theoretical and practical problems of transition into socialism, as well as about my standpoint regarding the relationship between the "existing socialism" and the Marxian theory of social formations.[3] I wish only to remark here that the thesis about the "initial stage of socialism" elaborated by the ideologists of the CPC obviously relies on the uncritical adoption of the subjective, idealist, and willful Stalinist criteria. According to these, if in a society - independent of its development level, the socialization of forces of production, and their internationalization - the "socialist transformation" of ownership of the basic means of production is implemented (i.e., if they are nationalized and collectivized) in any way and at any price, this society will already develop "on a socialist basis," that is, it is a socialist society as regards the substance of the matter. It follows that the leaders and ideologists of the Chinese party do not even question what kind of socialist society it is that is characterized for decades, even for almost a century, by poverty and backwardness. Or, if this question is put, they answer that this is but the initial stage of socialism. Nor are they apparently much disturbed by the fact that the "extreme-left" policy that has forced putting Utopian communist ideas into practice for two decades is accordingly a part of the same "initial stage," as is the transitory period of reforms aimed at radically changing the economic and political system established earlier, or the phase of mixed economy emerging as a result of reforms and opening, based on diversified forms of ownership, and of the development of a democratic, commodity-producing society.

This stubborn and rigid insistence on the myth of "existing socialism" is all the less understandable in view of the particular historical circumstances and development of the Chinese revolution; for the leaders of the CPC there offers itself a possibility and base of reference for "theoretical retreat" more advantageous than for any other communist party. The party, namely, which - according to its present organizational rules - places: "Mao Zedong's Thought" on an almost equal level with Marxism-Leninism, as the compass of its activities could easily retreat to Mao Zedong's theory of a "new democracy." Its substance was, namely, that in China (owing to its backward society and its semi-feudal, semi-colonial nature) between the democratic and socialist stages of the revolution a new democratic social development phase, lasting for several decades, is necessarily inserted, its economic base being a multisector market economy and its system of political superstructure the state power of a people's democratic dictatorship relying on a broad alliance of classes, including the national bourgeoisie - not the dictatorship of the proletariat. Mao Zedong revised and changed his ideas about the path of development only in the summer of 1953, after the death of Stalin, and it can be shown that he was led to do this by his efforts and illusions about China's becoming a great world power in a short time. And it was then that, treading in the footsteps of his great rival, he aimed at carrying out the "socialist transformations" in record time.

Today it is quite clear that even a century will not be enough time for China to move beyond a system of commodity production based on capital relations and establish a society operating on the basis of socialist principles. As a matter of fact, by the end of the "initial stage", in the middle of the twenty-first century this country can attain - even in the judgement of its present leaders - at most the level of medium-developed countries, as a result of its efforts at modernization. In addition, in this initial stage, in the interest of gradually building up a commodity economy and a democratic political superstructure capable of competing with capitalism, radical economic and political reforms have to be implemented that will more easily and harmoniously fit into the framework of a people's democracy than into any kind of "model of socialism." The unfinished task of uniting the country also speaks for such a "theoretical retreat" to be carried out in the spirit of the formula: "one country-two sytems." Theoretical and practical adherence to the social development path of a people's democracy would, at the same time, not violate the "four principles," which have recently been mentioned so frequently. As a matter of fact, the new democratic, or people's democratic development also means a "socialist path" as regards its goal. Its form of state power is a "people's democratic dictatorship," and the "leading role of the communist party" can also be asserted (if the party can convince the majority of the people about it); this would allow "insistence on Marxism-Leninism and Mao Zedong's Thought" and would even lend more concrete substance to the latter.

Issues Under Discussion

We have reviewed the theoretical foundation of Chinese economic reform on the basis of official declarations, adding our own remarks and comments. But the theoretical problems related to reform cannot be considered settled, even in China, with these official declarations. In academic and university circles, in scientific associations and institutions, and particularly in the press, a debate has been going on, for more than 10 years already, about these questions, and various diverging opinions and standpoints with more or less consistent sets of ideas and "schools" have emerged. From time to time these debates cool down, only to revive again, depending mostly on whether the reform process is on the upswing or declining. An attempt is made below to briefly review the most marked and characteristic standpoints taken on the most debated theoretical questions.

Present stage of Chinese social development

In spite of having elaborated the theoretical thesis about the "initial stage of socialism" and having raised it to the rank of official party opinion, some Chinese social science researchers are still of the opinion that Chinese society continues to be in the initial stage of the long historical process of transition from capitalism into socialism, which should not be confused with the "initial stage" of socialism. Thus, the society established in China in the 1950s is not yet a socialist one, nor will the one coming about be, if the present economic and political reforms are realized. Accordingly, the present Chinese society is a "transitory society" in which the elements of feudalism, capitalism, and anticipated socialism are mixed in a particular way, and this transitory state will continue for a long time. Some add even that "clear formations" are otherwise rarely found in the course of historical development, as social formation is itself a theoretical category and an abstraction, and its concrete form of appearance is always some kind of mix of the old, the even older, and the new formations.

There are some who maintain that Chinese society is not even in a state of "transition from capitalism into socialism," but in one of "transition to this transition," as in China before 1949 not even capitalism had become the ruling social formation and mode of production. This is one reason why China was not able to succeed in its transition to socialism from the semi--feudal and semi-colonial social state by skipping a phase of capitalism. For them the economic and political reforms open the way to the "natural, necessary and unvaoidable capitalist social development," as the "ground of commodity production can carry mass production only in capitalist form" (Marx). They believe that the most important task in the present state of development of Chinese society is a thorough, radical transformation of the political superstructure and creation of a democratic constitutional state, because without it the intended economic reforms cannot be realized. The official ideology declares this to be a "rightist," "bourgeoise liberal" viewpoint, while it refers to the former as a "dogmatic deviation," or "theorizing."

Finally, there are also some who reject the thesis about the "initial stage of socialism," together with the policy of reform and opening, from a genuine "leftist" standpoint, saying that both serve only to mask efforts at the "restoration" of capitalism. The advocates of this concept insist on the Stalinist and Maoist interpretation of socialism and socialist society and brand every kind of deviation from it as "revisionism." The representatives of this standpoint do not openly advocate this platform, but views they have expounded about some concrete problems of the reform reflect the traditional, dogmatic concept of socialism.

Target model of the economic reform

It has already been indicated that in the interpretation of the economic model relying on a linkage of plan regulation with market regulation significant differences may be found, depending on which kind of regulation is emphasized by whom. In reality, the problem is much more complex, as at least four "schools" may be distinguished among those advocating this model.

There are advocates of a planned commodity economy; they propose a model based on an organic unity of plan and market mechanisms which differs not only from the traditional, highly centralized, model of planned economy, but also from that of market economy. The model proposed by them is a mix of plan regulation based on market mechanism and market regulation guided by planning.

There are experts who believe that a market regulation subordinated to macroregulation guided by planning would be expedient, and they propose a target model with the following basic characteristics: the main forces should be concentrated on "enlivening" the enterprises, using economic methods as the main form of indirect control; the principle of material interest should be integrated with the principle of social justice, developing the horizontal associations on a wide scope.

The advocates of the model who wish to integrate the commodity economy relying on public ownership with planned economy denote the main goal of the reform as replacement of the old macrolevel regulatory mechanism of "product economy" (meaning natural economy) with a new macrolevel regulatory mechanism of commodity economy.

Those adhering to the model of a planned market economy are of the opinion that this model should integrate direct with indirect control (so that the main role falls to the indirect one); it should bring about harmony between the economic activities of enteprises and the market situation, and adjust the size and structure of aggregate social supply to aggregate social demand.

Phases of the economic reform

The phases of the economic reform is a particularly important aspect, which relates to selection of the target model and of the path leading to it. This is, namely, not a tactical question but one of strategic importance, and the success or failure of the reform process depends on the answer to it.

There were few, even among the Chinese theoretical and practical experts dealing with the problems of reform, who were of the opinion that in the wake of the introduction and implementation of a however well-considered and thoroughly prepared reform the new economic and management system could be attained in a few years and "in one round." This was not believed even by those who championed the cause of thorough preparation, over several years, of the reform and the exact elaboration of every detail, and who proposed to start with the simultaneous introduction of a large, complex comprehensive reform package. Even in this case, the reform process would fall into at least two phases: those of preparation and introduction.

The camp of those was much stronger who were for the elaboration and introduction of the reform in several phases, and intended to complete one or more tasks of crucial importance in each of them. Since the preparation of the comprehensive reform covered one and a half years, from the spring of 1983 to the autumn of 1984, this fact in itself divided the reform process that had started in agriculture in 1978-1979, into at least three phases:

1. The phase of partial reforms, considering reform of the organization and management of the rural economy to be the crucial task

2. The phase of many-sided reform experiments, aimed at the thorough preparation of a comprehensive reform

3. The phase of introduction and implementation of comprehensive reform

The real debates were, however, not conducted about these - either then or later. They were and still are much more about in what phases and with concentration on which crucial problems the comprehensive reform itself should be implemented. Opinions in this respect are rather strongly divided.

There were those who contended that the comprehensive program could be implemented in its substance in the space of about 5 years; thus, in the 1990s the Chinese economy would already be operating under the new economic system. During these 5 years a mixed, so-called double-track economic and management system would come about, in which initially the elements of the old economic system and economic mechanisms would be preponderant. However, with the progress of reform their weight and scope would diminish more and more. The elements of the new system and new mechanisms would gain ascendancy until they would completely oust the elements of the old system. Therefore, this natural process need not be broken into phases, since - according to the rules of formal logic - at most, such phases could be mentioned which mechanically state that the elements of one or the other system are preponderant, or just balance out each other.

The concept outlined above also has a version - represented by experts who doubt that the comprehensive reform could be implemented in so short a time - according to which implementation of the comprehensive reform and evolution of the new economic system might take even decades, and thus arrangements were needed to ensure the survival of the "double-track" system. According to the representatives of this view, the management system of a planned commodity economy oriented by the market could develop in China around the turn of the millennium, at the earliest, and this is a period long enough to allow for delimiting separate phases within it. These experts believed that one of the most important tasks was to decide which tasks were crucial to the acceleration of the reform process and would at the same time ensure that the elements of the new system increasingly and irrevocably replaced those of the old one.

Finally, there were and still are views according to which the "double-track" system is a kind of trap, easy to enter but difficult to leave. In an economy characterized by shortage such a system would create chances for speculation and subterfuge, which would result in a situation where neither plan regulation nor market regulation functioned properly. In fact, this would combine the rigidity of plan regulation with the blindness and spontaneity of the market, pushing the economy towards a state of chaos. Therefore, the "double-track system" has to be abolished, the sooner the better, and to do this "points of breakthrough" have to be found which will allow the rapid jettison of this lopsided system.

Keystone of the economic reform

In this respect eight different opinions have emerged among the Chinese experts:

1. The central link of the entire economic reform is <u>reform of the system of enterprise.</u> In modern societies enterprise is the subject of management and, at the same time, the subject of market activity as well. The enterprise is the basic unit of production and turnover. If the system of enterprise is not reformed, if the vital power of enterprises is not enhanced, then vitality will be missing from the entire economy. The main task is thus to further deepen the reform of enterprises, because only this can lead to growing supply, to changes in the structure of production, and to a more rational use of the factors of production - all of which are preconditions for successful implementation of the reform. Some of the advocates of this view are, however, of the opinion that enterprise reform is a point of breakthrough only in the initial stage of reform; in a more advanced phase of the change of mechanism it would lose its outstanding role.

2. In the initial stage of reform, macroeconomic control has become the weakest link in economic management. Thus, the decisive link of economic reform is now <u>to strengthen macroeconomic guidance and control as quickly as possible.</u> Since, in consequence of decentralization and liberalization already implemented, the traditional system of direct macroeconomic control has fallen apart, while the new, indirect system of macroeconomic control has not yet been established, the economic processes have become unmanageable. Therefore, if the reform of enterprise becomes the "breakthrough point" of the reform, then the original mechanism of macroeconomic control and management has to be restored. Obviously, this is the standpoint of those advocating recentralization.

3. China is still a basically agrarian country. In the initial phase of reform rural reform was the vanguard. Later this came to a halt, and this was reflected in the results of agriculture. If we now want to give new impetus to the reform, the main job in planning the whole reform process should be <u>exact elaboration of the second step of rural reform.</u> This should include further reform of land ownership and land use, of the rural turnover system, and of the organization system of collec-

tive farms. Without a developing agriculture there is not and cannot be any dynamic and balanced economic growth in China; nor can urban economic reform reach its goal without a further reform of the rural economy.

4. The keystone of economic reform is <u>price reform</u>. For the elaboration of reform plans, reform ideas, and reform programs it is indispensable that the internal relationship between the reforms of the price system and of ownership relations be correctly treated, that the role of price reform in the reform of the economic system be fully acknowledged, and that the central problems of price reform be analyzed. Without a price system correctly reflecting the socially necessary input as well as market supply and demand, a well-functioning economic system cannot be established.

5. A breakthrough might be attained through the reform of <u>ownership relations</u>. The key to this is improvement of the socialist system of ownership by developing rational mechanisms for the regulation of allocation in the interest of harmonizing different interests and incomes. The basis of every economic system is property, while the quality and success of its functioning depends on an adequate division of ownership and disposal rights.

6. The basic deficiency of the traditional economic system is weakness of the market system, its underdevelopment. Therefore, the fundamental target of the reform should be <u>perfection of the market system.</u> This should be used for developing the new economic system, the planned market economy. A well-functioning commodity economy cannot come about without a full-scope market system.

7. Success of the reform does not depend on the implementation of one concrete program, but rather <u>on the coordinated and harmonized simultaneous introduction of various interrelated reform measures.</u> Partial reforms, fragmented even over time, have nowhere led to adequate results; in fact, they have rather made the contradictions of transition from the old system to the new one more acute. Only the simultaneous introduction of a complex and comprehensive reform can be successful, as a complete change of model and system is at stake.

8. The key to the success of the reform is not in the reform of the economic system itself, but <u>in the radical transformation and rebuilding of society.</u> The breakthrough in economic reform should not be attained by transformation of the economic system itself, but through the reform of the political system and social consciousness. Without a radical change in the political system and in the consciousness, in the psychology of the people, even the best economic reform ideas and efforts are doomed to failure, as they will face strong "recalcitrance."

Reform of the ownership system

In this matter there are three basic opposing trends:

Adherents of <u>the first trend</u> wish to perfect the state ownership system by reconsidering its content and function. They mostly propose to separate, within the system of state ownership, the ownership right of enterprises from the rights of administration (management, disposal), thus allowing for various forms, modes, and methods of management. This trend takes a firm stand for maintaining the dominance of state ownership, only wishing to operate it in more diversified forms and with more flexible management methods. This trend enjoys the support of the majority of party and state leaders.

The <u>second trend</u> is toward transformation of the whole people's (state) ownership into enterprise ownership, where the enterprise has an autonomous legal right to management and takes full responsibility for the results, both for profit and for loss. The advocates of this concept set out from the theoretical consideration that a commodity economy capable of functioning cannot dispense with autonomous and independent commodity producers managing at their own responsibility and risk, i.e., with economic subjects and organizations who do not depend on decisions taken by higher authorities. Nor can a real competitive market develop without them.

According to the ideas of <u>the third school,</u> state ownership should be replaced by a system of joint stock companies. Thus, some state-owned property is transferred to ownership of the enterprise collective. Workers will buy shares and the state will found joint stock companies, thus ensuring that the enterprise is managed and used by the state, the enterprise, and the workers together.

As regards the concrete course of transformation, several different ideas and proposals were born even within each of the trends outlined above, and almost all of them received publicity in the Chinese press.

The reform of ownership relations is no longer merely a theoretical question in China; it has become part and parcel of everyday practice. The question is how far they should go with these reforms, so that the vital power and activity of enterprises may evolve, but China still remain on the "socialist road." This has become one of the central issues of recent research for Chinese economists.

Some economists are of the opinion that, setting out from the present development of forces of production, the most expedient proportions between the whole people's ownership, collective ownership, semi-socialist, and nonsocialist (individual or private) ownership would be 5:3:1:1.

According to others, for the emergence of rational relations among the various forms of ownership, the treble requirement of "quality, quantity, and measure" should be ensured. To attain "quality" the leading role of the economy in public ownership has to be ensured, allowing the simultaneous existence of individual and private economy and their parallel development with the other economic sectors. As regards "quantity," the absolute superiority of an economy based on public ownership should be aimed at. According to preliminary ideas, its seems expedient that 10%-20% of industrial output and 20%-30% of agricultural output should derive from the individual and private sector. This ratio may be higher in the sphere of trade and services. Finally, as regards "measure," the goal should remain to preserve socialist orientation and to secure rapid development of the social forces of production.

Debates about the system of shares

In recent years the system of shares has been the "hottest point" of theoretical debate among Chinese economists. Some maintain that there is a substantial difference between a socialist commodity economy and one relying on private ownership. Therefore, the system of shares is not an unavoidable and necessary consequence of the development of a socialist commodity economy. Its introduction cannot lead to a proper regulation of the relationship between government and enterprises; in fact, it brings further factors of uncertainty into this relationship. Introduction of the system weakens the economic expediency of enterprise activities to a certain extent and renders the evaluation of performance more complicated. The payment of dividends to shareholders would presumably lead to a boosting of the consumption fund, and thus one of the main deficiencies of the present management system would remain unresolved.

Other economists are of the opinion that the share system can be used only with definite conditions. The system may play a positive role in concentrating capital and in efficiently linking and uniting the various basic factors of production, but it cannot be made general, or introduced everywhere. It is particularly unsuited for enterprises making large profits.

There are some who cling to the view that the share system is important for reform of the state ownership system and, as a matter of fact, this system might become the main form of the ownership reform. They are of the opinion that the share system may render more exact the relationships among the various forms of ownership. In the framework of the share system it would be possible to do away with the situation where nobody takes responsibility for the property of the enterprise, for its proper use and augmentation, and a situation characterized by cooperation and mutual effects among the owners, managers, and workers of the enterprises would come about. This would be a step toward rationalizing the activities of enterprises and increasing their performance; it would promote the collection and controlled utilization of the free monetary assets of society and the intervention of shareholders in the interest of curbing the unjustifiably growing investments, and would thus result in a more rational allocation of social resources. As enterprise shares can also be bought by workers, the workers become directly interested in improving the enterprise's performance as well as in augmenting the property of the enterprise, and using it wisely, economically.

The contractual responsibility system

Although the contractual responsibility system (in Chinese: chengbao zerenzhi) - also called by some "contractual management system" (chengbao jingyingzhi) - has already been approved and widely used by the government, no uniform opinion has as yet emerged among Chinese economists about its usefulness and expediency.

The opponents of the system believe it hinders deepening of the reform. To support their opinion they advance the following two arguments:

1. Under the contractual system a chance for bargaining between the state and enterprises emerges, and this renders it difficult to work out and introduce a normative regulatory system.

2. The contracting enterprise follows its short-term or immediate interests and therefore uses the available assets and resources to make a quick profit. This has an adverse impact on long-term interests and creative activity as well as on the continuous renewal of the production and product structures.

Supporters of the contractual responsibility system maintain that it helps to alleviate the effects of the psychological shocks caused by the reform of ownership relations. In addition, it is in conformity with the existing technical and management standards. The preliminary - contractual - fixing of the base level of profit and of the part of profit to be left with the enterprise makes the budget and management of the enterprise more disciplined and more controllable - to a certain extent. As the relationship between the state and the enterprises takes a contractural form, this will certainly facilitate the separation of enterprise management from government control. According to the advocates of this standpoint, the contractual responsibility system also corresponds with the basic strategy of the reform, which intends to make progress under stable conditions and with steady efforts.

There are also some who approach the problem rather cautiously. They acknowledge that this system is in conformity with the present technical and management standards, yet they are of the opinion that the system may be regarded only as the most realistic and most efficient form of transition to deepening the enterprise reform; that is, it should be conceived as a necessary phase in the transition to a commodity economy. The final goal is to provide normative legal bases for the control and management of enterprises that will secure equal conditions and make identical requirements for everyone.

Labor as a commodity

The correctness and validity of the earlier statement, that under the relations of socialism labor is no longer a commodity, has been the subject of new research in China in recent years.

Those who continue to maintain it are of the opinion that labor can become a commodity only under capitalist relations. The opening of the labor market does not involve an automatic retreat from this theoretical conclusion, and the introduction of labor contracts does not lead to labor again becoming a commodity.

The opponents of this concept list several kinds of arguments, summed up in the following:

1. In socialism work is not merely a means of livelihood, but also the sole criterion for measuring performance. The dual nature of work thus makes labor a commodity also under the relations of socialism.

2. Socialism has not eliminated the two basic conditions under which work and labor assume commodity characteristics: first, the employees enjoy personal freedom (although this is

not asserted in China today in choosing one's place of work and working conditions - author's note); second, workers do not have any property, since the means of production are owned by the state or by various groups of workers, not by individual workers (except for those in the individual and private sector).

3. In socialism the workers have become the masters of society. This ruling position is determined not only by ownership, as various relations may exist between the ownership of the means of production and the right to use them and their yields. There is thus no contradiction between the commodity character of labor and the workers as masters of society.

Two further views may also be found in the Chinese professional literature:

1. Under socialist relations labor takes the dual character of "both commodity and not commodity."

2. Labor is not a commodity, but it does possess the character of a commodity or commodity features.

On the nature of wage work

The nature of wage work is also debated. Until now it has been held as self-evident that there is no exploitation in socialism. But reality evokes in people doubts about the validity of this theory.

Those who try to present wage work from the viewpoint of socialism are of the opinion that this mode of management is a "heritage of capitalism" and has persisted from the period when socialism was still underdeveloped. Thus, this mode of organizing work comprises capitalist elements.

Others think that wage work is semi-socialist in nature, since only a small part of the after-tax profit is used for collective accumulation or for rewarding blue- and white-collar employees.

Others, again, are of the opinion that wage work belongs to the private economy. This determines that the ownership of means of production (including their use) is separated from the employees, and thus the employers enjoy the fruits of the surplus labor of employees. But, because labor is not a commodity, this private economy differs from capitalist wage work.

Some experts maintain that wage work has a dual nature. On the one hand, since a part of the profit produced by wage workers goes to the employer, this is a kind of exploitation. On the other hand, since a part of the remaining profit goes to the workers' collective and another part to the state, it also has a socialist character. Since the employer uses a definite part of the net income for the wages of employees, the employment of wage labor simultaneously has a "unified-work" (community work) and a wage-work character.

Focal points of macroeconomic regulation

In recent years, parallel with the upset of macroeconomic equilibrium, the problems of macroeconomic regulation have gained growing importance in the theoretical debates of Chinese economists. As regards the points to be emphasized in macroeconomic policy, several proposals have been advanced, crystallizing around the four sets of views to be found below:

1. <u>Demand should be curbed.</u> Economists representing this view are of the opinion that macrolevel economic policy should be aimed first of all at restricting aggregate social demand. The Chinese economy belongs, namely, to the category of shortage economy in which demand - in consequence of the "soft budget constraint" - is inclined to grow fast. A growing budget deficit, excessive issue of paper money, and overconsumption of the national income in recent years have all shown that the situation in which demand exceeds supply could not be radically improved in China. At the same time, the reform requires a rather free economic environment. To attain such a situation it must be ensured that aggregate social supply exceed demand.

2. <u>Demand should be stimulated.</u> Macroeconomic policy ought to be aimed at boosting investments and stimulating demand in the interest of maintaining a sufficiently high rate of growth. Supporters of this view advance the following arguments: an equilibrium attained by curbing demand is a passive, short-term one, achieved by leaving existing capacities idle - even in respect of goods for which there is increased demand. This method curbs

economic development, whereas the free economic environment needed for the reform can be brought about only through development of the economy. It is not realistic to implement a reform when enterprises have already brought about the free environment.

3. <u>Supply should be boosted.</u> Macroeconomic policy ought to be aimed at boosting supply, as the curbing of demand does not address Chinese realities. Regulation of demand in itself is incapable of solving such problems as structural transformation and rational allocation of resources. Restriction of demand has no positive impact on supply. China possesses a backward industrial base; its structure by branches is obsolete, as is her productive equipment, and the infrastructure is underdeveloped. The rising tendency of consumption demands a boosting of the supply of investment goods as well as of infrastructural equipment and assets.

4. <u>Demand should be integrated with supply.</u> Both the curbing of demand and the boosting of supply have their advantages. The regulation of demand - through restriction or stimulation - works against cyclical economic growth, and promotes equilibrium between aggregate supply and aggregate demand. The aim of bringing about equilibrium is to increase future supply by enhancing the profitability of production and optimizing the allocation of resources. Efforts should be made in both directions. The first one cannot substitute for the second, the two-way efforts have to complete each other.

It is clear from the above how wide is the palette of standpoints taken by Chinese economists with regard to reform. Indeed, we have given only a summary of the most characteristic views.

Formation of the target system for economic reform

Elaboration of the target system of the Chinese economic reform began after the 12th national congress of the CPC, held in September, 1982. Following several lines and going through several phases, it continued until the summer of 1986. Organization and coordination of the research and the exchange of views related to the concept of comprehensive economic reform and to working out some of its elements were initially coordinated by the presidium of the Chinese Academy of Social Sciences. In May, 1983 - as has been mentioned - the State Reform Commission (SRC) was created alongside the State Council of the PRC, which soon became the main director and central workshop of theoretical and practical work related to the reforms. The Commission gathered together - and in some cases even included - the best reform experts of China, organized study tours abroad, and invited foreign reform economists to hold lectures and consultations in China. It also directly controlled the preliminary testing of various reform measures in the areas and cities selected for this purpose.

It was in autumn, 1984, that the first comprehensive draft of the reform of the Chinese economic system - extending to several years - was completed; it was then discussed and raised to the rank of a CC resolution at the 3rd plenary session of the 12th CC, CPC held in October, 1984. As regards the nature and function of this document, it may be best compared - as has been mentioned - to the CC resolutions of the HSWP of May, 1966, and of the CPSU of July, 1987 - with the difference that, although the Chinese CC resolution is less elaborate as regards some partial problems and concrete modes of solution, on the principal and theoretical problems of the reform it is more resolute and forward-looking. A contributing factor may obviously have been that, in the working out of the Chinese CC resolution they could rely to a greater extent on the positive and negative experiences of reforms carried out, or recently halted, in other socialist countries; they could also take into account the experiences with the reforms that had already taken place in the Chinese villages and those being carried out experimentally in the cities.

Although the CC resolution of 1984 dealt with almost every basic problem and task of the economic reform, and in questions of principle and theory mostly took a correct, forward-pointing, and consistent stand, it had not yet provided a theoretical foundation for and scientifically elaborated the complex target system of the comprehensive reform. This was done by Chinese reform experts only one and a half years later, after they had summarized the positive and negative experiences with the comprehensive reform also extended to cities and, not least, after a new and thorough analysis of the Hungarian reform process. The latter became necessary because, after introduction of the so--called urban reform to the Chinese reform process, almost the same negative phenomena and problems have emerged (imbalances, price hikes, inflation, growing demand of enterprises for subsidies, etc.) which appeared in our country and which could not be fought or solved in a reassuring manner - either here or there.

Elaboration of the target system for economic reform involved the fitting into a logical framework, reflecting definite objective interrelations and rules, of the concrete reform targets affecting the different economic activities. In the course of solving this task the Chinese economists and theoretical experts disclosed a chain of objectively existing interrelations which had hitherto mostly remained hidden from the planners and those implementing the reform. This ignorance may have been one of the greatest difficulties of the reforms implemented to that point. In order to exactly understand the substance of this recognition and its further importance for theory and practice, we must briefly review the target system worked out by a group of theoretical experts of the CASS in the summer of 1986.[4] Following the sequence in which the individual reform targets emerged and were identified, the various concrete reform goals were summed up in the four-level target system reviewed below:

On the first level are found the targets of reform related to the mechanism of movement and management techniques of the economy. They include: (a) expansion of the autonomy of economic units, and (b) making government control indirect. These are goals of reform which have occupied first rank up to now in the reform concept of every socialist country, and which aim at providing new bases for the relations between the state and the economic units. Here belongs also the elaboration of various ideas about the reform of the planning system and of laws regulating the legal status of enterprises. According to experience to date, every socialist economic reform first formulates and sets these targets.

Closely related to the above reform targets, on the <u>second level</u> of the target system may be found the economic and financial regulators (in the terminology of Chinese economists: economic parameters) to be transformed and made operative. They mean the following concrete targets: (a) the price system, (b) the wage system, (c) the taxation system, (d) the tariff system, (e) the interest rate policy, and (f) the exchange rate policy. Without a simultaneous and coordinated transformation of these economic and financial regulators the reform targets identified on the first level cannot be implemented. Each of the reform targets on the second level should contribute to working out an economic regulatory system adjusting to the requirements of the law of value. Although the necessity of the quick, coordinated implementation of these reform targets is relatively soon recognized and always emhasized by those elaborating socialist economic reforms, their implementation mostly proceeds slowly, dragging, inconsistently, and - what is most important - in an uncoordinated manner. Most reforms fail because a radical revision of the price system has been missing or has been inconsistently implemented, but also the establishment of a wage system in harmony with the requirements of the law of value (i.e., one reflecting actual performance) and of realistic exchange rates causes serious difficulties.

On the <u>third level</u> are found the reform targets related to creating a market system of full scope and bringing about actual competitive situations. They include: (a) development of markets for consumer goods; (b) creation of the market for means of production, inclusive of markets for land and other immovables, the leasing of productive equipment, as well as the markets for know-how, patents and licences; (c) creation of money markets, including every kind of security or money substitute (letter of credit, bond, share, bill of exchange, etc.) and the establishment of a stock exchange and money market proper, i.e., the operation of a real capital market; (d) creating and developing a labor market, which assumes the free choice of job on the part of the employees and the possibility of firing unsuited or redundant labor on the part of the employers.

As regards the goals to be found on this level, individual socialist reform ideas (where these exist) reflect rather different and restricted viewpoints, and these are frequently changed or modified - even within a country. There are countries where the expansion of a market and the creation of conditions for genuine market competition are not considered as targets of economic reform, and the regulation of economic processes through market methods is generally dismissed as a method foreign to socialist planned economy. Elsewhere attempts are made to bring about the market of means of production on a restricted scope, excluding, e.g., the market of land and other real estate. In several countries the existence of a capital market and a foreign exchange market is also deemed to be incompatible with socialist planned economy as well as with the traditional requirements of the state monopoly of foreign trade and foreign exchange management. With reference to the thesis that the commodity character of labor has ceased in socialism, the necessity and expediency of bringing about a labor market is also refuted and negated.

In recent years there has been a rather rapid change in China regarding these questions. The CC resolution of 1984 still held that "under the socialist conditions of our country, labor is not a commodity, nor is land, mines, the railways, nor are banks, state enterprises and resources."[5] In 1986, however, the commodity character of every factor of production was already being emphasized, and in 1987 money markets started operating in several cities (with restricted rights regarding foreign exchange), the market for land and real estate opened (though, for the time being, rather for foreigners), several loss-making state enterprises were offered for sale (true, only smaller ones), several stock exchanges started experimental operations, concessions were given to foreign firms for the extraction of sources of energy (crude oil, coal) with their own means, and several measures were taken to gradually establish a labor market.

Related to the reform targets to be found on this level, it is an important recognition of the Chinese reform experts that without creating a full-scope, smoothly functioning market system, the economic parameters, regulators cannot be properly employed. If actual market relations and a genuine competition are missing, the means of regulation are suited only for mediating the will of the state and serve only as substitutes for directive plan indicators. (It should be noted here that, in the opinion of the Chinese economists visiting Hungary, the most convincing proof for this is supplied by Hungary. As a matter of fact, Hungary has not succeeded in bringing about a full-scope and genuinely competitive market even during the two decades of reform. Only so much has changed in economic management: the direct central management has been replaced by indirect central control, whereby the economic and financial regulators do not reflect the actual market relations and the market value judgements, but rather the expectations and value judgements of the government control agencies. That is, in the terminology of Hungarian economists: "The plan bargain has been replaced by bargaining about the regulators."

Finally, on the <u>fourth level</u> of the target system can be found the goals related to transformation of the existing ownership relations: (a) diversification of the existing structure of ownership, i.e., establishing proper and rational ratios between the state (whole people's), collective (group), individual, and private capitalist sectors; (b) selection of adequate ownership relations within each sector and development of new, intersectorial mixed forms of ownership; (c) elaboration and application of an adequate government policy with regard to ownership, which should be aimed above all at accelarating the development of the forces of production and at securing the livelihood of the population.

The need for radical change in the relations and forms of ownership that evolved during the earlier stages of socialist construction, particularly in the rigid and bureaucratic system of sate ownership, earlier held to be "most socialist" and called "whole people's," was not at all recognized, or only rather late, by the economic reforms that took place in the socialist countries. In respect of their replacement by more up--to-date forms of public ownership, merely the legal framework has been established (Company Law, Transformation Law) and only the initial steps have been taken, even in Hungary, considered the pioneer of economic reform. Since 1986, various experiments have been made in China with separating ownership rights from rights related to management (disposal), as well as with the establishment of mixed forms of ownership. In a talk with leading executives of GATT in November, 1987, Zhao Ziyang, secretary general of the CPC, is reported to have said that the share of the state sector in the GNP would be reduced in the first half of the 1990s from the then prevailing more than 60% to about its half, i.e. to about 30%-33%. Reform of the ownership system is needed above all in order that enterprises and other economic units can appear on the competitive market as really autonomous subjects and entrepreneurs, managing themselves at their own risk and responsibility. Without such entrepreneurs a truly competitive market cannot develop.

To sum up: in the course of elaborating the above-outlined system of targets, the Chinese reform experts have recognized that not only a <u>horizontal</u> dependence exists between the reform targets on the individual levels, demanding adequate harmonization. There is also a <u>vertical</u> dependence between the individual levels - and that in a direction opposite to the order in which they were listed above. Without a radical reform of the ownership system established during an earlier stage of socialist construction, a competitive market comprising all factors of production and functioning according to the rules of a commodity economy cannot develop. Without the latter, however, the system of economic regulators cannot function according to the requirements of a planned commodity economy, either; that is, it cannot orient the economic units both to the demands and requirements of developments in a market situation and to those raised by government control agencies. In this case, however, the measures taken to increase the autonomy of economic units (enterprises) and to create their self-financing ability cannot achieve their goal. With this, the circle closes and, at the same time, we have one of the causes of failure of the reform experiments made up to now.

Footnotes to Chapter Eight

1. Sun Yefang, then director of the Economic Research Institute of the Chinese Academy of Sciences proposed already in 1963 that planning and ecomic management be implemented with the aid of indirect instruments (economic and financial regulators, commodity and monetary relations, price, wage and interest policies, by consciously using the law of value and market value judgement
2. Hungary, Rumania, Yugoslavia
3. See, among others, the following publications of the author:
   - A szocializmusba való átmenet néhány elméleti kérdése a társadalmi-gazdasági fejlődésben elmaradott országokban (Some theoretical questions of transition to socialism in the countries lagging behind in socioeconomic development) Doctoral thesis, Budapest, 1981. 288 p
   - A szocializmusba való átmenet preszocialista szakasza az elmaradott országokban (The pre-socialist stage of transition to socialism in the backward countries), Világosság (Light), no. 2, 1983, pp 75-84
   - A szocialista forradalmak történelmi padoxona - A szocializmusba való átmenet megváltozott történelmi feltételei korunkban (The historical paradox of socialist revolutions. The changing historical conditions of transition to socialism in our age), Világosság, no 2. 1984, pp 90-97
   - Átmenet és történelmi hátrány - A preszocializmus felépítményrendszeréről (Transition and historical handicap - On the system of superstructure of pre-socialism), Világosság, no. 12, 1984, pp 737-745
   - A kínai fejlődés főbb tendenciái (Main tendencies of the Chinese development), Világosság, no. 4, 1986, pp 252-258
   - A marxi szocializmusfelfogás és "forradalmi revíziója" (The

Marxian concept of socialism and its "revolutionary revision"), <u>Info-Társadalomtudomány</u> (Information on Social Sciences), no. 7, Budapest, December 1988, pp 19-27
- A "létező szocializmus" és a marxi formációelmélet (The "existing socialism" and the Marxian theory of social formations). In: Válaszúton: "Létező szocializmus" - Politikai átmeneti időszak? Szocializmus? Kapitalizmus? (At the crossroads: "Existing socialism" - A phase of political transition? Socialism? Capitalism?, ELTE, ÁJTK, Budapest, 1988, pp 63-81
- Mi a szocializmus? (What is the socialism?), <u>Új Fórum</u> (New Forum), no. 3, 1989, pp 26-31
4. See the article by Sun Yangyan and Wang Haidong: "The system of ownership: difficulties of the economic reform and the way out of the mess" in <u>Jingji Yanjiu</u> (Economic Research), no. 9, 1986, pp 32-38
5. <u>Renmin Ribao,</u> Oct. 22nd, 1984, p 2

Chapter Nine
INSTRUMENTS OF ECONOMIC REFORM IN CHINA

Means of Political and Economic Leaders for Realizing Reform Goals

For implementing their system of targets for economic reform the party and government leaders of the CPC and the PRC dispose of a relatively wide variety of political, legal, economic, and financial instruments that can be used alone or in combination. The efficiency of their implementation depends, however, to a significant extent on the expediency of these instruments, on how elaborate and coordinated they are, and, last but not least, on how much the social environment can be influenced and how receptive it is. Every factor comprises both objective and subjective elements.

The political instruments play a determining role. The introduction and implementation of reform and the identification and modification of the various reform targets in the past 10 years has always been done on the basis of political decisions. These were made partly by the leading bodies of the CPC and partly by the legislative and executive organs of the state (National People's Congress, State Council). These decisions were formulated and implemented mostly in the form of party resolutions, laws and legal decrees, orders, legal regulations, and instructions. With the progress of reform, the number of orders and prescriptions that were issued at lower levels of the party and state organizations, in the spirit of delegating and decentralizing the right of decision making, kept growing. This significantly complicated the situation and at times made it difficult to survey the extent to which economic activities were regulated. In several cases it channeled the reform processes in a direction which was not in conformity with or was even opposed to the central ideas. At the same time, it is a fact that in a country as large as China control cannot be exercised, in any respect, merely by issuing central instructions, particularly not in the field of economy, where there are huge differences between different parts and provinces of the country as well as between urban and rural areas as regards both the structure and level of development of the economy and the supply with various economic resources and factors of production. This is why in China, presumably, it is still not possible to introduce reform measures everywhere uniformly, at an identical rate, and in the framework of normative prescriptions. This will be the case for some time to come.

The legal regulation of economic processes is a novel and seemingly unsolvable task for the economic control organs and legislators of China. Although huge efforts have been made in this field in the past 10 years, with dozens of laws and several hundred legal decrees worked out and approved, most of them could not be implemented and required frequent modification. This was partly because of the "legal gaps" discovered in the meantime, and partly because of the incompetence or passive resistance of the local authorities and/or economic organizations. To date no Civil Code exists in China. Instead, "Legal Civil Principles" were enacted in April, 1986, by the 5th session of the 6th National People's Congress and they became effective on January 1, 1987. As has been mentioned, the "Enterprise Act" was approved - after much wrangling - by the first session of the 7th NPC and took effect on August 1, 1988. The Labor Code is awaiting modification, and a Trade Union Law must be worked out. Most laws and legal decrees were issued in China in the past 10 years in connection with foreign investments and the founding of foreign enterprises, but even these required repeated modification and completion. All this indicates that economic legislation and legal regulation of economic processes are still in the initial phase in China, and thus the development of a legal system for the economy is rather a goal than an instrument for reforming the Chinese economic system. In this field Chinese jurists and economists stress the study and utilization of international experience. They translate a large number of relevant books and articles into Chinese (as we have seen, also from Hungarian), they participate in international seminars dealing with economic legal problems, and several well-known experts from all parts of the world have been invited to China to lecture and for consultation.

In the implementation of the goals of economic reform an outstanding place is occupied by the administrative, economic, and financial instruments deployed by the government, as well as by the government policies for their improvement, for creation of a market, and for transformation of ownership relations. Since these instruments and policies are extremely extensive and complex, it seems expedient to review their most important characteristics in a logical grouping conforming to the system of targets for the economic reform, pointing out at the same time the problems and difficulties with their implementation.

Instruments of Administrative Regulation

A modern economy cannot operate without deploying instruments of administrative control and regulation. The traditional model of a "socialist planned economy" - owing to its economic philosophy and to the economic and political power centralized in the hands of the ruling élite - relied for the control and regulation of economic processes almost exclusively on command methods and instruments of administrative coercion. In this system even such categories of commodity economy as price, wage, rate of interest, and rate of exchange had an administrative character as their measures were centrally prescribed and were mandatory for everyone. This is why one of the main requirements of economic reform is to ease the administrative restrictions on economic activities and to gradually shift the control and regulation of economic processes from direct (command) methods to indirect ones (to economic and financial instruments).

The paradox is that the party and government leaders committed to reform are forced to help the transition from administrative management to economic and financial control mainly by administrative methods, voluntarily renouncing certain decision-making rights and delegating them to lower-level authorities or economic organizations. Separation of the functions of the party from those of the state, as well as those of government organs and enterprises, takes place in a similar way.

Thus, one of the main directions of reform measures implemented in an administrative manner is <u>decentralization</u>, that is, delegation of authority and rights earlier exercised by central or higher-level economic management organs and institutions to lower-level ones, right down to enterprises themselves, and in the countryside even to peasant families. This process began in China as early as in 1978 and significant progress was achieved in the first half of the 1980s. In its course, the scope of authority and rights of government organs in the economic management of provinces and cities significantly have increased in the past 10 years. In consequence of the budgetary reform this was coupled with great financial autonomy, particularly in the case of the coastal provinces and so-called open cities receiving special treatment in the framework of "outward opening." The coastal provinces and "open cities" were allowed to retain a greater part of budget revenues for local infrastructural investments promoting foreign trade and foreign investments (e.g. construction of highways and railways, building up the telephone network). But the people's governments of counties, rural towns, districts and villages also received significant autonomy, as did the economic units and enterprises under their supervision. Perhaps it was the autonomy of large and medium-sized state enterprises that increased the least, though their rights were significantly expanded in 1984.[1]

No exactly outlined and uniformly interpretable official standpoint has emerged in the past 10 years on the expedient, desirable, and permissible extent of <u>enterprise autonomy</u>. On the whole, everyone agrees that the autonomy of enterprises has to be increased and that in some way they should become self--financing, but opinions differ about how, when, and with what methods this might be attained. The recentralizing efforts, which have intensified since the autumn of 1988, allow us to conclude that this question will not be removed for a long time from the agenda of Chinese economic reform.

The actual extent of enterprise autonomy otherwise depends in China on several factors, above all on the size of the enterprise, then on the form of ownership, and, finally, on the superior organ of the enterprise. The position of large firms was on the whole the same - independent of their belonging to the state or the cooperative sector. In the past 2 or 3 years this situation has changed, insofar as, with the development of groups and groupings of enterprises, these firms that organized themselves both horizontally and vertically (in which also firms operating under different forms of ownership may participate) received greater autonomy and broader rights, including the right to cooperate with foreign firms. These groups of enterprises extend their activities to several provinces, or even to the whole country, and they mostly operate under the direct control and management of the central economic authorities, which holds more advantages than disadvantages for them. The autonomny of medium-sized and small state enterprises is usually greater than that of large state-owned ones but smaller than that of enterprises of the same size in collective ownership. These operate mostly under the control and supervision of local governments, and thus the extent of their autonomy frequently depends on the approach and style of the local leaders. It is small and medium-sized collectively owned enterprises that enjoy the greatest freedom, although it is true that they have to rely on their own resources and cannot expect state support. Their number has suddenly grown since the mid-1980s, mainly as a result of the mushrooming of rural industrial and service ventures.

One of the main instruments for the administrative regulation of enterprise management is the <u>drawing off of profit</u>, or the <u>system of taxes</u>. In the case of state enterprises mostly the former, in that of individual and private firms rather the latter method is used. Beginning in 1978 with state firms, the so-called <u>paying-in-of-profit system</u> was in force, which left only a minimum of profit with the firms - barely 2%-3% - for premium and welfare funds. The part of realized profit due to the enterprise was then established - similar to subventions - individually and ulteriorly by the supervisory authorities. Beginning in the early 1980s, several experimental forms for the division of profit were introduced in the state enterprises. One of these was the <u>system of leaving profit behind</u>, under which the portion of profit to be left with the enterprise was determined in advance, ranging between 5% and 10%, according to branches and regions. Another form was the <u>system of undertaking profit</u>, whereby not the rate but the sum of the profit was predetermined and the enterprise committed itself to pay this sum. If it complied with this commitment, it could freely dispose of any re-maining profit. The third form was the <u>profit tax system</u>; an attempt was made to introduce it beginning in 1983 (though with some state enterprises it had been used even earlier, but a general introduction finally failed in 1985-1986, above all because of the huge differences in the profit-producing ability of the Chinese state enterprises. With the firms unsuited for normative profit taxation, they made attempts to "level out" the profit remaining or missing after deduction of the profit tax, determined at 55% of the realized profit, by levying a "regulatory tax" or granting a subsidy so that 10%-15% of profit should remain for the formation of the obligatory enterprise funds. Such "normative" profit taxation did not make much sense; thus, beginning in 1987, they again reverted to modified forms of undertaking profit. Several versions exist, depending on the conditions under which the enterprise obliges itself to pay a predetermined amount of profit into the state budget. In the case of losing enterprises there is also a form of contract in which the firm obliges itself to maintain the loss level or reduce it. If the commitments undertaken in the contract are fulfilled of overfulfilled, the enterprises receive various favors and premiums, which are similarly stipulated in in the contracts.

Beyond the profit tax, or the undertaking of profit payment substituting for it, in recent years new kinds of taxes have been introduced in order to "cool down" the "overheated" economy and to restore the balance of supply and demand. The most important of these are the so-called <u>energy and transport development tax</u> (usually 10-15% of the after-tax profit, with rates varying by regions) and the <u>premium tax</u>, to be paid on earnings other than wages. (In a calendar year, premiums corresponding to the wages of 4 months at most can be paid above wages.) Following from the conditions of the country, the tax system differs by regions. Further major taxes are: turnover tax, various product taxes, property tax, personal income tax. The latter is levied only on incomes above 400 yuan/month. (Up to an income of 800 yuan monthly only a 15%, so-called adjusting tax has to be paid; beyond it, however, the rate steeply increases, reaching 45% on an income of 12 000 yuan/month.) The collectively and privately owned enterprises pay in general a 55% profit tax, to which, however, other local taxes or dues may be added. In the case of starting and carrying on activities in the public interest, these firms may receive various tax exemptions. The taxation of joint Chinese-foreign ventures, coming about in the wake of investments of foreigners, of cooperative enterprises, and of private firms owned exclusively by foreigners, as well as repatriation of profits deriving from the activity of such firms, is regulated by separate laws and decrees. Taxation conditions are generally more advantageous for foreigners, particularly in the special economic zones and the so-called development districts. Foreign capital investors also enjoy tax reductions for several years if they import world-standard technologies.

Among the administrative tools for the regulation of enterprise management may be mentioned the <u>official prescriptions relating to the formation and use of the various enterprise funds</u>. These strictly define the proportions in which the profit left with the firm has to be divided among (a) the production development fund, (b) the research and development fund, (c) the welfare fund, and (d) the premium fund. In some enterprises a reserve fund is formed in addition to the four funds listed. The manner in which these funds may be used is regulated by separate decrees.

The system of planning also belongs to the administrative instruments of economic management. Its comprehensive reform was initiated, as mentioned, on January 1, 1985. By virtue of the document issued by the Planning Commission on August 31, 1984, and approved by the State Council on October 4, 1984, entitled: "Some temporary dispositions about the improvement of the planning system," the number of mandatory plan indicators significantly diminished from 1985 on, and so did the weight of the output and turnover prescribed by them in total output and trade. Besides the <u>mandatory plans</u> the <u>guidance plans</u> appeared; these usually contained value quotas, not concrete plan targets relating to kinds of products (the guidance plans were generally worked out by the enterprises themselves). The state organs do not secure materials and technology for the volume of products figuring in the guidance plans; the enterprises have to secure these themselves, through contracts made with other firms, who satisfy them from product quotas figuring in their own guidance plans. In principle, for these products the enterprises make autonomous agreements also on prices and conditions of delivery. In the case of prices, however, they have to observe the limits set by the State Office for Prices, and may exceed the "mandatory plan prices" by only 15%-20%. Thus, the "guidance plan prices" are not free prices, but belong to the category of maximized official prices - even if the contracting parties do not always observe the prescriptions of the price authorities when setting their prices. The scope of the products (and their volume) included in the mandatory and the guidance plans may change from one year to the next - depending on supply and demand - and this is a factor of rather serious uncertainty in the reformed system of planning in China. Regarding the relation between directive and guidance planning, no uniform opinion has yet emerged among the Chinese economic leaders and economists. Differences in opinion appear not merely in respect of the volume of the two spheres of planning, i.e., their expedient or possible limits; judging from the experience of recent years, it is also debated whether the prevailing guidance planning is actually of a "guiding" or orienting nature, or is rather a looser, "modernized" form of directive planning. As a matter of fact, owing to the ever more frequent interference by authorities, the current guidance plans are becoming increasingly similar to the mandatory ones.

Nor has a uniform opinion emerged among the Chinese economic and political leaders, economists, and social scientists regarding the rate, extent, and most expedient forms of transition to <u>indirect</u> management of the economy. On the whole, there is agreement that the government-level economic control agencies will have to engage in the future in the comprehensive, strategic problems and tasks of macrolevel planning and control and that, accordingly, the management of everyday activities of economic organizations and even the formulation of enterprise strategies have to be entrusted to the organizations themselves. This is also reflected by the standpoints taken by the party and state leaders on the role and management of the market, formulated in the repeatedly quoted slogan: "The state regulates the market and the market orientates the enterprises." These are, however, all too generally formulated principles which do not provide sufficiently concrete guidance for practical economic management activity. This is why differences in opinion and debates are concentrated around the specific fields where direct and indirect control methods should be employed, on their relative proportions, as well as on the extent to which the former can be replaced by the latter. Three marked standpoints can be identified from these debates:

According to the first, in China it is absolutely necessary that the production of goods most important for the development of the national economy and for satisfying the needs of society and, particularly, the large and medium-sized firms engaged in their production and trade should be managed even in the future mainly by direct methods, i.e., with mandatory plan indicators and centrally controlled price and credit policies. With the management of medium-sized firms that are of secondary importance for the national economy and public welfare it is expedient to use some combination of plan regulation and market regulation. Finally, in the case of small firms - the number of which already exceeded 5 million in industry and 12 million in trade and services at the end of 1985 - basically market regulation and taxation policy should gradually be allowed to control their activities.

The second standpoint holds that the forms and methods of government control should be differentiated first of all according to the forms of ownership, not to the size of firms. Differences in the latter should be observed - also with a view to their nature and importance - only in second place. Accordingly, with state-owned (whole people's) enterprises combined forms and methods of direct and indirect, i.e., of plan and market regulation should be used, considering the size and character of the firms. With enterprises belonging to the collective and individual sectors and those owned by Chinese and foreign private capitalists, further, in the case of Chinese-foreign joint ventures, market regulation should assert itself exclusively.

Finally, representatives of the third standpoint believe that the basic target of the economic reform is an organic linking of planned economy with commodity economy, i.e., the simultaneous and coordinated use of plan regulation and market regulation. They are of the opinion that, for every form of ownership and every size of enterprise, state control is permissible only with indirect instruments, i.e., with so-called guidance plans and various economic and financial regulators. Therefore, they urge a shift to such control methods as soon as possible. They think that the things most urgently needed to achieve this end are a radical transformation of the state (whole people's) system of ownership, separation of ownership rights from those of disposal, and, on this basis, the fastest possible development of a full-scope competitive market extending to all factors of production.

Economic Regulators

It will have become clear from the above that in developing the target model of Chinese economic reform, i.e., a functioning planned commodity economy, a distinguished role falls to the economic regulators, or economic parameters, as they are called by some Chinese economists. It is, namely, with the help of these that they intend to gradually transform the up to now mostly direct control of the economy with administrative instruments into an indirect one. Below we briefly review two basic categories of the economic regulators: prices and wages, the related reform measures, and important features of further reform ideas and conceptions. (We remind the reader that - as opposed to the overwhelming majority of Chinese economists - we do not consider the system of taxation to be an economic regulator, but list it among the administrative instruments of economic control and management.) In the next section separate mention will be made of the financial regulators which belong to the armory of monetary policy (issue of money, rate of interest, rate of exchange, foreign exchange management rules, etc.).

The price system

The Chinese price system that prevailed prior to 1978 served as a control only to an extremely restricted extent and mostly through transmissions - using administrative brakes and barriers, as well as various supports (subsidies, donations, price subsidies, tax benefits). For the fundamental raw and basic materials and an extremely wide range of consumer goods, producer and consumer prices, the wholesale and retail price margins, and the prices of most services were established according to the guidelines and price formation rules of the central price authority, taking into account certain local characteristics. The state procurement prices for the most important agricultural products and export articles were a separate category. For these, a state trade monopoly was in force for three decades, from 1954 until 1984. The government economic control agencies aimed throughout at price stability, and thus the relative prices were modified only to the extent that they should have no essential impact on either producer or consumer price levels. The agricultural price scissors opened rather wide but were stable and calculable. The role of market prices was negligible, because the rural and urban free markets - when they existed at all - transacted only a fraction of retail trade.

The reform of the price system began in the autumn of 1979, with the raising of procurement prices (covering 18 products by 20%-50%) and continued in the years that followed. Between 1979 and 1984 the procurement price level of agricultural products and of goods produced by the rural complementary enterprises increased by altogether 53.6% relative to 1978, corresponding to an annual rate of 7.4%. At the same time - parallel with the spreading of the contractual responsibility system - the free market trade of agricultural produce that exceeded the contracted volume also expanded, and in this area prices changed in conformity with supply and demand. In this period the government price policy also became more flexible; efforts were made to introduce incentive prices for the most up-to-date and sought-after products, also using the method of "price adjustments" and partial "freeing of prices."

Essential changes took place in the Chinese price system after 1984, in consequence of the expansion of enterprise autonomy and transition to the new system of planning. Although this could not yet be called a comprehensive and radical price reform (it was at about this time that this goal had been formulated in the party resolution on the reform of the economic system), the changes implemented brought about a qualitatively new situation. By 1985 three price categories had emerged in China:

1. There are fixed prices (ding jia in Chinese) which continue to be determined by the state price authorities, with national or regional validity, for the products most important for the national economy and people's welfare. This is why these are also called official prices (pai jia). Since for these products definite production quotas are prescribed in the mandatory plans, and the procurement and sale (more exactly: allocation) of these quantities takes place with the mediation of the state materials management bureaus, for these quotas also the term mandatory plan price (zhiling xing jihua jiage) is used - instead of "fixed price" or "official price".

2. There are floating prices (fudong jiage), which develop on the basis of agreements between producers and users, or producers and state commercial organs and enterprises taking over the produce for sale. To some extent they already reflect the supply and demand relations as well as differences in quality of the products. Since the parties mentioned agree on these prices gen-

erally within the framework of supply or procurement contracts, these are also called <u>contractual prices</u> (yi jia). A third term exists for them: <u>guidance plan price</u> (zhidaoxing jihua jiage), which derives from the fact that a considerable portion of the products sold at such prices figures in the so-called guidance plans in the form of plan targets formulated in terms of quantitative or value quotas. In this case even the term <u>maximized price</u> could be used, as, according to the regulations, the prices of products produced and sold in this manner can exceed the level of mandatory plan prices by at most 20%. (In recent years, however, this limit has rarely been observed by the enterprises.)

3. Finally, there are <u>free prices</u> (ziyou jiage), which flexibly adjust to the momentary supply-and-demand situation on the market and thus basically express the market value judgement. This is why they are also called <u>market prices</u> (shi jia). In consequence of the continuous "price liberation" this price category already covers the overwhelming majority of industrial articles for mass consumption and a considerable portion of foodstuffs. The fast rise of these prices expresses best the upsetting of the market equilibrium in recent years: demand far exceeding aggregate supply and decline of the domestic purchasing power of the yuan - i.e., inflation.

The basic problem of the Chinese price reform derives not so much from the simultaneous coexistence and functioning of these three price categories, but from the fact that in the current "double-track" system of planning and management the same product may have three kinds of prices. This depends on whether it has been produced on the basis of mandatory or guidance plans, or perhaps above plan targets, even outside the plans, using free capacities of the enterprise. Thus, there are significant differences in the level of prices belonging to the different categories, depending on the sphere of turnover (state allocations, interfirm sales, free market sales). It is therefore a basic interest of every producing and trading firm to withdraw the greatest possible portion of its products and sales from the scope of mandatory plans and to fulfill its supply contracts only if the ordering party is willing to pay a "quality surcharge" approximating the free market price for its products, or to compensate for the "price loss" of the enterprise obliged to deliver by supplying its own product at lower guidance or mandatory plan prices. This system provides opportunity for speculation and abuses while accelerating inflation with its price--raising tendency.

One of the biggest and most debated problems of the Chinese economic reform is how to implement the price reform in the process of transition from the old economic system to the new one without disorganizing the economy with the radical transformation of the price system, and how to avoid an even bigger inflation spiral. The basic problem is the depressed prices of energy, raw and basic materials, and of the most important agricultural products (grain, cotton, oil-bearing plants). For a long time already, these prices have not covered the costs of production, and production could be maintained and increased only with instruments of administrative coercion (mandatory plan targets). A sudden big or repeated small rise of these prices would entail - by secondary effects - a general rise of producer prices in the manufacturing industry and also of consumer prices, and this process would be difficult to control and brake. This is why no uniform concept has developed to date in respect of how to implement the price reform. The draft proposals and concepts of Chinese experts may be grouped around six opinions:

1. The most widespread opinion is - and most government leaders agree - that the price reform should be implemented in stages, step by step, avoiding major shocks. In the first stage it is expedient to carry out merely the adjustment of producer and wholesale prices; a major adjustment of consumer prices can take place only in the second stage. Those who hold this opinion propose that the approximation of domestic and foreign trade prices to each other, their greater harmony, should be brought about through a corresponding modification of the rate of exchange in the third stage. According to this concept, one should begin at every stage with minor adjustments, later to be fol-

lowed by major modifications of irrational relative prices. The whole system of price formation can be radically revised and modified only when all three stages have been implemented and a clearer picture can be obtained about a rational price system.

2. Diametrically opposed to the former is the minority opinion, according to which the price reform has to be implemented in close harmony with the reforms of the tax, financial, and credit as well as the foreign trade systems, simultaneously, in the framework of a major "reform package," as a price reform cannot succeed alone. Some propose inclusion of wage reform in the package as well, while others treat it as a separaate "package," together with the reform of social policy.

3. There are experts who believe that the price reform should be coupled first of all with market organization and market development and with the transformation of the whole turnover system, because a well-functioning price system cannot be developed without a well-functioning market. The market is merely a necessary but not a sufficient condition of price liberalization. For this also the operational rules of the market have to be worked out. At the same time, in the interest of bringing about genuine market relations, it is urgent to put state trade on a business basis, and further, to gradually eliminate "planned allocation" and replace it with government orders.

4. The past 1-2 years have seen an increase in the number of economic experts who stress that the development of strong macrolevel control is a basic and indispensable condition for successful price reform. If, namely, the gap between aggregate social demand and supply is too broad, forced price reform carries great dangers, above all an acceleration of inflation.

5. Some are of the opinion that in the process of the gradual liberalization of prices and the gradual liquidation of administrative price controls a distinction should be made between the competitive and the monopolistic spheres. In fact, even within the latter, the branches where the monopolistic situation derives from the nature of the products (e.g., tobacco, spirits, or enterprises satisfying national demand alone for some rare product) should be treated in a manner different from that to be

used in branches where monopolistic situations are created by the formation of cartel-like groups. For the latter, the elaboration and introduction of an antimonopoly law is absolutely necessary. Otherwise, the prices of all products will not be able to develop exclusively and completely under the spontaneous impact of changes in supply and demand. For certain products the official fixing of prices will be necessary even in the future.

6. The final standpoint acknowledges the existence of the "double-track" system, more precisely, of several kinds of prices for the same product in the initial stage of the reform, since even this system shakes the old one of administrative price formation. However, it must not be maintained for long; otherwise, its harmful effect will grow stronger. Parallel with the progress of the reform, the double-track system has to be replaced by a market price system in a growing number of fields. Where the necessary conditions do not yet exist, the market price system should be approximated gradually, with official price fixing and price control. The "guidance plan prices" offer a good opportunity to do this, as they are partially market prices and partially officially maximized prices, with levels usually between those of official fixed prices and those of free market prices.

All these diversified opinions do not change the fact that from the price reform package declared in 1984, only the first step was implemented in the course of the first 5 years. Further ones have been repeatedly delayed because of the upsetting of market equilibrium and accelerating inflation.

The wage system

The essential features of the current Chinese wage system developed in the mid-1950s, at the time of the first 5-year plan, and they have not changed substantially in the past 10 years. Although the concrete sums of the eight-grade wage scale used in state enterprises slowly increased in consequence of the growing inflation, no basic changes have taken place in relative wages, in the criteria for setting wages, and in wage components. The same can be said about state enterprises in other branches of the economy and about the 30-grade wage scale for employees of government offices and institutions. (The difference between the lowest and the highest wage is 3-3.5-fold in the case of the eight-grade wage scale, and 12-15-fold in the case of the 30-grade scale.) In collectively owned enterprises there has never been any centrally or officially established or prescribed wage schedule or wage scale. In these the establishment and payment of wages is effected in conformity with the income level and considering the local living conditions, in some cases on the basis of collective agreements, but mostly individually. (In these enterprises the workers - provided they are also part-owners of the enterprise - also receive profit shares above their wages.) The situation is similar for the workers in private firms, excepting those owned by foreigners or jointly owned by Chinese and foreigners, where wages are a matter left exclusively to the management, and official prescriptions relate only to the social security fund of employees and to the maintenance of certain welfare institutions.

As regards the level of wages, it is highest in the enterprises owned by foreigners, in the joint ventures of Chinese and foreigners, and in some private Chinese enterprises. In these firms the average wage fluctuates between 200 and 250 yuan/month, which is about double the average wage paid in the state sector (about 120 yuan/month). There are also significant differences in wage levels in the state sector - of 30%-40% - depending on the size of the enterprise and the nature of the work. The average wage of those working in the collective sector approximates the lower wage zone in the state sector (70-80 yuan/month). Workers in small rural enterprises usually attain this level. However, workers in the state sector enjoy significant payments over and above wages (premiums, bonuses) and also various favors (cheap factory canteens, cheap housing, free medical supply, pension, and, less frequently, free holidays and travel facilities). This puts them in a privileged position relative to other groups of workers. A particular advantage for them is that their job is secured until they reach the age of retirement (called in China the "iron rice bowl") and when they retire, the enterprise is obliged to employ in their place one of their descendants. Beginning in 1986, efforts were begun to put an end to this system by no longer employing workers "for a lifetime," but rather under contract for a definite period (usually 3-5 years). At present, about 10% of those working in state enterprises, that is, about 10 million blue- and white-collar employees, work under the new contract system.

In the last 4 years there have been partial initiatives at reforming the wage system in two directions and in two fields. With some industrial state enterprises (about 7000) wage-bill management has been introduced and the amount of the wage bill is determined depending on the success of enterprise management. In recent years this system has been built into the contractual profit-undertaking or management responsibility system, making the wage bill dependent on the amount of profit. But the system has not been introduced generally. In 1986 an experiment was carried out with a new wage system for workers in government institutions; it differentiates to a greater extent than earlier, according to individual capabilities, position, and actual performance of the employee. In this system the wages of an employee are composed of four elements: (a) basic wage, (b) wage according to duty, (c) age bonus, and (d) the premium for quality performance. The last is paid once a year as a lump sum, generally at the end or the beginning of the year. In the end, the introduction of this system was passed over as well, mainly because its advocates wanted to link the filling of a post to an aptitude test and professional examination in the framework of competition and to delegate the determination of premiums to the members of collectives working together.

As regards the further course of wage reform, ideas are rather uncertain and hazy. On the whole, there is general agreement that, in the long run, with the development of a commodity economy, the level of wages has to be determined and regulated by the supply and demand relations on the labor market (only those who deny the commodity character of labor disagree). This should also lead to diminishing sectorial differences and to the development of a wage system proportionate to performance. But the way leading to such a situation seems to be long and rough and full of pitfalls.

First of all, the current wage system - in spite of the sectorial differences mentioned - still bears the signs of a leveling wage policy characteristic of former decades. From among the forms of wage payment, performance wage is rarely used, even where conditions exist for it. Time wage is the most widespread form, in rare cases complemented by extras for night shifts and dangerous work. This is partly because in most productive establishments the management cannot ensure regular work, and thus a considerable number of workers would earn essentially less through no fault of their own. This situation is due partly to the chronic disturbances in the supply of materials and energy, and partly to the surplus staff (overemployment), estimated at 25%-30%. (Where performance wages are still used, the "standstill" is reckoned as overhead cost, and a time-proportionate part of average wages is paid to the "workers" who actually do not work.)

Second, owing to the different levels of development of the various areas and branches, as well as to the huge differences in the size and technological equipment of individual firms, the productivity of live labor and the income-producing ability of the various economic units cover an extremely wide scale. This is why wage payment according to uniform principles can hardly be introduced, even within one branch or a single area. Beyond the above, the main obstacle to reducing and eliminating wage differentials among enterprises belonging to different forms of ownership and sectors is that the income of those working in the state sector (including bonuses above wages and various other favors) is too high, and the collective sector will not be able to catch up in any foreseeable period of time. This would require a complete transformation of the social insurance system and of social policy practice, and the number of those covered by this insurance would multiply. China will dispose of the necessary materials and finances only after several decades of effort.

Finally, also the effect which the development of a genuine labor market may have on the price of labor in the country with the biggest population of the world is extremely problematic and carries great risk. In this market there will be excess supply. (As a matter of fact, there already is one.) The current official statistics show as unemployed, or as "those waiting for work," only the urban young people actually waiting for work and those dismissed from state enterprises. (According to the latest official statistical publication their number was merely 3.6 million.) The number of peasants filtering into the cities and seeking jobs is a multiple of that even now, and then we have not yet mentioned the rural "underemployed", the latent unemployed (their number may be about 60-70 million), and the "indoor" unemployed in the now-operating enterprises and institutions (their number is estimated to be about 30-35 million). This means that at least one fifth of the 550 million people recorded as being employed in the cities and villages are actually unemployed. Such a mass of unemployed workers would exercise unbearable pressure on the wage level - certainly not high even now - if the labor market were free.

Financial Regulators

It must be said right at the beginning that China still has a predominantly controlled, not market-like economy. Thus, in the course of the reform up till now the financial regulators (the issue of banknotes, the state budget, credit policy, and rates of interest, as well as foreign exchange management and exchange rate policy) have functioned much more as administrative regulators than as actual financial ones. The reform of the financial system has taken the form mostly of such organizational measures as decentralization of budget revenues and expenditures, increasing the weight in investment financing of repayable bank loans, reform of the banking system, and the creation of money markets promoting the flow of money among enterprises and granting short-term credits. In recent years, in some large cities (Guangzhou, Nanjing, Shanghai, Shenyang and Wuhan) as well as in one of the special economic zones (Shenzhen) securities exchanges and foreign exchange markets have been set up, but these operate only with territorial restrictions and on an experimental basis. In financial policy the emphasis is now on consolidating macroeconomic control and management, and with economic units, on strengthening financial discipline.

Regulation of the issue of money

In the PRC exclusively the central bank, the People's Bank of China is entitled to issue money. It supplies the specialized banks with money, thus the Industrial and Commercial Bank, the Agricultural Bank, the Bank of Construction, and the Bank of Communication. The Bank of China, the foreign trade and external economic relations bank of the country, enjoys a particular status: it centralizes the foreign exchange management related to foreign trade and also a portion of foreign trade transactions. But the national network of branches is structured hierarchically with every bank, in conformity with the levels of administrative sub- and superordination, and the heads of banking organizations of the different levels are personally closely dependent on the leaders of the local party and government organs (without whose approval they can be neither appointed nor relieved). Also the granting of credits depends considerably on the views and will of the local leader. This may be one explanation for the fact that - in spite of several resolutions and some attempts at making money tight - it has never been possible to keep the issue of money within the planned limits. It followed that the rate at which paper money was issued was double or treble the growth rates of the GNP and commodity trade. Thus, the issue of money cannot be considered to be an effective tool of financial regulation in China today.

The state budget

The above summary statement may also be said to hold for the state budget, with the difference that the effects of decentralization assert themselves to an even greater extent in budgetary management. The revenues and expenditures of the state budget are today transacted mostly in the scope of authority of the regional organs; only a portion - about 40% - flows into the budget of the central government. The regional government organs frequently levy various surtaxes in order to cover their expenditures; they even draw away a part of the depreciation funds of enterprises. The result of this is that budget management becomes increasingly difficult to oversee and controll, and expenses regularly exceed revenues. Thus, in order to complement its revenues, the state is forced - at both the central and the regional level - to issue state bonds and raise foreign credit. The Chinese press has been full of news about the wasteful spending of government bureaus and institutions "managing themselves" with fiscal money. In spite of the various decrees and orders issued year after year, the budget deficit has not diminished; rather, it shows a rising tendency. The mere fact that hardly one third of investments of the state sector are financed from budget resources ought to have reduced the budget expenses. (This did not happen however, because of the rising demand for subsidies of the state enterprises. In 1989, the subsidies granted under various titles and through various channels amounted to more than one third of the total budget expenditure.)

Credit policy and interest rates

We can speak about a credit policy in China only after the beginning of reform experiments, particularly after the reform of the banking system, implemented in 1984. The substance of this reform was the introduction of a two-tier banking system. Besides the central bank of issue, the People's Bank of China, there are now five specialized banks active in the country: the Industrial and Commercial Bank, the Agricultural Bank, the Bank of Construction, the Bank of Communication and the foreign trade bank, or the Bank of China. Among them, the Bank of Construction is not quite of a business nature, as it finances the large state investments implemented from budget sources. In addition, in order to transact bond issues abroad and for the investments of foreign firms in China, the Chinese International Trust and Investment Company (CITIC) has been created, and in the special zones the opening of branches of foreign banks has been allowed, as has the creation and operation of banks jointly owned by Chinese and foreigners. The banking system is complemented by about 1500 major and more than 60 000 smaller rural credit cooperatives.

The issue of credit takes place basically according to quotas allocated by the central bank of issue and further broken down to the provincial level by the specialized commercial banks. In the ensuing further allocation also the government organs of different levels have important roles. Within the credit limits the banks procure their resources basically from the deposits placed with them (the mandatory reserve rate is 20%), as well as from the interbank money market. (In 1987 the interbank money turnover was 240 billion yuan.) Money substitutes (checks, letters of credit, deposit certificates, bills of exchange) are not sufficiently widespread and are not readily used by enterprises. However, beginning in 1988 - owing to the tight money supply - they have increasingly been forced to resort to these instruments. The bond and stock markets have started to operate only in the past 2 years, and their turnover is about 10%-15% of the total volume of credit. (In 1987 bonds and shares of stock were issued on the domestic market in the amount of about 100 billion yuan; at the time of writing no data were yet available for 1988.) The issue of bonds is restricted, in order to prevent the higher interests of bonds from "sucking off" the bank deposits. The rates of interest have been raised since 1988 on three occasions. Their average rate was 9.5% in early 1989, and even this was barely more than half of the rate of inflation in the preceding year. On the interfirm money markets granting short-term loans the rates of interest were - depending on supply and demand - 5-10 percentage points higher than those of bank credits.

Two thirds of investments are financed from bank credits, one third from budget allocations. (In the early 1980s the proportion still was fifty-fifty.) The investment credit limits are determined by the central planning agencies, but these are exceeded each year, mainly in consequence of interference by the local organs. In investment financing a growing role is intended to be given to the so-called investment companies, which operate as ventures under the direct supervision of the Investment Bureau of the State Planning Commission. (By the end of 1988 eight such companies had been established in various industri These companies, or rather their branches in the provinces and towns, no longer allocate the credit limits made available to them in an administrative manner; rather, they consider the profit motive. It is intended to abolish the investment credits at favorable rates of interest beginning in 1989, and to raise the rates to the level of medium-term development credits. It is also planned that later the state will not contribute from the state budget even to large individual projects, but will secure credit resources for them exclusively through the investment companies, or earmarked funds. In the future the investment credit will have to be repaid from after-tax profit, in contrast with the present situation where it is deducted from pre-tax profit, i.e., it is a factor reducing profit.

As regards personal savings by the population, the rate - around 8% in villages and 14% in cities - is considered low by Chinese banking experts, in spite of the fact that the stock of deposits increased even in 1988 by 23.8% and exceeded 380 billion yuan at the end of the year. In the last one and a half years the interest rates on these deposits were also raised, but they still reached barely half of the rate of inflation. In the autumn of 1988 - curiously, just after the raising of the interest rates - for some months personal bank deposits declined in consequence of the "purchasing fever" that had developed among the population, and this was moderated and braked only in early 1989.

Summing up, it may be stated that credit policy and interest rate policy in China have not yet had any substantial impact on either the structure and rate of investments or the saving propensity of the population. In order to achieve a positive effect an essentially higher development level of market relations -

particularly of the money and capital markets - would be needed, and the real rate of interests should exceed the rate of inflation by at least 2%-4%, especially where personal savings are concerned. In the enterprise sphere, efforts should be made to give efficiently producing and profit-making firms access to the necessary development credits, through competition and with conditions of interest that will transform even banking activities into business ventures, instead of the administrative allocators of money they are at present.

Policy on foreign exchange and exchange rates

Foreign exchange management has for years been one of the most debated problems in the reform of the Chinese financial system. Many Chinese experts - but even foreign ones and those of the World Bank - do not agree with the measure taken in the early 1980s under the slogan of decentralization and the policy of "outward opening," under which a kind of <u>foreign exchange retention system</u> was introduced. As a result, although a decisive portion of the foreign exchange revenue continues to go into the central till (about 60%), about 15% is given to the provincial governments and 25% is shared by the producing and foreign trading firms. (Many are of the opinion that this amounts to violating the monopoly of foreign trade and foreign exchange management, also laid down in the constitution. The development of the sizeable trade deficit is traced back mainly to this measure.) The joint Chinese-foreign ventures may fully retain their foreign exchange earnings, but they do not get any central foreign exchange allocations. The other firms can buy foreign currencies necessary for their permitted imports with domestic currency through various channels from the central resources. The central government also directly allocates foreign exchange to the provinces and preferred key enterprises.

For some years now, enterprises have been allowed to sell the foreign exchange retained or allocated them by the central authorities - if momentarily not needed - at the <u>currency exchanges</u> established in some large cities and provincial seats. In these transactions the local authorities may also participate, in addition to the enterprises. In the last one and a half years at these exchanges rates exceeding the official rate of exchange by 70%-90% developed (1 US $=8-9 RMB). The official exchange rate is usually adjusted by the financial government only every 1.5-2 years. The now valid official rate of exchange was established in 1989 (1 US $=4.72 RMB) and the exchange rates of other currencies adjust to that. In 1980 the exchange rate started at 1 US $=1.49 RMB and it rose above 3 yuan only in 1985 (1 US $=3.22 RMB). A major devaluation of about 50% was intended in the autumn of 1988, so as to approximate the official exchange rate to the one of 6-6.5 yuan/dollar developed at the currency exchanges, and thus to stimulate exports and brake imports. Because of the dangerously accelerating inflation, this idea was finally discarded, as devaluation would certainly have given a big push to inflation. According to many experts, the "purchasing fever" that erupted in the autumn of 1988 could also be attributed to the rumors about devalution.

For the practical implementation of foreign exchange management and the control of the foreign currency exchanges the responsible agency is the Currency Bureau, subordinated to the State Council but functioning as a department of the central bank of issue. Its tasks include the compilation of the balance of payments, the balance of foreign exchange, and other statistics relating to foreign exchange, the supply of information and statements about external debts, the making of payments related to foreign trade, and the control of foreign exchange management of enterprises. Foreign exchange transactions related to foreign trade are transacted - as already mentioned - by the Bank of China, the foreign trade bank. The principles of foreign debt policy and the plans by markets are worked out at a department of the State Planning Commission organized for this purpose. One of the starting points of economic policy for the next several years is China's continuing need for external resources to accelerate economic development and deepen the reforms. It is believed that doubling the current rate of debt - barely 10% - is permissible. This would allow the stock of China's debts, amounting to about US $40 billion at the end of 1988, to rise as high as US $80 billion, if terms of expiry and interest conditions remain the same on the whole until 1995. (According to the latest information at the time the manuscript was completed, the stock of debts of the PRC amounted to US $42 billion at the middle of 1989. The debt service burdens increased from US $7 billion in 1988 to 10 billion in 1989.) The raising of external loans is decentralized within the government. The loans granted by the IMF and by international regional organizations are taken by the central bank of issue. Contacts with the World Bank are maintained by the Ministry of Finance, while government loans are transacted by the Bank of China. In the coastal regions several provinces were given the right to establish external credit relations. It may be of interest to mention that, in spite of the operation of the foreign currency exchanges and of exchange rates differing from the official one, the Chinese financial authorities never confessed officially to the IMF that double or multiple rates of exchange existed in the country.

It is a financial curiosity, or rather one of currency policy, that besides the official currency, the renminbi (RMB) - since the declaration of the policy of opening the yuan certificate, issued to foreign tourists and businessmen, as well as to the employees of foreign representations (embassies, trade offices or representatives of private firms) in China - is used as a domestic instrument of payment. In certain shops (foreign-exchange shops), hotels, and restaurants payment can be made only with this convertible yuan, in consequence of which an "exchange rate" exceeding that of the "people's yuan" by 70%-80% has emerged on the black market. On leaving the country, foreigners may change this yuan certificate into any convertible currency - provided they can prove that they acquired it through their earlier change of convertible currency. In the special economic zones, too, yuan certificates are generally used as a means of payment, although in shops, hotels, and restaurants the American dollar or the Hong Kong dollar are also accepted. Also the Chinese blue- and white-collar workers there employed get a part of their wages in yuan certificates, but in some warehouses and restaurants and on the market they can buy consumer goods and foodstuffs also for renminbi. The Chinese financial authorities planned to abolish the circulation of yuan certificates several times, and even announced it, but this has not yet been implemented.

Reform of Foreign Capital Investments and Trade

The instruments for reforming foreign economic relations are similar to those used in reforming the entire economic system. Thus we may speak about administrative, economic, and financial instruments, but we may also encounter instruments and methods used exclusively in this area of the Chinese economy of outstanding importance. Such are the various measures and decrees facilitating and regulating the drawing in of foreign capital, the special economic zones and development areas in different provinces of China, and the various cooperation or jobwork contracts concluded with foreign governments and firms, relating to productive and construction activities partly within the country and partly outside it. The system of instruments for foreign economic reform is called upon to serve the policy of "opening" declared by the Chinese leadership in 1979-1980 and promotes its practical implementation and concrete realization in foreign economic relations.

Administrative regulation of foreign economic activity

In spite of the decentralization and liberalization carried out in several steps since 1979, in some fields of foreign economic activity a good many restrictions persisted even in the tenth year of the reform process (1988), and in the eleventh year (1989), their number even increased in consequence of recentralization.

First of all, the Ministry of Foreign Economic Relations and Trade of the PRC (henceforth: MOFERT) extended the decentralization and liberalization of foreign economic and foreign trade activities only to some of the transactions concluded in freely convertible currencies, up to a certain value limit, and merely for export and import products *not* figuring in the mandatory plans. In trade with the socialist and developing countries transactions continue to be dependent on MOFERT lincenses. These licenses are usually granted only if the items covered by the transaction figure in the quotas set in interstate agreements. Similarly, the import or export of kinds of products figuring in the mandatory plans and settled in free convertible currency are linked to license. Their number changes every year, depending on the balance of the economy and foreign trade. Beginning in 1986 it was made possible for the Soviet Union and the Eastern-European socialist countries to develop direct exchange of commodities or cooperation embodied in mutual deliveries with selected provinces and cities above the agreed quotas. But the export and import lists have to be presented to the MOFERT in this case as well. Also, the conclusion of intended export and import deals or cooperation agreements with capitalist firms is linked to a central license, if the value limits allowed in the given area are exceeded. (The value limits are presently US $5 million, 10 million and 30 million, depending on whether the area in question is on the mainland, a coastal province or so-called open town, or a special zone or special development district.)

Decentralization covered the branch and territorial management system of foreign economic relations as well as the wide network of productive and foreign trade enterprises, vertical and horizontal economic associations, banks, and research and development institutes. In effect, decentralization meant abolition of the earlier monopolistic sitution of the MOFERT and the foreign trade firms subordinated to it, which created for them a certain competitive situation. The MOFERT made efforts to reorganize its apparatus accordingly. New functional organs were created in addition to the MOFERT; their tasks were accomplished earlier by the ministry itself, but now these organs operate as bureaus with authority on a national scale, for example, the State Customs Office and the Office for Quality Control of Export and Import Products. In the provinces and cities foreign economic and foreign trade directorates have been set up, under whose control and management provincial and urban export-import firms with the right to trade abroad operate. The right to export and import was gradually extended, first to several hundred and then to several thousand large and medium-sized productive enterprises and groups of enterprise which, even earlier, had sold a considerable part of their output abroad.

Liberalization, which affected mainly those products "freed" from export-import licensing, was rather characteristic of the first and second stages of the reform, i.e., the years 1979-1982 and 1983-1984. Beginning in 1985 - owing to the growing trade deficit - the number and weight of products linked to export-import licenses increased again. While in 1982 80-85 export products and 20-25 import products were subject to licensing, by 1986 the numbers increased to more than 200 and more than 50 respectively. At the end of 1985 the turnover of commodities linked to license reached 33% of the total in imports and 54% in exports (in terms of value). In recent years this tendency has continued, and lately even withdrawal of the right to independent foreign trade from several thousand firms has been contemplated.

In China the main tool for the administrative regulation of foreign economic relations and foreign trade was and has remained the system of licensing. Beyond commodity trade, it also extends to money and credit turnover transacted with foreign firms, to the transfer of capital, and to the purchase of licenses. As a matter of fact, the Chinese system of customs duties, introduced in 1982, may also be regarded as administrative regulation, as may the official exchange rate policy and the foreign exchange management prescriptions. However, since to a certain extent these fulfill regulatory functions in economy and finances as well, they will be discussed together with the economic and financial regulatory instruments of the reform of foreign economy.

Indirect regulation through economic and financial regulators

Following from the original concept and logic of the Chinese economic reform, the intent was to give a growing role to regulation using indirect - economic and financial - instruments also in the management and control of foreign economy. The long-term objective was to gradually replace direct, administrative regulation with indirect regulation - at a pace depending on competitiveness of the Chinese economy on the world market and on the improvement of its external economic balance. However, in consequence of deterioration of the conditions mentioned, this seems to be a more distant goal today than it did 4 or 5 years ago, and this continues to strongly limit the scope and effectiveness of the indirect regulators. One of the most widely used instruments in foreign trade activity is the stimulation of export and the subsidization of export. This is done with various methods and through various channels, using partly economic and partly financial instruments. The economic ones include taxation, credit and tariff favors, facilitation of imports, and the preferences given to enterprises specializing in export. Financial ones are the price-leveling mechanism and the price subsidy. The former automatically levels out - up to a certain limit - the difference between the foreign trade price converted at the official rate of exchange and the domestic producer price, using a "domestic exchange rate." (In 1981 this was 2.8 yuan/dollar, with an official rate of 1.7 yuan/dollar; in 1989 it was 8 yuan/dollar, while the official rate was 4.7 yuan/dollar.) The price subsidy is used with a rather wide range of export goods, mainly with finished goods, and is given in excess of price leveling.

Also the system of foreign exchange retention, used in China for almost 10 years, may be considered a stimulating financial instrument. From the viewpoint of foreign exchange management it may be considered liberalization. Initially, it was used only in two coastal provinces of South China (Guangdong and Fujian), and in the four "special economic zones" created in them; later it was extended to other regions of the country. The part of foreign exchange left with the enterprise producing for export - the extent of retention - was initially 25% (in the special economic zones 70%), but the firm got only 2/5 of it (10%) and 3/5 went to the budget of the province. The rate of foreign exchange retention was later raised, first to 30% and then to 40% (in the special economic zones to 90% and then to 100%), and from this the exporting companies already received a 20% or 25% share. (As has been mentioned, this latter part is divided in a proportion of 2/3:1/3 between the productive and the foreign trade firms, if the former has no right to export independently.) In recent years, with the spreading of the contractual responsibility system, the exporting firms have undertaken contractual commitment also for the sum of foreign exchange to be paid into the state budget annually, and then 80% of the foreign exchange acquired above it remains in the region (with the province and the firm).

On the import side, the main tool of economic regulation is the new <u>tariff system</u>, introduced in 1982, which levied customs duties of 10%-50% on more than 40 products also in the case of exports. This tariff system was further "refined" in March, 1985, to make it conform with the prescriptions of GATT. (The PRC had announced its intention to join GATT earlier.) The Chinese tariff system applies two kinds of customs clerance procedure to commodities arriving from abroad in the framework of commercial deliveries. In the first case, the ordinary tariff rates are applied, in the second "the lowest" ones, that is, preferential rates. Both are applied in the case of reciprocity. For the time being, however, because of various export subsidies and administrative import restrictions, the GATT officials see no chance for China to join on the basis of the now operating tariff system (as happened in the case of Hungary when she actually joined the GATT in 1973); similar to the Polish accession, they demand a commitment that imports will be increased annually by a definite percentage. Also the various preferences given in the case of import-substituting investment projects are aimed at an economic regulation of imports.

Instruments for regulating the inflow of foreign capital

Ever since the announcement of the policy of opening, China has made efforts to attract as much foreign capital as possible to develop its economy. This is why great attention was paid from the beginning to the creation of a climate and conditions favorable for foreign investment. Since it would have taken quite a long time to create such an attractive climate throughout the country, the Chinese proceeded step by step. In 1979 the provinces Guangdong and Fujian obtained special rights to develop economic, commercial, and financial relations with foreigners, and to establish four special economic zones in the coastal areas (Shenzhen, Zhuhai, Shantou, Xiamen). In 1984, 14 coastal cities and the island of Hainan were opened to direct foreign investments, and in 1985 these open areas were further extended to include the delta regions of the Pearl river and the Yangtze river and, in the southern part of Fujian province, the triangle of Changzhou-Quanzhou-Xiamen. In 1986, first the Liaoning and then the Shandong peninsula was opened. In the spring of 1988 the island of Hainan, which had earlier belonged to Guangdong province, was raised to the rank of province and qualified as a special investment zone. With this, an open zone of about 320 000 km^2 with about 160 million inhabitants has been established. At the same time, the value limit of foreign investment that may be permitted by the authorities of provinces was raised in these areas to US $30 million instead of the earlier 10 million, in the case of the mainland provinces to USA $10 million instead of 5 million.

Beginning in 1979 the PRC made great efforts to regulate foreign investments with legislation. The act on joint Chinese-foreign ventures (with joint capital and management) - the so-called act on joint ventures - had already been passed in July of that year. In September, 1980, the income tax act covering these enterprises was born, prescribing a rate of 30%+3% (the 3% going to the provincial authorities). But in cases where up-to-date machines are imported and advanced technologies are introduced, the foreign investor gets tax relief. The same exemption is due to him if he does not repatriate his profit but invests it in China. In September 1983, the act on joint ventures was completed by a decree governing its implementation, which clarified a number of questions not treated in the act itself (e.g., the mode of creation and registration of joint ventures, the organizational forms and the registered capital, the mode of drawing away capital, transfer of technology, the right of land use and the charge to be paid for it, tax liabilities and tax reliefs, the rules of foreign exchange management, the recording of property and bookkeeping, rights and duties of the employees, the place and role of trade unions in the joint ventures, settlement after expiry of the contract, dissolution and final accounting, settlement of debated questions). The act on enterprises with exclusively foreign capital was passed and introduced in March 1986.

Foreign capital investments are realized in four main forms: (a) Chinese- and foreign-funded ventures (zhong-wai hezi jingying qiye), (b) Chinese-foreign cooperative enterprises (zhong-wai hezou jingying qiye), (c) Chinese-foreign cooperative development agreements (zhung-wai hezou kaifa), and (d) exclusively foreign-founded enterprises (waishang duzi jingying qije). Let us call them, for the sake of simplification, (a) joint enterprises, (b) cooperative enterprises, (c) joint developments, and (d) foreign firms. In the 10 years between 1979 and 1988, the planned and actually used foreign capital investments of US $28.2 billion and 11.6 billion, respectively were distributed as shown in Table 6.

It may be seen from the data that - with the exception of off-shore oil prospecting - foreign investments and ventures are characteristically not very large. The average amount of capital investment per firm in the three enterprise forms is US $1-2 million on the contract basis, while the amount actually used ranges only between US $0.5 and 0.6 million. Foreign investments made in the special economic zones do not differ in this respect; in the oldest and largest zone Shenzhen, in the past 10 years foreign entrepreneurs committed themselves in the framework of 6179 contracts to invest capital in the amount of US $5

Table 6. Distribution of foreign capital investment according to use between 1979-1988

Use	Number of ventures	Contracted	Actually used
		amounts (US $ million)	
Joint enterprises	8 532	9 889	4 810
Cooperative enterprises	6 778	13 863	3 974
Joint developments	51	2 925	2 488
Foreign firms	594	1 524	294
Total	15 955	28 201	11 566

Source: Beijing Review, no. 10, 1989, March 6-12, p 23

billion, of which US $2276 million was actually invested up to the end of 1988, creating 1333 joint enterprises, 715 cooperative enterprises, and 152 foreign firms in this zone. Beyond the founding of these 2200 enterprises, some of the contracts concluded related to the building of infrastructural establishments. The export performance of enterprises in the Shenzhen region in 1988 approximated US $2 billion.

In spite of the considerable increase in foreign capital investments over the past 10 years, in addition to the recent political problems, several unsolved problems and negative experiences continue to hinder a major expansion of joint ventures in China. Administration is too slow and bureaucratic; there are a great number of "internal orders" which are inaccessible to foreigners; there is a lack of foreign exchange on the part of the Chinese partners; the infrastructure is poor, with frequent difficulties in raw materials and energy supply. These are the complaints generally voiced by foreign investors. There are troubles with the work performance and discipline of Chinese employees, and with the wages and premiums demanded by trade unions. This is why no spectacular development may be expected in external economic relations in this very important area.

Other methods of opening to foreign economic activities

In the spirit of the slogan and directive of "opening outward - reviving the economy inward," the government organs of the PRC have made efforts in the past 10 years to develop their foreign economic relations in such a way as to allow the continuous modernization of industry, agriculture, science and technology, and defense, i.e., to ensure attainment as soon as possible of the long-term strategic objectives of the "four modernizations." To this end, beyond the import of up-to-date productive equipment and the introduction of modern production processes and management methods (also promoted by attracting direct foreign investment), great emphasis has been placed on developing <u>technical and scientific cooperation</u> with the industrialized countries, on the training and advanced training of Chinese experts at Japanese and Western-European universities and scientific institutions. In the past 10 years more than 35 000 young Chinese experts have been trained alone in the USA, partly at government costs, partly self-financed or with the support of relatives living abroad. Up to now, the majority of these students have returned to China on completion of their studies, but it is doubtful whether this trend will continue. At present, more than 40 000 young Chinese are studying at foreign institutions of higher education.

Since 1979, the PRC has spent almost 20 billion US dollars on the <u>purchase of licenses,</u> mainly in engineering and the electronics industry. The main suppliers of technology are Japan, the USA and the FRG. In recent years, however, China itself has sold licenses and production technologies, primarily in mining, the oil industry, electronics, and light industry. The sale of Chinese licenses is greatly promoted by the country's active participation in various international fairs and specialized exhibitions, where, besides exhibiting its products, China also makes efforts to sell its licenses.

In the past 10 years, mainly in order to earn foreign exchange, China has undertaken various <u>construction projects abroad,</u> with increasing frequency. Between 1983 and 1987 almost

4350 such "contracts for undertaking work performance" (chengbao laowu hetong) were signed with 112 countries. Work to the tune of US $4 billion was completed by the end of 1987, with the participation of about 25 000 people. In China more than 70 firms are engaged at present in such "work services," that is, in the export of manpower. Up to now, Chinese have worked mainly in African, Middle-Eastern, and Southeast-Asian countries and in islands of the South Pacific. Recently, however, participation in construction projects in the USA, Canada, and the USSR has also been contemplated.

In the 1980s a spectacular rearrangement of the <u>economic aid policy</u> earlier conducted by China was witnessed. While earlier, economic aid had been granted by China almost exclusively on a bilateral basis, keeping political objectives in view, from 1979 on such aid was increasingly paid through the multilateral UN organizations and without any political conditions. China actively participates in most of the specialized UN agencies - above all in the UNIDO, UNCTAD, and FAO - and several leading posts in these organizations are filled by representatives of the PRC. Since 1982, close cooperation has been established with the IMF and the World Bank, and the latter participates in the financing of several Chinese development programs.

Footnote to Chapter Nine

1. In May 1984 the State Council issued a temporary decree on "Further expansion of the autonomy of state enterprises," which significantly expanded the decision-making rights of firms in the following fields: (a) production and management planning, (b) product sales, (c) price setting, (d) procurement of materials, (e) use of monetary assets, (f) disposal over the property of the firm, (g) developing enterprise organization, (h) personnel and labor affairs, (i) determining wages and premiums, (j) bringing about economic associations. All this was closely related to the reform of the planning and commodity turnover system then under preparation, which was introduced on January 1, 1985.

Chapter Ten
TWO KEY ISSUES OF CHINESE ECONOMIC REFORM: MARKET BUILDING AND FORMS OF OWNERSHIP

It follows from the target model of the Chinese economic reform and its system of goals that key issues in the whole reform process are the creation of markets and a thorough reform of the existing property system. Regarding the first, the goal is to create a fullscope market system extending to every factor of production. This unified national market must also be closely and directly linked to the world market, particularly to the most dynamically growing regions, i.e. the Far East and Southeast Asia. This is all the more important for China as shortly before the turn of the century Hong Kong and Macao (in Chinese, Xiangkang and Aomen) will become part of the PRC, albeit as special administrative areas. As regards Taiwan, it has been a firm intention of the government of the PRC for almost a decade to create the conditions necessary for the peaceful return of this flourishing island country to the motherland, on the basis of the principle "one country - two systems."

As regards reform of ownership, thanks to the activity and enlightening work of theoretical experts, the Chinese political and economic leaders have become increasingly aware that this is an indispensable condition for the development of an effectively functioning market system and genuine competition on the market. Property reform extends to the development of new forms of ownership within the individual sectors and between them. It also means the elaboration of a flexible government policy towards ownership, which above all keeps in view the most efficient possible exploitation of resources, and thereby acceleration of the development of productive forces and a steady and lasting growth of welfare for the population. Such a policy has to create equal conditions for every sector and every form of ownership in order that genuine competition can develop among them, because an optimal distribution and use of resources as well as dynamic and balanced growth can be secured only in this way.

Position of Certain Market Elements in China Today

An approximately realistic picture of the current position of the market and market relations, the extent of their development, and their operation can be obtained only if we take the individual components in turn, with their characteristics and properties. Today these market elements are at diverse stages of development, thus their operation and effects can be judged only in a differentiated manner. Considering their combined impact, these market elements do not yet work in a coordinated way, or in the same direction; the impact of individual elements is frequently opposed or deviating, and thus they are incapable of integrating the economy. In fact, in some cases they produce expressly disintegrating effects. In spite of reforms that have been going on for a decade, the economy of China today is not yet a genuine commodity economy, let alone a market economy, although some elements of these can already be seen. Nor is it a planned economy in the traditional sense of the word, but a particular mix of the two, a "double-track" economic system, in which there are innumerable connecting tracks between the old and the new tracks, but where most of the "switches" can be set in only one direction, shifting the "train" from the new track back to the old one.

The commodity markets

Based on the considerations above, it would be more accurate to speak about a product market, since on this market, in spite of purchase and sale, products do not become genuine commodities, as they are not exchanged at prices developing on the market and reflecting real inputs.

The commodity markets best conforming to the theoretical requirements of a market in China are the <u>rural and urban free markets</u>. Here, mostly products coming from the agriculture and rural sideline activities, as well as from small-scale urban industries and trades, are sold, partly by the producers themselves and partly by full-time or occasional middlemen. Most of these are foodstuffs (various grains and vegetables, mill products, meat, poultry, eggs, fish and other seafood; the smaller part consists of clothing, household equipment, second-hand goods, medicinal plants, etc. At these markets there is a genuine, animated "market life," with browsing, picking, bargaining, gathering of information, and, of course, buying and selling. Prices change every day, depending on the quantity and quality of the commodities offered for sale and on supply and demand but they do not fluctuate too broadly within a season. These markets took an upswing and began to flourish after the rural economic reform, since it is here that peasants tend to sell what remains of their products after sale to the procurement agencies according to their contracts. This is also why individual and private entrepreneurs have proliferated in recent years: it is generally here that they find buyers for their undemanding (and frequently tasteless) products. Local authorities have made efforts to make these markets more cultured and organized (by building covered halls and stalls), and in villages weekly, fortnightly, or monthly fairs are arranged.

The consumer goods market may be said to be well organized in China and well developed - relative to the general development level of the economy. Even in 1988, almost 88% of the total retail turnover consisted of consumer goods; hardly more than 12% was represented by means of production sold to peasants and other small-scale producers. (Of the total turnover, 36%-38% in recent years has been transacted by state trade and 18%-20% by private traders, while the remaining 6%-8% was free-market sales and those of joint ventures.) The network of shops is well developed in the cities, as are the buying and selling cooperatives in villages. Consumers can easily buy, without queuing, and can make their choice from a wide range, which is no small matter in a country with such a large population. There are shortages, of course, but nowadays these tend to be in luxury articles or brand-name goods (e.g., imported and home-produced color televisions, household refrigerators, automatic washing machines, bicycles).

A <u>producer goods market</u> exists only where, and to the extent that, the purchase and sale of means of production produced in the framework of guidance plans or above plan targets have become organized, i.e., where producers and the authorities make efforts to bring together buyers and sellers in a single place. In recent years the number of exhibition halls and transaction bureaus has increased significantly, and territorial or specialized markets for means of production are organized with growing frequency. Nevertheless, the bulk of trade in means of production is still transacted through channels organized and directed by the state, at centrally determined plan-prices. In the production of and trade in the means of production in the framework of the guidance plans some elements of market economy are already found, but these are rather restricted and are exposed to various manipulations. This sphere of turnover strongly resembles the barter transactions known from foreign trade where products are exchanged for other products, and where prices and means of payment serve rather as means to facilitate the transaction. A real market for the means of production has developed only in the similarly restricted free-market sphere. It satisfies mainly the demand for raw and basic materials, as well as for machinery and equipment, on the part of the collectively owned small rural and village workshops, and of urban artisans - not infrequently from the idle stocks of the state enterprises and their productive equipment written off to zero. Brand new means of production rarely get to this market and then in greatly restricted quantities. The problem of supplying peasant farms with means of production is not at all solved. Peasants have access to small machines, fertilizers, insecticides, and particularly fodder only by long waiting, queuing up, bribing, or paying usury prices, because of the inadequate quotas of the purchasing and selling cooperatives.

The development of a viable market for the means of production is thus of key importance for the Chinese economic reform. In its framework a market has to be created also for patents and licences, in accordance with the requirements of the international market, as chaos still prevails in this field. Chinese industry - also in the state sector - copied for decades foreign machines, production lines, and technologies and sold them as its own products, without suffering any financial consequences. This "tradition" must be quickly abandoned. This was one of the aims of the patent law elaborated and enacted by the PRC in April 1985.

The money and capital markets

In former years only initial steps were taken to develop the money and capital markets. In some of the preceding chapters the creation and operation of money markets have already been mentioned. Their activities are still rather restricted today, mainly because not banks, but separate organizations under administrative control (interfirm money markets, exchanges) are engaged in money-market transactions. Only experimental attempts were made at establishing product and money exchanges in some large cities and in the special economic zones. Establishment of the real value, and regular market evaluation and trading of bonds and shares issued meets with great administrative and economic obstacles in the prevailing "double-track" economic system. Among the obstacles we find the prevailing multiple price system, the formal nature of the valuation and recording of fixed assets, a lack of normativeness in profit taxation, as well as the great dependence of the economic units on the administrative and political organs and institutions of economic management. But the restrictions on labor management and on the setting and payment of wages and premiums, independent of actual performance, are also serious obstacles. This is the system usually called in China "eating from the big common pot."

The land and estate market

Here, too, only the first faltering steps have been taken. For a long time, the concept prevailed that land in public ownership and buildings belonging to the whole people cannot become commodities in socialism; they cannot become objects of purchase and sale. In recent years, however, the Chinese leaders have become aware of the fact that land in China - particularly its cultivable part, now less than 10% of the total area of the country - continues to increase in value and can no longer be managed as a factor of production "of no value," i.e., without a price.

In consequence of industrialization, urbanization, the development of infrastructure, and, last but not least, rapid population growth, the size of cultivable land decreased in China by 16.7 million hectares in the more than three decades between 1957 and 1988, in spite of the fact that virgin lands were brought under cultivation. The area lost corresponds to the total cultivated area in three significant provinces (Liaoning, Sichuan, and Hobei). While in 1957 111.8 million hectares of land were under cultivation, the amount had decreased by 1988 to hardly more than 95 million hectares. The picture is even more gloomy when the land area is projected per inhabitant: in 1957, 0.17 hectares fell to one inhabitant, while in 1988 this was only 0.09 hectares, that is, hardly more than half of the figure 31 years earlier. Under such conditions, protection of the cultivable land is a vital problem for China; this is done, in part, by determining the value of land, its price, or the fee for its use (land rent). The legal possibilities for this were created by the land management act modified in the summer of 1988, and by a modification of the constitution in the spring of 1988, at the first session of the 7th NPC.

The core of a land and estate market developed in the special economic zones and in some of the so-called open cities, linked to the founding of enterprises and leasing contracts of foreign firms. These contracts were usually concluded for 30-50 years, stipulating in detail the rights and duties of the lessor and the lessee. The rent for the land made available was defined for foreigners in terms of convertible foreign currency, taking into consideration the land and site prices established in the neighboring Southeast-Asian countries. Later, the rents for Chinese firms were adjusted to those set for foreigners. For peasants, advantageous rents were established, but the contracts were also made for 30-50 years. The peasants are allowed to transfer the right to land use to their descendants or to cede it to other peasants under the same conditions, in the latter case, in the form of tenancy, meaning that the tenant has to pay rent to the lessor in a definite amount or in kind (e.g., rice or other grain corresponding to the ration) for the use of land.

The labor market

The development of a labor market is also in the initial phase. There has been an organized form of labor exchange to place the unemployed, operating as an economic unit, ever since 1980 in the cities, the so-called labor service enterprises (laodong fuwu gongsi). These are engaged mainly in finding jobs for young people who had finished school and for those who were dismissed for whatever reason by the state enterprises. In many cases this is done by creating new jobs - with minor investments - for the unemployed in small-scale industry doing piecework, or in various service industries. They frequently mediate skilled workers and qualified personnel to foreign firms and joint Chinese-foreign ventures operating in China. But they can place and employ only a relatively small portion of those looking for jobs (less than one million people annually). The majority of those seeking jobs move from villages into the cities, to the spontaneously developing labor markets, where mostly seasonal or occasional workers are sought. Their number amounts to millions in the various large cities and on a national scale it exceeds even 20 million. Because of the excess supply, wages are extremely depressed on this labor market; they do not attain even 60% of the average. For the major construction projects organized recruiting of labor goes on in the villages; thus, the construction enterprises do not satisfy their demand for labor from these "slave markets."

Reform of the Ownership System

The reform of the ownership system has been, right from the beginning, an organic part of the ideas about the reform of the Chinese economic system and it has proved to be a success in the rural economy. Nevertheless, in the concept and practice of the comprehensive economic reform, also extending to the cities, it was not until 1986 that it became obvious that the key to success of economic and political reform was a deep and radical reform of the ownership system. At the same time, this is one of the most difficult areas to change in the socialist countries, because maintenance of the system of ownership developed in earlier decades of the "socialist construction" (characterized above all by the overwhelming weight and determining role of state ownership) is the prime interest of the party and political elite in power. The fundamental economic basis of the traditional socialist political superstructure, of the monolithic and bureaucratic party state and party dictatorship, is precisely the system of state ownership, i.e., a state monopoly on the means of production. This centralizes an economic and political power greater than any other form of statehood in the hands of the political leaders who control the party and government machinery. This is why the progress of ownership reform depends not only on the recognition of economic interrelations and necessities, but also on the power relations between the forces committed to reform and those fearing or opposing it - both within and outside of the party. In this sense, the reform of ownership depends mainly on the reform of the political system. The reason is that the pluralistic structure of ownership and the diversified forms of it developing in the wake of the reform of ownership demand quite a new political superstructure and different methods of exercising power.

As has been mentioned, the reform of the ownership system has three main goals: (a) gradual transformation of the structure of ownership, (b) selection and development of ownership forms ensuring efficient management, and (c) elaboration and application of an adequate ownership policy on the part of the government organs. In recent years, some progress has been made in all three fields, although in the present phase of the reform process this amounts much more to experimenting than to planned and organized implementation. Below are presented not only the results of ownership reform in these three fields to date, but also the various ideas about further progress, independent of the chances and probability of implementation in the coming years. This is all the more justified, as the reform of ownership is one of the most debated areas of socialist economic reform, a kind of terra incognita about which international experience is extremely scarce; thus, we cannot speak about tested and safe methods.

Transformation of the ownership structure

By transformation of the ownership structure we mean a change in the percentual distribution of the types of ownership (economic sector) of economic units, expressed with the aid of some synthetic value indicator. Already, various types of ownership can be found in the economy of the PRC, and thus it may justly be called a multisector mixed economy. Within it, however, the determinant sectors are, for the time being, the sector of the state (or whole people's) ownership and collective ownership. This developed in the 1950s, partly by nationalization and partly by collectivization, then became consolidated, and in the second half of the 1960s - in the course of the "cultural revolution" - it was complemented by the joint state-private companies that came about in the wake of the "socialist transformation" of capitalist industry and trade. The state investments financed from the central and local budgets strengthened the state sector from the very beginning. In 1978 the state and collective sectors represented 98%-99% in the gross social product, gross national product, and national income of the PRC, while the individual and private sectors, as well the joint state-private companies "resuscitated" from 1977 on, merely had a 1%-2% share. The miniature household-plot farms of the peasants are not included, as they basically satisfied the needs of peasant families and hardly produced anything for the market.

There are no uniform or generally accepted criteria in China for the classification of economic sectors. Statistical publications usually distinguish four or five types of ownership, depending on the branch of economy in question.[1] Some scientists maintain that it is sufficient to distinguish four types on the basis of ownership relations: state, collective, individual, and private, within which several forms of ownership may exist, and in statistical records even an "other" category may be included, mainly for the mixed types that develop from the associations of the different types of ownership. Others propose to distinguish five types of ownership by separating the state capitalist sector to comprise the joint state-private and Chinese-foreign ventures. Chinese scientists emphasize that the systems analysis and complex research of different types of economic ownership are indispensable because their development falls into the scope of long-term policies. The constitution of the PRC makes equally possible the development of whole people's, collective, and individual economic units, as well as of the private and joint ventures founded with Chinese and foreign capital. Table 7 shows the changes that occurred in the ownership structure of the Chinese economy between 1980 and 1987.

Table 7. Changes in the ownership structure of the Chinese economy

		Share of the sectors (%)			
		State	Collective	Individual	Other
Of the gross output value of industry	1980	78.7	20.7	–	0.6
	1987	59.7	34.6	3.6	2.1
Of the value of transport performance	1980	–	–	–	–
	1987	86.3	2.6	–	11.1
Of total retail trade	1980	84.2	11.9	0.7	3.2
	1987	38.6	35.7	17.4	8.3

– No data available

Source: Zhongguo Tongji Nianjian 1981, 1988 (Statistical Yearbook of China)

This strong growth of the collective sector in industrial production may be attributed primarily to the fast expansion of rural industrial activities. Agricultural productive activity is not classified by forms of ownership. Earlier it was recorded as being completely in collective ownership, but today this may be challenged from several aspects. On the one hand, the collectively owned lands are cultivated by peasants mostly as family farms under contractual leasing; on the other hand, the number of specialized peasant farms employing wage labor is slowly growing as well, and these increase their land area by leasing or redeeming leased lands of peasants who are looking for other sources of livelihood. In addition, a growing number of enterprising peasants are engaged in mediating trade, transportation, the repair of agricultural and household machinery, handwork and cottage industry, the gathering and sale of medicinal herbs, or unlawful lending of money.

In the past 7-8 years the number of urban and rural retailers, small cook-shops tradesmen, and those performing various services has suddenly increased. At the end of 1988 more than 2 million people nationwide were engaged in such activities, mostly in the form of family undertakings. Private industry and private trade of a capitalist nature started growing extensively, mainly in the wake of foreign capital investments and usually in the form of joint ventures, primarily in manufacturing, the hotel trade, and the mediatory trade with Hong Kong. The private sector is the largest in the special economic zones. In 1988 it was the private sector that developed fastest among all economic sectors. Following the political change in early June 1989, the campaign started against the tax frauds of the private entrepreneurs put a strong brake on this development and even reversed it. By the end of the year the number of private ventures had dropped by more than 3 million, and the number of those who earned their living from them by about 5 million relative to the beginning of the year.

Development of diversified forms of ownership

As a result of experiments in the framework of the reform of ownership, diversified, mixed forms of ownership, frequently uniting deviating types of property, have developed in China in recent years in several fields of economic activity.

The greatest problem of the reform of ownership is the <u>transformation of state (whole people's) enterprises into more efficient forms of ownership</u> and their successful functioning. Several ideas have emerged and several of them have already been tested in practice. The greatest concern is that one fifth of the state enterprises make losses and their subsidization consumes more than one third of the revenues of the state budget. Although the act on state enterprises and the bankruptcy law have created the possibilities for closing down continually losing enterprises, the Chinese leadership does not resort to these instruments - for political reasons and social considerations. (Not a single state enterprise has been closed down as yet, and merely two bankruptcy procedures have been initiated in two rural towns, in both cases against smaller collectively owned enterprises.) In the case of smaller losing enterprises, the local authorities prefer the methods of contractual leasing, transfer to the ownership of enterprise collectives, or sale.

The <u>leasing of state enterprises</u> usually takes place via tenders, with competitive bidding. The conditions of leasing are set by the local authorities as owners. The lessees may also be workers in the enterprise, or a smaller group of them, but outside entrepreneurs, groups of managers, and private individuals may also submit tenders for the leasing of such enterprises. For 1 or 2 years the condition for leasing may also be the elimination of the loss, and in this case the lessees receive only a salary corresponding to their job; later, however, the profit remaining after payment of taxes and the rent is due them.

In recent years the Chinese press has reported on numerous such successful ventures under leasing, even on ones where the annual profit of the lessees was several hundred thousand or even several million yuan. These entrepreneurs used the overwhelming part of the profit for the expansion and modernization of the enterprise, thus becoming partial owners themselves, and in this way the leased enterprise has turned "in a natural way" into a state-private share company. There also have been cases where the enterprise's workers contributed to the development of the enterprise with surplus work or money and received shares in exchange. Thus, the share companies in reality united three types of ownership: state, collective, and private. This form of leasing and transformation into a share company was used mostly with small commercial and service firms owned by the state, and only rarely with industrial enterprises.

The <u>handing over into collective ownership</u> of state (whole people's) enterprises occurred mostly with enterprises that had originally been in collective ownership but were nationalized in the course of the "cultural revolution." In such cases the collective is obliged to repay, in installments, the value of additional investments made by the state, less depreciation. This method is also used in the case of continually losing small and medium-sized state enterprises which, in the judgement of the economic management organs, cannot be made profitable even in the long run and cannot be leased, as nobody applies for them. In such cases, closing down is the only solution, but this would entail the dismissal of the staff. The collective is then offered the enterprise free of charge or for a merely symbolic sum, if they are willing to take it over and operate it at their own risk.

Some smaller commercial and service firms have been <u>sold</u> to other enterprises, groups of enterprises or private individuals. In some large coastal cities, medium-sized obsolete and losing firms have been offered for sale to already operating or newly organized joint Chinese-foreign ventures or private firms established with exclusively foreign capital. The latter have bought them, not mainly for their equipment and production capacities, but to use the sites and buildings in order to expand or start new ventures. In this case they were even willing to take over, retrain, and employ some of the workers of the enterprise bought, provided they proved to be suited. Over 20 000 smaller state shops and repair shops have been sold annually in recent years, mainly to private individuals or family undertakings.

The overwhelming majority of theoretical Chinese economists believe that the most expedient and most acceptable way of making big and medium-sized state enterprises more efficient is to transform them into share (joint-stock) companies. The literature on the advantages and drawbacks of share companies written in the past 2-3 years could fill several libraries. Most of the studies and articles emphasize the advantages of the share company system and its transitory character, pointing beyond the capitalist mode of production and leading to socialism. They frequently quote Marx's words from vol. III of The Capital: "The capitalist stock companies, as much as the cooperative factories, should be considered as transitional forms from the capitalist mode of production to the associated one, with the only distinction that the antagonism is resolved negatively in the one and positively in the other."[2] If this is so under capitalist relations, it is even more true under the conditions of China, now in the "initial phase" of socialism, according to Chinese economists. But this form also best answers the theoretical requirement of the Chinese reform of ownership that the right to ownership gradually be separated from the right of management or disposal, which is a basic tendency of the development of modern commodity economies. In this context, the following sentences of Marx are most frequently quoted:

"In stock companies the function is divorced from capital ownership; hence also labor is entirely divorced from ownership of the means of production and surplus labor. The result of the ultimate development of capitalist production is a necessary transitional phase towards the reconversion of capital into the property of producers, although no longer as the private property of the individual producers, but rather as the property of associated producers, as outright social property. On the other hand, the stock company is a transition towards the conversion of all functions in the reproduction process wich still remain linked with capital property into mere functions of associated producers, into social functions."[3]

The Chinese economists feel it is necessary to support the transformation of the bulk of enterprises traditionally in "whole people's ownership" into joint-stock companies with theoretical and ideological arguments as well. They emphasize that under socialist relations the share company is one of the most efficient forms of public ownership. In addition to the executives, it makes the other employees interested in improving the results of management and also strengthens their feeling of ownership. The form of share company facilitates the collection of fragmented monetary assets, the flow of capital, and provides opportunity for the horizontal and vertical integration of firms of different ownership types. This form is advantageous also for the development of a market system, the socialist market economy, since with the development of the share market the performance of enterprises is directly measured on the market. But this is also favorable for the shift from management in physical terms to one in value terms, as well as for the attraction of foreign capital.

At present the reorganization of existing enterprises into share companies and creation of new ones takes place in the following four ways:

1. The enterprise issues shares or share certificates for its own staff, mostly at low nominal value and in restricted quantities.

2. The share company comes about from the association of or joint investment by various enterprises. Several share companies were formed in this way, mainly in the wake of the proliferation of horizontal economic associations.

3. Shares are issued for the general public and for social organizations, mostly to create communal service (public utility) share companies.

4. Joint Chinese-foreign mixed share companies are created with the participation of foreign capital.

In 1988, more than 6000 share companies were already active in China. At the beginning of the year their combined registered capital amounted to about 20 billion yuan. By issuing new shares in the course of the year they obtained more than 100 billion yuan in additional resources. Although this is not a large sum relative to the 380 billion yuan deposited by the population with banks and credit cooperatives (at the end of 1988) and to the cash in the hands of the population, estimated at about 170 billion yuan, it is nevertheless a beginning.

Associations based on uniting capital operate in China not exclusively in the form of share companies. Other forms of economic associations may also be found, from cooperative associations, through various limited partnerships, to limited liability companies. We frequently find service associations of young people with little money, as well as joint ventures of peasant families brought about for the transportation of their products to the market and for selling them. The number of associations in which several types of property are united is growing: state, collective and private property, and in some cases even foreign property, or some (partial) combinations of these. Some Chinese economists are already speaking about the coexistence of nine or ten types of ownership and believe that the main direction of the reform of ownership is the further enrichment and rapid spread of these diversified forms and of mixed forms. It is also emphasized at the same time that the development and spread of these colorful and diversified forms of ownership does not endanger the domination of communal or public forms of ownership in the Chinese national economy, but even strengthens them by the participation of the state property in the various mixed forms of ownership and facilitates indirect manegement and control by the state.

Establishment of an adequate government policy on ownership

Ownership policy is the most delicate and most neuralgic point of government economic policy. Every stand and every measure taken on this question is not only of political but also of ideological importance, particularly in a society such as the Chinese one, which was educated for decades in the spirit of "extreme left" politics and ideology. This is why both theoreticians and practical economic policy makers exhibit great caution and consideration in working out an ownership policy conforming to the target model and system of goals of the economic reform. The permissible limits to the development of the "nonsocialist" forms of management are usually not prescribed, nor is their development restricted, but it is still held that an economy and a society can be considered socialist only if the social or public forms of ownership predominate in it, primarily in the fields of production of key importance. The general opinion is that one cannot, nor is it expedient to, establish in advance rational proportions between the various types of ownership and economic sectors, because these will develop in any case via an evolutionary process of natural selection on the market. Those forms should exist and develop which can more efficiently operate under equal market conditions; for those, however, which cannot operate without state subsidies, these subsidies should be linked to definite conditions and abolished after a few years. Thus, the bankruptcy of firms which are unprofitable for a long time will become unavoidable, and this becomes an actual stimulant for increasing economic efficiency.

As regards the leveling of conditions of activity of various types of management, i.e., the development of equal conditions in competition, significant differences in opinion may be found among Chinese economists, particularly in judging the existing advantages or drawbacks. Some of them point rather to the ideological and political aspects and maintain that the situation and treatment of the individual and, particularly, the private sector are discriminatory, as most of the population is still permeated by the traditional "extreme left" negative attitude. Others, taking the degree of autonomy of the economic units as the basis of their judgement, believe that it is precisely the individual and private economic units that are in the most advantageous position, since nobody "commands" them, followed by the units in collective ownership, and finally by the state enterprises, whose "hands and feet are bound."

In working out the government's ownership policy the economic management organs on different levels are influenced by effects, pressures, and coercion coming from various directions. One such pressure is their responsibility for supply, which prompts them to ensure supply of the population with basic necessities, if possible, with the aid of state-owned industrial and commercial firms under their direct control and management, that is, with the state sector. At the same time, the growing burdens of state subsidies needed for the operation of the enterprises of the state sector stimulate them to get rid of the losing firms and look for ways of transforming them into other forms of ownership. Also the pressure of finding employment for the annually growing labor force works to faster develop the collectively owned units and the individual or private sector, which can be done without major state investments. Another circumstance also speaks for this solution: the so-called tertiary sector, the sphere of services, was neglected for decades in China, and its "restoration" is "cheaper" for the state through the development of the collective economic units and of the individual and private sectors using the savings of the population.

The rapid development of the private sector also demands a new approach to such questions of ideological portent as wage labor, exploitation, differentiation by property, and the social polarization deriving from these. The substance of all these questions is to find out how real the danger of reverting to capitalism, the danger of "capitalist restoration," is in China. In recent years, Chinese reformist propaganda has been directed precisely at explaining these problems. A wide range of popular scientific works have been published; the central and local press has published writings of outstanding scientitists or the texts of interviews made with them, and letters sent by readers, i.e. the answers to the questions contained in them, are published. Leading experts appear on television, and the social problems as well as the negative phenomena coming to the surface are boldly treated in various dramas and films. With their aid, efforts are made to convince the wide masses that diversification of the forms of management and ownership and a greater differentiation of incomes depending on the efficiency of management and on individual performance are necessary concomitants of social progress and modernization, and that they do not at all contradict the socialist principles. The political changes in the wake of the events at Tienanmen Square brought significant shifts in emphasis also in this field, in consequence of the ideological campaign launched against "bourgeois liberalization." Afterwards, efforts were made to attribute the differentiation of property - similarly to other negative phenomena - to "bourgeois liberalization," as if it were a consequence of the latter.

In their proposals to elaborate a government ownership policy the Chinese reform economists and policy makers set out from the Marxian concept that, in the interest of efficient management, the forms of ownership have to be brought into harmony with the given level of development of production and with their operation. The gravest mistakes in ownership policy were made in the last decades, when, independent of the actual state of the forces of production, there was forced expansion of the form of whole people's ownership, regardless of the costs. In China today, beside the big modern factories (numbering hardly ten thousand) several hundred thousand small workshops can be found (let alone the several hundred million of rural and urban small-scale producers). In these small establishments mechanization has hardly begun, and the overwhelming amount of work is done with hand tools. It is more expedient and more efficient to continue such production in smaller work organizations, whether individually or as private undertakings, because there is direct interest in better work and no need for extensive administration. In theory, the growth of the forces of production would, by specialization and spread of more efficient production processes, foster the demand for consolidation and cooperation of the small producers relying on their own labour power or on that of their family. This will stimulate the voluntary organization of economic units. While this process ought to be supported by the state with economic, financial, and legal instruments, it must not be forced. This is an extremely important lesson to be learned from the earlier mistaken policy of collectivization.

Footnotes to Chapter Ten

1. Industrial statistics distinguish the following economic sectors: whole people's ownership, collective ownership (within it separately the rural industries), urban and rural individual industry (together), and industry belonging to "other" economic sectors. In agricultural statistics the whole people's sector is not separated (only the state farms); their order of magnitude may be deduced indirectly from the data of production on virgin lands and from investments. (On virgin lands, namely, mostly state farms operate.) The total value of retail trade turnover is given in a breakdown by whole people's, collective, joint venture, and individual sectors, and the direct sales on the market of peasants (as producers or on commission) are separately shown.
2. Karl Marx: The Capital, Book III, sect. V, chap. 27. Progress Publishers, Moscow, 1966, p 440
3. Ibid., p 437

Chapter Eleven
CONCEPTS FOR REFORMING THE POLITICAL SYSTEM

Already in a relatively early period of the reform process that started in 1979, the Chinese party and government leaders had come to the conclusion that the "four modernizations" and the radical transformation of the economic system could not be successfully completed without a thorough reform of the systems of party and government leadership, that is, if reform of the economic system was not accompanied by reform of the political system. This idea was first formulated by Deng Xiaoping in August 1980, at the extended session of the PB of the 11th CC, in his speech entitled "On the reform of the system of party and state leadership." Besides listing the gravest deficiencies of the established political system, in this speech Deng Xiaoping outlined the main directions for reforming the system and its most important steps, emphasizing that the reform could be realized only as a result of deliberate and consistent efforts over a long period. In its course the resistance of a considerable number of party and government cadres would certainly have to be fought, and their resistance would take the most diverse forms.

Although in the first half of the 1980s - as already indicated in those chapters that reviewed the major events and developments in individual phases of the reform process - certain steps were taken and some progress was perceptible also as regards the political reforms, this task received greater emphasis beginning in the autumn of 1986, mainly in relation to preparations for the 13th congress of the CPC, at which - according to the original idea - reform of the political system was to have been an independent point on the agenda. As has been mentioned, the subject was not independently discussed at the 13th congress and constituted only one (though the longest) chapter of the report to the congress. Although this part of the report - together with the other chapters - was approved as a resolution of the congress, the thorough reform of the political system continues to be primarily a target; its implementation proceeds slowly, reluctantly, and with conflicts, with forward and backward steps. In 1989 this produced growing dissatisfaction and unrest among ever wider groups of the population, particularly intellectuals, students, and cadres committed to the reforms. This became manifest in diverse proposals, demands, petitions, strikes, and demonstrations.

The cause of the dissatisfaction may be found first of all in the fact that the negative phenomena, deficiencies, and distortions listed and analyzed by Deng Xiaoping in his speech delivered in August 1980 had not ceased to exist; in fact, in some fields and in some respects they had even gathered momentum and become more manifest in the 9 years that had passed since then. (The complete text of the speech was published on July 1, 1987 - on the 66th aniversary of the founding of the CPC - and thus the entire Chinese society became acquainted with it.) Such phenomena were misuse of power by the leaders, corruption of party cadres, routine administration, proliferation of bureaucracy, etc. Thus, lack of reform of the political system has become, also in China, an obstacle to the renewal of the social system, of the progress of economic reform and, at the same time, the main source of social unrest.

Main Deficiencies of the Existing Political System

It will be helpful to begin by listing the main deficiencies of the existing political system, briefly reviewing the above-mentioned speech of Deng Xiaoping. These anomalies and deficiencies have not been formulated more succinctly and comprehensively by anyone in China since. In his speech Deng Xiaoping criticized first of all the deficiencies of the system of party and state leadership, as well as those of the cadre policy, but from this speech almost every feature characteristic of the political system of a bureaucratic party-state can be learned. If you like, the Chinese political system is the typical "veterinary horse" on which every "disease" of the "feudal-socialist" system can be demonstrated.

"As far as the leadership and cadre system of our party and state are concerned, the major problems are bureaucracy, over-concentration of power, patriarchal methods, life tenure in leading posts, and privileges of various kinds,"[1] said Deng Xiaoping in the third part of his speech, where he subjected the deficiencies of the existing political system to analysis. At this point he did not even mention the lack of democracy, direct representation of the people, and the constitutional state, since he took it as self-evident that with the existing negative features the development of these was out of the question. He denoted bureaucracy as a particularly grave concern which had deep historical roots in China, and thus its extermination met with extremely great obstacles and resistance.

The main forms in which this phenomenon manifested itself were listed by the speaker with almost unprecedented thorougness: "standing high above the masses; abusing power; divorcing oneself from reality and the masses; spending a lot of time and effort to put up an impressive front; indulging in empty talk; sticking to a rigid way of thinking; being hidebound by convention; overstaffing administrative organs; being dilatory, inefficient, and irresponsible; failing to keep one's word; circulating documents endlessly without solving problems; shifting responsibility to others; and even assuming the airs of a mandarin, reprimanding other people at every turn, vindictively attacking others, suppressing democracy, deceiving superiors and subordinates, being arbitrary and despotic, practicing favoritism, offering bribes, participating in corrupt practices in violation of law, and so on."[2] He could have added the wasting of public money, the arrogance of bureaucrats, sticking to position and power, submissiveness to superiors, servility and flattery, careerism, the feeling of being above the law, etc. This wide range of forms of manifestation clearly indicates that only a part of these phenomena can be eliminated with institutional reforms. For their complete elimination the social, economic, and ideological bases of the existing political system, its moral and legal norms, as well as its whole functional mechanism have to be radically transformed.

Since the party is at the center of the Chinese political system, the reform of this system is inconceivable without changes in the tasks, scope of authority, and working style and methods of the party. The overcentralization of power - also indicated by Deng Xiaoping - is characteristic first of all of the party, of the party committees on various levels. Its consequences were also underlined by Deng: "Overconcentration of power means inappropriate and indiscriminate concentration of all power in party committees in the name of strengthening centralized party leadership. Moreover, the power of the party committees themselves is often in the hands of a few secretaries, especially the first secretaries, who direct and decide everything. Thus, 'centralized party leadership' often turns into leadership by individuals."[3] This, too, contributed to the development of a paternalistic style in the party, so that finally "... only one person has the say and makes important decisions, practicing the cult of personality and placing individuals above the organization."[4] Deng also mentioned the name of Mao Zedong, but made it clear that the problem had not been solved with his death, as the roots of the system reached deeper and were more ramified. "Many places and units have their patriarchal personages with unlimited power. Everyone else has to be absolutely obedient and even personally attached to them."[5]

Further on in his speech Deng Xiaoping discussed in detail the causes of the other negative features, their roots in history and in the movement, as well as the forms in which they become manifest. Then he summarized, in five points, the tasks related to reforming the obsolete system of party and state leadership:

1. The constitution of the PRC has to be modified so as to guarantee the citizens' rights to control the power organs, including the right to relieve leaders who no longer deserve the trust of the masses.

2. An advisory body or commission has to be created besides the leading bodies, to which the old cadres could retire, ceding their place to younger and more qualified cadres.

3. An effective working machinery of government has to be developed, beginning with the State Council, right down to the local governments. In this context, the activity of party committees on various levels should be restricted to guidance on principles and political control. (It was in this form that the demand for separating the functions of party and government organs first appeared.)

4. Congresses or conferences of representatives of workers and office staff should be introduced in all enterprises and institutions. These would have the right to make decisions on questions of concern to the institution and to make proposals for the appointment of leaders or their recall.

5. Party committees at all levels should combine collective leadership with individual responsibility. It should be clearly delimited which questions require collective discussion and where individual responsibility is needed in decision-making.

This speech of Deng Xiaoping offered important guidance in starting and gradually developing the political reforms. In the earlier chapters we have already reported, in chronological order, the initial steps and some achievements. Below we review the ideas which were formulated in the report of the CC submitted to and debated by the 13th congress of the CPC, and which were finally raised to the rank of resolution at the plenary closing session on November 1, 1987.

Standpoint and Resolution of the 13th Congress of the CPC in Connection with Political Reform

The ideas related to reforming the political system received rather wide publicity in the Chinese press from May 1987 on, and the subject was not even later removed from the agenda of debated problems. Nevertheless, in this question it is the standpoint and guidelines formulated at the 13th congress of the CPC that may be considered most authentic, and the results achieved in this field may best be measured by reviewing them. Chapter Five of the report about "Reforming the political system"[6] denoted the following as being the most important tasks:

1. Separating party and government
2. Reforming government organs
3. Delegating powers to lower levels
4. Reforming the personnel system relating to cadres
5. Establishing a system of consultation and dialogue
6. Improving a number of systems relating to socialist democracy
7. Strengthening the socialist legal system

We believe that the ideas related to the reform of the political system can most expediently be presented in the light of these tasks, together with the situation and perspectives of their implementation, also showing the most important obstacles in the way of the reform. Before going into detail, let us briefly survey the arguments with which the leaders of the CPC justified the need for and timeliness of the political reforms. In this context, the introduction to Chapter Five of the report to the congress reads as follows:

"The deepening of the ongoing reform of the economic system makes reform of the political system increasingly urgent. The process of developing a socialist commodity economy should also involve the building of a socialist democracy. Without reform of the political system, reform of the economic system cannot succeed in the end. The Central Committee of the Party believes that it is high time to put reform of the political system on the agenda for the whole Party. Comrade Deng Xiaoping's speech, 'On the Reform of Party and State Leadership,' delivered to an enlarged meeting of the Political Bureau of the Central Committee in August 1980, is a guide to the reform of the political system.

"The purpose of reforming both the political and economic system is, under the leadership of the Party and the socialist system, to better develop the productive forces and to take full advantage of the superiority of socialism. In other words, we shall catch up with the developed capitalist countries economically and, politically, we shall create a democracy that is of a higher level and more effective than the democracy of those countries. We shall also try to produce more and better-trained professionals than they do. The merits of the reform should be judged on the basis of whether these objectives are attained.

"China is a socialist country under the people's democratic dictatorship, and its basic political system is good. However, there are major defects in our system of leadership, in the organizational structure and in our style of work. Chief among these defects are overconcentration of power, a serious degree of bureaucracy, and feudal influences that are far from eliminated. The purpose of reforming the political system is to promote what is beneficial and eliminate what is harmful and to build a socialist democracy with Chinese characteristics. The long-range goal of reform is to build a socialist political system with a high degree of democracy and a complete set of laws, a system that is effective and full of vitality. And that is something which cannot be achieved without sustained effort.

"Like the development of a socialist commodity economy, the building of a socialist democracy is a gradual, cumulative process. Confronted as we are with the complicated social contradictions that arise in the drive for modernization, we need a peaceful social and political environment. We shall never again allow the kind of 'great democracy' that undermines state law and social stability. The system of the people's congresses, the system of multi-party cooperation and political consultation under the leadership of the Communist Party, and the principle of democratic centralism are the characteristics and advantages of our system. We shall never abandon them and introduce a Western system of separation of the three powers and of different parties ruling the country in turn."[7]

The first four paragraphs of the relevant chapter in the report to the congress have been quoted here at full length because almost every sentence has political weight. It also reflects a rather resolute and clear ideological stand. Clearly, its idelogical and political base is the theoretical thesis about the "primary stage of socialism" - not at all free from internal contradictions and utopianism - expounded by the CC in Chapter Two of the same report (reviewed and analyzed in the preceding chapters of this book). The lines quoted above make palpable the present limits and constraints of the Chinese political reforms. By listing the "particular and positive features" of the existing political system they also make it clear how far these reforms can go without endangering - at least according to the leaders of the CPC now in power - the legal order of the state and the stability of society. In this context it is worth reminding the reader that in the autumn of 1988 and the spring of 1989, the restrictive and recentralizing measures were taken under the slogan and in the interest of restoring legal order and stability. These measures put a brake on and even froze the economic reforms that had already begun. It was with reference to them that the demands of several leading intellectuals and representatives of students to expand democracy, to exercise human rights to freedom without restriction, and to relieve the unsuited and corrupt leaders, as well as to continue the promised political reforms were rejected. But the base of reference was the same in the summer of 1989 when the "legal order" was restored by deploying armed forces and merciless reckoning with the "troublemakers."

Separation of party and state

In the "party-states" that developed in the wake of the traditional Stalinist and Maoist model of "socialist construction," separation of the party from the state is of prime importance for the reform of the political system. Without its consistent realization every further reform measure remains a half-solution or sham measure - not only in the political but also in the economic sphere. In this respect, the report to the congress contains many concrete hints, albeit in a rather defensive spirit. It tries to show the advantages of separating from each other the party and state functions, mainly from the aspect of the party's tasks, of making party work more efficient. It establishes several "basic truths," known to the parties in power but not enforced in practice, or even acted against. It emphasizes that the separation of party and state functions has to be consistently implemented on all levels, and it stresses the importance of separation for the autonomous and responsible management of enterprises.

Some progress has been made during the past 2 years in separating party and state functions - mainly at lower levels of economic units and in some state institutions of nonpolitical character - but on the whole the solution of this task is only in the beginning phase. No qualitative change has taken place in the earlier concept and interpretation of the party's leading role. Decisions on the substance of all important political questions - affecting both the economy and society - continue to be taken in a relatively narrow circle of party leaders (in the Political Bureau or its Standing Committee), and afterwards the leading bodies of the party and the state mostly only approve them, or at most modify them in some respects. (For example, Prime Minister Li Peng and Deputy Prime Minister Yao Yilin, chairman of the planning commission, are at the same time members of the Standing Committee of the PB, of the "five-in-hand" and, similarly, on province and township levels the leaders of local governments are members of the "peak leadership" of the corresponding party committees.) All this precludes from the outset a consistent organizational and functional separation of the party and the state, and this cannot fail to have an impact on the progress of political reform.

Delegation of power to lower levels

In this respect the principles have also long been well known: decisions should be made where the best conditions exist for actually knowing the situation, and the masses should handle their own affairs, as far as this is possible. In spite of this, in delegating power to lower levels substantial progress has been made only in economic management and economic activities, as a result of some measures taken in the framework of the economic reform. Where political decisions are concerned, the fundamental approach prevails that it is expedient and useful to ask for the opinion and approval of the higher authorities in every important matter, and it is even better if a decision is made by the latter, since in this case also the responsibility is theirs. Thus, no real progress can be reported in this field, either.

Reform of governmental organs

This is the field where spectacular efforts have been made and reorganization has occurred. Yet bureaucracy and the number of bureaucratic phenomena have not diminished. This is why the report to the congress proposed that "... the State Council begin immediately to work out a plan for restructuring the organs of the Central Government and that the plan be submitted to the First Session of the Seventh National People's Congress for examination and approval and then implemented."[8] This actually happened in the spring of 1988 when, as mentioned, several ministries and government commissions with national authority were amalgamated and others separated. On the whole, however, the staff of the central government machinery was reduced only minimally (by about 10 000). In organizational reforms the guideline of the report to the congress was much respected, according to which:"To ensure the smooth progress of the structural reform, we should make appropriate personnel changes in the organs to be restructured, seeing to it that proper arrangements are made for everyone that work proceeds normally."[9] But the viewpoint, formulated in an earlier passage, that "to avoid repeating the old practice of 'streamlining - swelling - re-streamlining,' we must concentrate on a change of functions, which is the key to structural reform"[10] was less heeded. In this respect little happened on either the central or the local level.

Reform of personnel and cadre work

Among the tasks related to the reform of the political system, there can be no doubt that the most original and most interesting initiatives and ideas were born in this field. For a proper evaluation it must be explained that in China, "cadre" (in Chinese: ganbu) means a social function and rank different from those in most socialist countries. In China the party and state cadres (the distinction is only of formal importance, as most of the latter are also party cadres) constitute a social group with special rights and duties, possessing various privileges. In a sociological sense they may be considered to be the "ruling class" or "privileged class."

These cadres owe unconditional obedience first of all to the party and to the leaders of the party at all times. As "good soldiers" they have to carry out the commands and instructions coming from above in a disciplined manner and, where instructions are lacking, they are obliged to represent the current party "guideline" and to enforce it within their own scope of authority. In return, the party "cares" for them, ensures their accommodation and livelihood, and this care may even extend to the members of their families. Up to a certain (though rather broad) limit, this also involves some protection against mistakes, blunders, human weaknesses (of character), and frailty. (Cadres violating the law are mostly called to account by the party's disciplinary committees; their cases come only rarely and in extremely grave cases before the courts.) In China at present there are nearly 25 million such "cadres" in the party and state machinery on various levels; i.e., almost half of the party membership of 48 million are cadres.

One of the main directions of the reform of personnel and cadre work - related to the efforts at separating the party from the state - is to distinguish party from state cadres, or political from professional cadres (i.e., experts) and to handle them according to different criteria. (This is all the more justified, as in the past decade the notion of "cadre" has become "diluted" and has frequently been applied to outstanding scientists, teachers, artists, and even sportsmen, whether they were party members or not.)

Later efforts were concentrated for some time on transforming the classification and recording system of public servants, distinguishing the public servants attending to political tasks from the employees directing and performing professional work. In this context the report to the congress laid down the following: "Public servants in the political-affairs category, whose tenure in office will be for a specified period of time, must be managed strictly in accordance with the relevant provisions of the Constitution and the Organic Law and be subjected to supervision by the public. The Central Committee of the Party and local Party committees at various levels will recommend candidates in the political-affairs category at the corresponding levels to the national or local people's congresses, through legal procedures, and will supervise and manage those public servants in this category who are Party members. Public servants in the professional-work category, whose tenure in office is to be permanent, will also be managed in accordance with statutory standards and procedures. Their promotion, demotion, reward, and punishment will be based mainly on their work results. Their rights to training, wages, welfare, and retirement will be guaranteed by law."[10] It is conspicuous in this passage that the selection and supervision of public servants attending to political tasks are treated in merely three sentences and, essentially in conformity with the prevailing practice, are entrusted to the party organs on various levels. In contrast, in the case of public servants attending to professional matters, it is intended to proceed according to a complicated method, circumscribed in laws and legal rules, comprising various examinations and regular evaluation of their work.

Transformation of the personnel system was begun in the enterprises in 1986 with the introduction of the manager responsibility system. Next, in the framework of the planned wage reform, the drafting of a new classification system of employees of state institutions was also begun, but - as mentioned earlier - this was interrupted and put off. The system of competition was also used mostly in the enterprise sphere for the filling of leading jobs (though not in full scope even here), as well as in the filling of teaching and research posts in some universities, other institutions of higher education, and research institutes. Efforts were made at every work place to assert the general requirement of rejuvenating and increasing professional expertise in filling the various leading posts, and in this respect substantial result have been achieved in recent years.

Developing a system of social consultation and dialogue

This effort is aimed at learning and influencing the atmosphere of social public opinion with methods more direct than those used up to now. The report to the congress says the following about this: "To correctly handle contradictions and reconcile various social interests is an important task in a socialist society. Only when the leading bodies at all levels listen attentively to the views of the masses can they gear their work to actual conditions and avoid mistakes. And only when they let the people know what they are doing and what difficulties they face can they secure the people's understanding. There should be channels through which the voices and demands of the people can offer suggestions or pour out any grievances they may have."[12]

This system of social consultation and dialogue has not developed to date. In fact, one cannot even see any recent effort at creating the institutional forms of such a system. On the contrary, in the past one to one and a half years there have been several indications that the party leaders on all levels react nervously to criticism coming from below and do not exhibit adequate tolerance to opinions deviating from the official party stand. This was evidenced in the spring of 1989 by the confiscation and pulping of certain issues of several newspapers and periodicals and the replacement of editors-in-chief and editors, not to mention the various forms of retaliation following the bloody suppression of the students' demonstrations in April and May. In other words, it seems that the party leaders act in this question contrary to the spirit of the stand taken by the congress.

Expanding democracy

In this context the report to the congress applies the complicated and rather hazy term: "Improving a number of systems relating to socialist democracy." In the introduction it lays down that "The essence of socialist democracy is that the people are masters of the country, genuinely enjoying all citizens' rights and the power of administering the state, enterprises, and institutions." True, this ideal goal-setting is immediately qualified by the statement: "In building socialist democracy at the present stage, we should place emphasis on practical results and on arousing the initiative of the grass-roots units and the people. We should start with things we are able to do, concentrating on improving a number of basic systems."[13]

The report then deals in turn with the tasks related to improving the work of such political institutions and mass organizations as the National People's Congress and its Standing Committee, the People's Political Consultative Conference, the system of local people's congresses on different levels, trade unions, the youth organization, the women's association, various democractic parties, and other mass organizations. It separately discusses the further development of the election system towards selection of several candidates so that voters have a genuine choice. It emphasizes the need for legal guarantees for the exercise of democratic rights; for the passing of laws which regulate the work of the press, the rights of publication, association, assembly, and marches; and for the creation of a system for popular appeals. At the same time, it points out that with the same laws the abuse of rights and freedom should be prevented. In the past one and a half years, more and more Chinese leaders have emphasized the need for gradual progress in broadening democracy and the "immaturity" of the Chinese society for democracy.[14]

Strengthening socialist law and order

In this context the report to the congress underlines the close link between democracy and legal order, as well the importance of order and calm. "Socialist democracy is inseparable from a socialist legal system. Without stability and unity throughout the society, we can succeed neither in economic development nor in the reform of economic and political systems. In exercising democracy and dictatorship in all spheres of activity - political, economic, and social - we should see to it that there are laws to abide by, that laws already enacted are observed and enforced to the letter, and that violators are brought to justice,"[15] reads the introduction to this part of the report.

It is emphasized in the following that construction, reform, and the strengthening of legal order should be dealt with simultaneously and that tightening legal order should permeate the whole of the reform process. It is acknowledged that in this field - owing to historical circumstances - China is still at the beginning of the process, and that this is a huge, difficult, and complicated task, requiring resolute but circumspect political work and a high degree of expertise. This is why the reform cannot be implemented at one stroke. The Chinese experts drafting laws and the legislative bodies have done much in the past 8-10 years to develop the socialist legal order of the PRC, but it is still too little. In this huge country several basic laws and legal rules have not yet been codified; in some fields the traditional common law or the "revolutionary legality" that developed in the period of revolution still assert themselves, and this provides an opportunity for taking justice into one's own hands and for actions violating the law.

Interdependence and Mutual Conditionality of Political and Economic Reforms

In every country where reform of the traditional "socialist" socioeconomic and political systems has begun, the relation to each other of political and economic reforms is one of the most debated questions today. China is no exception, although the need for reform of the political system was recognized relatively early, in the initial stage of the reform process in the wake of reform and opening policy - together with an awareness of the close interrelations between the political and economic reforms. A deeper investigation of the interdependence and mutual conditionality of these reforms from theoretical aspects started in China only in the autumn of 1986, in the wake of the resolution passed at the 6th plenary session of the 12th CC, CPC, entitled: "On the guidelines of building up a socialist spiritual civilization."

In this resolution it was pointed out that "the whole of the building process aimed at the socialist modernization of our country is made up of the following elements: putting economic construction into the center, the reform of the economic system has to be resolutely continued, the building of spiritual civilization has to be resolutely strengthened, harmonization of these elements has to be achieved, so that they mutually support each other."[16] Later the resolution added: "The reform of the political system, recently emphatically raised by the CC, means that - on the basis of insistence on the leading role of the party and on the dictatorship of a people's democracy - the system of party and state leadership have to be reformed and perfected, socialist democracy has to be expanded, and the socialist legal system has to be perfected, so that all these conform to the requirements of socialist modernization."[17]

These formulations make it quite clear that the strategic objective of the activities of the Chinese party leaders is socialist modernization of the country and society, centered on economic construction. All other elements of the policy serving this goal - reform of the economic and political systems and the development of a socialist spiritual civilization - are conceived of as, on the whole, equal instruments which should be harmonized with each other by all means. Most Chinese theoretical experts basically agreed with this concept; the only subject of discussion was whether these instruments were really of equal rank, or whether some order of importance or priority existed among them. In this respect, opinions are divided.

There are some who, in agreement with the official standpoint, emphasize the importance of continuing the economic, political, and ideological reforms simultaneously and in a harmonized manner. They believe that reforms in these three basic fields of social life have to proceed parallel to and in close interaction with each other. A slowdown or neglect of reforms in one or the other sphere would sooner or later adversely affect the reforms in other spheres, thus braking and delaying them. This concept seems to be confirmed by practical experiences in some phases of the reform process, though not quite unequivocally.

Another opinion emphasizes the priority of consistent implementation of the economic reform, setting out from the fact that economic construction is of outstanding importance and plays a central role from the viewpoint of attaining the strategic objective ("the economy is the base on which the political, ideological, and legal systems of superstructure are built." If the planned reform can be implemented successfully in the economy, if the development of the forces of production accelerates in their wake, and if living standards rise, it will be much easier to implement the political and ideological reforms. The representatives of this standpoint most frequently refer to the example of the reform of urban economy and to the experiences of other socialist countries - among them Hungary - where reforms began in the economy and later only gradually extended to the various components of the political and ideological superstructure.

There are some who believe that in the socialist reform process priority should be given to political reforms, as without them, even the economic and ideological reforms cannot advance at a proper rate. In fact, sooner or later they run into the opposition of persons and organizations interested in maintaining the old political structure; thus, the whole reform process is braked and a "rearrangement" starts. The advocates of this concept rely partly on Eastern-European experiences, and partly on the events and developments in China in the past one and a half years. To support their view they also advance the argument that in socialist systems the leading role of politics has always been asserted, and economic and ideological reforms were made possible by the changes and turns in the political sphere. It follows that political reforms should continue to play the role of transmission gear or "engine" in the reform process, as otherwise the machine or the "train" will stop.

Finally, opinions also exist which emphasise the priority of ideological reform, setting out from the assumption that without ideological clarity and a firm ideological basis both the economic and the political reforms "are groping in the dark." A basic deficiency of the old system is that it was built upon mistaken theoretical and ideological assumptions. If the substance of these mistakes is not clarified and the erroneous beliefs are not rooted out, the reform steps will be guided by forced manoeuvring dictated by practical considerations or the situation at any time. This is why, for a planned and consistent implementation of the reform process, above all a scientifically founded, firm theoretical and ideological base has to be created. Some of its elemens already exist, but political boldness and the ability to systematize are still lacking; these would arrange all these elements into a coherent and consistent system adequately reflecting reality, and would then serve as a "compass" for harmonizing the reform processes going on in various fields and spheres.

Each of the differing opinions reviewed above evidences a certain truth and logic. The question is, which of them has more, and which reflects better the actually exsisting inner logic of the individual elements of the reform process? In the system of goals of the economic reform it was easier to find the "decisive link" in the reform of ownership, although - as could be seen - this is still debated by many. The author adheres to the view reflected in the fourth opinion. For already a decade I have made efforts to provide ideological foundations for the economic and political reforms with my theoretical works, wishing to prove that the "existing socialism" is actually nonexistent as socialism and thus in our age the aim of surpassing the capitalist mode of production in a historical sense (i.e., in the sense of the theory of social formations) is ill-advised. It is my deep conviction that until we comprehend that efficient production and management can be carried on in our age only in a pluralistic commodity economy, relying on capital relationships, and that this necessarily entails an actual pluralistic (multi-party) system of political and legal superstructure and institutions, our political and economic reforms cannot achieve their goals, and in social progress we shall continue to chase after utopian dreams. The greatest pitfall of the Chinese economic and political reforms is also the lack of ideological clarity, the rigid insistence on the fiction of "realized socialism" and on the mistaken theoretical thesis of the "primary phase of socialism" based on it.

In the 10 years during the development of the Chinese reform process - interspersed with new starts and backward steps, upswings and "readjustments" and "creating order" - it was clearly seen how complicated, difficult, and painful a process the radical reform and thorough transformation of the economic and political system established in former decades is. Such reform is particularly difficult in such a vast country as China, with a huge population, unevenly developed and on the whole backward, a country that lagged behind the development of civilization by whole historical epochs in the past several centuries. The situation is further complicated by the fact that this vast country, owing to its particular circumstances, tried to overcome its backwardness in a revolutionary way with the aid of a socio-economic development model that has proved to be a blind alley, even in more developed countries and societies. In fact, this model led the development of these societies not in the direction of historically surpassing capitalism, but towards the survival and institutionalization of precapitalist social and production relations in the framework of a "socialist system."

Footnotes to Chapter Eleven

1. Selected works of Deng Xiaoping (1975-1982), Foreign Language Press, Beijing, 1984, p 309
2. Ibid., p 310
3. Ibid., p 311
4. Ibid., p 313
5. Ibid., p 313
6. "Advance along the road of socialism with Chinese characteristics" - Report delivered at the 13th National Congress of

the CPC on October 25, 1987, by Zhao Ziyang. Beijing Review, vol. 30, no. 45. Nov. 9-15, 1987, (Centerfold) pp XV-XXI
7. Ibid., p XVI
8. Ibid., p XVII
9. Ibid., p XVIII
10. Ibid., p XVII
11. Ibid., p XVIII
12. Ibid., p XIX
13. Ibid., pp XIX-XX
14. This was also shown by a statement of Deng Xiaoping in a talk with President George Bush: "Our final goal is to develop socialist democracy, but it would do no good if we acted rashly. If we now held elections among one billion Chinese, certainly such chaos would ensue as prevailed during the "cultural revolution." ... The need for stability pushes every other problem to the background." (Quoted by the Hungarian daily Népszabadság, August 9, 1989, p 4)
15. Report to the party congress, op. cit. (note 6). p XXI
16. ZJN 1987, I, p 41
17. Ibid., p 44

SUMMARY

Since the 3rd plenary meeting of the Central Committee elected by the 11th Congress of the Communist Party of China, held in December 1978, China has taken a promising political turn, seeming to break with the abnormal circumstances and phenomena existing for more than two decades in the socieconomic and political-ideological development of the most heavily populated country of the world. This put China on its way to creating a modern society, conforming to the requirements of the late twentieth century and adapting organically to the system of international relations.

In China there was no lack of attempts at transforming society even in previous decades. However, due to the strategy of social development based on erroneous ideological hypotheses of the leaders of the CPC and their impatience, violence, and willfulness feeding on ill-concealed power ambitions, these attempts led to a distorted economic structure and an anachronistic political superstructure. This economic structure and political superstructure were characterized by an economic development that focused on the military industry, a chronic backwardness in agriculture, and a stagnation of the living standard on the one hand, and by the uninhibited dictatorship by a narrow group of party leaders and an unbounded personality cult of the "great leader" Mao Zedong on the other hand.

In connection with this brief characterization of the circumstances before the political turn in 1978/1979, however, it should be observed that both the stagnation and temporary decline of the living standard and the unconditional respect paid to persons at the top of the power structure were not new phenomena for the Chinese people, who have fought, for several thousand years, against various elemental disasters, and the devastation caused by wars, who have been little influenced by foreign ideologies, and who were nursed mainly on Confucian ideology. This explains as well why relatively great numbers of the Chinese people accepted, at the beginning still with a certain amount of expectation and enthusiasm, later simply with indifferent resignation or acquiescence, the repeated attempts by the leaders of the CPC to change society with political and ideological campaigns. Only a relatively thin stratum of Chinese society - the intelligentsia, amounting to 20-25 million persons - has tried, from time to time, to resist these attempts at transformation and reeducation, in most cases without any success and with rather grave and painful consequences. In the past four decades - excepting former landowners and rich peasants, as well as "counter-revolutionists" at all times - no stratum of Chinese society has been so stigmatized, humiliated, and repressed as the intelligentsia and their families.

It is not by chance that the ideological and political renewal process that was launched with such slogans as "Let's have free thinking!" and "Let's find the truth starting from the facts!" after Mao Zedong's death in 1977 and has led to the already mentioned political turn, found the warmest response and the most enthusiastic support precisely among the Chinese intelligentsia. Neither is it by chance that the overwhelming majority of the intellectual cadres - being at that time numerous among the members of the CPC as well - wanted to realize ideological and political renewal primarily by way of radical transformation and deep reform of the economic and political system, and by changing the policy of seclusion and self-isolation that China had followed for decades. This has been clearly and unanimously expressed in the policy of reform and opening. During the 10 years of pursuing this policy - in spite of the problems and difficulties encountered - outstanding and lasting results have been achieved in China in most areas. The 10 years from 1979 to 1988 have proved to be the most successful period in the 40 years since the establishment of the PRC, in regard to economic growth, modernization of production, and an improved standard of living for the Chinese people.

Results and Problems

As in Hungary, economic reform in China began in agriculture, or in the rural economy in the broad sense, where it achieved in a relatively short period resounding success. Consequently, one of the most important results of the Chinese reform policy is undoubtedly the radical reorganization of the rural economy, which has helped the overwhelming majority of about 800 million peasants living in villages and townships to considerably better and more advantageous living and working conditions. It can also be said that the principal beneficiary of the Chinese reforms has been the peasantry.

What are these advantageous changes? First of all, the system of rural people's communes that had been hamstringing the development of the rural forces of production for more than a quarter of a century was abolished over a 5-year period. Agriculture and household farming are done primarily within the compass of the family, and small-scale and service industry activities are accomplished in rural and township collective enterprises. In villages the ownership system was deeply influenced, too, by the reform: while the dominant role of collective ownership has been preserved, individual ownership has been expanded and development of the private ownership sector has also begun. Following the quick upswing of productive activities outside agriculture, the sectorial structure of the rural economy has undergone considerable changes, and within agricultural production, stock breeding, forestry, fishery, and various traditional secondary rural occupations have notably increased. At the end of 1988, more than 80 million people in Chinese villages were engaged in activities outside agriculture, i.e., more than one fifth of the rural labor force.

The rapid increase in the number of small firms and enterprises in rural areas and townships has essentially changed the former relations and the division of labor between cities and villages in China, and has given a great impetus to the process of industrialization in the country. By "readjusting" the agricultural price policy, raising state purchase prices repeatedly, and setting "free" (i.e., liberalizing) prices for a relatively wide range of agricultural products, new possibilities for contractual production and procurement as well as for rural and urban free-market trade have been created. All this has considerably contributed to the expansion of rural commodity production and to gradual development of a commodity-producing economy at a national level. A particularly great result is the fact that the average pace of growth of agricultural production in China over the past 10 years - even without considering the performace of rural industy - has more than doubled the average annual pace of growth reached in the preceding 26 years.

In spite of these results, a number of problems are still unresolved in Chinese villages; moreover, a whole series of new problems and contradictions has emerged as well. For example - contrary to former assumptions - the technical equipment and supply of agriculture has not changed considerably during this decade. Up-to-date family and collective farms specializing in commodity production have not been established in great numbers. Indeed, in the field of irrigation and the management of water, as well as in the use of chemical fertilizers and pesticides, a certain decline or stagnation can be observed; neither has there been any serious progress in the mechanization of agricultural enterprises. Because of repeated postponement of the promised price reform, it has not been possible to ease tensions and reduce troubles arising from the excessively low profitability, and even losses in the production of cereals, cotton, and several other industrial crops. All these factors together - after a rapid development between 1979 and 1984 - have led in the past 5 years to a decline and stagnation in the production of cereals and cotton. In turn, the different measures taken to offset price losses - for example the sale of cheaper chemical fertilizers or fuels to farmers - have often presented opportunities for the local cadres to commit various abuses. In spite of the rapid enrichment of the rural households in more developed regions and in the agricultural zones near cities, and the considerable increase in the average peasant's earnings, about 100 million peasants still live under extremely difficult conditions, at the subsistence level, or simply vegetate in the poorer and backward regions of the country. Thus, in the past several years a widening gap in the pecuniary standing and an increasing social polarization have become evident in a considerable number of Chinese villages. This exerts an unfavorable influence on the mood of the population and strengthens the antireform endeavors in the end.

In contrast to the rural economic reform, the reform of the urban economy has not seen any resounding success in the past 10 years; moreover, it has recently faced ever-increasing difficulties and obstacles and has brought to the surface a number of new problems. Their causes are extremely different and far-reaching, but their common root is the intertwining of the traditional "socialist" economic and political system and primarily the exclusive rule and influence of the party, which supervises directly the policy and the economy, disregarding all kinds of social control. This situation could be amended by a radical and sweeping reform of the established political system, but today the chances for it are very slight.

The beginning of urban reform has concentrated on decentralizing power in economic management and control, i.e., on delegating certain decision-making rights from the central to the regional (provincial and municipal) administration organizations and economic units (enterprises or groups of enterprises). These measures have been received by party and state leaders of different regions with mixed feelings. The leaders of the developed coastal provinces and cities have generally given decentralization a favorable reception, as it offers them greater independence and broader powers, and they have made the best of this opportunity. However, the leaders of remote and poorer provinces and cities would have preferred less independence if it had been accompanied by more central support. In most cases, they are unable to make use even of possibilities presented by the foreign economic "openness". Extending the scope of powers of enterprise managers has met with serious opposition even in more developed regions, since some local party and state leaders have seen these reforms as limiting their own scope of power and rights.

Decentralization measures have launched positive processes in several fields, though they have no doubt had negative consequences as well. On the basis of greater enterprise independence, as well as the separation of rights of ownership and disposal, very different economic forms of contractual operation and leasing have been established in the state sector, and they have improved, in most cases, the economic efficiency of these enterprises and instructed economic leaders to manage "on a business basis." In recent years, considerable results have been obtained in establishing and operating various horizontal economic unions, which have broken through the former stiff sectorial and regional dividing lines and have given a great impetus to the spread of different forms of association operating on a shareholder basis. While the dominance of state ownership has been preserved, in the past 10 years the ownership structure of the urban economy in China has changed significantly. In the past 4-5 years, within the areas of production and services, the share and importance of the individual and private sector, as well as the cooperative sector representing collective ownership by smaller groups, have increased at a rapid pace. In addition, different mixed forms of undertakings and types of joint ventures have also appeared. Particular attention and treatment are given to joint ventures and cooperative enterprises established with both Chinese and foreign capital investment; these operate mainly in coastal "open cities" and so-called special economic zones.

In spite of all these results, the urban economic reforms, which were continually extended, failed and came to a dead-end in the second half of the 1980s. They have caused at least as many problems and troubles for the economic leadership as they have settled. Therefore, the comprehensive economic reform - introduced in China at the end of 1984 and at the beginning of 1985 - has produced only contradictory results. It has maintained a dynamic development in the economy, but at the same time it has also overheated it and therefore exacerbated imbalances and started an inflationary spiral. In several fields, it has tried to swing the established "product economy" of China in the direction of a commodity-producing economy, but it was unable to develop an indirect system of regulators for economic management characteristic of commodity-producing economies, primarily because China lacked independent producers and market clients, managing on their own responsibility and at their own risk. Instead, a management system and a trade mechanism on a "double track" have been established, combining the negative features of planning and market regulation - the inflexibility and the spontaneity - but not the positive features of both methods; this has led to a "neither plan nor market" economy in China. Weakening of macroeconomic management and control and loss of control over the microeconomic processes have encouraged the economic and political leaders of the PRC in their endeavors to recentralize.

Among the negative consequences of the comprehensive reform for the whole national economy, two-digit inflation is the greatest problem. This inflationary spiral began right after the launching of the reforms, and what is more, it has taken place in a country which already suffered devastating inflation with a total economic downfall 40 years ago. In the more than three decades that followed, the people of China grew accustomed to a price stability that was artificially maintained, and they considered it one of the greatest achievements of the socialist economic system. This is why the new inflation in China is not only an economic problem, but also an ideological and political problem of vital importance which concerns and troubles a wide strata of the population. Though this problem has its origin in the traditional directive-planned economy and can be traced back to the unreasonable pricing methods and relative prices of the former price system, both the objective economic and subjective political conditions necessary for their solution are missing in China. The Chinese economy continues to be one of scarcity, contradictions, and tensions, which were increased and aggravated by the "overheating" of recent years. At the same time, the inflation is caused by the economic and political leaders themselves, by undertaking losing enterprises in the state sector on the one hand, and by maintaining and "supporting" the enormously swollen bureaucratic party and state apparatus on the other hand. Moreover, the ever-growing budget deficit is financed by issuing banknotes without any real backing. This situation can be changed only by a radical reform of the political structure and the power system. However, efforts in this direction have failed, one after the other, in recent years because of the opposition of political forces who want to protect the existing structure and power system. Nevertheless, without a sweeping reform of the political system, the further development of economic reform is questionable, as even the best reform concepts are defeated at the outset if their realization can be easily hindered or sabotaged, on all levels, by political leaders in key positions of power.

In the field of developing and widening foreign economic relations, the reform and opening policy launched 10 years ago can register considerable success. At the same time, imbalances and tensions, as well as the loss of several billion US dollars due to inappropriate planning and lack of coordination, have become rather frequent in this area as well. In the past 10 years China has made use of a considerable amount of foreign capital, resources, up-to-date technology, and special knowledge to modernize and develop its economy, but all this has proved to be insufficient to meet the enormous claims of the "four modernizations." The volume of debt, exceeding US $40 billion, of the People's Republic of China does not seem very high in comparison with that of several other countries of the world, especially when we consider that China's debt service burden of about US $8-10 billion a year does not exceed the 20% of its foreign exchange income from exports. The total foreign trade turnover on the order of US $100 billion a year is already an important factor in world trade, though it is not as high as the foreign trade turnover of the small insular country Taiwan, with 20 million inhabitants, not to mention the differences in the commodity structure and in the balance of trade of the two parts of China. Balancing trade presents more and more trouble from year to year, and represents an unresolved problem for the economic management in China, because of the slowly changing commodity structure of exports, on the one hand, and the unsatisfying quantity, quality and choice of the Chinese export products, on the other hand. In consequence of the Chinese "export offensive," enforced at any price and strongly subsidized by the state, the importation of certain products from China encounters quantitative restrictions or prohibitions against dumping in several countries of the world. Tourism, which had begun to develop at a good pace, has suffered a setback - at least temporarily - due to the unfavor-able international reception and wide-ranging comdemnation of the events that took place in Beijing in the summer of 1989. It is also questionable whether many of the thousands of young Chinese intellectual cadres pursuing their studies or receiving postgraduate training abroad will return home in the coming years, in view of the sanctions and disciplinary actions that followed the students' demonstrations in April and May of 1989, as well as the campaign of "ideological re-education by means of physical work," affecting a rather large number of the intelligentsia and reminiscent of methods applied at the time of the "cultural revolution." Perceiving this persistent fear of the penetration of "bourgeois ideas" and "bourgeois liberalization," the outside observer is under the impression that the leaders of China want to realize their "open policy" in such a way that their country is open to receive foreign technologies and capital only, but that their society is closed and protected against foreign ideas and conventions. However, in the last decade of the twentieth century, the formula "open country and closed society" seems a completely anachronistic and unrealizable requirement which can result only in renewed isolation and backwardness.

In spite of these contradictory results, during the 10 years of the reform and opening policy the horizon of the Chinese people has widened considerably and their knowledge of the world beyond China has been broadened and enriched. In the past decade, the Chinese intelligentsia - recruited also from talented young workers and peasants - has produced in itself an open--minded and well-educated group of reformers who will not give up, even in the face of provisional difficulties and sorry attempts, the reform targets they judge to be right. This is why we may be sure that the economic and political reform processes launched 10 years ago will be continued in China sooner or later. Social progress and development has no other way, even in China, than the radical transformation of the existing socioeconomic and political-ideological system, i.e., a total change of the social system.

Experience and Lessons

During 10 years of economic reforms and political reform attempts a manifold positive and negative experience has been gained in China, the summing up and systematization of which seems to be reasonable and profitable, since it allows us to draw some theoretical and practical lessons that may be useful for reform movements of other countries as well. In the past one to one and a half years several reform economist and theoretical experts in China have tried - in shorter or longer studies and papers - to sum up the most important experience of the reform process that started in 1979, and to draw and draft from them some generalizable lessons and recommendations. These papers are characterized mainly by an attempt at a "positive explanation," i.e. they did not make any critical observations and evaluations directly and explicitly, though the summaries and recommendations contained such negative elements and criticism in an indirect and implied form. The message in papers of this kind can be summarized as follows:

 1. The practice of reform without any proper theoretical basis cannot lead to the desired goal. However, the rightness of the theoretical foundations for reform can be justified only by success in practice. Therefore, in a reform process there is a constant need for closely joining theory with practice and for parallel and continuous development "by means of mutual control and adjustment." This fully corresponds to the epistemological axiom according to which "the criterion of the truth is the practice."

 2. The theoretical foundation of economic and political reforms has to start by "breaking through" the framework of traditional socialist economic theory and "rethinking" views and conceptions formed earlier on socialism, as well as with "up-to-

-date interpretation" of the original (authentic) texts of Marx and Engels; people have to throw off the shackles of dogmatic thinking.

3. The economic reform has to be linked with the development of the economy and technological progress; otherwise it becomes autotelic. The target of economic reform is to develop productive forces, more exactly: to conform relations of production to the existing requirements for developing productive forces. Therefore, the efficiency of reform can and should be measured, first of all, by a developing economy, an up-to-date production and consumption structure, and a higher standard of living and improved living conditions.

4. It is reasonable to start the economic reform by reforming the ownership system, because it is a decisive link in transforming relations of production and distribution and adjusting them to the requirements of the development of productive forces. Without reform of the ownership system, a complete market system, constituting the "heart" or "brain" of the commodity-producing economy, cannot be created, not to mention the market mechanism constituting the "blood vessel system" or "nervous system" of the commodity-producing economy. Reform of the ownership system in China - except in agriculture and the rural economy - began relatively late, and this circumstance has produced difficulties in the reform process. (The ownership reform was stopped following the summer of 1989.)

5. Harmony has to be established between plan and market and between the state and enterprises, or more exactly: between macroeconomic direction and control by the state and the microeconomic activity of enterprises conforming to market demands and requirements and regulated by the market. This can be achieved only by strengthening macroeconomic direction through indirect means, by improving permanently its regulation system and set of tools, and by creating the self-financing faculty of enterprises constituting autonomous market subjects. In this respect, Chinese economic reform has taken only the first steps.

6. The short-term reform measures have to harmonize with medium- and long-term reform targets and cannot be permitted to be

detached from them; the reform process should not take a direction different from or even opposite to the long-range targets. Consequently, the state organizations supervising reforms have to be in possession of reform programs and plans for a longer term.

7. Reform of the urban economic system should be bound to reform of the rural economic system. Reforms in these two fields should not be realized independently or more than temporarily detached from each other, as sooner or later tensions and conflicts will occur which slow down and set back the reform processes.

8. Reform of the economic system should be joined with reform of the political system; absence of the latter hinders or dooms to failure the former. Economic reforms without any political reforms function in a vacuum, and for lack of support they will sooner or later die.

These recommendations drafted by Chinese economists and theoretical experts - explained in considerably greater detail in the studies and papers mentioned - reflect relatively authentically the competent and moderated opinions and evaluations which developed among the reform intelligentsia in China by the end of 1988 and the beginning of 1989. It is important to recall them, as since June of 1989 there have been published evaluations which differ considerably from those above. Naturally, some party and state leaders and various strata of the population even earlier made critical observations and expressed their uncertainty and doubts concerning the course of the reform process; these have sometimes appeared explicitly in antireformist views and attempts to influence public opinion. However, the 10--year reform process, taken as a whole up to the summer of 1989, has been judged as an essentially positive one, and attempts have been made only to liquidate and "cut off" some of its negative consequences and offshoots in the framework of "improving the economic environment" and "setting the economy in order" over a period of 2 years. Today, however, considerably more is going on, with radical revision of the former ideas and conceptions regarding economic and political reforms and annulment of a series of former reform measures. A kind of "retreat" is being made, back to the previous situation in economic management and control.

It must be pointed out that these recommendations that claim to be theoretical generalizations are really based only on empirical experience that does not go beyond the framework of the 10-year Chinese reform process. Only one or two authors refer sporadically to the fact that it might be worthwhile to compare the Chinese reform experience in economics and politics with that of the Soviet Union and of some Eastern-European countries. Therefore, I would like to call attention to some aspects of this broader experience which can serve as lessons with a more general value.

Perhaps we have to proceed from the fact that economic and political reforms unfolding in countries with "existing" or "real socialism" are considered unprecedented undertakings in the history of mankind, because they want to transform a planned "product economy," directed centrally and "commanded" with totalitarian methods, into a planned commodity-producing economy or regulated market economy, and a dictatorial party state, based on a power monopoly, into a democratic, constitutional state based on the division of power. There are no tested prescriptions for this transformation; indeed, it is possible to follow this path only as the Chinese people have characterized it figuratively: "to cross the river, groping for the stones" (in Chinese: mozhe shitou guo he), i.e., persuading oneself step by step that one is really following the right path, the shallows. As regards the nature of this reform process, it is a "peaceful revolution" initiated from above, by those in power, and it generally coincides with the wishes and endeavors of a broad spectrum of the population; this is why it can rely on support from below as well. The purpose of this "revolution" is to transform or to "rebuild" (perestroit') radically the economic and political system that was established in the preceding decades and named "socialist" - on the basis of the Stalinist misconception of social formations - i.e., to effect a qualitative change of the existing social system. Practically speaking, this is a total change of system, though many, even among the political leaders, are not aware of it, or are afraid to acknowledge it for various reasons, and they prefer to speak euphemistically only about a "change of model." Since these reforms are tied to ideological and political questions of primary importance, or, more precisely to a strategic reversal which questions the correctness and expedience of the entire social development strategy followed by the communist and workers' parties in power till now, it is not unimportant how these initiatives coming from above are received and supported from below. These reforms, in their final outcome, cut to the center of the ruling, privileged strata; consequently, they can hardly meet with enthusiastic support from this area. An essential question is how, which strata of the society can be won over to the cause of the reforms, and how they can be convinced of the fact that they should also make sacrifices and endure the tensions and difficulties involved in order to make the reforms successful.

The interrelation and interconnection of reforms and economic development become extremely important precisely at this point, as Chinese authors point out. Support for the reforms from below can be established and broadened only when these reforms provide something to the masses. The first manifestation must not necessarily be in material goods, though these are important. For a certain period greater freedom, a guarantee of the enforcement of essential human rights, free speech and openness, the free flow of people and ideas, possibilities for political and social organization and assertion of interests are values which can improve the general feeling of people in these societies and can win them over to these reforms. But they are not sufficient for long. In an economy in stagnation or recession and with declining living standards or deteriorating living conditions, it is extremely difficult and, with time, almost impossible to carry out successful reforms, and to retain the necessary mass support. Hungary, Poland, and the Soviet Union can serve as examples in this regard.

Nevertheless, the experience of Hungary and China shows without a doubt that it is much easier to begin the economic reforms in the rural economy than in the urban economy, i.e., than in the national economy as a whole. This is obviously connected with the clearer production and distribution relations in the rural economy, and the simpler division of rural labor. There, at the start, it is enough to "leave peasants to produce" and to make it possible for them to sell a part of their products on the free market, with the other part bought up by the state at reasonable prices. However, in more developed countries this simple solution does not suffice, because rural producers are also increasingly dependent on industry, trade, transport, and financial organizations. Consequently, Chinese authors correctly see that rural economic reform must go hand in hand with urban economic reform.

All Chinese authors have mentioned the primary importance of a theoretical foundation for reform. This is crucial when the whole ideological system is to be revised. Theory and ideology can serve as a compass for the reform process only when they operate with clearly interpretable notions and adequately reflect reality. In this respect, the reform theories expounded in China and elsewhere to date leave room for improvement. Notions which have been regarded as a "theoretical breakthrough" - for example, "socialist" and/or "planned commodity economy," "primary stage of socialism," and "public ownership" - are really hazy and scientifically indefinable and can be interpreted quite arbitrarily. The notion of "public ownership" (in Chinese: gongyouzhi) means nothing more in China than "modernization" (i.e "renaming") of the formerly used expression "whole people's ownership" (in Chinese: quanmin suoyouzhi), so it is essentially equal to state ownership. In comparison with these abstract categories, such new economic categories as "family-size production responsibility system" (in Chinese: jiating shengchan zerenzhi) or "family contracted responsiblity system" (in Chinese: jiating chengbao zerenzhi) and "contracted management responsibility system" (in Chinese: chenbao jingying zerenzhi), established in the practice of Chinese economic reform, are already an improvement, since these expressions - which perhaps seem to us somewhat complicated and ponderous at first hearing and in a word-for-word translation - have concrete meaning exactly understandable and interpretable for the simple Chinese peasants and workers.

Finally, as regards the linking up of political and economic reform, we should not be surprised after all at the opposition and objection of the aged Chinese leaders, or even at their brutal reply to the ever louder young intelligentsia urging political reforms. In fact, this brutal reply is dictated by a reflex developed during decades of wielding power exclusively and by an instinctive insistence, at whatever cost, on power gained through hard and painful struggles. Economic and political reforms unfolding in the countries with "existing" or "real socialism" have a strict - specified by the objective regularities and requirements of the social development - inherent logic which leads inevitably to the negation and liquidation at its foundations of this system, wrongly named socialism. In order to explain it more clearly, we have to make a short theoretical detour.

Willful attempts at "historically outdoing" capitalism have thrown these more or less backward societies late in their socioeconomic development, back, not simply to "presocialist" but to explicitly precapitalist socioeconomic conditions. Presocialist conditions could have been developed - in a formation-theoretical sense - in these societies only if, after the victory of their radical people's revolutions, they had gone the way of people's democratic social development, appearing as an atternative to bourgeois democratic social development, i.e., if they had tried to surmount their backwardness and make up their civilization deficit in the framework of a multisectorial market economy based on mixed ownership forms, as well as through a people's democratic state power with a multiparty system, based on a broad class alliance. Now they have to effect a newer - possibly peaceful - revolution in order to get from their precapitalistic state to a bourgeois or people's democratic development (or to a certain mixture of both and to a commodity-production and market economy based on capital relations, by liquidating their "product economy" and organizing the civil society. These factors constitute the objective content and formation-theoretical essence of economic and political reforms unfolding in the countries with "existing" or "real socialism."

For precisely this reason - because of the inherent logic of social development - these reforms come inevitably to the point where party leaders who enjoy a monopoly of power have to decide whether to follow through consistently and liquidate, step by step, the economic, political, and ideological basis of their own power, or whether to call a halt and to stop those who have taken seriously their promises of radical reform, qualitative transformation, and revolutionary change. Experience to date shows that the former, "enlightened" and "civilized" solution is chosen by leaders of ruling parties only in countries where the economic and political system of "socialism" has already come to a general, ever increasing crisis, to such an extent that any attempt to maintain the system by violence carries the threat of a civil war, i.e., a national catastrophe and perhaps international conflict. As of the summer of 1989, the leaders of the Communist Party of China - in like manner as some former leaders of ruling communist parties in Eastern Europe - did not view the situation as being so critical, and they decided, consequently, to choose the latter alternative. How much longer this system can be maintained in China - by means of party power - will be shown by events and developments in the coming years.

APPENDIX

Basic Indicators of Economic Growth in the People's Republic of China, 1952-1988

Denomination	Unit of measure	1952	1957	1965	1978	1988	Average annual growth rate between 1953-1978 (26 years) percent	1979-1988 (10 years)
A PHYSICAL INDICATORS								
I Demography and employment								
1. Population (end-year)	millions							
cities and rural towns		574.8	646.5	725.4	962.6	1096.1	2.0	1.3
of which: cities		71.6	106.2	130.4	172.5	540.6+	3.4	12.1+
rural towns		-	69.0	92.5	119.3	300.8+	2.8 (20 years)	9.7+
Villages		-	37.2	37.9	53.2	239.8+	1.8 (20 years)	16.3+
		503.2	540.3	595.0	790.1	555.5+	1.8	-3.6+
2. Rates of natural change	per mille							
- Birth rate		37.0	34.0	38.1	18.3	20.8	-2.7	1.3
- Death rate		17.0	10.8	9.6	6.3	6.6	-3.9	0.5
- Rate of natural increase		20.0	23.2	28.5	12.0	14.2	-2.0	1.7
3. Employment (end-year)	millions							
- Urban workers		207.3	237.7	286.7	401.5	543.4	2.6	3.1
- state sector		24.9	32.0	51.4	95.1	142.7	5.3	4.1
- collective sector		15.8	24.5	37.4	74.5	99.8	6.1	3.0
- private sector		0.2	6.5	12.3	20.5	36.3	19.5	5.9
		8.9	1.0	1.7	0.1	6.6	-18.8	52.0
- Rural workers		182.4	205.7	235.3	306.4	400.7	2.0	2.7
- in agriculture		-	-	-	274.9	314.6	-	1.4
- in industry		-	-	-	17.3	34.1	-	7.0
- in other branches		-	-	-	14.2	52.0	-	13.9

+ The sudden increase in the number of inhabitants of cities and rural towns is a consequence of the administrative reform implemented in 1983-1984. Adjacent villages were annexed to these cities and rural towns, and thus their population was thereafter included in the latter.

- No data available

(Table continues)

(Continuation)

Denomination	Unit of measure	1952	1957	1965	1978	1988	1953-1978	1979-1988
II Annual output of major industrial products								
1. Hard coal and lignite	mn tons	66.0	131.0	232.0	618.0	980.0	9.0	4.7
2. Crude oil	" "	0.4	1.5	11.3	104.1	137.1	23.9	2.8
3. Electric energy	bn kWh	7.3	19.3	67.6	256.6	545.2	14.7	7.8
4. Steel	mn tons	1.4	5.4	12.2	31.8	59.4	12.8	6.5
5. Cement	" "	2.7	6.9	16.3	65.2	210.1	13.0	12.4
6. Timber	mn m^3	12.3	27.9	39.8	51.6	63.0	5.7	2.0
7. Fertilizers (effective substance)	mn tons	0.0	0.2	1.7	8.7	17.4	20.8 (20 years)	7.2
8. Cotton cloth	bn m	3.8	5.1	6.3	11.0	18.8	4.2	5.5
9. Paper and cardboard	mn tons	0.4	0.9	1.7	4.4	12.7	9.7	11.2
10. Sugar	" "	0.5	0.9	1.5	2.3	4.6	6.0	7.4
11. Bicycles	mn pieces	0.1	0.8	1.8	8.5	41.4	18.6	17.1
12. Sewing machines	" "	0.1	0.3	1.2	4.9	9.8	16.1	7.3
13. Household washing machines	" "	–	–	–	0.0	10.5	–	187.5
14. Household refrigerators	" "	–	–	–	0.0	7.6	–	75.1
15. Tape recorders	" "	–	–	–	0.1	23.4	–	65.0
16. Television sets	" "	–	–	0.0	0.5	25.1	–	47.4
of wich: Color televisions	" "	–	–	–	0.0	10.3	–	117.4
III Annual output of major agricultural products								
1. Grain crops	mn tons	163.9	195.1	194.5	304.8	394.1	2.4	2.6
Rice	" "	68.4	86.8	87.7	136.9	169.1	2.7	2.1
Wheat	" "	18.1	23.6	29.2	53.8	83.4	4.3	4.5
Corn	" "	16.9	21.4	23.7	56.0	77.4	4.7	3.3
Soybeans	" "	9.5	10.5	6.1	7.6	11.7	-0.9	4.4
Tuber crops	" "	16.3	21.9	19.7	31.7	27.0	2.6	-1.6
Other cereals	" "	34.7	30.9	28.1	18.8	25.5	-2.4	3.1
2. Cotton	" "	1.3	1.6	2.1	2.2	4.1	2.0	6.7
3. Oil-bearing crops	" "	4.2	4.2	3.6	5.2	13.2	0.8	9.7
4. Sugar-bearing crops	" "	7.6	11.9	15.4	23.8	61.9	4.5	10.0
5. Tea	thousand tons	82.0	112.0	101.0	268.0	545.0	4.7	7.4
6. Fruits	mn tons	2.4	3.2	3.2	6.6	16.7	3.9	9.8
7. Meat (excl. poultry)	" "	3.4	4.0	5.5	8.6	21.9	3.6	9.9
8. Aquatic products	" "	1.7	3.1	3.0	4.7	10.6	4.0	8.6

(Table continues)

(Continuation)

Denomination	Unit of measure	1952	1957	1965	1978	1988	1953-1978	1979-1988
IV Agrotechnical supply								
1. Hauling power of machines, total	mn kW	0.2	1.2	11.0	117.5	265.8	27.8	8.5
2. Big and medium-sized tractors	thousand pc	1.3	14.7	72.6	557.4	870.0	26.3	4.6
3. Hand tractors (below 20 HP)	mn pieces	–	–	0.0	1.4	6.0	–	15.7
4. Pumping capacity	mn kW	0.1	0.4	6.7	48.2	65.7	26.8	3.1
5. Area of cultivated land	mn ha	107.9	111.8	103.6	99.4	95.7	-0.3	-0.4
irrigated land		20.0	27.3	33.1	45.0	44.1	3.2	-0.2
tractor-ploughed land		0.1	2.6	15.6	40.7	40.7	26.0	0.0
6. Fertilizer consumption								
– effective substance, total	mn tons	0.0	0.4	1.9	8.8	21.4	12.6 (20 years)	9.3
– per unit of area	kg/ha	0.0	3.0	18.0	88.5	222.0	13.9 (20 years)	9.6
7. Electricity consumption in rural areas	bn kWh	0.0	0.1	3.7	25.3	71.2	23.7 (20 years)	10.9
V. Transport and communications								
1. Length of railway lines (end-year)								
– total	thousand km	22.9	26.7	36.4	48.6	52.8	2.9	0.8
– electrified	"	–	–	0.1	1.0	5.7	–	19.0
2. Length of highways	"	126.7	254.6	514.5	890.2	999.6	7.8	1.2
3. Length of internal waterways	"	95.0	144.1	157.7	136.0	109.4	1.4	-2.2
4. Length of domestic airline routes	"	8.0	22.1	34.9	93.6	245.5	9.9	10.1
5. Length of pipelines	"	–	0.0	0.4	8.3	14.3	–	5.6
6. Volume of freight transport	bn ton/km	76.2	181.0	346.3	982.9	2382.5	10.3	9.3
7. Volume of passenger transport	bn person-km	24.8	49.6	69.7	174.3	620.7	7.8	13.5
8. Number of telephone subscribers	mn subscrib.	0.4	0.7	1.3	1.9	4.7	6.7	9.4
– in cities		0.3	0.5	0.8	1.2	3.6	5.5	11.8
– in rural areas		0.1	0.2	0.5	0.7	1.1	10.2	4.2
VI Supply indicators								
1. Per capita food consumption	kg/year							
– grain (unprocessed)		197.7	203.1	182.8	195.5	249.1	-0.0	2.5
– edible oil		2.1	2.4	1.7	1.6	5.9	-1.1	13.9
– meat (excl. poultry)		6.8	6.2	7.3	8.4	16.5	0.8	7.0
– poultry		0.4	0.5	0.4	0.4	1.8	0.0	16.2
– eggs		1.0	1.3	1.4	2.0	5.8	2.7	11.2
– aquatic products		2.7	4.3	3.3	3.5	5.7	1.0	4.5
– sugar		0.9	1.5	1.7	3.4	6.3	5.2	6.4

(Table continues)

(Continuation)

Denomination	Unit of measure	1952	1957	1965	1978	1988 (1983)+	1953-1978	1979-1988
2. Per capita calorie consumption	cal/day		2270		2311	2877	0.1 (20 years)	4.5 (5 years)
– in cities	"	–	–	–	2715	3182	–	3.2 (5 years)
– in villages	"	–	–	–	2224	2806	–	4.8 (5 years)
3. Housing supply	m²/head							
– living space in cities	"	–	–	–	4.2	8.8	–	7.7
– living space in villages	"	–	–	–	8.1	16.6	–	7.4

Notes: + No data available for 1988, only for 1983; – No data available for these years

B VALUE INDICATORS

a) At constant prices of 1980:

I Gross industrial output value	bn yuan	27.1	60.6	119.6	433.4	1444.9	11.4	12.8
– light industry	"	18.5	33.9	63.7	185.8	749.7	9.3	15.0
– heavy industry	"	8.6	26.7	55.9	247.6	695.2	13.8	10.9
II Gross agricultural output value	"	88.3	110.1	121.0	176.3	322.0	2.7	6.2
– plant production	"	74.5	90.2	93.1	127.9	200.5	2.1	4.6
– animal husbandry	"	12.0	16.7	20.0	28.9	71.0	3.4	9.4
– other occupations	"	1.8	3.2	7.9	19.5	50.5	9.6	10.0
I+II Gross industrial and agricultural combined output value	"	115.4	170.7	240.6	609.7	1766.9	8.2	11.3
III Gross output value of other productive branches	"	21.9	39.9	48.5	116.8	336.7	7.9	11.2
I+II+III = Social product	"	137.3	210.6	289.1	726.5	2103.6	7.9	11.2
IV National income (generated)	"	71.4	109.2	140.9	323.7	782.2	6.0	9.2
National income	bn US $*	47.6	72.8	93.9	215.8	521.5	6.0	9.2
Per capita national income	US $	83	113	129	224	476	3.9	7.8
V Gross national product (GNP)	bn yuan	82.5	128.4	176.7	385.3	964.1	6.1	9.6
– extracting branches	"	–	–	–	128.7	223.7	–	5.7
– manufacturing branches	"	–	–	–	176.8	507.1	–	11.1
– servicing branches	"	–	–	–	79.8	233.3	–	11.3
Per capita GNP	yuan	144	199	244	372	880	3.7	9.0
Per capita GNP	US $*	96	132	162	248	586	3.7	9.0

Note: * Converted at the official exchange rate of 1980 to US $ (1 US $ = 1.5 RMB)

(Table continues)

(Continuation)

Denomination	Unit of measure	1952	1957	1965	1978	1988	1953-1978	1979-1988
b) At current prices:								
VI National income (used)	bn yuan	60.7	93.5	134.7	297.5	1209.9	–	–
– for consumption	" "	47.7	70.2	98.2	188.8	797.1	–	–
– for accumulation	" "	13.0	23.3	36.5	108.7	412.8	–	–
VII State budget								
– Revenues	" "	18.4	31.0	47.3	112.1	258.8	7.1	8.7
– Expenditures	" "	17.6	30.4	46.6	111.1	266.8	7.4	9.2
– Balance	" "	+0.8	+0.6	+0.7	+1.0	-8.0	–	–
VIII Investment in capital construction	" "	–	–	–	–	449.7	–	–
– in the state sector	" "	4.4	15.1	21.7	66.9	276.3	11.1	15.2
of which: from budget	" "	3.7	13.1	16.3	41.7	40.3	9.8	-0.3
IX Retail sales	" "	27.7	47.4	67.0	155.9	744.0	6.9	16.9
Retail price index	%	100.0	108.5	120.4	121.6	210.0	0.8	5.6
X Incomes of inhabitants								
1. Average net income of a rural inhabitant	yuan/year	57	73	–	134	545	3.3	15.1
of which: real increase	%						2.4	11.5
2. Average income spent on living of a rural inhabitant	yuan/year	62	79	100	132	479	2.9	13.8
of which: real increase	%						1.8	8.1
3. Average per capita wages of blue- and white-collar workers	yuan/year	445	624	590	615	1747	1.3	11.0
of which: real increase	%						0.4	4.2
4. Average income spent on living of an urban inhabitant	yuan/year	148	205	237	383	1281	3.7	12.8
of which: real increase	%						2.9	5.9
5. Average income spent on living by an inhabitant of China	yuan/year	76	102	125	175	639	3.3	13.8
of which: real increase	%						2.2	7.6
XI Savings of inhabitants								
Saving deposits (end-year)	bn yuan	0.9	3.5	6.5	21.1	330.1	12.9	33.5
– in urban areas	" "	0.9	2.8	5.2	15.5	265.9	11.6	32.9
– in rural areas	" "	–	0.7	1.3	5.6	114.2	11.0 (20 years)	35.2

(Table continues)

(Continuation)

Denomination	Unit of measure	1952	1957	1965	1978	1988	1953-1978	1979-1988
XII Foreign trade turnover, total	bn US $	1.9	3.1	4.2	20.6	102.8	9.6	17.4
– export		0.8	1.6	2.2	9.7	47.5	10.1	17.2
– import		1.1	1.5	2.0	10.9	55.3	9.2	17.6
– balance		-0.3	+0.1	+0.2	-1.2	-3.1	–	–
Per capita foreign trade	US $	3	5	6	21	94	7.8	16.2
Bilateral turnover with the most important partner countries:	bn US $							
– Hong Kong and Macao		0.3	0.2	0.5	2.7	30.8		27.3
– Japan		0.0	0.1	0.5	4.8	19.0		14.7
– United States of America		0.0	–	–	1.0	10.0		26.0
– Federal Republic of Germany		0.0	0.1	0.1	1.4	4.9		26.9
– Soviet Union		1.1	1.4	0.4	0.4	3.3		22.3
– Singapore		–	–	0.1	0.3	2.5		23.9
– Italy		0.0	0.0	0.1	0.4	2.3		20.5
– Canada		0.0	0.0	0.1	0.7	2.2		12.9
– United Kingdom		0.0	0.1	0.3	0.7	1.6		8.8
– France		0.0	0.0	0.1	0.4	1.5		13.5
– Australia		0.0	0.0	0.0	0.8	1.5		5.8

Sources: Zhongguo Tongji Nianjian 1981, 1984 and 1988
Fenjin de sishi nian 1949-1989
The Development of China (1949-1989)
Guoji Maoyi, 5/1989, p 59

Main Structural Proportions of the Chinese National Economy, 1952-1988 (percent)

Denomination	1952	1957	1965	1978	1988
I Of the gross industrial output value					
- light industry	64.5	55.0	51.6	43.1	49.3
- heavy industry	35.5	45.0	48.4	56.9	50.7
II Of the gross agricultural output value					
- plant production	83.1	80.6	75.8	76.7	55.9
- animal husbandry	11.5	12.9	14.0	15.0	27.2
- forestry	0.7	1.7	2.0	3.4	4.7
- fisheries	0.3	0.5	1.7	1.6	5.5
- sideline occupations	4.4	4.3	6.5	3.3	6.7
III Of the combined gross industrial and agricultural output value					
- agriculture	56.9	43.3	37.3	24.8	24.3
- light industry	27.8	31.2	32.3	32.4	37.3
- heavy industry	15.3	25.5	30.4	42.8	38.4
IV Of the total value of the social product					
- agriculture	45.4	33.5	30.9	20.4	19.6
- industry	34.4	43.8	52.0	61.9	61.1
- construction	5.6	7.4	6.6	8.3	9.9
- transport and communications	3.5	3.7	3.4	3.0	2.8
- trade	11.1	11.6	7.1	6.4	6.6
of this: proportion of the social product produced in rural areas		(1978)	(1980)	(1985)	
		29.8	32.7	38.2	42.0
- agriculture		68.6	68.9	57.1	46.8
- industry		19.4	19.5	27.6	38.1
- construction		6.6	6.4	8.1	7.1
- transport and communications		1.7	1.7	3.0	3.5
- trade		3.7	3.5	4.2	4.5
V Of the national income (generated)					
- agriculture	57.7	46.8	46.2	32.8	32.4
- industry	19.5	28.3	36.4	49.4	46.2
- construction	3.6	5.0	3.8	4.1	6.7
- transport and communications	4.2	4.3	4.2	3.9	3.7
- trade	15.0	15.6	9.4	9.8	11.0

(Table continues)

(Continuation)

Denomination	1952	1957	1965	1978	1988
VI Of the national income (used)					
- for accumulation	21.4	24.9	27.1	36.5	34.1
- for consumption	78.6	75.1	72.9	63.5	65.9
VII Of the gross national product (GNP) produced		(1978)	(1980)	(1985)	
- extracting branches		28.4	30.4	29.7	27.3
- manufacturing branches		48.6	49.0	45.4	47.0
- service branches		23.0	20.6	24.9	25.7
VIII Share of budget revenues in national income	29.5	34.2	34.1	37.2	22.0
IX Distribution of budget revenues by origin					
1. From enterprises	31.2	46.5	55.8	51.0	1.8
of which: industrial enterprises	11.7	19.1	45.7	39.3	-
2. Tax revenues	53.2	49.9	43.2	46.3	88.5
of which: industrial and commercial tax	33.3	36.5	35.0	40.3	58.7
agricultural tax	14.7	9.6	5.4	2.5	2.0
3. Bond issue	4.6	2.3	-	-	9.7
4. Other revenues	6.9	1.3	1.0	2.7	-
X Of budget expenditures, spent					
- for investments	26.6	40.7	34.0	40.7	24.4
- for educational, scientific, and health purposes	7.7	9.1	9.8	10.1	18.0
- for defense	33.0	18.1	18.6	15.1	8.7
XI Share of investments in the state sector in national income	7.2	16.7	15.6	22.2	23.5
			(Average) (1963-1965)		
XII Of investments in capital construction					
By destination:					
- productive projects	66.9	73.3	79.4	79.1	65.9
- nonproductive projects	33.1	26.7	20.6	20.9	34.1
of which: housing construction	10.3	9.3	6.9	7.8	13.0
By main branches:					
- agriculture	13.4	8.3	17.6	10.6	3.0
- light industry	9.3	7.7	3.9	5.8	7.4
- heavy industry	29.5	42.8	45.9	48.7	44.8
of which: energy	10.2	15.7	15.1	22.9	26.9
- transport and communications	17.5	14.4	12.7	13.6	13.7

(Table continues)

(Continuation)

Denomination	1952	1957	1965	1978	1988
XIII Pattern of consumption (by retail sales)					
– foodstuffs	56.4	54.5	55.4	51.8	54.2
– clothing	19.3	18.7	19.1	22.0	17.0
– daily necessities	15.0	14.8	11.7	12.4	14.7
– entertainment goods	2.6	2.9	2.9	3.3	7.1
– books and other printed matter	0.8	1.1	1.1	1.0	1.2
– pharmaceuticals and other medical goods	2.6	3.8	4.7	5.1	3.2
– fuels	3.3	4.2	5.1	4.4	2.6
XIV Commodity pattern of foreign trade				(1985)	
1. Export pattern:			(1980)		
– materials	83.4	–	50.3	50.6	30.4
– manufactured goods	16.6	–	49.7	49.4	69.6
2. Import pattern:					
– materials	18.7	–	34.8	12.5	18.2
– manufactured goods	81.3	–	65.2	87.5	81.8

Note: – No data available

XV Educational standards of population (Census data over the age of six)		(1964)	(1982)	(1987)	
1. Higher qualification (3–5 years)		0.4	0.6	0.9	
2. Secondary school, higher section (3 years)		1.3	6.6	6.9	
3. Secondary school, lower section (3 years)		4.7	17.8	21.2	
4. Primary school (6 years)		28.2	34.5	36.2	
5. Incomplete primary school		31.8	15.9	13.9	
6. Semi or completely illiterate		33.6	23.7	20.9	

Source: Fenjin de sishi nian 1949–1989
The Development of China (1949–1989)

BIBLIOGRAPHY

Dailies

Renmin Ribao (People's Daily) - Beijing
Jingji Ribao (Economic Daily) - Beijing
China Daily (in English) - Beijing
Világgazdaság (World Economy), daily of the Hungarian Chamber of Commerce - Budapest

Wceklies

Beijing Review (in English, also published in Arabic, French, German, Russian and Spanish) - Beijing
Far Eastern Economic Review (FEER) - Hong Kong
Liaowang (Outlook) - Beijing
Shijie Jingji Daobao (World Economic Herald), suppressed in May 1989 - Shanghai

Periodicals

Forthnightlies

Ban Yue Tan (Fortnightly Talks) - Beijing
Hong Qi (Red Flag), theoretical periodical of the CPC, published until June 1988 - Beijing
Qiu Shi (Search for Truth), theoretical periodical of the CPC, published since July 1988 - Beijing

Monthlies

Guoji Maoyi (Intertrade), monthly of the Research Institute for International Trade of MOFERT - Beijing
Jingji Guanli (Economic Management) - Beijing
Jingjixue Wenzhai (Abstracts from Economic Science) - Beijing
Jingji Yanjiu (Economic Research) - Beijing
Nongye Jingji Wenti (Problems of Agricultural Economy) - Beijing

Xinhua Yuebao (New China Monthly), monthly collection from Chinese Press, second publications - Beijing
Zhongguo: Fazhan yu Gaige (China: Development and Reform), perodical of the Research Institute of the State Reform Commission; discontinued November 1989 - Beijing
Zhongguo Jingji Tizhi Gaige (China's Economic Structure Reform), periodical of the State Reform Commission - Beijing
Zhongguo Jianshe (China Reconstructs), published in seven languages until 1989; since 1990 under the new title of Qinri Zhongguo (China Today) - Beijing
Zhongguo Nongcun Jingji (Chinese Rural Economy), periodical of the Chinese Agricultural Society and the Agricultural Research Institute of the Chinese Agricultural Academy - Beijing
Zhongguo Tongji Yuebao (Monthly Bulletin of Chinese Statistics), published by the State Statistical Bureau of the PRC - Beijing

Bimonthlies

Guoji Wenti Yanjiu (International Studies) - Beijing
Jingji Gaige (Economic Reform), periodical jointly published by the Economic Reform Commission and the Academy of Social Sciences of Shaanxi Province - Xi'an
Jingji Lilun yu Jingji Guanli (Economic Theory and Business Management), periodical of the Chinese People's University - Beijing
Problemy Dal'nego Vostoka (Problems of Far East), periodical of the Far-Eastern Institute of the Academy of Sciences of the USSR - Moscow
The China Business Review. The magazine of the US-China Business Council - Washington, D.C.
Xuexi yu Tansuo (Study and Exploration), periodical of the Academy of Social Sciences of Heilongjiang Province - Haerbin
Zhongguo Jingji Wenti (Chinese Economic Problems), periodical of the Economic Research Institute of Xiamen University - Xiamen
Zhonguo Shehui Kexue (Social Sciences in China), periodical of the Chinese Academy of Social Sciences - Beijing

Quarterly

Makesizhuyi Yanjiu (Studies on Marxism), published by the Institute of Marxism-Leninism-Mao Zedong Thought of the CASS - Beijing

Yearbooks

Zhongguo Jingji Nianjian. Jingji Guanli Chubanshi (Almanac of China's Economy. Economic Management Publishing House) - Beijing issues. The Almanac is also issued every year in English in Hong Kong

Zhongguo Tongji Nianjian. Zhongguo Tongji Chubanshi (Statistical Yearbook of China. Chinese Statistical Publishing House) - Beijing

Documents

Zhonghua Renmin Gongheguo guomin jingji de diyige wunian jihua 1953-1957. Renmin Chubanshi (First 5-year plan of the national economy of the PRC 1953-1957. People's Publishing House) - Beijing, 1955, 238 p

Zhonghua Renmin Gongheguo guomin jingji he shehui fazhan diqige wunian jihua 1986-1990. Renmin Chubanshi (Seventh 5-year plan of the development of the national economy and society of the PRC 1986-1990. People's Publishing House - Beijing, 1986, 218 p

Statistical compilations, records of events, handbooks

Weida de shinian. Zhonghua Renmin Gongheguo jingji he wenhua jianshe chengjiu de tongji. Guojia Tongjiju bian. Renmin Chubanshi (The great decade. Statistics of economic and cultural building in the PRC. Edited by the State Statistical Bureau. People's Publishing House) - Beijing, 1959, 198 p

Jushi zhumu de ba nian (1978-1986). Zhongguo fazhan yu gaige jishi. Sichuan Renmin Chubanshi (Eight years that aroused world attention - 1978-1986. Chronicle of development and reform in

China. Sichuan People's Publishing House) - Chengdu, 1987, 472 p
Jingji tizhi gaige shouce. Wang Jiye yu Zhu Yuanzhen bian. Jingji Ribao Chubanshi (Handbook of the reform of the economic system. Edited by Wang Jiye and Zhu Yuanzhen. Economic Daily Publishing House) - Beijing, 1987, 1060 p
Fenjin de sishinian: 1949-1989. Guojia Tongjiju bian. Zhongguo Tongji Chubanshi (The elevating 40 years: 1949-1989. Edited by the State Statistical Bureau. Chinese Statistical Publishing House) - Beijing 1989, 481 p
The Development of China (1949-1989). Beijing Review Press - Beijing 1989, 33 p

Books

Bachman, David M.: Chen Yun and the Chinese Political System. Institute of East Asian Studies, Berkeley, California 1985, 185 p
Chiu, Huangdah, ed.: Survey of recent development in China (Mainland and Taiwan) 1985-1986. Occasional Papers/Reprint Series in Contemporary Asian Studies, No. 2/1987 (79). School of Law University of Maryland, Baltimore, Maryland, USA
Dong Fureng zhubian: Shehuizhuyi jingji tizhi jiqi youyuexing. Beijing Chubanshi (Dong Fureng, ed.: The socialist economic system and its adventages. Beijing Publishing House) - Beijing, 1981, 257 p
Dong Fureng: Da zhuanbian de Zhongguo jingji lilun wenti. Shandong Renmin Chubanshi (Dong Fureng: Theoretical questions of the Chinese economy undergoing great changes. Shandong People's Publishing House) - Jinan 1981. 308 p.
Dutt, V.P., ed.: China: The Post-Mao View. Allied Publishers Private Limited. New Delhi-Bombay-Calcutta-Madras-Bangalore--Hyderabad 1981. 196 p
Feng Lanrui: Laodong baochou yu laodong jiuye. Zhongguo Zhanwang Chubanshi (Feng Lanrui: Remuneration of labour and employment. Chinese Prospects Publishing House), Beijing, 1982, 149 p
Feng Lanrui: An lao fenpei - Gongzi - Jiuye. Jingji Kexue Chu-banshi (Feng Lanrui: Distribution according to work - Wages

-Employment. Economic Science Publishing House), Beijing, 1988, 365 p

Gao Qian zhubian: Zhongguo de shehuizhuyi gaige. Heilongjiang Renmin Chubanshi (Gao Qian, ed.: The socialist reform of China. Heilongjiang People's Publishing House), Haerbin, 1986, 343 p

Goodman, David S.G., Lockett, Martin, and Segal, Gerald: The China Challenge. Adjustment and Reform. Chatham House Papers 32. The Royal Institute of International Affairs. Routledge and Kegan Paul, London, New York, and Andover, 1986, 86 p

He Jianzhang, Wang Jiye zhubian: Zhongguo jihua guanli wenti. Zhongguo Shehui Kexue Chubanshi (He Jianzhang, Wang Jiye, eds.: Problems of plan-direction in China. Social Sciences in China Publishing House), Beijing, 1984, 729 p

Hu Hua zhubian: Zhongguo geming jiangyi. Shang-Xia. Zhongguo Renmin Daxue Chubanshi (Hu Hua, ed.: Curriculum of the history of the Chinese revolution, vols. I-II. Chinese People's University Press), Beijing, 1979, 804 p

Huang Da, Chen Gong yu qita zuozhi: Shehuizhuyi caizheng jinrong wenti. Shang-Xia. Zhongguo Renmin Daxue Chubanshi (Huang Da, Chen Gong, et al.: Problems of socialist finance and banking, vols. I-II. Chinese People's University Press), Beijing, 1981, 600 p

Klenner, Wolfgang: Ordnungsprinzipien im Industrialisierungsprozess der VR China. Planung - Organisation - Unternehmenskonzept. Verlag Weltarchiv GmbH, Hamburg, 1979, 364 p

Kraus, Willy: Wirtschaftliche Entwicklung und sozialer Wandel in der Volksrepublik China. Springer, Berlin Heidelberg New York, 1979, 738 p

Li Zhongjie, Xu Yaoxin, Wei Li bian: Shehuizhuyi gaige shi. Chun-Qiu Chubanshi (Li Zhongjie, Xu Yaoxin, Wei Li, eds.: History of the socialist reforms. Spring-Autumn Publishing House), Beijing, 1988, 851 p

Liao Jili: Zhongguo jingji tizhi gaige yanjiu. Zhongguo Caizheng Jingji Chubanshi (Liao Jili: Research into the reform of the Chinese economic system. Chinese Financial and Economic Publishing House), Beijing, 1985, 316 p

Linder, Willy: Die chinesische Wirtschaftspolitik. Chansen,

Irrtümer und Hypotheken. Verlag Neue Zürcher Zeitung, Zürich, 1983, 89 p

Liu Guoguang: Shehuizhuyi zaishengchan wenti. Shenghuo-Dushu-
-Xinzhi San Lian Shudian (Liu Guoguang: Questions of socialist reproduction. Life-Reading-New Knowledge Three United Publishers), Beijing, 1980, 277 p

Liu Guoguang zhubian: Zhongguo jingji fazhan zhanlue wenti yanjiu. Shanghai Renmin Chubanshi (Liu Guoguang, ed.: Study of the strategic questions of Chinese economic development. Shanghai People's Publishing House), Shanghai, 1984, 603 p

Liu Suinian, Wu Qungan zhubian: Zhongguo shehuizhuyi jingji jianshe (1949-1983). Heilongjiang Renmin Chubanshi (Liu Suinian, Wu Qungan, eds.: China's socialist economic construction 1949-1983. Heilongjiang People's Publishing House), Haerbin, 1985, 480 p

Liu Suinian, Wu Qungan, eds.: China's Socialist Economy. An Outline History (1949-1984). Published by <u>Beijing Review</u>, Beijing, 1986, 700 p

Liu Zheng, Song Jian, et al.: China's Population: Problems and Prospects. New World Press, Beijing, 1981, 180 p

Ma Hong, Sun Shangqing zhubian: Zhongguo jingji jiegou wenti yanjiu. Shang-Xia. Renmin Chubanshi (Ma Hong, Sun Shangqing, eds.: Research into the structural problems of the Chinese economy, vols. I-II. People's Publishing House) Beijing, 1981, 808 p

Polonyi, Péter: A Kínai Kommunista Párt IX. kongresszusáról. Kossuth Könyvkiadó (Péter Polonyi: On the 9th Congress of the CPC. Kossuth Publishing House), Budapest, 1970, 153 p

Polonyi, Péter: Kína története. Kozmosz Könyvek (Péter Polonyi: History of China. Cosmos Books), Budapest, 1988, 228 p

Su Shaozhi, Feng Lanrui zhubian: Zai xinde lishi tiaojian xia jianchi he fazhan makesizhuyi. Renmin Chubanshi (Su Shaozhi, Feng Lanrui, eds.: Marxism has to be applied and developed under new historical conditions. People's Publishing House), Beijing, 1983, 298 p

Su Shaozhi, Zhang Xianyang zhubian: Shiyijie san zhong quanhui yilai makesizhuyi zai Zhongguo de fazhan. Renmin Chubanshi (Su

Shaozhi, Zhang Xianyang, eds.: Development of Marxism in China since the 3rd plenary session of the 11th CC. People's Publishing House), Beijing, 1988, 368 p

Sun Shangqing zhubian: Lun jingji-jiegou duice. Zhongguo Shehui Kexue Chubanshi (Sun Shangqing, ed.: On treating the economic structure. Social Science in China Publishing House), Beijing, 1984, 513 p

Wang Guichen, Zhou Qiren, et al.: Smashing the Communal Pot - Formulation and Development of China's Rural Responsibility System. New World Press, Beijing, 1985, 200 p

Zhongguo de da qushi. Wen Yuankai tan gaige. Shanghai Renmin Chubanshi (China's great trend. Wen Yuankai talks about the reform. Shanghai People's Publishing House), Shanghai, 1984, 152 p

Xu Tixin: Lun shehuizhuyi de shengchan, liutong yu fenpei. Du "Zibenlun" biji. Renmin Chubanshi (Xu Tixin: On socialist production, turnover and distribution. Notes made when reading "The Capital". People's Publishing House), Beijing, 1979, 615 p

Xu Tixin: Zhongguo guomin jingji de biange. Zhongguo Shehui Kexue Chubanshi (Xu Tixin: Transformation of the national economy of China. Social Science in China Publishing House), Beijing, 1982, 464 p

Xue Muqiao. Zhongguo shehuizhuyi jingji wenti yanjiu. Renmin Chubanshi (Xue Maqiao: Research into the poblems of China's socialist economy. People's Publishing House), Beijing, 1979, 273 p

Yu Guangyuan, ed.: China's Socialist Modernization. Foreign Languages Press, Beijing, 1984, 775 p

Yu Guangyuan zhubian: Zhongguo shehuizhuyi xiandaihua jianshe (1981-1985). Renmin Chubanshi (Yu Guangyuan, ed.: China's socialist modernization construction 1981-1985. People's Publishing House), Beijing, 1987, 698 p

Zhou Taihe zhubian: Dangdai Zhongguo de jingji tizhi gaige. Zhongguo Shehui Kexue Chubanshi (Zhou Taihe ed.: Contemporary China's reform of the economic system. Social Science in China Publishing House), Beijing, 1984, 825 p

Selected writings, collections of speeches, and articles

Chen Yun Wenxuan (1926-1949). Renmin Chubanshi (Selected works of Chen Yun 1926-1949. People's Publishing House), Beijing, 1984, 313 p

Chen Yun Wenxuan (1949-1956). Renmin Chubanshi (Selected works of Chen Yun 1949-1956. People's Publishing House), Beijing, 1984, 368 p

Chen Yun Wenxuan (1956-1985). Renmin Chubanshi (Selected works of Chen Yun 1956-1985. People's Publishing House), Beijing, 1986, 391 p

China unter neuer Führung. Hintergründe und Analysen zur Entwicklung von Gesellschaft, Wirtschaft, Wissenschaft und Kultur nach dem Sturz der "Vierbande" im Herbst 1976. Ostasiatisches Seminar der Freien Universität Berlin. Studienverlag Dr. Brockmayer, Bochum, 1978, 301 p

Selected works of Deng Xiaoping (1975-1982). Foreign Languages Press, Beijing, 1984, 418 p

Dong Fureng: Shehuizhiyi zaishengchan he guomin shouru wenti. Shenghuo-Dushu-Xinzhi San Lian Shudian (Dong Fureng: Questions of socialist reproduction and the national income. Life-Reading-New Knowledge Three United Publishers), Beijing, 1980, 308 p

Fang yan lu. Renmin Ribao lilun banduan wenxuan. Sichuan Renmin Chubanshi (Taking a broad view. Collection of theoretical articles from Renmin Ribao. Sichuan People's Publishing House), Chengdu, 1985, 655 p

Gaige yu fazhan 1983-1987. Zhongguo Jihua Chubanshi (Reform and Development 1983-1987. Chinese Plan Press), Beijing, 1987, 455 p

Gaige: women mianjian de tiaozhan yu xuanyi. Zhongguo Jingji Tizhi Gaige Yanjiusuo diaochazu bian. Zhongguo Jingji Chubanshi (Reform: the challenge and the decision alternative before us. Edited by the investigating group of the Research Institute of the Reform of the Chinese Economic System. Chinese Economic Press), Beijing, 1986, 305 p

Gui Shiyong zhubian: Lun Zhongguo hongguan jingji guanli. Zhongguo Jingji Chubanshi (Gui Shiyong, ed.: On China's macroeconomic management. Chinese Economic Press, Beijing, 1987, 852 p

Hidasi, Gábor: Gazdaság és politika a Kínai Népköztársaságban. Kossuth Könyvkiadó (Gábor Hidasi: Economy and politics in the People's Republic of China. Kossuth Publishing House), Budapest, 1979, 380 p

Jingji gaige de zhengzhi jingjixue wenti tantao. Zhongguo Shehui Kexue Chubanshi (Research into the problems of political economy of the economic reform. Social Science in China Publishing House), Beijing, 1982, 331 p

Jinian Makesi shishi yibai zhounian wenji. Zhongguo Renmin Daxue Kexue Yanjiu Chu (Collection of articles for the 100th anniversary of Marx's death. Scientific research section of the Chinese People's University), Beijing, 1983, 528 p

Liu Guoguang zhubian: Guomin jingji zonghe pingheng de ruogan lilun wenti. Zhongguo Shehui Kexue Chubanshi (Liu Guoguang, ed.: Some theoretical questions of the complex equilibrium of the national economy. Social Science in China Publishing House) Beijing, 1981, 416 p

Mao Zedong xuanji. Diyi juan. Renmin Chubanshi (Selected works of Mao Zedong, vol. 1. People's Publishing House), Beijing, 1951, 296 p

Mao Zedong xuanji. Dier juan. Renmin Chubanshi (Selected works of Mao Zedong, vol. 2. People's Publishing House), Beijing, 1952, 516 p

Mao Zedong xuanji. Disan juan. Renmin Chubanshi (Selected works of Mao Zedong, vol. 3. People's Publishing House), Beijing, 1953, 342 p

Mao Zedong xuanji. Disi juan. Renmin Chubanshi. (Selected works of Mao Zedong, vol. 4. People's Publishing House), Beijing, 1960, 406 p

Mao Zedong xuanji. Diwu juan. Renmin Chubanshi (Selected works of Mao Zedong, vol. 5. People's Publishing House), Beijing, 1977, 500 p

Mao Ce-tung: Beszédek és írások 1956-1974. Kossuth Könyvkiadó (Mao Zedong: Speeches and writings. Kossuth Publishing House), Budapest, 1978, 664 p

Sun Yefang: Shehuizhuyi jingji de ruogan lilun wenti. Renmin Chubanshi (Sun Yefang: Some theoretical problems of socialist economy. People's Publishing House), Beijing, 1979, 376 p

Sun Yefang: Shehuizhuyi jingji de ruogan lilun wenti (Xuji). Renmin Chubanshi (Sun Yefang: Some theoretical problems of socialist economy. (Further articles. People's Publishing House), Beijing, 1982, 292 p

Xue Muqiao. Shehuizhuyi jingji lilun wenti. Renmin Chubashi (Xue Muqiao: Theoretical problems of socialist economy. People's Publishing House), Beijing, 1979, 201 p

<u>Zhongguoshi de shehuizhuyi jingji tizhi.</u> Hong Qi Chubanshi (The socialist economic system of Chinese type. <u>Red Flag</u> Publishing House), Beijing, 1984, 244 p

Zhuo Jiong: Lun shehuizhuyi shangpin jingji. Guangdong Renmin Chubanshi (Zhuo Jiong: On the socialist commodity economy. Guangdong People's Publishing House), Guangzhou, 1981, 452 p